A WORLD BANK

Inequality and Economic Development in Brazil

THE WORLD BANK
Washington, D.C.

TABLE OF CONTENTS

TABLES

FIGURES

ACKNOWLEDGMENTS

This report is the result of collaboration between the Instituto de Pesquisa Econômica Aplicada (IPEA) and the World Bank between 2000 and 2002. The task was jointly managed by Carlos Eduardo Vélez (World Bank), Ricardo Paes de Barros (director of social studies, IPEA, Rio de Janeiro), and Francisco H. G. Ferreira of the Pontifical Catholic University of Rio de Janeiro (PUC-Rio).

The report was prepared under the overall guidance of Roberto Martins (president until 2002, IPEA), Gobind Nankani and Vinod Thomas (country directors, 2000–02), Ernesto May (sector director), Norman Hicks (sector manager), and Suman Bery and Joachim von Amsberg (lead economists, 2000–02).

Part I consists of the Policy Report, prepared by Carlos Eduardo Vélez, Francisco H. G. Ferreira, and Ricardo Paes de Barros.

Part II contains the background papers commissioned for the report, which diagnose income inequality in Brazil, present relevant international experience, and discuss the policy implications. The authors of the papers are Juliano Assunção (PUC-Rio de Janeiro), Andreas Blom (World Bank), François Bourguignon (DELTA and World Bank), Chris Elbers (*Vrijei* Universiteit, Amsterdam), Jean Olson Lanjouw (Yale University), Francisco H.G. Ferreira (PUC-Rio), Peter Lanjouw (World Bank), Phillipe G. Leite (PUC-Rio), Marcelo Medeiros (IPEA), Luis Carlos Magalhães (IPEA), Marta Menendez (DELTA, Paris), Serguei Soares (IPEA), Fernando Gaiger Silveira (IPEA), Carlos Eduardo Vélez (World Bank), and Salvador Vianna (IPEA).

We acknowledge many valuable comments to preliminary versions of this report. First of all our appreciation to Joachim von Amsberg for very detailed and useful comments, at several stages of the development of this task. François Bourguignon, Gobind Nankani, Guillermo Perry, Martin Ravallion, and Mike Walton provided very helpful feedback to earlier versions of Part I. The main findings and policy messages were presented at the *II World Bank Development Forum* in Brasilia. Distinguished panelists and participants at that event also influenced the form and contents of Part I. Discussants and participants met at a two-day seminar *A Desigualdade no Brasil: Dimensoes, Peculiaridades e Politicas Publicas* in Rio de Janeiro on August 30–31, 2001 to discuss the background papers, which influenced the form and content of papers included in Part II. The team expresses its appreciation to Mauricio Blanco, Rosane Mendonça and Renata Orofino, the IPEA-Rio team that successfully organized the seminar and facilitated the involvement of more than 100 participants from the research community in Brazil (academia, nongovernmental organizations, public sector). Valuable research assistance was provided by Samuel Franco at IPEA-Rio and Natalia Millán, Taizo Takeno and Juanita Riaño at the World Bank. Excellent editorial assistance was provided by Anne Pillay.

The peer reviewers for this task were Martin Ravallion and Mike Walton.

Finally, we wish to acknowledge the continued collaboration of the Government of Brazil and the close partnership with IPEA in the development of this task.

ABBREVIATIONS AND ACRONYMS

CEA	*Centro de Estudos Agrícolas*
CPMF	*Contribução Provisoria sobre Movimentação Financeira*
CPS	Current Population Survey
DELTA	*Département et Laboratoire d'Economie Théorique et Appliquée, Ecole Normale Superieure, Paris*
DITAR	Dalton-Improving Tax Reforms
ENDEF	*Estudo Nacional da Despesa Familiar*
ENIGH	*Encuesta Nacional de Ingresos y Gastos de Hogares*
FAO	Food and Agriculture Organization of the United Nations
FGTS	*Fundo de Garantia do Tempo de Serviço*
FGV	*Fundação Getúlio Vargas*
FUNDEF	Fund for Development and Maintenance of Elementary Teaching and Teacher Development
GDP	gross domestic product
GIE	Gini income elasticity
IADB	Inter-American Development Bank
IBGE	*Instituto Brasileiro de Geografia e Estatística*
IBRE	*Instituto Brasileiro de Economia*
ICMS	*Imposto sobre Circulação de Mercadorias e Serviços*
IFPRI	International Food Policy Research Institute
INCRA	*Instituto Nacional de Colonização e Reforma Agrária*
IPEA	*Instituto de Pesquisas Economicas Aplicadas*
IPI	*Imposto sobre Produtos Industrializados*
ITR	*Imposto Territorial Rural*
LAC	Latin America and the Caribbean
LSMS	Living Standard Measurement Survey
MECF	marginal efficiency cost of funds
Mercosur	*Mercado Común del Sur*
OLS	ordinary least squares
PIS	*Contribução para o Programa do Integração Social*
PNAD	*Pesquisa Nacional por Amostra de Domicílios*
POF	*Pesquisa de Orçamentos Familiares do IBGE*
PPP	Purchasing Power Parity
PPV	*Pesquisa sobre Padrões de Vida*
PRONAF	*Programa Nacional de Fortalecimento da Agricultura Familiar*
PSE	public social expenditure
PUC-Rio	Pontifícia Universidade Católica do Rio de Janeiro
RGPS	Public Pensions System for Private Sector Workers
RJU	Federal Government Pensions programe (Regime Jurídico Único)
SAEB	Sistema Nacional de Avaliação da Educação Básica
VAT	value added tax

Currency Equivalents
US$1.00 = R$2.84

Fiscal Year
January 1–December 31

EXECUTIVE SUMMARY

Brazil is a continent-sized nation, marked by profound contrasts and diversity. Some of these are geographic or climactic in nature, others are racial or ethnic. Brazil's population draws on Native American, African, and European roots, and successive waves of immigrants, principally from Asia and Europe, have added to the mix. Yet other contrasts are social in nature and generally less welcome. Living conditions for Brazil's 170 million people vary dramatically, and income disparities in Brazil are significant—not only across regions but also between metropolitan centers, nonmetropolitan urban centers, and rural areas.

This report is motivated by the coming together of three widespread perceptions about inequality, two somewhat newer and one long-standing. The two newer ones are that inequality may matter for the country's economic development, poverty reduction, and social progress, and that public policy and reforms, for example in the areas of social security and taxes, can and should do something about it. The old perception, which is well borne out by the facts, is that Brazil occupies a position of very high inequality in the international community.

Why do Inequalities Matter for Brazil?
Excessive Income Inequality Is Unfair and Could Be Inefficient
Income inequality matters because high inequality means that there will be more poor people at a given average level of income. It also means that the poor will benefit relatively less from economic growth than in a more equal society. Also, inequality matters beyond its impact on poverty. There is increasing evidence that high inequality adversely affects growth and health outcomes, undermines social cohesion, and increases crime. Besides, dynamic growth modeling shows that weak social mobility and excessively unequal initial conditions are likely to lead to its persistence or even more inequality. This perverse cycle is more likely in countries—like Brazil—where fertility differentials between educated and uneducated parents are much stronger. Finally, many consider that the inequality of opportunities—social mobility determinants that are outside the control of the individual-, which explains one third and one half of the Brazilian income inequality—is unfair and undesirable on ethical grounds.

Why is Brazil so Unequal?

Brazil's Income Inequality Is Very High and Persistent over Time

Brazil's income inequality is very high and persistent over time, and it has deep historic and regional roots. With an income share of the richest 20 percent of the population equal to 33 times the corresponding share of the poorest 20 percent, Brazil has one of the highest levels of income inequality in the world. The Gini coefficient for the distribution of household incomes per capita is 0.59; that is, the expected difference in income per capita between any two Brazilians chosen at random is nearly 1.2 times the average income per capita.

High inequality remains a fundamental characteristic of Brazil despite some important qualifications:

- New analysis shows that Brazil's income inequality has likely been overestimated as a result of limitations in the household survey data. Previous analysis also suggests an overestimation of inequality to the extent that cost-of-living differences are not fully reflected. But even with better data, income inequality would still be high.
- Even though aggregate measures in income inequality do not show much change over time, there have been important income improvements for the poorest, especially since stabilization in 1993, and possibly some further improvements in the last three years.
- Brazil has achieved major improvements in social indicators, particularly health and education. Although these were not immediately translated into less income inequality, they improve the quality of life of the poor and create the conditions for reduction of inequality in the future.

Income differences among the Brazilian population by gender and skin color account for an important part of overall income inequality, and this is due to disadvantages in wages, schooling, or both. Some 12 percent of income inequality in Brazil is accounted for by income differences by skin color. The same figure for the United States is 2.4 percent. Educational attainment is also widely unequal; by years of schooling, blacks fare only two thirds as well as whites. Earnings of women are on average 29 percent lower than earnings of men, even though Brazilian females entering the labor force get nearly one more year of education than males. Although, the current gender gap has the same magnitude as that of the 1920s, this time it is against men. In summary, whereas skin color gaps are cumulative, gender gaps are asymmetric.

Regressive Public Transfers, Inequitable Distribution of Education, and High Skill Wage Differentials

The excessive income inequality of Brazil is due to three factors: more regressive public transfers, less equitable distribution of education, and higher wage differentials. One approach to better understanding Brazil's high income inequality is to analyze what accounts for the excess inequality of Brazil compared with other countries. The 14 percentage point difference between the Gini coefficient for Brazil and the United States (a country that also has relatively high income inequality in international comparison) can be decomposed as follows:

- Public transfers are less progressive in Brazil, accounting for 39 percent of the excess inequality. Although most social programs are progressive, retirement pensions, especially pensions for public sector employees, consume the largest share of social spending (above 50 percent) and are heavily biased in favor of higher-income groups. In fact, the share of pensions to the richest 20 percent in Brazil is more than twice the corresponding share in the United States—61 versus 26 percent. Moreover, despite having nearly half the percentage of beneficiaries than the United States, Brazil devotes a much higher share of its resources (5 percentage points above) to these entitlements.
- The unequal distribution of education in Brazil accounts for 29 percent of excess inequality. Brazil has a considerable skill gap in the labor force when compared with the

United States, but also compared with Mexico and Colombia. The percentage of high school graduates—not to mention workers with postsecondary education—is only 35 percent. In the United States, it is 94 percent, and in Mexico, 52 percent. This reflects a long-standing neglect of and inequity in education that has been addressed only recently through substantial education system improvements.

▦ Finally, higher skills premiums (wage differentials by skill level) in Brazil account for 32 percent of excess inequality. The Brazilian differential has been increasing during the 1990s and is 50 percent greater than the differential in the United States and also well above Mexico's. This means that the unequal asset distribution is projected into an even more unequal distribution of labor market incomes. Besides, these two factors are mutually dependent. The skill premium—the relative price by skill—is partially determined by the distribution of education (the supply of skills). In fact, this premium has increased over time as a result of both technological change and a relative shortage of highly skilled workers.

Partially Counterbalanced by the Progressive Effect of Other Social Expenditure Programs and Direct Taxation, and the Moderate but Regressive Impact of Indirect Taxation

Fortunately, despite the regressive incidence of pensions described above, the distribution of the *other* half of public social expenditures is egalitarian and unambiguously progressive and contributes substantially to the reduction of inequality. Although most of the social programs (excluding pensions) are not in cash but in kind and do not enter the household income as such, they represent an important contribution to current nonmonetary household welfare. In particular, these are the best-targeted programs directed to infants and children and to basic infrastructure *favela* (shanty town) upgrading. Overall, the subsidies, which are implicit in social programs, contribute to income equalization. Once public social expenditure (PSE) subsidies are added to income, inequality is considerably smaller relative to inequality of income alone the Gini coefficient is 5.6 percentage point slower. However, although the share of the poorest income groups in total PSE subsidies is relatively low—12 percent for the poorest 20 percent of the population, the welfare of the poor is quite sensitive to social policy targeting. In fact, in 1997 the average household in the first quintile received as much from income as it did from government subsidies in cash or in kind.

Contrary to the progressive quality of PSE, overall household taxation has a moderate regressive impact on income distribution: 0.7 percentage points of the Gini. The magnitude of taxation on households is considerable in magnitude, and the incidence of direct and indirect taxation operates in opposite directions—that is, progressive and regressive, respectively. In fact, the tax burden on the economy increased by nearly 3.5 percent of gross domestic product during the 1990s (more than 1.5 percent was via indirect taxation), and current indirect tax revenue triples the revenue from direct taxation. Henceforth, currently indirect taxation revenue is approximately three times as large as direct taxation and displays very heterogeneous tax rates across goods and services. The burden of direct income taxation is mostly (96 percent) concentrated on households that belong to the richest 20 percent in Brazil, but the opposite occurs with indirect taxation. Out of total indirect taxation, 16 percent is paid by the poorest 40 percent, although their share of income is well below 10 percent.

Despite Progressive Social Public Expenditure, Access to Education Remains Quite Regressive and Deficient

Despite the magnitude and progressive nature of social expenditure, access to education remains quite deficient and regressive across income groups and regions. The burden of educational inefficiencies—chronic repetition and dropout—falls mostly on the poor and, consequently, they experience many more difficulties going through the education system. While average grade 9 completion is below 10 percent for the poorest 50 percent, it was 79 percent for the 10th income decile in 1999.

In summary, Brazil's excessive income inequality is associated to both market and nonmarket forces, which operate in opposite directions and compensate partially. First, insufficient and unequally distributed education endowments and excessive wage skill premiums contribute in similar proportions to excess inequality when compared with the United States and jointly explain 60 percent of income inequality. Second, the regressive nature of Brazilian retirement pension transfers provides the largest contribution to excess inequality: 40 percent. Third, this situation is marginally worsened by the regressive impact of indirect taxation (nearly half of the endowment effect, 1.6 percentage points of the Gini). Fortunately, some compensatory and progressive effects follow from direct taxation and PSE—that is, nonpensions. This is moderate in the case of former (1 percentage point of the Gini) and clearly progressive and substantial for the latter (−3.8 Gini points), similar in magnitude and opposite in sign to the endowment effect in the U.S.-Brazil comparison.

What Should Public Policy Do About Income Inequality?

This report recommends that, among possible strategies for fighting inequality, Brazil should focus on those policies that are good for reducing inequality, good for reducing poverty, and good for increasing efficiency, competitiveness, and growth. In the key areas recommended for action, there are thus no tradeoffs between equity and efficiency or between the reduction of inequality and the reduction of poverty. This does not mean that these policies benefit everyone. They do involve political choices, and they do involve the dismantling of privileges such as those implied in excessive public sector pensions.

The Long-Term, Aggressive Expansion of Education to Narrow the Gap with the Rest of the World

The most important area for action is education. Over the last two decades, each age cohort has achieved higher average educational attainment with less inequality within the cohort. The rate of progress has been much faster in the last decade than during the 1980s and strong compared to most other countries. Yet compared to international and Latin American standards, educational attainment in Brazil is still lagging behind. Two decades ago, Brazil's educational attainment for young cohorts was close to Ecuador's and better than Mexico's, but cohorts born two decades later are on average 1.5 years of schooling behind Mexico and more than 2 years behind Ecuador. Moreover, when compared with South Africa, Brazil shows rather slow progress in education and a persistent educational gap against nonwhites.

Expansion of Education Is Desirable for Both Equity and Efficiency

Educational expansion is also unambiguously desirable because it is likely to lead to faster and better quality growth by correcting the inefficiencies induced by inequality (in particular, insufficient human capital investment of the poor). This would reduce the underlying inequality of human capital endowments and, finally, save the economy from converging toward even more unequal equilibria in the future—as it is moving toward more a level field of opportunities.

Before the Demographic Window of Opportunity Expires

Given that Brazil is in the middle of the demographic transition, time is running short for Brazil to reduce inequality through education. After experiencing a monotonic ascent during the 20th century up to 1970, the population share of the youngest cohorts entering the labor force started to fall and is expected to converge to a stable minimum—half of the maximal demographic weight—by the end of the 2010s. The current generation of students is coming from a relatively large age cohort, but 10 years from now, new graduates will represent a 25 percent smaller share of the population. Hence, demographic opportunities to raise the level of schooling of the whole labor force by improving education of younger cohorts are fading away as they are gradually losing share in the population of working age.

A Patient, Long-Term Perspective in Educational Policy

Educational policies are necessary to address the structural determinants of inequality and poverty, but they only render their benefits in the long term. It is frustrating to report that, according to our demographic models, even the most important policies for reduction of inequality—the expansion of the quantity and quality of education—will not reduce income inequality in the short term. Even very strong improvements above the current trend of schooling attainment take more than two decades to show up as higher educational endowments for the whole working age population. This is because demographic transition forces in Brazil determine the time lag required to extend the educational improvements enjoyed by the younger cohorts to the whole labor force (the stock-to-cohort time lag). Under these circumstances, policymakers' faith in education should go together with patience, taking demographic inertia into account and monitoring educational policy with a clear long-term perspective.

Additional Benefits of Educational Expansion: Faster Extension of the Benefits of Education to the Whole Population and Reduction of Long-Term Inequality

Taking advantage of the window of opportunity of demographic transition to expand education not only would accelerate the achievement of educational attainment goals for the *whole* population, but also reduce the long-term inequality of educational attainment and, consequently, labor income. If the educational expansion of the 1990s had occurred one decade earlier—before the demographic transition started—then that temporary acceleration would have permanently reduced the stock-to-cohort time lag from 25 to 20 years and cut long-term inequalities of schooling and labor income. Two decades later, the simulated variance of schooling would have become 7 percent smaller than expected, with obvious implications for labor income inequality. Furthermore, additional reduction of inequality will follow from the induced decline in the wage skill premium.

The Medium Term: A More Educated Labor Force Will Help to Lower the Wage Skill Premium

Unless high wage differentials by skill are reduced, efforts to bring higher and more equitable access to education will not produce substantial reductions of income inequality in the medium term. Although, large shifts toward a more skilled labor force have taken place in the last two decades, they have been insufficient relative to the demand shift. According to this report, around 60 percent of the increase of the skill premium to tertiary education can be attributed to supply shortage. The remaining 40 percent is due to a shift in labor demand toward highly skilled labor. Brazil needs to vigorously expand the supply of postsecondary education with the help of the private sector and increased cost recovery linked with credit programs. This strategy would permit the necessary expansion of postsecondary education without requiring additional public spending. Also, at this time, the massive expansion of secondary education is still a critical precondition for the equitable and efficient expansion of postsecondary education.

More Cost-Efficient Public Education Requires Multilevel Interventions

To achieve higher and more equitable educational attainment, the education system in Brazil has to become more efficient for the poor (reduce the repetition and dropout rates). This basically means taking all actions that reduce the cost of helping the children from poor families complete high school and enter postsecondary education. This also implies taking action at multiple levels in the education system: schools, households, and subnational governments: This could be achieved within school programs to reduce chronic repetition, alternative supply programs aimed at expanding school availability for the poor, extension of Fund for Development and Maintenance of Elementary Teaching and Teacher Development (FUNDEF) (the subnational public finance incentives to promote efficient expansion of basic education in the poorer states) to secondary education, and family-focused social assistance programs, such as Bolsa Scola, linked to school attendance and subsidies of school supplies for the poor. Finally, addressing persistent inequality of opportunities should include raising access to childcare and preschool education where the poor experience a considerable consumption gap relative to the middle- and high-income households.

The Short Term: Cutting Excessive Retirement Benefits to Free Public Resources for Better-Targeted Social Policies

After education improvements, further deep reform of Brazil's social security system, in particular substantial reduction of currently excessive retirement benefits for civil servants, would address an important source of income inequality, contribute to fiscal sustainability, and eventually free resources for targeted social policies. The current social security reform and its follow-up provides an important opportunity. Although programs such as the Old Age Program are well targeted—mostly to rural and female-headed households—and the Public Pensions System for Private Sector Workers (RGPS) improved after the recent reform, the Federal Government Pensions program (RJU) remains the most problematic. The RJU absorbs excessive funds and violates basic principles of fairness of public expenditure—namely, vertical, horizontal, and intergenerational equity.

Indirect Tax Reform Could Be Both Efficient and Equitable

Finally, there are possible budget-neutral reforms to the indirect tax system that could increase efficiency and potentially improve welfare. The current structure of indirect taxation—heterogeneity of tax rates, excessive burden, and regressive incidence—could be improved to reduce the efficiency cost of taxation, reduce tax heterogeneity (lowering collection and enforcement costs), and reduce inequity. Also important would be not to give special privileges and exemptions to physical and financial capital, which would stack incentives in favor of capital relative to labor and contribute to a worsening of the income distribution. The tax reform agenda is an opportunity to address these issues. A relatively larger reliance on direct taxes would merit consideration, given the progressive impact of such change.

*   *   *

In summary, to reduce inequality, public policy must be active in four areas. First, raising the level and reducing the inequities of educational attainment, which would involve making the education system more efficient for the poor (reduce the repetition and dropout rates) and taking advantage of transient demographic opportunities to cut the educational gap between Brazil and middle-income countries. Second, reducing the wage skill premium of postsecondary education by promoting its expansion and increasing their availability in the labor market. Third, reallocating public expenditure away from excessive and regressive transfers, such as the implicit subsidies imbedded in the Federal pensions regime. And finally, taking advantage of the opportunity to implement an indirect tax reform that can reduce the inequity of indirect taxation avoiding any additional efficiency costs.

PART I

POLICY REPORT

INTRODUCTION

Brazil is a continent-sized nation marked by profound contrasts. Some of these are geographic or climactic in nature, and they add to the variety of settings and scenes of which Brazilians are proud. Others are racial or ethnic: Brazil's population draws on Native American, African, and European roots, and successive waves of immigrants, principally from Asia and Europe, have added to the mix. Such a combination of races and cultures, spread over more than 8 million square kilometers, inevitably makes for enormous diversity.

Yet other contrasts are social in nature and generally less welcome. Living conditions for Brazil's 170 million people vary dramatically, both across the country's regions and states and within them. Spatial variations can be marked. Life expectancy at birth ranges from 63.2 years in Alagoas to 71.6 years in Rio Grande do Sul.[1] Adult literacy ranges from under 70 percent in Alagoas and Piauí to almost 95 percent in the Federal District (IBGE 2000). Poverty incidence rates range from 3.1 percent in metropolitan São Paulo to more than 50 percent in the rural northeast. Income disparities in Brazil are significant not only across regions but also between metropolitan areas, nonmetropolitan urban centers, and rural areas. Moreover, inequality across gender and racial groups is also important.

The present Report is motivated by the coming together of three widespread perceptions about inequality, two somewhat newer and one long-standing. The two newer ones are; (i) that inequality may matter for the country's economic development, and (ii) that public policy can and should *do* something about it. The old perception, which is well borne out by the facts, is that Brazil occupies a position of very high inequality in the international community. Therefore, this report tries to explain what makes Brazil so unequal and to what extent the interaction of labor

---

1. Life expectancy at birth statistics are based on the 2000 census and are still treated by the IBGE as preliminary.

market forces and public policies—or the lack of them—contribute to this undesirable outcome. For instance, in what measure is social mobility becoming more independent of family background thanks to progressive public policies in basic education, health and nutrition.

Accordingly, the report is organized around three basic questions. The first section asks *why inequality might matter for the country's economic development*. Why it matters for poverty reduction, for social justice equality of opportunities and social mobility, and for economic and political efficiency. The second section asks *why Brazil is so unequal*. It seeks a deeper understanding of what lies behind Brazil's position as one of the most unequal countries in the world, as shown in typical international comparisons, the dynamics of income inequality, and the magnitude of inequality across regions, racial groups, and gender. Then, it attempts to shed light on why this may be so. It investigates the causes of Brazil's excess inequality in four dimensions: the distribution of assets (human and nonhuman), the price of those assets, the behavioral difference in the labor market and fertility, and, finally, the distribution of state transfers and entitlements (public expenditure and taxation). The third section asks *whether there is a role for public action aimed at reducing inequalities*, and considers some lessons from theory and evidence on the relative effectiveness of alternative approaches. First, it considers how the provision of education might affect not only the distribution of human assets in the long run but the relative prices of human capital for different levels of skill. Second it examines how public policy toward rural land use must take into account inefficiencies that are closely linked to inequities of land distribution. Finally, it investigates how taxation and public expenditure policies reduce income inequality and inequality of access to basic social services. The fourth section concludes.

CHAPTER I

WHY DO INEQUALITIES MATTER FOR BRAZIL?

W hy does the fact that Brazil is a highly unequal society, along various dimensions to be discussed below, matter for the quality of life and for economic development in the country? In order to find out whether inequality matters for Brazil, the following questions must be answered: Is the current situation fair and opportunities equally available? Does family background account for too much, and effort too little for the standard of living available to a typical Brazilian—or vice versa. Secondly, is this state of affairs economically efficient? Or has inequality become a burden for the economy, because investments of low income households is insufficient and sub-optimal, and it is pulling GDP below its maximum potential. Finally, to what extent do growth dividends for poverty reduction, get weakened by excessive inequality.

In this Chapter we draw on some economic theory—old and new—as well as on some recent empirical findings, to try and shed some light on this question. We consider three broad areas: those related to links between inequality and poverty reduction; those related to social justice, equality of opportunities, and social mobility; and those related to the likely impacts of inequality on both narrow productive efficiency and the external costs of inequality (and hence to a broader concept of efficiency) and; those related to links between inequality and poverty reduction.

Social Justice, Inequality of Opportunities and Persistent Inequality

The concept of social justice is inherently normative, which means that departing from different views about what constitutes fairness could very well lead to radically different perceptions of whether the Brazilian society, unequal as it is, is or is not fair.[2] Two rather different approaches have been influential. The first is utilitarianism, which views social welfare as a weighted sum of

---

2. It goes beyond the remit of this report to attempt a review of this literature. See Atkinson and Stiglitz (1980) for an excellent summary.

individual levels of wellbeing. Most advocates of this view consider that the weights should decline with individual wealth or income, possibly as a result of supposing that the marginal utility of income falls as people become richer. Because this implies that, all else equal, overall social welfare should rise as a result of a progressive transfer, many have interpreted the prescriptions of utilitarianism as requiring egalitarian outcomes.

However, economists know that all else seldom *is* equal. If a transfer is made from a richer man to a poorer one, and the former anticipates this, he might very well feel less inclined to work as hard. As a result, the overall level of output available to be shared in the first place might decline. Similarly, if the transfer is made to the poorer man independently from his own efforts, he too might have less incentive to produce, thereby adding a separate source of reduction in aggregate wealth. Because such incentive effects must be internalized when deciding which feasible allocation is best for society as a whole, unequal outcomes are in general perfectly consistent with a utilitarian view of social welfare.

What utilitarianism does imply, however, is that choosing the best allocation for a society will, in general, entail a tradeoff between equity and efficiency. In other words, although a utilitarian voter will take the effect of incentives into account when choosing her optimum, she will also bear in mind that a dollar gained by a poorer man is "worth more" to society than a dollar lost by a rich man. This implies that the socially optimal amount of efficiency forgone for the sake of greater equity is in general positive.

Making a leap from such abstract concepts to the complex reality of the policymaker is usually a difficult thing to do. It is quite plain, however, that a distributionally neutral—or even regressive—state in a country as unequal as Brazil is unlikely to correspond to the optimal amount of redistribution, unless the rich are exceedingly more potentially productive than the poor. As we will see below, there are many reasons why this is unlikely to be the case.

The second influential approach is based on the concept of equality of opportunities. This approach departs from the view that fairness consists not of ensuring that all persons enjoy the same outcomes, regardless of ability or effort, but instead ensuring that, to the maximum extent possible, they all have the same chances in life. In an influential treatment of this issue, John Roemer (1998) suggested that relevant outcomes (such as income, consumption, wages, etc.) may be seen as determined by two large sets of variables. Those that, to various extents, are within their individual control are called *effort* variables. And those that help determine outcomes but are beyond the control of the individuals concerned, are called *circumstance* variables. In Roemer's framework, opportunities are equalized if the circumstances that can be modified—not predetermined—do not produce systematic differences in individual outcomes. Only differences in outcomes that arise from differences in individual efforts are regarded as fair.

Any empirical implementation of this framework is fraught with difficulties. In the first place, no known data set contains all the circumstance and effort variables that really play a role in determining individual outcomes. Second, even among the variables that existing data sets do contain, there are some whose classification between effort and circumstance is inevitably somewhat arbitrary. Nevertheless, if one were prepared to take a data set such as the PNAD and classify the characteristics of the households and individuals recorded there as either efforts or circumstances, it would be possible to simulate an equalization of circumstances and decompose overall observed inequality into a "minimum" component, due to opportunities, and a residual, which is at least in part associated with efforts (but also with luck, transitory variations, etc.).

This is what Bourguignon, Ferreira, and Menendez (2002), whose work is included in Part II of this report, do. They consider one's own educational level and one's decision to migrate as efforts, and they take the set of circumstances to include parental schooling and occupation, gender, race, and region of birth. They into account the fact that the efforts are themselves influenced by the circumstances, estimating separate models for them. They find that between 8 and 12 points of the Gini coefficient (of 0.55) for the distribution of male earnings, and between 8 and 14 points of the Gini coefficient (of 0.57) for the distribution of female earnings, are accounted for by inequality of opportunities. If one bears in mind that all omitted characteristics are being treated as efforts, and that the R^2 (of 0.42) of the earnings regression places an absolute upper bound in the share of inequality that can be attributed to circumstances, this 14–25 percent share of overall inequality that can be ascribed only to those circumstances identified with parental education and occupation, region of birth, race and gender, is quite high.

When each of these circumstances is equalized separately, it turns out that the one with by far the greatest impact on reducing inequality is the mean education of the individual's parents. As we saw above, this works through both an impact on the child's educational attainment and an additional direct impact on her income. Equalizing race came second.[3]

Furthermore, in a dynamic context, weak social mobility could lead to a perverse cycle of increasing inequality in Brazil. Cross-country evidence shows that the fertility differentials between educated and uneducated parents are stronger in more unequal countries like Brazil.[4] If children of uneducated parents are less likely to become educated, the fertility differential will induce an increasing proportion of unskilled workers in the next generation, which in turn tends to depress their wages and increase their chances of having more children and so on.[5] Based on a dynamic framework of fertility and education inequality across generations, Kremer and Chen (2002) show that depending on the initial inequality conditions, the economy is more likely to converge to high or low inequality scenarios: "If the initial proportion of skilled workers is too low, inequality will be self-reinforcing and the economy may approach a steady state with a low proportion of skilled workers and greater inequality between the skilled and unskilled (p. 77)."

Auspiciously, Kremer and Chen also find that the timely enhancement of educational opportunities for the children of the poor is critical in putting the economy on a path leading to a more egalitarian equilibrium, with a more balanced distribution of skilled and unskilled workers. According to their findings, even a temporary increase in schooling opportunities for the children of the poor that raises the share of skilled workers above a certain critical value would induce a virtuous dynamics of education equalization across generations.[6] Moreover, they also show that if fertility is endogenous to skill wage differentials, temporary policy interventions can have even larger multiplier effects.

However, the window of opportunity for this policy intervention is expiring: As time passes the economy moves away from the desired qualification of the labor force, hence the effort required to reach the critical share of skilled workers becomes larger. Velez, Medeiros and Soares (2002)—included in Part II of this report—show that the otherwise welcome trend of decreasing average fertility in Brazil has been reducing demographic weight of younger cohorts, thus constraining the leverage of current educational policies to modify the distribution of schooling for the whole labor force. In Chapter 3 this report explores in detail the relationship between the expansion of education, demographics transition and income inequality.

Inequality as Efficiency Burden: Insufficient Investment by the Poor, Inefficient Political Outcomes and Induced Crime

Further, this situation might be both unfair and inefficient. Social justice considerations, based on the idea that people somehow value equity for its own sake, whether in the space of outcomes or of opportunities, are not the only reasons why inequality would be undesirable. Economists are no longer convinced that most economies operate in a range where every concession to equity comes at some positive cost in efficiency. Although tradeoffs certainly do operate at the level of the

---

3. See Bourguignon, Ferreira and Menendez (2002) for details.

4. See Kremer and Chen (2002). They also show that for most Latin American countries fertility are very high differentials, well above the predicted level conditional on inequality.

5. Assuming the substitution effect dominates the income effect.

6. As a corollary, Kremer and Chen (2002) show that any effort to reduce the unit cost of helping the children of the poor to reach high educational attainment has the same consequences. Hence a whole range of handles can contribute to the goal, namely improvements in nutrition and childcare and public finance incentives to reduce unit cost and improve the allocation efficiency of public funds for education.

individual tax or transfer instrument, economists have, in the past decade or so, identified a number of reasons why inequality and/or poverty may lead to aggregate economic inefficiencies.

Chief among these reasons is the simple fact that capital markets—notably, the market for loans to small producers—are imperfect. Informational asymmetries between lenders and borrowers mean that many credits are made only if collateral can be provided or, alternatively, are supplied only at interest rates that are higher than those charged to more established borrowers. Both of these rationing mechanisms, whether by price or quantity, result in a flow of lending to poor entrepreneurs that is below the socially optimal level, in the sense that profitable loans are not made to finance profitable projects, which are therefore not implemented.

The market failure that lies at the origin of this inefficiency is either the informational asymmetry between lenders and borrowers or the inability to enforce contracts in certain markets. Yet, a key implication of these types of credit market imperfection is that the larger the number of people in poverty—or at least, excluded from these markets—the farther the economy is from its output potential.[7] Given a mean income that is not too low relative to the lending threshold, it can be shown that higher inequality means more poverty.[8] Similar arguments can be made for failures in the insurance markets, which imply an undersupply of insurance contracts (to the rich or the poor, depending on the model), and thus a suboptimal amount of investment under uncertainty.

There are other reasons. It has been suggested that excessive inequality might lead to political equilibria in which the chosen amount of efficiency-augmenting redistributions—such as investing in better public education—is inefficient or suboptimal.[9] The basic mechanism at work is that if political power is somehow related to wealth, the dominant coalition in society might be a group that prefers to underfund basic public services, so as to pay less tax, even though total output might have been higher if those productive public services had been produced, so that the poorer beneficiaries would have been able to compensate the richer taxpayers for the extra tax paid.[10]

Inequality Weakens the Benefits of Growth for the Poor

A third set of arguments is that, quite apart from whether inequality leads to inefficiencies and thus may lower the rate of economic growth, there is plenty of evidence that it weakens the link between growth—at whatever rate—and poverty reduction. This link is the poverty reduction elasticity of growth, and Ravallion (1997) has shown that this elasticity is negatively related to inequality in a cross-country sample. These arguments deserve attention in Brazil, where the combination of sluggish growth and high inequality has prevented poverty from declining in a substantive way during the last two decades (see Barros, Henriques, and Mendonça 2000).

Not surprisingly, despite its level of development, the excessive level of income inequality prevalent in Brazil induces excessive poverty. According to Barros (2002) in income per capita (PPP) Brazil occupies the 82nd percentile among all countries in the *World Development Indicators* (2002) in the 1990's, but at the same time is in the 40th percentile when those same countries are ranked in decreasing level of poverty according to the $1 a day poverty line. As Figure 1.1 shows, the excess inequality of Brazil relative to other world countries explains nearly 18 percentage point of its "excessive" poverty.

Moving on from narrowly defined economic efficiency in terms of output, growth, and poverty reduction, there is also substantial international evidence that high levels of inequality are associated—perhaps causally—to a number of other costs for the functioning of the economy and of the society. Chief among these is the evidence that crime and violence levels are statistically

---

7. Or Pareto frontier.

8. See Galor and Zeira (1993) and Banerjee and Newman (1993) for two different formal treatments of this idea, and Banerjee and others (2001) for empirical evidence in the context of sugar cooperatives in India.

9. Suboptimal allocations in the sense that Kaldor and Lorenz-dominant equilibria. That is, allocations with both higher overall output and less inequality. See, for example Bénabou (2000) and Ferreira (2001).

10. This is an application of the well-known Kaldor criterion.

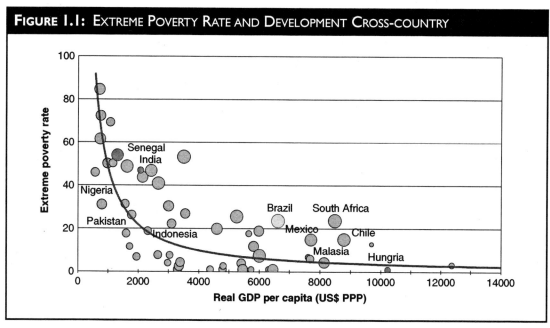

FIGURE 1.1: EXTREME POVERTY RATE AND DEVELOPMENT CROSS-COUNTRY

Source: World Development indicators, 2002.

significantly associated with inequality (see Fajnzylber, Lederman and Loayza (1998)). In Brazil, recent research has estimated that the direct cost of violent crime in terms of life and health may be very large (see Lisboa and Viegas 2000). And these costs are those that are easiest to quantify. In addition, there are likely to be significant indirect costs *in* terms of resources devoted to (public and private) security provision. More tentatively, some have hypothesized that the dilution of the perception of common ownership or stake in society, which is associated with very high inequality, may contribute to some erosion of society-wide social capital, such as respect for rules, trust in institutions or in strangers, and so on.

Rural Land Inequality and Low Agricultural Productivity Induced by Missing Markets for Credit and Insurance

Brazil is a highly urbanized country where the gap between the living conditions in rural and urban areas is persistent, and where overall agricultural productivity remains low and heterogeneous across landholdings. Small farms generate the largest share of employment in rural areas with the smallest share of land. Only one-third of the total area available has been used by family-based farms, which employ 77 percent of the rural labor force. Most of the agricultural land is in large landholdings, with a much lower performance per hectare—less than half the average land productivity of family-based farms—despite having similar levels of investment per hectare.

Brazilian land distribution is found to be not only unequal but inefficient. Based on an equilibrium model of the land market—where land has an alternative nonagricultural use as collateral, induced by imperfections in the markets for credit or insurance—Assunção (2002) finds three necessary conditions for inefficiency of land distribution hold in Brazil.[11] Namely: (1) heterogeneity in access to agricultural technologies across landholding types; (2) nonagricultural benefits derived from land property; and (3) malfunctioning land rental market. These conditions

---

11. He draws on the ideas of Stiglitz e Weiss (1981); Feldstein (1980); Brandão e Rezende (1992), among others.

generate the *inverse* relationship between farm size and productivity, observed by Barros and others (2000). As a result, both inequity and inefficiency in land use will tend to persist as long as the structural determinants to demand land for nonagricultural use remain.

*   *   *

In summary this chapter has shown why excessive inequality is undesirable for economic development. Current inequality will be perceived as a lack of social justice and unfair if differences between individuals are weakly dependant on effort and strongly dependent upon unequal distribution of avoidable circumstances. Besides, excessive inequality not only restrain economic growth by inducing inefficient levels on investment among the poor but also as it provokes political outcomes with excessive taxation and compensatory expenditures. Finally, excessive inequality also obstructs poverty reduction efforts as it hampers the benefits of growth that the poor derive from it. Consequently, the following chapter seeks to understand what lies behind Brazil's inequality.

CHAPTER 2

WHY IS BRAZIL SUCH AN UNEQUAL SOCIETY?

This chapter tries to understand why Brazil is such an unequal society. Is inequality being driven mainly by disparities in the distribution of human assets or in their relative prices? Does nonlabor income and entitlements matter for income inequality today? Does public policy and social programs help to reduce inequality today and tomorrow? In view of those questions this chapter explores two main issues: identifying the main inequalities in Brazil and appraising alternative explanation of Brazil's excessive inequality. Moreover, it provides separate assessments of the incidence of labor market forces *vis a vis* social policy programs.

The first section describes the key dimensions of income inequality in Brazil and provides an considers the accuracy of those measures when compared to more precise consumption aggregates. The second section explores the cause of inequality in relation to asset distribution (human and non-human), asset price differentials, and entitlements to estate transfers (mainly retirement pensions). In this case, the method used to appraise the alternative explanations of Brazil excess inequality is to use cross country comparison with the United Sates and Mexico. Finally, the third section studies the impact of public policy on equity. In particular, measuring to what extent transfer (in kind and monetary) implicit in the public provision of social services are able to produce a more equitable distribution of welfare among Brazilians.

Inequality in Brazil
High and Persistent Inequality
With a Gini coefficient of 0.59 in the distribution of household incomes per capita, Brazil has one of the highest levels of income inequality in the world. Although the Gini coefficient can, by construction, range from zero (for perfect equality) to one (for distributions in which all income is in the hands of a single unit), in practice, Gini indexes for income distributions range from just

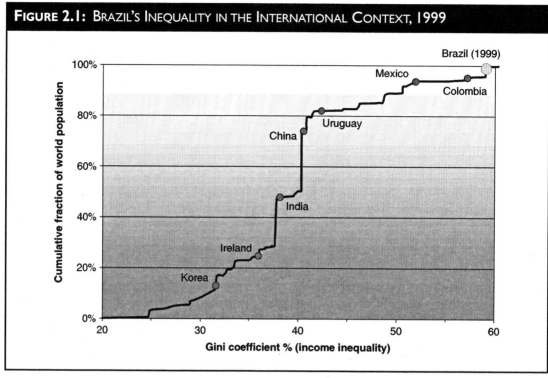

FIGURE 2.1: BRAZIL'S INEQUALITY IN THE INTERNATIONAL CONTEXT, 1999

Note: Includes 108 countries. Data from 1993–1999.

Source: World Bank Indicators, 2002.

under 0.3 to just over 0.6.[12] Figure 2.1 presents the cumulative distribution of Gini coefficients for all 108 countries for which the World Bank judges it has reasonably reliable data, with each country given a weight proportional to its population. Comparability problems abound across the surveys on which these data are based.[13] In the case of Brazil, some upward inequality bias is due to incomplete measures of income, in particular in poor rural areas. Hence, holding any other inequality determinants the same, Brazil will appear more unequal when compared to other countries where rural household data is not collected (only urban) and/or *income* inequality estimates are unavailable and, use—typically lower—consumption inequality measures. Finally, Brazil has arguably an extensive set of programs that provide basic services to the poor, with the result that income inequality overestimates inequality of a broader welfare measure. Based on these concerns, one can question Brazil's relative position—99th percentile of the world's population. However, the fact remains that Brazil has extremely high inequality.

Brazil has the fifth largest population (170 million) and the eighth largest gross national product (GNP) in the world.[14] Brazil is not only unequal in terms of income and social indicators, but also unequal given its level of economic activity. Figure 2.2 compares the inequality and GDP per capita of Brazil's with other low and middle-income countries. Although most unequal societies (for example, Sierra Leone, Nicaragua, the Central African Republic, Paraguay, and Guatemala) tend to be countries with a lower level of development, Brazil's level of inequality

---

12. Values for distributions of consumption expenditures are generally lower, because some of the dispersion arising from transitory income components is smoothed away through the consumption behaviour of households.

13. Some of these are further discussed below.

14. World Development Indicators, 2001 (figures correspond to 1999).

FIGURE 2.2: BRAZIL'S INEQUALITY AMONG UPPER MIDDLE-INCOME ECONOMIES

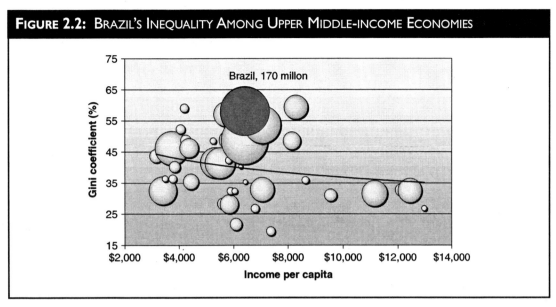

Note: Bubbles reflect population size.
Source: World Bank Indicators 2002.

FIGURE 2.3: TIME SERIES OF INEQUALITY IN BRAZIL

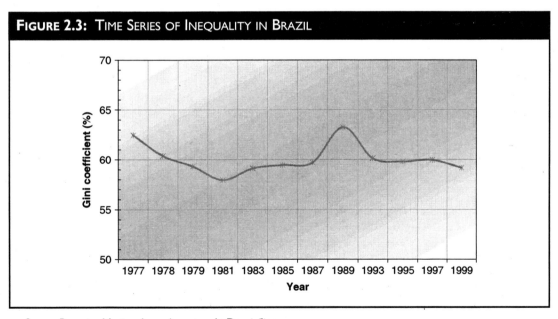

Source: Pesquisa Nacional por Amostra de Domicílios.

appears more prominent when compared with other middle-income countries (figure 2.3). Such levels of inequality become even more prominent when Brazil's size is taken into account.

In addition, these high levels of inequality have been remarkably stable in Brazil. As Figure 2.4 (Bourguignon, Ferreira and Leite (2002a)) indicates, during the entire period for which we have reasonably reliable survey information (1977–99), the Gini coefficient has never strayed outside the 0.58–0.62 range, except for an unexplained upward blip to 0.64 in 1989. This striking persistence is part of what the authors refer to as "the unacceptable stability" of Brazil's inequality.

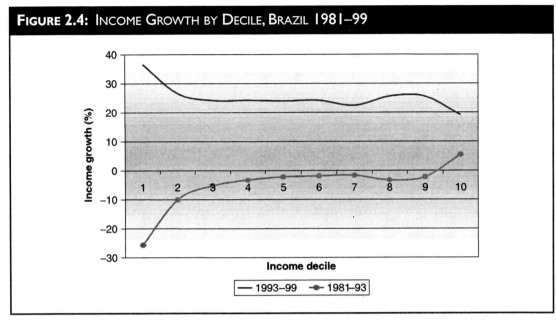

FIGURE 2.4: INCOME GROWTH BY DECILE, BRAZIL 1981–99

Source: PNAD, Barros 2002.

Despite the persistence of inequality in the long term, there is some evidence that the mid- to late 1990s represented a period of inequality reduction in Brazil. Figure 2.5 shows that during that period income growth was nearly homogeneous across income groups except for the top and lowest deciles of the population. For the first decile, income grew 25 percent below average from 1981 to 1992, but it was 10 percent above average from 1993 to 1999. Something similar happened for the second decile but in a smaller order of magnitude. Somewhat symmetrically, income growth for the top decile was 5 percent above average in the first period and 5 percent below during the second.

Income disparities in Brazil are also significant across regions and between metropolitan areas, nonmetropolitan urban centers, and rural areas, as well. Figure 2.6 shows the mean household per capita income by region and by area (rural and urban) for Brazil in 1999. Across areas, there is a uniform trend across the country: Metropolitan areas have substantially higher income per capita than nonmetropolitan areas, and between nonmetropolitan areas, urban areas have higher income than rural ones. As figure 6 shows, this trend is particularly acute in the center-west region, where the difference between the income per capita in the metropolitan area (Brasília) and the income in other urban areas is of some R$250. The difference between metropolitan and rural areas in terms of income is R$353. Across regions, income disparities are considerable as well, and they increase for all the areas as one moves from the northeast region toward the southeast. An early study pointed out the large extent of these regional and urban-rural inequalities and also how the nominal differences are reduced when price differences are accounted for (Thomas 1987). A recent study of Ceará found how much difference the accounting for educational transfers makes to the poverty estimates and their trends (World Bank 2003).

The reduction in mean-income differences across regions appears to be significant for poverty, than the reduction of regional differences on income inequality.[15] In fact simulations of poverty changes associated to elimination of regional differences in inequality and income reveal strong

15. For example, the Sudeste regions is not only richer but a bit less unequal than the other Brazilian regions—Gini coefficient equal to 0.58 versus 0.60 for the whole country.

FIGURE 2.5: MEAN HOUSEHOLD PER CAPITA INCOME BY REGION AND AREA (RURAL–URBAN)—BRAZIL, 1999

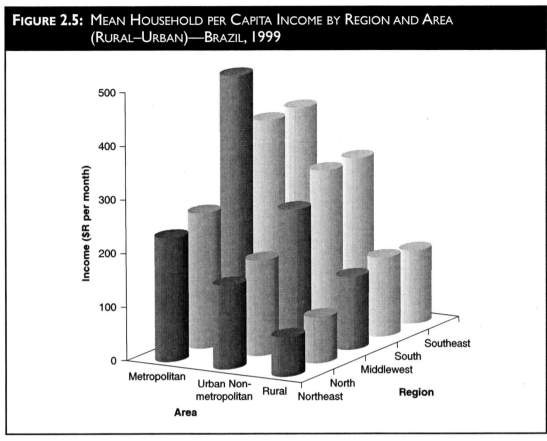

Source: PNAD 1999.

FIGURE 2.6: LABOR EARNINGS BY GENDER—BRAZIL, 1999

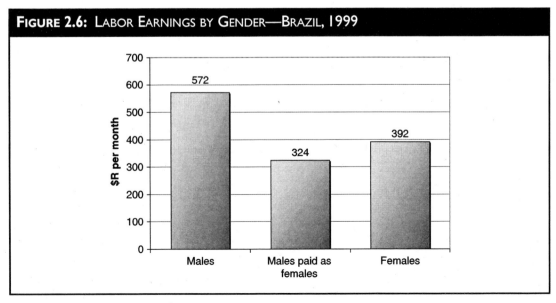

Source: PNAD, 1999.

TABLE 2.1: EFFECT OF REGIONAL DIFFERENCES ON POVERTY: BRAZIL

Simulations	Poverty Rate	Extreme Poverty Rate	Mean Income	Income Inequality
Observed	35	15	298	0.60
Elimination of regional differences of				
1. Mean income				
standardizing for the mean	31	12	298	0.58
standardizing for the Sudeste	23	8	376	0.58
2. Income Inequality				
standardizing for the mean	35	14	298	0.60
standardizing for the Sudeste	30	11	298	0.58

Source: Barros (2002).

discrepancies (Table 2.1). While eliminating regional mean income differences can reduce poverty and extreme poverty by 4 and 3 percentage points, eliminating regional differences of inequality has negligible effects on poverty. Moreover standardizing by mean income in the Sudeste region reduces poverty and extreme poverty by 12 and 7 percentage points, while doing the same for inequality reduces poverty by 5 and 1 percentage points, respectively. Even though these unconditional comparisons are true, they should be interpreted as a puzzle of determinants of regional differences in mean income and to as a simple policy prescription. For instance, are regional differences mostly associated to lack of human capital or infrastructure, or to labor markets segmentation or discrimination. The answer to this question would provide a framework for the most appropriate Federal policies to address regional inequality.

Yet, the regional dimension is by no means the only one. However well-integrated within neighborhoods and households, living conditions still vary dramatically across Brazil's racial groups. Mean earnings for whites are R$585 per month, whereas they are only R$279 per month for blacks.[16] Those of Asian origin earn R$1,155 per month. In terms of household income per capita, some 12 percent of all inequality in Brazil is accounted for by inequality between races. The comparable figure for the United States is 2.4 percent.[17] Also, incomes do not differ that much by color. Educational attainment is also widely unequal; by one measure, completed years of schooling, blacks fare only two-thirds as well as whites: 4.43 years for the former compared with 6.54 years for the latter (Lam 1999).

Gender inequalities are also important. Although the gender gap in wages has been diminishing steadily over time, unconditional differences are still very large. Figure 2.7 shows that mean earnings for women in 1999 were 29 percent lower than those of men. Remarkably, this differential actually rises to 34 percent after controlling for age, education, and hours worked, reflecting the fact that women in younger cohorts are on average more educated than men.[18]

---

16. Comparison based on main occupation.

17. Where inequality is measured by the Theil-L or by the Theil-T indices. See Bourguignon, Ferreira and Menendez (2002).

18. Note, however, that, as elsewhere in the world, the actual work experience of each worker is not observed. Because women are, on average, likely to have been out of the labor force for longer periods than men (as a result of childbirth and childcare duties), these differences are likely to reflect errors in the measurement of actual experience and therefore cannot be ascribed only to discrimination.

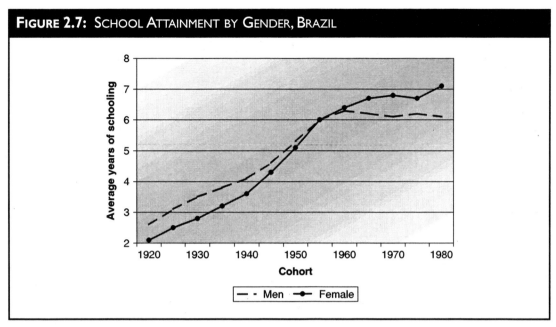

FIGURE 2.7: SCHOOL ATTAINMENT BY GENDER, BRAZIL

Source: Silva. M.C and S. Wajnman (2000).

Further, women are at a disadvantage not only in the labor market: female representation at top decisionmaking positions is still tiny in both the private and public sectors.

There are also some newer, and perhaps less common, gender inequalities that also present policy challenges. Figure 2.8 shows the educational attainment by gender for Brazilian cohorts born since 1920. The educational gender gap against women that existed since 1920 in Brazil was systematically reduced until it disappeared in the 1950s, when girls started to study longer than boys. Today, the gender gap has broadened, again reaching the 1920s magnitude, but this time it is against men. Male-specific difficulties in the learning process are as serious a problem as female-specific ones, and they may be related to increasing exposure to violence among young men in many of the country's metropolitan regions.

Accuracy of Measurement: Caution Is Needed when Interpreting Brazilian Data

Before the data analysis proceeds, it should be recognized that current knowledge about the distribution of living standards—however and wherever measured is intrinsically imprecise. At its best, it is based on answers provided by a sample of households to interviewers. Measurement errors arise from the nature and design of the samples, from the ways questions are asked and understood, from the manner in which answers are recorded, and even during the process of transcoding replies from questionnaires onto electronic storage.

Most of the (abundant) existing work on poverty and inequality in Brazil has been based on the data sets of the *Pesquisa Nacional por Amostra de Domicílios* ([PNAD] household survey), which is conducted annually by the *Instituto Brasileiro de Geografia e Estatística* (Brazilian Statistical Institute [IBGE]) and is representative of the whole country, except for rural areas in the northern region. Recently, however, as researchers learned more about the way in which respondents may misreport incomes depending on certain characteristics of the questionnaire, doubts have emerged about whether the information drawn from the PNAD was reliable, particularly as regarded incomes in rural areas, the informal sector, and capital incomes (Ferreira, Lanjouw, and Neri 2000).

FIGURE 2.8: HEADCOUNT POVERTY MEASURES BY REGION FOR DIFFERENT DATA SERIES

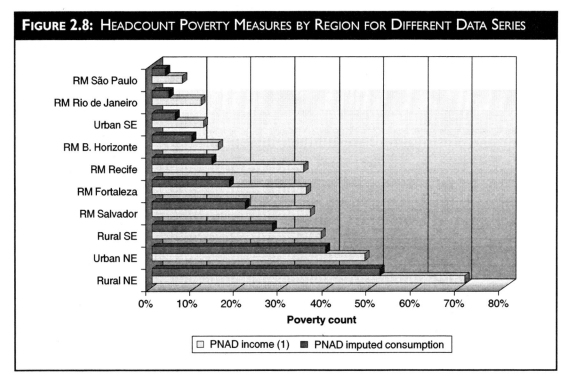

Notes: Poverty line of R$65.07 in 1996 São Paulo (see Ferreira, Lanjouw, and Neri [2000]). PNAD per capita income, PPV per capita consumption, and PNAD-imputed per capita consumption have been adjusted for spatial price variation (see Ferreira, Lanjouw, and Neri [2000]).
Source: PNAD 1995, 1996, and 1997.

The IBGE has responded quickly and aptly by radically redesigning the *Pesquisa de Orçamentos Familiares* Family Expenditure Survey [POF]), which is currently in the field. This survey is planned to be nationally representative, and it will provide detailed income and consumption expenditure data from the same survey instrument, with that level of representativeness for the first time since the *Estudo Nacional da Despesa Familiar* (National Study of Family Expenses [ENDEF]) study of 1975. Although it is likely that future measurement and analysis of poverty and income distribution in Brazil will draw heavily on the new POF, in the meantime, it was still necessary to form a judgment on the reliability of the estimates, poverty profiles, and inequality decompositions based on a time series of a quarter-century of PNADs.

This was done for this report by relying on yet another IBGE survey, the *Pesquisa de Padrões de Vida* ([PPV]), fielded in 1996. The PPV contains detailed information on household consumption expenditures, as well as incomes. It has been used for national analysis less often, because of its incomplete geographic coverage and small sample size. However, recent developments in statistical techniques have allowed researchers to rely on common variables surveyed in both PPV and PNAD samples, and to estimate models that allow consumption estimates from the PPV to be imputed into the PNAD sample.[19] Elbers, Lanjouw, and Leite (2002), whose work is included in Part II of this report, describe the methodology in detail and present results for Brazil as a whole, for its individual states, and for other spatial disaggregations.

---

19. See Elbers, Lanjouw and Lanjouw (2001) for the pioneering description of this methodology.

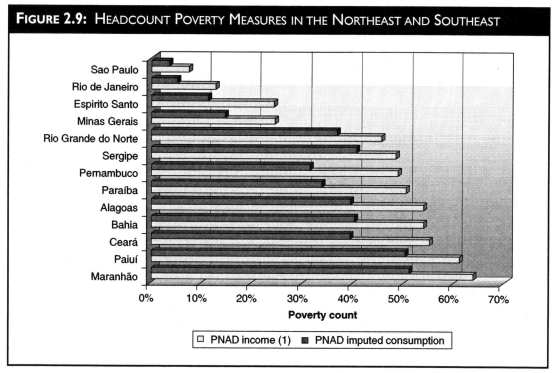

FIGURE 2.9: HEADCOUNT POVERTY MEASURES IN THE NORTHEAST AND SOUTHEAST

Notes: PNAD per capita income, PPV per capita consumption, and PNAD-imputed per capita consumption have been adjusted for spatial price variation (see Ferreira, Lanjouw, and Neri [2000]).

Source: PNAD 1996, 1997. *Note:* Poverty line of R$65.07 in 1996 São Paulo (see Ferreira, Lanjouw, and Neri [2000]).

Although their findings are rich in detail, two main results arise that are fundamental for the analysis in this report:

1. *Consumption-based poverty and inequality levels are much lower than those measured for income,* in accordance with the international evidence. Nevertheless, when compared with other countries that measure consumption inequality, Brazil is still very unequal.
2. *Qualitatively and in relative terms, however, income-based poverty and inequality profiles in the country are remarkably robust in terms of poverty ranking between regions of Brazil.* Figures 2.9 and 2.10 show that the rankings of states and regions by poverty incidence change little as we move from the original PNAD income distributions to those based on imputed income. The graphs for inequality, which are broadly similar, can be found in Part II of this report.

This suggests that although we should be careful about attaching excessive value to the absolute levels that have been reported in some previous work, it is reassuring to know that the main conclusions about the nature and incidence of poverty across regions, areas, occupations, and educational levels are generally robust. These "poverty profiles" are generally of greater importance in guiding policy decisions than the absolute value of specific poverty or inequality measures. Insofar as one guards against paying too much attention to specific levels, it would seem that the existing time series of PNAD data, and the excellent work that has been built on it, can still teach us a great deal about the patterns of distributional behavior in Brazil over the 1976–2000 period.

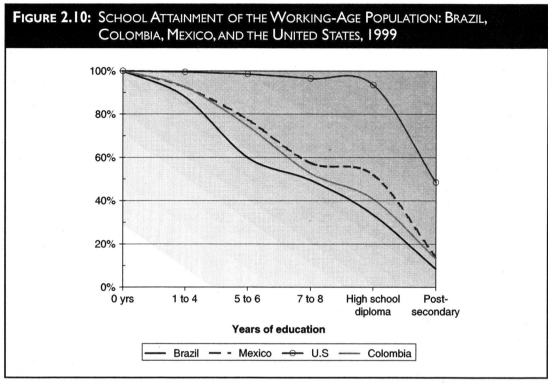

FIGURE 2.10: SCHOOL ATTAINMENT OF THE WORKING-AGE POPULATION: BRAZIL, COLOMBIA, MEXICO, AND THE UNITED STATES, 1999

Source: Bourguignon, Ferreira, and Leite [2002a] and Velez and others [2002b].

The distribution of imputed consumption constructed by Elbers, Lanjouw, and Leite (2002), is most valuable in providing guidance about the strengths and weaknesses of the PNAD data, and would also allow for detailed poverty mapping at a much greater level of disaggregation than the PPV and with less bias than the PNAD, but it is not intended for statistical analysis at the individual level. In the discussion that follows of the determinants of Brazilian inequality, we therefore rely on the urban-only PNAD income data.

The Causes of Inequality

Having established that Brazil is indeed among the worlds highest in terms of inequality, whether it is measured in terms of household incomes or consumption expenditures, and that the basic structure of inequality within the country known from previous studies is reasonably robust, we now turn to the main purpose of this section of the report, namely to investigate the causes of Brazil's excess inequality. Why is it that Brazil lies so far along the top tail of the distribution of Gini coefficients in the world, as shown earlier in figure 2.

There are four main candidate explanations:

1. The underlying *distributions of assets across the population* might be more unequal than in other countries. Important assets are educational attainment, land, and capital.
2. Price differentials of these assets—notably education—might be steeper in Brazil than elsewhere. If the wage differences for each extra year of schooling in Brazil are much higher than in comparable countries, then more income inequality would be generated from the same underlying distribution of education.
3. It could be that Brazil's excess inequality arises neither from unequal distributions of assets nor excessive wage differentials by skill, but from *behavioral differences* or differential

patterns of use of these assets. *Labor force participation, occupational choice, and fertility decisions* could account for very substantial differences in the distribution of household per capita incomes.

4. The distribution of claims and entitlements to state transfers might be less progressive than in other countries. Particular interest should be paid to retirement pension programs.

The evidence presented below shows that all of those explanatory factors are present in the case of Brazil, albeit to different extents. This subsection is divided into four components. We look first at the evidence on the magnitude and importance of inequality in the distribution of assets— mostly years of education and land. We then turn to an international comparison of wage differentials by education and other features of the labor market. In particular, we provide a cross-country appraisal of alternative explanations of Brazil excessive *urban* inequality, both market and non-market determinants.[20] Finally, we divide our discussion of the role of the state into evidence on the incidence of its expenditure and evidence on the incidence of its tax revenue-raising efforts.

Asset Distributions: Brazil in an International Perspective

The distribution of school attainment among the population of working age is more unequally distributed that in the United States, Mexico, or Colombia, to name a few. One explanatory factor behind wage differentials in Brazil is, therefore, simply the skill gap in the Brazilian labor force. Compared with the United States, Brazil has a much wider gap of labor force skills. As figure 2.11 shows, in Brazil, 35 percent of the working-age population finished secondary education, but in the United States, this 94 percent finished secondary school—and in Mexico, 52 percent, and in Colombia, 41 percent. The gap is even larger, in relative terms, for the postsecondary level. In the United States, almost half of the working-age population has postsecondary education, but in Brazil, this number is below 10 percent—and in Mexico and Colombia, 14 and 13 percent, respectively.

Another asset that has historically been of the utmost importance, and remains crucial to the one-fifth of Brazil's population who still dwell in rural areas, is agricultural land. Although this asset also is distributed very unequally in Brazil, the country is not as much of an international outlier in terms of the distribution of land as it is in terms of income. This can be seen from Table 2.2 below, which lists Gini coefficients for land distributions obtained for a sample of seventeen countries.

Table 2.2 above, drawn from Assunção (2002) reveals an enormous dispersion across land inequality measures, ranging from a Gini index of 0.38 in Japan to 0.91 in Peru. Brazil's Gini of 0.86 is certainly at the high end of this distribution, alongside some other land-abundant countries like Argentina, Australia, and Venezuela, but also nations with very different patterns of agricultural ownership, such as Spain or Peru.

As in many other countries, Brazil's distribution displays clear regional differences. At the risk of oversimplifying, one might distinguish a more unequal pattern of land ownership in the northeast of the country, as well as in the "newer" agricultural regions of the center-west and the north, whereas the south and the southeast show somewhat lower Gini indexes, at levels close to those of the national land distributions in the United States or Colombia. These regional patterns and their temporal evolution can be seen in figure 2.12, also drawn from Assunção (2002).

The overall picture that emerges, then, is one of a country with deep inequalities in the underlying distributions of the assets that determine how productive people are, such as human capital and land, which lead to correspondingly unequal distributions of primary income.

---

20. Since it is a cross-country comparison of *urban* income inequality, this report does not provide a measure of the impact of rural land distribution on income inequality.

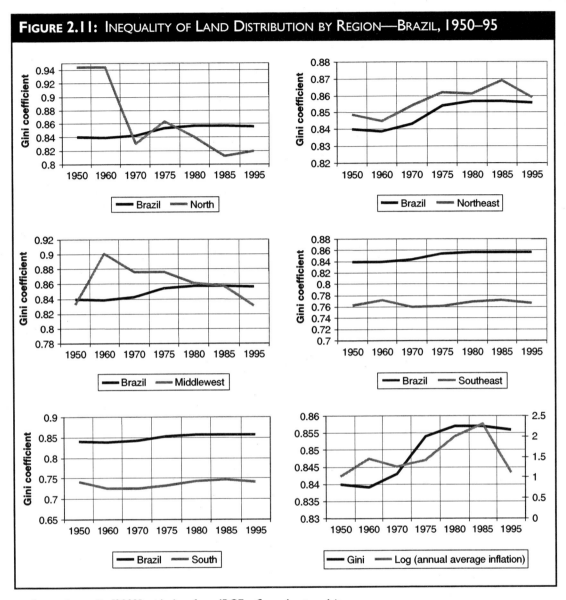

FIGURE 2.11: INEQUALITY OF LAND DISTRIBUTION BY REGION—BRAZIL, 1950–95

Source: Assunção [2002] with data from IBGE—*Censo Agropecuário.*

Wage differentials by Skills are a Also Part of the Picture

An unequal distribution in the endowments of land and education is, however, only part of the story. It turns out that the market wage differentials to additional schooling are also higher in Brazil than in a number of other countries, at least over part of the range of years of education. This means that an already unequal asset distribution is projected into an even more unequal distribution of market incomes. Returning to the country comparisons we made in the previous subsection, we find that the wage-skill premium in Brazil is also higher when compared with the United States and Mexico, but less than in Colombia. Figure 2.13 shows that, on average, individuals with postsecondary education earn 3.7 times the labor earnings of individuals with incomplete primary education. The Brazilian differential is 50 percent greater than the differential in the United States (2.5) and also well above that in Mexico (3.3). It is, however, slightly below that of Colombia (4.3). Differences are also pronounced when high school graduates are

TABLE 2.2: GINI COEFFICIENT FOR LAND DISTRIBUTION; SELECTED COUNTRIES

Country	Year	Gini Coefficient
Peru	1972	0.911
Venezuela	1971	0.910
Australia	1990	0.903
Spain	1989	0.858
Brazil	**1995**	**0.856**
Argentina	1988	0.850
Uruguay	1980	0.803
Paraguay	1991	0.784
Colombia	1990	0.774
Bolivia	1989	0.768
United States	1987	0.754
Italy	1990	0.739
Germany	1990	0.667
United Kingdom	1990	0.621
India	1985	0.592
Bangladesh	1977	0.419
Japan	1990	0.382

Source: Assunção [2002] see Volume 2 of this Report.

compared with individuals who have incomplete primary education. In this case, Brazil leads with 2.4, followed by Colombia (2.0), Mexico (1.9), and the United States (1.6).

Moreover, the dynamics of wage-skill premia during the 1990s have also been detrimental to income inequality. Blom and Vélez (2002) in Part II show that if the marginal returns to tertiary education had remained at the 1988 level (that is, 19 instead of 24 percent), the total reduction of wage inequality wage differentials by education would have been *two more percentage points* of the Gini. Moreover, if wage differentials by education would have fallen to U.S. levels (13 percent), the additional reduction in wage inequality due to changes in these differentials would have been twice as large and would have reduced wage-inequality from 0.575 to 0.530. Similar simulations for changes in wage differentials by education at lower levels of schooling show that they have much smaller influence on wage-inequality.

These simulations reveal the potential of reduction in the skill premium to attain more equitable income distributions. That is, hypothetical increase in supply (or reduction in demand) for workers with postsecondary education that causes schooling wage differentials might bring important reductions in wage income inequality. This finding motivates inquiring about how far policymakers can influence the skill premium and thereby reduce wage inequality. Chapter 3, below, examines whether increasing skill premium in Brazil has been associated to insufficient supply or increasing demand or both.

Unequally Unequal: Segmentation and Discrimination

The labor market affects the distribution of incomes primarily through the projection of differences in levels of human capital, but not exclusively so. Although the generation and

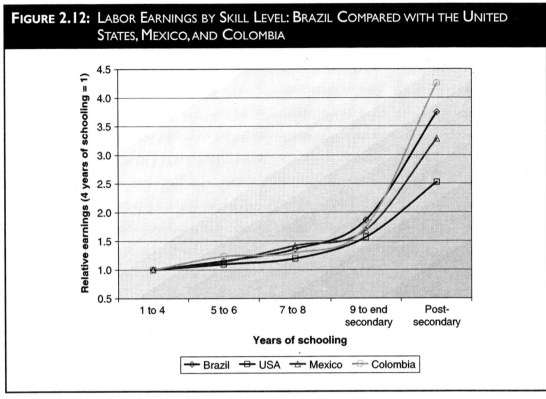

FIGURE 2.12: LABOR EARNINGS BY SKILL LEVEL: BRAZIL COMPARED WITH THE UNITED STATES, MEXICO, AND COLOMBIA

Source: Bourguignon, Ferreira, and Leite [2002a] and Velez and others [2002b].

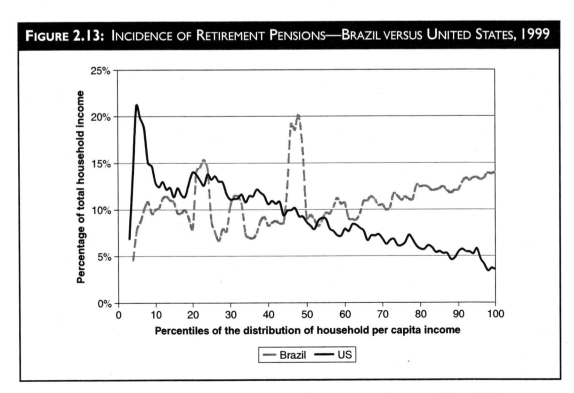

FIGURE 2.13: INCIDENCE OF RETIREMENT PENSIONS—BRAZIL VERSUS UNITED STATES, 1999

Source: Current Population Survey (CPS) 2000; PNAD 2000; Bourguignon, Ferreira, and Leite 2002a.

TABLE 2.3: LABOR MARKET AND SCHOOLING CONTRIBUTION TO INCOME INEQUALITY IN BRAZIL

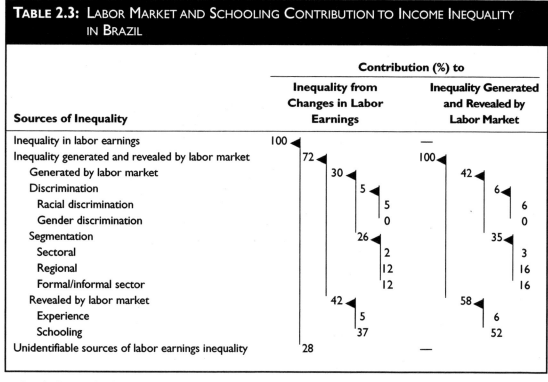

Sources of Inequality	Contribution (%) to	
	Inequality from Changes in Labor Earnings	Inequality Generated and Revealed by Labor Market
Inequality in labor earnings	100	—
Inequality generated and revealed by labor market	72	100
Generated by labor market	30	42
Discrimination	5	6
Racial discrimination	5	6
Gender discrimination	0	0
Segmentation	26	35
Sectoral	2	3
Regional	12	16
Formal/informal sector	12	16
Revealed by labor market	42	58
Experience	5	6
Schooling	37	52
Unidentifiable sources of labor earnings inequality	28	—

Source: Barros [2002]. PNAD.

reproduction of Brazil's inequality can be understood, in economic terms, through the continuing interplay of unequal distribution of assets, amplified by considerable price differentials to these assets (chief among them, education) the importance of historical, political, and cultural factors cannot be underplayed. The role of history is of obvious importance. The present distribution of land cannot be understood without reference to the history of colonization, just as present racial inequalities originate in slavery.[21] To this day, segmentation and discrimination in the labor markets appear to play an important role in the persistence of inequality.

Table 2.3 drawn from Barros (2002), indicates the relative importance of segmentation and discrimination effects as compared, for instance, with the effect of projecting educational inequality into the labor income distribution. The role of spatial and formal or informal segmentation, in particular, clearly cannot be ignored. Also, the evidence of discrimination, although quantitatively less important, is sufficiently substantial to warrant attention as well. Table 2.3 shows that 72 percent of total inequality in Brazil is either revealed or generated by the labor market 52 percent reveals the inequality of education among employed, 6 percent the variability in experience and the rest is generated by the labor market as segmentation (35 percent) and discrimination (6 percent). Therefore, although more than half of the labor earning differentials are coming from differences of schooling, the impact of segmentation and discrimination has the *same* order of magnitude. Notably, regional differences still account for almost half of inequality generated by labor market segmentation. Which confirms that the substantial income differentials across regions mentioned above are not only based upon human capital endowments but also on some other determinants of productivity such as infrastructure and the quality of government services, among others.

---

21. Although we do not see it as this report's comparative advantage to further the analysis of this historical background, that does not mean that it is any less important.

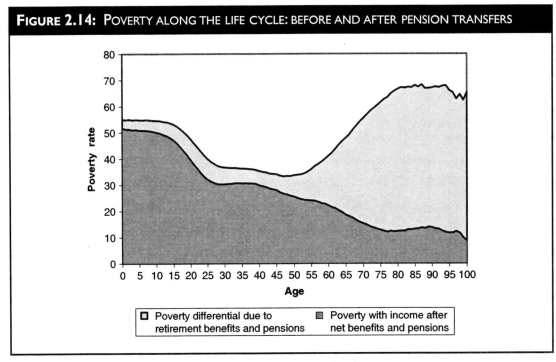

FIGURE 2.14: POVERTY ALONG THE LIFE CYCLE: BEFORE AND AFTER PENSION TRANSFERS

Note: Poverty defined by Brazilian domestic poverty line.

Source: Pesquisa Nacional por Amostra de Domicílios (PNAD) de 1999. Barros [2002].

Appraising Alternative Explanations: Market versus Non-market Determinants

Our international comparisons across countries were not restricted only to market determinants of incomes. Brazilian *public transfers*—chiefly retirement pensions—are also highly regressive when compared with those of the United States. Figure 2.14 shows clearly that in Brazil the incidence of public pensions increases monotonically with income for the top two quintiles relative to the rest of the population. On the contrary, in the United States, retirement pensions are progressive: Incidence decreases monotonically with income as meant. The share of pensions on total income is the highest for the poorest 10 percent, but for the top 5 percent, the share is approximately one-third. As a result, the share of pensions to the top 20 percent in Brazil is more than twice the corresponding share in the United States—61 and 26 percent, respectively. Moreover, a similar comparison for the poorest 40 percent shows a disproportionate 1:3 ratio—9 and 29 percent, respectively. Notwithstanding, despite having only half the number of pensioners that the United States has, Brazil devotes a much higher share of resources to cover that population.[22]

The *relative importance of alternative explanations of excess inequality* was measured by cross-country simulations. To investigate the importance of each of these candidate explanations (or indeed, whether there are others), Bourguignon, Ferreira, and Leite (2002a) compared the structure of Brazil's urban income distribution with those of two other large countries in the Western Hemisphere, the United States and Mexico. The importance of wage differentials by skill was investigated by estimating wage regressions in both countries and then simulating the distribution that would result if, say, Brazil had the U.S. or Mexican structure of wage differentials. The importance of assets was investigated with respect to two broad asset types:

---

22. Pension transfers represent 12 percent of household income in Brazil, and only 7.2 percent in the United States.

TABLE 2.4: ACCOUNTING FOR BRAZIL'S EXCESS INEQUALITY RELATIVE TO THE UNITED STATES: MICROSIMULATIONS

Distribution	Gini Coefficient[a]	% of Total Difference
Brazil, observed	0.569	
Brazil, with U.S. wage differentials	0.530	32
Brazil, with wage differentials and educational endowments[b]	0.495	28
Brazil, with wage differentials educational endowments, and labor incomes	0.448	39
United States, observed	0.445	I

a. The Gini coefficient is for the distribution of household per capita incomes, in the urban areas only.

b. Educational endowments working directly as well as through effects on fertility and participation decisions. See Bourguignon, Ferreira, and Leite (2002a) for details and disaggregated results, as well as for other measures of inequality, poverty measures, and simulations for male and female earnings distributions.

Source: CPS 2000, PNAD 2000.

education and entitlements to public transfers.[23] For education, discrete educational choice models were estimated to allow for the conditional distribution of educational attainment on other characteristics. Once these were estimated for both countries, the authors simulated the income distribution that would result if, say, Brazil had the U.S. or Mexican educational choice parameters.

For public transfers, we simply replaced the observed distribution of transfers in Brazil by the mean normalized distribution of transfers in, say, the United States, preserving the rank by the distribution of earned incomes of the receiving households. The importance of preferences, regarding labor supply, occupational choice, and fertility, was investigated by estimating discrete choice models for these decisions and replacing the observed Brazilian parameters with those estimated for other countries. Details of the data used for each country, and of the methodology, are available from Bourguignon, Ferreira, and Leite (2002a) in Part II of this report.

In essence, it appears that three factors account for most of Brazil's extreme levels of inequality relative to the United States: unequally distributed endowments of human capital, substantial wage differentials by education, and, last but not least, the highly regressive nature of public transfers, chiefly retirement pensions. Table 2.4 summarizes the results from Bourguignon, Ferreira, and Leite (2002a).

Take the *underlying distribution of education* first. If Brazil's conditional distribution of education were replaced by those of Mexico or the United States and nothing else changed, overall income inequality would be substantially reduced. In the U.S. comparison, this effect alone accounts for some six Gini points, 28 percent of the 12.5-point difference. This effect becomes even more pronounced when one allows for the additional indirect effects of a higher educational endowment on fertility and participation behaviors. The combination of U.S. educational, fertility, and participation behaviors contributes a nearly one more Gini point decline.

However, it is not only an unequal distribution of years of schooling that explains Brazil's high levels of inequality. The fact that wage differentials by skill are steeper in Brazil than in the two comparator countries constitutes another source of excess inequality. In particular, adopting the U.S. structure of wages would subtract some further four points of the Gini—32 percent of

---

23. More will be said about land distributions later. The distribution of nonland physical and financial assets is essentially unknown in Brazil, and estimates for other countries are also regarded as very unreliable.

the total difference between Brazil and the United States. In summary, education contributes to Brazil's excess inequality through both quantities and prices.

In Table 2.4, we report first the effects of adopting the U.S. structure of wage differentials by schooling. It lowers the Gini from 0.57 to 0.53. Importing educational-choice behaviour—and its consequences on fertility and participation as well as wage differentials by schooling—lowers the Gini further to approximately 0.50.[24] The remaining five points of the Gini (39 percent) turn out to be accounted for by imposing on Brazil the distribution of U.S. nonlabor incomes, principally that of pensions. Once this effect is added, we move to the result of the complete simulation, in the penultimate row of Table 2.4. The Gini of this simulated distribution, at 0.448, is remarkably close to the observed U.S. Gini in 1999, attesting to the power of the decomposition in accounting for the actual sources of differences between the U.S. and Brazilian distributions.

The large role of nonlabor incomes, identified in the last step of the decomposition, led us to investigate in greater detail the effects of each of the various sources of unearned income. Although the PNAD measures for capital income are more suspect than those for other sources, the decompositions by source reported by Bourguignon, Ferreira, and Leite (2002a) leave little room for doubt that the bulk of the effect is caused by importing into Brazil the incidence of U.S. retirement pensions. In other words, replacing the regressive nature of Brazilian pensions by the incidence pattern observed in the United States accounts for almost 5 full points of the 12.5-point difference observed between the Gini coefficients of both countries.

Moreover, retirement pensions are associated with strong inequities along the life cycle, specifically against younger cohorts. Figure 2.14 shows how the probability of being poor is "U" shaped and peaks at both extremes of the life cycle. While for the older population beyond 75 years of age, the probability of being poor when income excludes pension transfers is above 65%, for the cohorts between 25 and 55 years old is between 30 and 40 percent, and for the 0 to 15 years old is close to 55 percent. However, once state retirement pensions ("aposentadorias") are included they are quite effective in reducing poverty for older individuals. In fact, poverty falls below 20 percent for all individuals aged 65 or older. Obviously, one should consider that other programs directed towards the young population are progressive, hence poverty reducing as well. However, the fact that all programs directed to the young population (up to 17 years old) are one fourth of the total pension subsidies, while their relative population size is three times larger than the population 55 years and older shows clearly the magnitude of the inter-generational inequities of public policy.[25]

The striking importance of the regressive incidence of pensions as a determinant of Brazil's excess inequality relative to a country such as the United States shows that, in this case, the potential equalizing role of the Brazilian state is scarce. Approximately two-thirds of Brazil's federal expenditures, which amount to some 20 percent of gross domestic product (GDP), are grouped under the general heading of social expenditures. Retirement pensions, the incidence of which we have just considered, account for nearly half of that.

Public Policy and Equity

Public Social Expenditure and Targeting: Excluding Pensions, Incidence is Progressive

The previous section has shown to what extent three different determinants of income generation—that affect both labor and non-labor components—explain excess inequality in Brazil, relative to two large economies like the United States and Mexico. Despite this fact, the actual distribution of welfare across households also depends upon other very important determinants: in particular public social policy programs. In other words, household's welfare not only depends

---

24. The decomposition into endowment and wage-differentials effects is not perfectly additive in nature, so that the combination of these two effects accounts for 7.5, rather than 10.0, points of the Gini.

25. Assuming universal coverage of both population the disproportion of subsidies per capita would be close to 1 to 12 in against the younger population.

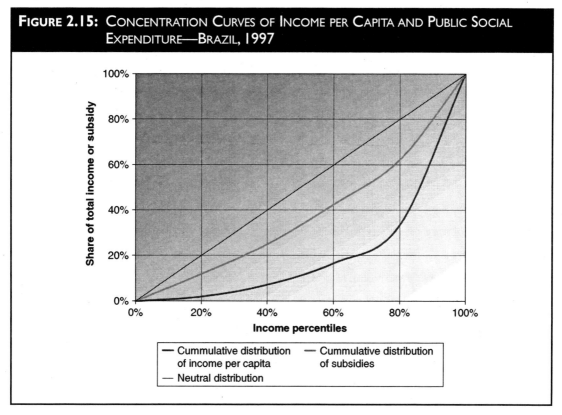

FIGURE 2.15: CONCENTRATION CURVES OF INCOME PER CAPITA AND PUBLIC SOCIAL EXPENDITURE—BRAZIL, 1997

Source: PPV 1997, authors' calculations.

upon monetary income per capita as such but on in-kind transfers implicit in the public provision of social services, as well. For instance, government programs in education, health care, urban investment in water, sewerage, housing and *favela* upgrading, nutrition, childcare and labor programs—including unemployment subsidies. Most of these services are in-kind transfers of assets and therefore—together with other subsidies in cash—affect welfare distribution in the short run to the extent that they substitute household expenses in social services or constitute a net increase in consumption. On the other hand, public social policy also affects income distribution in the long run to the extent that it shapes the distribution of human and non-human assets of the next generation of workers, a major determinant of tomorrows income distribution. However, this section we concentrate only on the distributional impact in the short run and, for that purpose, examine briefly the incidence patterns of the key publicly provided programs across the Brazilian distribution of household income.

Public Social Expenditure (PSE)—including pensions—in Brazil *reduces inequality.* In 1997, public social expenditure represented approximately 17 percent of income per capita for the average Brazilian, and its distribution is moderately regressive (Figure 2.15 and Table 2.5). That is to say, PSE benefits the poor less than proportionally. The share of the top quintile of the distribution in public social expenditure is 38 percent, but the share of the two poorest quintiles is just 25 percent. Nevertheless, because PSE is distributed less regressively than household income, inequality of income after PSE subsidies is well below the inequality of income alone. The Gini coefficient of household *income plus subsidies* is almost six percentage points –5.6, smaller than the Gini coefficient of household income.

TABLE 2.5: SUMMARY OF RESULTS OF ANALYSIS OF DISTRIBUTIONAL INCIDENCE OF PUBLIC SOCIAL EXPENDITURE—NORTHEAST AND SOUTHEAST BRAZIL, 1997

| | Subsidy Size | | Targeting Share by Quintile (%) | | | | | | Gini[2] | Subsidy Redistributive Effect Gini-Coeff-Reduction | | |
	Value (R$ billions)	Share	Q1	Q2	Q3	Q4	Q5	Concent.[1] Coefficient	Income Elasticity	Change in Gini[3]	%	RRE[4]
PSE categories												
Pensions	68	56%	7%	8%	15%	19%	51%	0.39	0.63	-1.85	33%	0.6
Non-pensions PSE	54	44%	18%	20%	20%	21%	22%	0.04	0.06	-3.76	67%	1.5
Non pensions PSE without higher education	49	40%	19%	22%	22%	21%	16%	-0.03	-0.05	-3.81	68%	1.7
Total	121	100%	12%	13%	17%	20%	38%	0.23	0.38	-5.61	100%	1.0
Incidence by quintile[5]												
Non-pensions PSE			66%	29%	16%	10%	3%					
Non pensions PSE without higher education			66%	29%	16%	9%	2%					
Total			101%	44%	32%	20%	10%					

Notes: (1)Concentration Coefficient for subsidy x, CCx = 2*COV (x, F(quantile of income)) / mean (x). (2)Gini Income Elasticity for subsidy x, GIE x = CCx / Gini (income), (3) Change in Gini (x): Sector x's contribution to redistribution as change in Gini Coefficient. (4) RRE (x): Relative Redistributive Effectiveness of sector x, redistributive power per unit of expenditure. RRE(x) is equal to the ratio of the sector x's share in contribution to Gini change to the sector x's share in total expenditure. Note that RRE(x) = [GIE(x) −1]/[GIE (total subsidies)−1]. (5) Incidence by quintile:subsidy as a share of income.

Source: "Attacking Brazil's Poverty" (World Bank, 2000),Authors calculations.

Although the share of the poorest income groups in total PSE subsidies is relatively low, the *poor's welfare is quite sensitive to social policy targeting*. In fact the incidence ratios for the first and second quintiles of the distribution are 101 and 44 percent. Which means that the average household in the first quintile receives as much from income as it does from government subsidies in cash or in kind. Obviously, that proportions tends to fall for higher quintiles where poverty is less severe, but its magnitude remains is still sizeable—32 percent for the average household of the third quintile. Moreover, this numbers tend to underestimate the incidence of subsidies on the typical beneficiary of social programs, because many other households in the same income group arc excluded from access to those services. Consequently, any policy changes that modify targeting and access to social services will induce significant gains or losses in the welfare of the poor.

Fortunately, despite the regressive targeting of pensions described in the previous section, the distribution of the other half of these public social expenditures is egalitarian, with clearly progressive impact on the distribution of household welfare. Table 2.5 shows how non-pensions PSE subsidies are distributed in almost equal proportions among income quintiles[26] Non-pensions PSE subsidies have an unambiguous progressive impact on income inequality, reducing the Gini coefficient by 3.76 percentage points. It is also worth noting that in spite of their smaller expenditure share relative to pensions (44 vs. 56 percent), they explain 67 percent of the redistributive effect of PSE as a whole.

Across social sectors, incidence is far from homogeneous. The impact of PSE subsidies by sector on inequality depends on both their targeting (the share of the poor) and their magnitude. After controlling by their size, the ones that have the largest redistribution impact are those where the share of the poor tends to be the largest—namely, kindergarten, children's services, *Favela* upgrading, maternal nutrition, basic education, childcare *"crèche,"* and school lunches (Figure 2.16 and Table A.2). For that reason, their contribution to income redistribution is above their share in expenditure: twice the average or more for all the sectors mentioned (Table A.2).[27] Just the opposite happens with tertiary education, pensions, sewerage connections, and housing (*carta de credito*). In those sectors, the share of the poor tends to be less than proportional and correspondingly their redistribution impact is below their share on expenditure (Figure 2.17).[28] The remaining sectors—universal public health care, unemployment insurance, water connection, urban public transport, and secondary education—are moderately progressive and their corresponding redistribution impact is just above their expenditure share.[29]

One way to understand the implications of heterogeneous targeting across social sectors for income distribution is to ask the following hypothetical question: What is the redistributive potential of changing benefits per household across programs, maintaining total expenses constant? For example by expanding subsidies for best targeted programs and reducing them for the worst shows that redistributive potential is higher for kindergarten, *favela* upgrading, maternal nutrition and basic education programs. Marginal incidence calculations based on Table A.2 show that in order to obtain an effect on inequality equivalent to an additional subsidy of R$100 per individual in kindergarten, the required subsidy rise in other sectors should be much similar for Favela Upgrading (R$106), Maternal Nutrition (Milk Programs) and basic education (R$108),

---

26. Therefore its Concentration Coefficient or quasi-Gini is nearly zero −0.06 and, much smaller that in the case of pension −0.39.

27. Those same sectors have the most negative concentration coefficients (see Table A.2), given the negative covariance of their subsidies with income per capita. They are −0.33 for kindergarten and child assistance services, −0.28 for *favela* upgrading, −0.26 for maternal nutrition programs, and −0.19 for primary education. This property is expressed by the Relative Redistribution Effectiveness parameter (RRE).

28. RRE parameter tends to be below unity (0.6 for pensions, 0.8 for housing, 0.6 for sewerage, and—worst of all −0.2 for tertiary education (see Table A.2)). It is negative for tertiary education because its distribution is more regressive than the distribution of income.

29. RRE parameters have values from 1.1 to 1.5. The two highest values, 1.5 and 1.4, correspond to two key social insurance programs: health care and unemployment insurance.

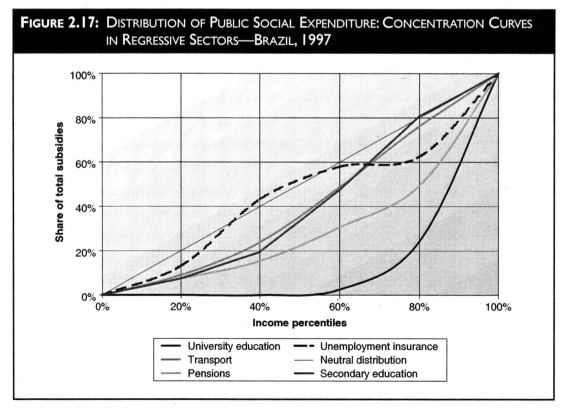

Figure 2.16: Distribution of Public Social Expenditure: Concentration Curves in Progressive Sectors—Brazil, 1997

100%
80%
60%
40%
20%
0%
Share of total subsidies
0%
20%
40%
60%
80%
100%
Income percentiles
Kindergarten and child services
Basic education
Favela upgrading
School lunch

Source: PPV 1997; authors' calculations.

Figure 2.17: Distribution of Public Social Expenditure: Concentration Curves in Regressive Sectors—Brazil, 1997

100%
80%
60%
40%
20%
0%
Share of total subsidies
0%
20%
40%
60%
80%
100%
Income percentiles
University education
Unemployment insurance
Transport
Neutral distribution
Pensions
Secondary education

Source: PPV 1997; authors' calculations.

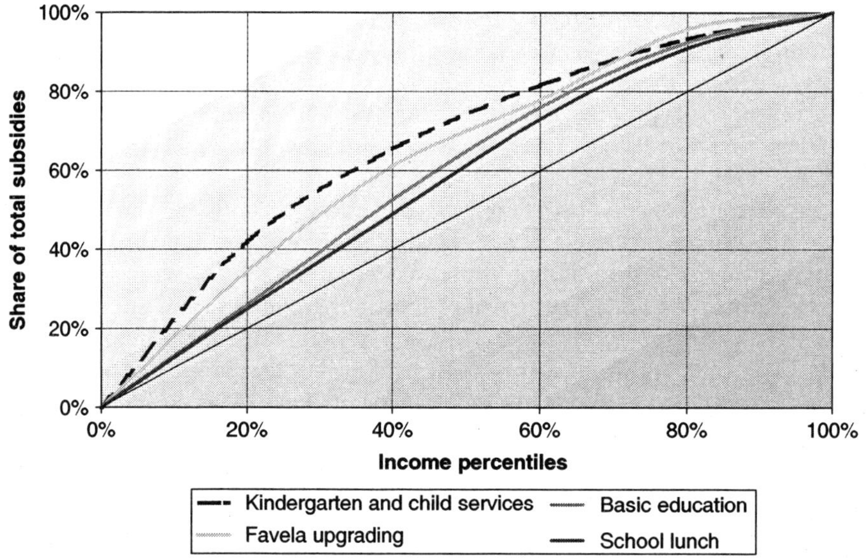

TABLE 2.6: SCHOOL ATTENDANCE AND HOUSEHOLD CHARACTERISTICS (10–15 YEARS OLD)

	Not Studying	Working and Studying	Studying	Total
Population share	6.1%	16.8%	77.1%	100%
Household per capita income	80.9	104.5	202.0	178.3
Years of schooling	2.9	3.9	4.1	4.0
Years of schooling of the most educated parent	3.2	4.0	6.4	5.8
Region				
North	6.1%	5.6%	6.0%	5.9%
Northeast	40.4%	45.6%	29.9%	33.2%
Southeast	32.8%	26.1%	43.5%	39.9%
South	14.1%	15.9%	13.7%	14.1%
Center-West	6.0%	6.7%	6.9%	6.9%

Source: Bourguignon, F., Ferreira, F. and Menendez, M.(2002) Volume 2.

but much larger for pensions ($422), Housing (Carta de credito) ($332), and nearly two fold in Unemployment Insurance, Water Connection, and Urban Public Transport. Therefore, considering the fact that pensions and tertiary education represent 56 and 4.5 percent of total PSE, the reduction excessive benefits in pensions and tertiary education, in order to apply it in almost any other sector—with better targeting—would bring produce reductions in welfare inequality.

Despite Progressive Social Expenditure, Access to Education Remains Quite Regressive

Due to internal efficiency problems, considerable differentials in access to education persist across both income groups and regions. The recent World Bank report on secondary education in Brazil (Rodriguez and Herran [2000]) showed that in 1996, out of 100 18-year-olds only 66 completed fourth grade, 43 completed eighth grade, and 25 finished secondary education.[30] Almost universal net enrolment (95 percent) in primary school hides two key internal efficiency problems: chronic repetition and large percentage of students in grades much lower than they should be, given their age. For instance, high school graduates remain in school 14 years on average, and eighth grade survivors remain in school 10.3 years. These deficiencies affect mostly the children of the poor.

Educational inequities are significantly correlated to income and region differences. Table 2.6 shows the difficulties that children from low income households experience going through the basic education system. The household per capita income of 10 to 15 years old children out of school is approximately 40 percent of the level corresponding to full time students. Moreover, those children who are entirely devoted to study, have on average 4.1 years of schooling, while those who do not—but work—have barely 2.9 years. It is also worth mentioning the strong correlation between the parents' educational attainment and the children' school attendance. On average, most educated parents of full time students have 3.2 years of schooling more than parents of children who are not studying at all. Regional inequities are also quite significant, while only 6.0 percent of children between 10 and 15 years old exclusively attends school in the poor states

---

30. Nevertheless, these numbers show clear improvements relative to 1981, when the corre
completion rates were 43, 31, and 18 percent. See table 2.1 in Rodriguez and Herran (2000).

in the North, 43.5 percent of children are exclusively studying in the more developed states of the Southeast. The next chapter shows to what extent conditional cash transfers might raise school enrolment of poor children.[31]

Regressive Tax Incidence: Regressive Indirect Taxation Dominates Progressive Direct Taxation

Public policy also affects household income through taxation and similarly to the case of social expenditures, taxation does not play a neutral role on income distribution. The magnitude of taxation on households income is not only considerable, but the incidence of direct and direct taxation operate in opposite directions. This subsection explores the evolution of total tax burden and decomposes the incidence by key components.

Tax burden on the economy increased during the 1990s by nearly 3.5 percent of GDP, and more than 1.5 percent of the increase occurred via the creation or modification of indirect taxes. Currently, indirect taxation revenue is approximately three times as large as income taxation and enforces very heterogeneous tax rates across goods and services (see Table 2.7). The main motivation behind this trend was increasing public revenues to correct public sector imbalance, especially at the federal level—mostly by the creation of new taxes, preferably those that could generate revenues with the lowest administrative costs. Hence efficiency and equity concerns were not the main concern of public administrators (for example, the financial transaction tax). Additional difficulties in the design of efficient and equitable taxes come from the fact that some Brazilian states are in the middle of a "fiscal war" to attract investors and stimulate job creation.

Total taxation has a regressive effect on income distribution, despite direct taxation being mildly progressive. The burden of income taxation (96 percent) is mostly concentrated on households that belong to the richest 20 percent in Brazil and is greater than their share of income (between 60 and 70 percent). However, relative to the share of income, the burden of direct taxation falls more than proportionally on poor households (see Table 2.7). Although the poorest 40 percent pay 16 percent of total indirect taxes, their share of income is well below 10 percent. For this reason the Gini coefficient of after tax is not very different from pre-tax income—0.7 percentage points of the Gini. The end product of a reduction of 1 percentage point due to direct taxation plus the increase of 1.6 percentage points due to indirect taxation

*   *   *

This chapter has shown that Brazil's excessive income inequality is associated with both market and nonmarket forces, which sometimes operate in opposite directions. The main findings can be summarized in two groups. First, when Brazil is compared to the United States and México, excessive inequality is explained by three factors: 1) insufficient and unequally distributed education endowments, 2) excessive wage-skill premia, that contribute in similar proportions to excess inequality relative to the United States—and jointly explain 60 percent of the difference, and 3) the regressivity of retirement pension transfers contributes in the largest proportion to raise inequality—40 percent of the difference.

Second, overall public policy instruments have a progressive impact on income inequality, but some of those instruments have a detrimental effect. In fact, In addition to the regressive factors identified by cross country comparisons, the situation is worsened by the regressive impact of *indirect* taxation –1.6 percentage points of the Gini, which is nearly half of the impact of importing to Brazil the United States human asset distribution. Fortunately, considerable compensatory and progressive effects follow from direct taxation and social public expenditure

---

31. An ex-ante evaluation of Bolsa Scola transfers. For detailed explanations see Bourguignon, Ferreira, and Leite (2002b) in Part II.

TABLE 2.7: REDISTRIBUTIVE IMPACT OF DIRECT AND INDIRECT TAXATION BY COMPONENTS: BRAZIL, METROPOLITAN AREAS, 1999

	Percentage of GDP	Share	Concentration Coefficient	Targeting Top 20%	Share of Poorest 40%	Redistributive Effect Delta Gini % Points	Relative Redistributive Efficiency
Indirect taxation	22.0	70%	0.417	50%	15.5%	1.6%	3.5
ICMS goods and services [1/]	14.3	45%	0.424	49%	16.7%	1.0%	3.4
PIS [2/]	3.4	11%	0.402	49%	16.3%	0.3%	3.8
IPI	4.4	14%	0.406	50%	15.8%	0.4%	3.8
Direct taxation	9.5	30%	0.735	96%	0.2%	−1.0%	−4.8
Income tax	6.8	22%	0.853	67%	7.0%	−0.9%	−6.0
Urban real state tax	1.6	5%	0.608	80%	2.1%	0.0%	−0.7
State private vehicle tax	1.1	3%	0.735	89%	1.6%	−0.1%	−3.4
Total	31.6	100%	0.798	62%	12%	0.7%	1
Total redistributive after re-ranking by after-tax income.						0.7%	

a. Relative redistributive efficiency is equal to the ratio of the redistributive effect of each tax relative to its share of aggregate tax revenue. Positive is regressive and negative is progressive.

b. Imposto sobre Circulação de Mercadorias e Serviços: state value added tax (VAT), tax on goods and services.

c. Contribução para o Programa do Integração Social: contributions to social funds.

d. Imposto sobre Produtos Industrializados: tax on industrial products.

Source: Versano and others1998, Pesquisa de Orçamentos Familiares, POF 1995/96." (Income-Expenditure Survey) IBGE, authors' calculations.

excluding pensions. These are moderate in the case of direct taxation –1 percentage point of the Gini- and clearly progressive and substantial for public social expenditure –minus 3.8 Gini points-. The magnitude of the latter is similar to the human asset distribution effect in the US-Brazil comparison. Finally there is a notable contrast between pensions and non-pensions PSE in relation to equity, while the former constitute 56 percent of PSE they only account for half of the redistributive impact obtained with a smaller amount of resources devoted to non-pensions PSE –which includes education, health, nutrition programs and others.

CHAPTER 3

WHAT CAN AND SHOULD PUBLIC POLICY DO ABOUT INEQUALITY IN BRAZIL?

The arguments presented in the last section do not establish scientifically that Brazil suffers from too much inequality, because this will always ultimately remain a value judgment. However, they do suggest that excessively high inequality can have substantial costs for a country, be it in terms of social justice and economic and political efficiency, or erosion of social capital. As the second chapter established, Brazil does suffer from very high inequality—of both outcomes and opportunities—overall, across its regions, between men and women, and across its racial groups.

This still would not imply that government policies should be used to try and reduce this inequality. The benefits from so doing would have to be weighed against the costs. However, in the context of a government that already spends very large sums seeking to achieve "social objectives," it would appear that there is scope for reforming and redirecting its existing programs so as to actually achieve some reduction in inequality. In this section, we consider some key policy instruments the government has been using, as well as possible effective reforms that the preceding analysis might point to. Throughout, we take the view that the only sensible way to reduce inequality is to seek to improve the lot of the poor—today and tomorrow. In addition to improving the effectiveness of public social expenditure, this objective might include making the tax burden more equitable, without raising the efficiency costs that price distortions induce on the Brazilian economy. In other words, good inequality reduction is inextricable from poverty reduction.

Our diagnosis was basically that Brazil's egregious levels of inequality arise from persistent inequalities in assets, notably education, land, and access to public transfers and services. This was compounded by price differentials for some of these assets, in particular wage differentials by education. We do not, however, advocate an income policy aimed at forcing the price of skills to deviate from its equilibrium schedule. Neither do we advise attempts to forcibly alter the pattern of technological change so as to reduce the demand for skills or increase the demand for unskilled work.

Separately from changes in supply, this leaves only one plausible tool to address wage differentials by skill: reductions in the state-driven indirect costs of employing unskilled workers. The "Brazil Jobs Report" (World Bank 2002c) has shown that binding minimum wages and mandated benefit legislation price out low-skilled workers of formal sector jobs, which in turn creates significant inequities of access to formal safety-net mechanisms. Consequently, increasing flexibility of labor contracts would help to boost safety-net access for poor households. Other costs arise from the existence of a number of fiscal wedges associated with high payroll taxes and social security obligations, including the severance payment system known as *Fundo de Garantia do Tempo de Serviço* (FGTS).

Human Assets and Land: Endowments and Prices
Despite Rapid Expansion of Education in the Last Decade, Education Attainment Remains Stubbornly Low

The fundamental way in which economies achieve a reduction in the skilled-to-unskilled wage ratio is by raising the skilled-to-unskilled balance in the supply of workers. This is most convenient, because it can basically be achieved through an educational expansion, which also contributes to a reduction in the inequality of human capital and adds to the aggregate stock of this important asset. The expansion of education—understood as both more years in school for all, and better schools in which to spend those years—is unambiguously good because it (a) is desirable in human terms quite apart from other economic consequences, (b) is likely to lead to faster and "better" growth, (c) is ultimately likely to reduce the underlying inequality of human capital endowments and thereby is also likely to reduce the wage differentials by skills, and, finally, (d) could save the economy from converging to even more unequal distribution of income in the long term—as Kremer and Chen 2002 explain.

Nevertheless, one facts bear highlighting in the face of such unusual certainty in recommending a policy. First, although Brazil has, over the last six to eight years, been engaged in a period of greater investment in education, this has simply not been long enough to bring the country's aggregate educational stocks into line with other countries with similar levels of GDP per capita. Let us consider both the good news and the bad as they relate to the long-term dynamics of educational attainment in Brazil.

Long-term improvements in educational attainment show that successive cohorts have achieved ever *higher* average schooling, with *less* internal inequality. Figure 3.1 shows average school attainment for successive Brazilian cohorts from 1908 to 1992, and each successive cohort attains a final educational level superior to that of its predecessors. Cohorts born from 1908 to 1928 (who where attending school as 12-year-olds from 1920 to 1940, as displayed in the graph in the cohort year + 12 axis) displayed a rather small improvement in school attainment over the period—approximately one year of schooling in two decades. Clear improvement was visible for cohorts born between 1938 and 1958 (see Figure 3.1, 1950–70 in the cohort year + 12 scale), with 2.5 additional years of school attainment in two decades. The following decade showed very little progress. Finally, cohorts born after 1973 (who were attending school as 12-year-olds after 1985) saw an acceleration in the pace of growth of school attainment up to the 1990s—nearly two additional years of school attainment in the last 15 calendar years. Symmetrically, the inequality of the distribution of education showed a monotonously decreasing trend, with a higher slope in the earlier decades of the 20th century.

Nevertheless, a long term comparison with other Latin American countries shows how education in Brazil is still lagging behind. Figure 3.2 compares average education in Brazil with that in a set of Latin American countries by cohorts older than age 25.[32] Four decades ago, Brazil

---

32. The reader should be aware of the limitations of this comparison, as it excludes the cohorts born after 1970, which have benefited the most from the mid and late 1990's expansion in education in Brazil (see details below).

FIGURE 3.1: AVERAGE SCHOOLING AND INEQUALITY OF EDUCATIONAL ATTAINMENT BY COHORT—BRAZIL, 1908–92

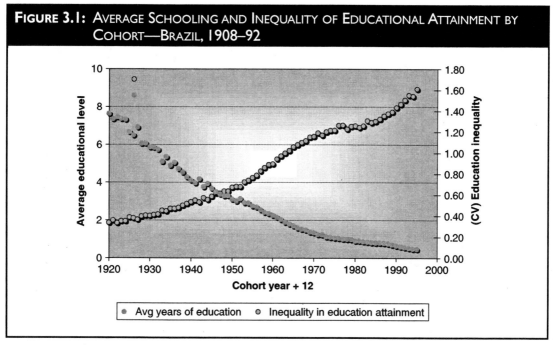

Note: CV stands for Coefficient of Variation.

Source: Vélez, Soares, and Medeiros 2002.

(black line) was close to Ecuador (pink line) and better off than Mexico (coral line), but Brazilian cohorts born two decades later (in the 1970s) are on average 1.5 years of schooling behind Mexico and more than 2 years behind Ecuador. It is evident from Figure 3.2 that Brazilian schooling lags relative to the selected countries and improvement is insufficient: Cohorts born in the 1970s in Brazil are behind those born in Colombia, Costa Rica, Ecuador, Mexico, Panama, Paraguay, and Venezuela. Moreover, whereas Brazilian cohorts born in the 1950s had on average 1.3 years of schooling more than their counterparts in Honduras (which has the lowest number of years of schooling among these countries), cohorts born in 1970 have the same schooling.

Moreover, when put side by side with South Africa, Brazil shows rather slow progress in education and a persistent educational gap against nonwhites. Figure 3.3 illustrates average years of schooling by age for white and nonwhite populations in Brazil and South Africa. According to Figure 3.3, in South Africa, the educational gap against nonwhites has decreased substantially, though it is still significant. For individuals who are 50 years old, the educational gap is on average 5.8 years, but for individuals who are 25 years old, it has been reduced to 3.2 years. On the contrary, in Brazil, the gap remains unchanged: The educational gap against nonwhites for individuals who are 25 years old is on average 2.5 years, and it is similar for individuals who are 45 years old. Even in comparing schooling of white individuals in Brazil with white individuals in South Africa, Brazilians show slow progress. On average, 25-year-old white South Africans do better than their Brazilian peers by 3.2 years, and nonwhite South Africans of the same age outperform Brazilians by almost the same amount, 3.3 years.

However is worth to mention that at the cohort level Brazil performance has shown important improvements during the last decade. While the average education for cohorts born between 1972 and 1983 grew 1.8 percent per year, the average schooling of cohorts born between 1960 and 1970 grew at a much smaller pace (0.5 percent per year). The former cohorts corresponds approximately to the policy period between 1985 to the late nineties, when those cohorts of students became teenagers.

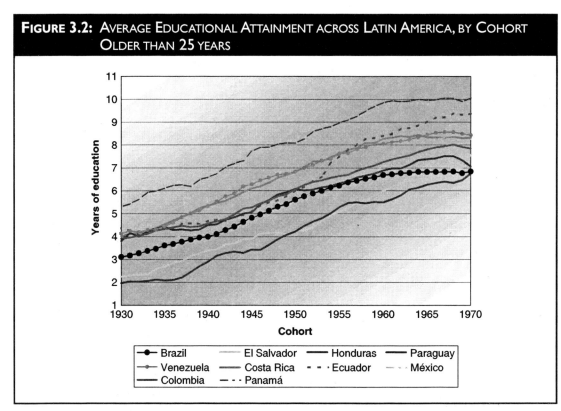

FIGURE 3.2: AVERAGE EDUCATIONAL ATTAINMENT ACROSS LATIN AMERICA, BY COHORT OLDER THAN 25 YEARS

Source: Household surveys: Brazil (1998), Colombia (1995), Costa Rica (1995), El Salvador (1995), Ecuador (1995), Honduras (1996), Mexico (1994), Panama (1995), Paraguay (1995), and Venezuela (1995).

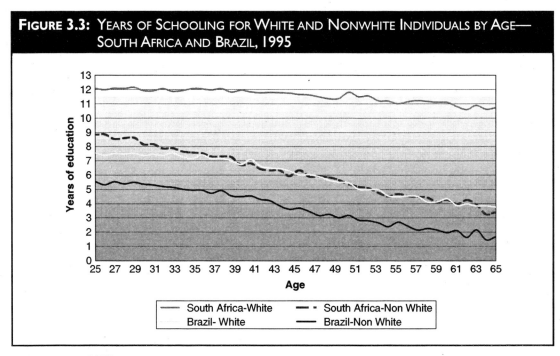

FIGURE 3.3: YEARS OF SCHOOLING FOR WHITE AND NONWHITE INDIVIDUALS BY AGE— SOUTH AFRICA AND BRAZIL, 1995

Source: Lam (1999).

So, despite some progress in education of the younger cohorts in Brazil, the average level of education of the *whole* labor force (individuals aged 16–70) remains stubbornly low (and its inequality stubbornly high). Average schooling for the whole labor force lags approximately four years behind average schooling for the most recent cohorts. That is, although average schooling was approximately 9 years for the new cohorts entering the labor force in 1996, average schooling for the whole labor force remained close to 5.2 years. Analogously average inequality for the whole labor force was nearly four times larger the corresponding value for the youngest cohort.[33]

The relatively inelastic behavior of the educational attainment of the whole labor force relative to the much larger investment in education for younger cohorts—in recent years—is linked to strong demographic forces. Empirical evidence suggests that it takes more than two decades to see the benefits of increasing educational attainment for the younger cohorts reflected on the whole labor force.[34] One way of looking at how contemporary educational policy affects the distribution of educational endowments of the whole labor force is to measure how many years it takes for the whole labor force to reach the level of educational attainment of one cohort—the stock-to-cohort time lag. Our observations show that the labor force of 1970s had the same number of years of education as the cohort born in 1940, which on average was finishing school in 1951 (entering school at seven years of age and attaining nearly four years of schooling). This resulted in a time lag of 19 years between 1951 and 1970. That time lag grew over time to a maximum of 25 years at the end of the century.[35] That is, the labor force of 1998 had 6.5 years of schooling, which was the same educational attainment obtained by the cohort born in 1960 (which on average was leaving school in 1973–74).

Further Aggressive Expansion of Education Should Happen
before Demographic Opportunities Expire

What should be the impact of a substantial expansion of education on the stock-to-cohort time lag? It depends on the timing relative to the demographic transition. During the last quarter of the 20th century the gap between the cohort and the whole labor force grew more than the marginal increase in schooling. That is, while the gap became 6 years larger, mean school attainment increased by 2.5 years. This phenomenon is linked with the *demographic transition of Brazil:* the decreasing demographic weight of the youngest cohort of the labor force (16–20 year olds) that started in the 1990s. Figure 3.4 shows the demographic share of the youngest cohorts on the whole labor force every 10 years from 1950 to 2000, and provides some forecast for the period 2010 to 2040. It is notable that for the labor force of 1970, the demographic share of the youngest cohorts peaks (19.6 percent) and then falls significantly for the labor force in 1990 and 2000 (close to 16 percent). Therefore, as younger and relatively more educated cohorts lose share within the labor force, the time gap between the youngest cohorts and the whole labor force grew in size. Thus, although the consequences of educational push of the 1990's were positive they are becoming weaker, because as the demographic transition gets deeper the time lag becomes larger.

Then, what would have happened if the educational expansion of the 1990s had occurred *one decade earlier*, coinciding with the peak of demographic "replacement" and before the demographic transition had started. Simulations by Vélez, Soares, and Medeiros (2002) show that a *temporary* acceleration of improvements in education during a period of highest demographic growth *permanently* accelerates the extension of educational benefits from cohorts to the whole labor force. More specifically, this alternative policy path would have reduced the stock-to-cohort time lag from 25 to 20 years and cuts long-term inequalities of schooling and labor income. Figure 3.5 shows the alternative policy as a temporary deviations in the cohort path that

---

33. See Velez, Medeiros, and Soares (2002) in Part II.
34. Ibid.
35. See Figure 3.5 below for an illustration. The increase in the stock-to-cohort time lag is represented by the difference between the two segments BB' and AA'.

FIGURE 3.4: DIMINISHING SHARE OF 16–20 YEARS OLDS ON WORKING AGE POPULATION

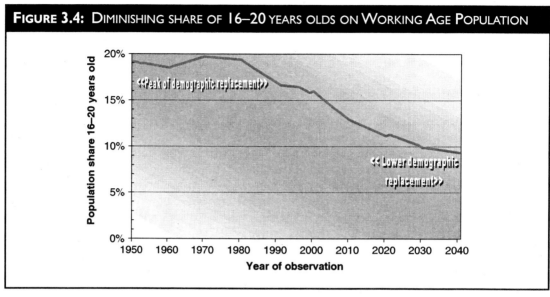

Source: Vélez, Soares and Medeiros (2002).

anticipates by nearly one decade the improvements of the educational system enjoyed by younger cohorts during the 1990s (the light blue line versus the yellow line, between points A and B).[36] For example, the *simulated* average education of the individual born in 1970 (who was leaving school in 1984) was nearly seven years of schooling, the same as the value *observed* for the person born in 1980 (who was leaving school by 1994). An alternative interpretation of the alternative cohort path would be as sustaining the rate of growth of educational attainment enjoyed by the previous cohorts born in the 1940 and 1950s, for the generations born in the 1960s and early 1970s.[37] The consequence of the alternative policy for the school attainment of the whole labor force is a permanent gain or northwest shift (from A'B' to A"B" or from the blue line to the orange line). The magnitude of the shift is considerable, 5 years to the left (represented by B'B" in Figure 3.5) and 0.6 year upward for the year 2002, which means that the time gap falls from 25 to 20 years.[38]

This result and the fact that the demographic transition has not yet been completed in Brazil, provides a rationale for raising educational investment in the first decade of the 21st century. Raising the level of schooling of the whole labor force by improving education of younger cohorts. Taking advantage of the demographic opportunities that are fading away as the younger cohorts are gradually losing share in the population of working age.

Furthermore, the policy simulation shows that taking advantage of the window of opportunity of demographic transition to expand education also reduces long-term inequality of educational attainment and labor income.[39] Figure 3.6 shows the *observed* and *simulated* paths of educational attainment for the whole labor force (mean and variance schedule) for Brazil in the period

36. The cohorts born after the mid 1970s, which benefited the most of the 1990's expansion of education.

37. A feasible rate of growth for Brazil -disregarding public finance constraints.

38. Note that the number of years represents by BB' is nearly four decades. And it is equal to the stock-to-cohort time lag *plus* the number of years of educational attainment of the 1984's cohort, plus the number of years before entering first grade (approximately 7 years).

39. Notice that this is a *temporary deviation* from the cohort path. Putting *more* effort earlier—in the 1970s and 1980s—implies doing *less* than was observed in the 1990s.

FIGURE 3.5: Schooling by Cohort and for the Whole Labor Force, Observed and Simulated—Brazil, 1940–2015

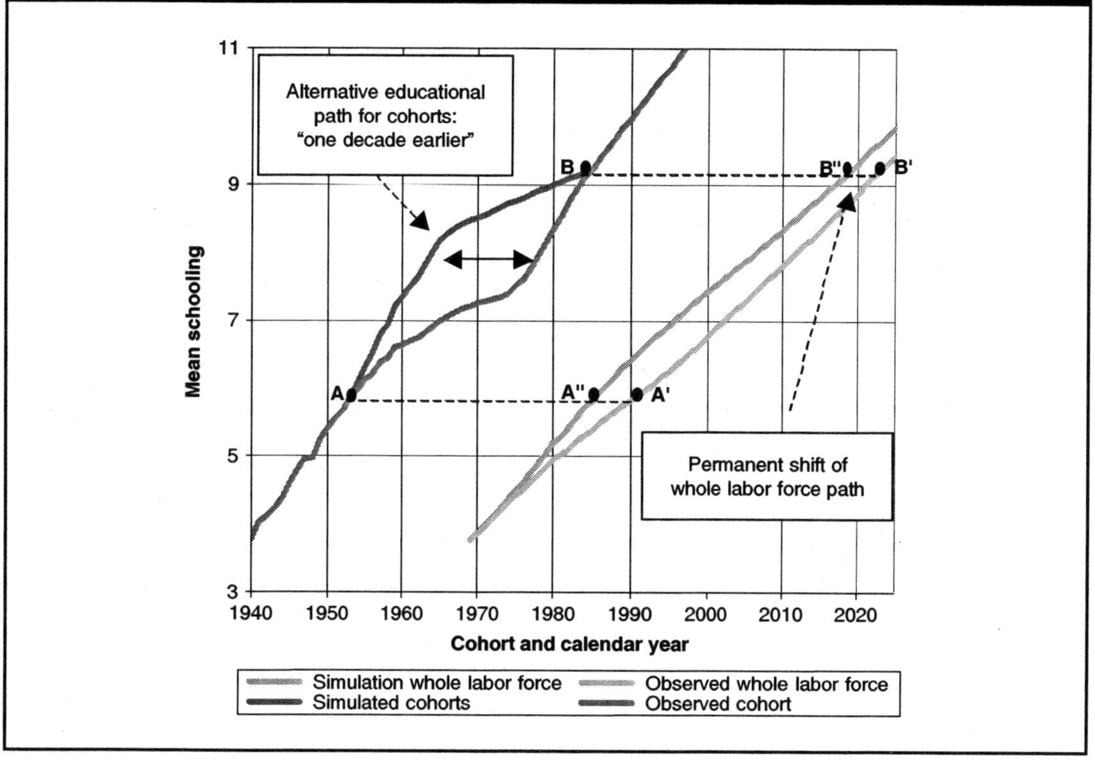

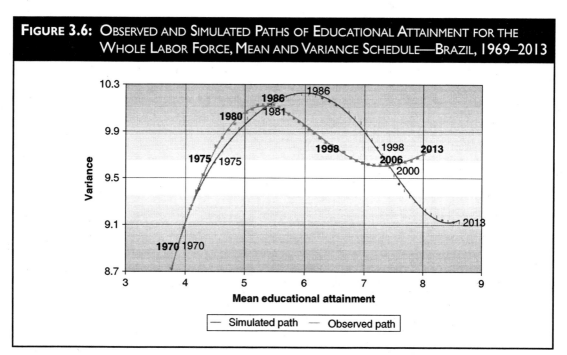

Source: Vélez, Soares, and Medeiros 2002.

FIGURE 3.6: Observed and Simulated Paths of Educational Attainment for the Whole Labor Force, Mean and Variance Schedule—Brazil, 1969–2013

Note: Labor force includes individuals 14–65 years old.

Source: Vélez, Soares, and Medeiros 2002.

1969–2013. By the year 2013, a relatively short period of time, the simulated variance of schooling becomes approximately 7 percent smaller than expected—without policy change. This is particularly significant if we take into account that the inequality of individual labor income is proportional to the variance of educational endowments of employed workers.[40]

Indirect equalizing effects induced by this educational policy might be important as well. The equalizing impact of supply changes—expansion of schooling—will be amplified by the expected reduction in the skill premium (see wage-skill premium subsection below). Moreover, as Kremer Chen (2002) pointed out, the multiplier effect of this type of temporary educational policy interventions for social mobility and inequality reduction can be even larger if fertility is endogenous to skill-wage differentials. Consequently, long-term reductions in labor income inequality, induced by educational expansion contemporary to a pre-demographic-transition period, should be of a magnitude similar or larger than the reductions in the variance of educational attainment.

Nevertheless, in the short run the consequences of this type of policy could be the opposite of the long term equalizing effect. Somewhat unexpectedly, once the aggressive equalizing expansion of education (simulated) takes place, both the variance and the inequality of schooling overshoot *temporarily*.[41] Figure 3.6 shows that in the range of mean educational attainment (5.2 to 7.4 years of schooling) in Figure 3.6, the simulated schedule is above the observed one. And when mean educational attainment is close to 6.5 years of schooling, the increase in variance reaches a maximum—approximately 0.4. However, in the long run the variance is smaller. This short-run effect dies down once the initial burst of inequality *between* cohorts is erased by the diminishing weight of less educated generations.

In summary, the level of schooling of the labor force in Brazil is clearly insufficient, and efforts to make educational attainment higher and more equitable should be vigorously emphasized when demographic opportunities are available. Nevertheless, policymakers and policy observers should be aware that any expected impact of education on inequality of income at the household level must be evaluated with a long-term perspective. Delaying a vigorous educational push beyond demographic opportunities would have a significant permanent cost in terms of extending the benefits of current educational policy to the whole population and catching up with the rest of the world.

Improvement of Educational Attainment Requires Simultaneous Policy Programs Applied at Multiple Levels: Households, Schools, and Subnational Governments

The recent World Bank and Inter American Development Bank (2000) report on education in Brazil shows that to improve the equity of educational attainment, policy efforts must be applied in multiple fronts. Programs should attend to three types of stakeholders:

1. Within-school programs to reduce chronic repetition by offering alternative options to fulfill the graduation requirements, such as *Classes de Aceleração* and *Escolas Nas Férias* (summer school), academic credit systems, internal reorganization to facilitate transition to middle and upper secondary school, accreditation exams (*supletivo*) for the terminal grades, alternative delivery options (*telesalas noturnas*), and so forth;
2. Alternative supply programs that expand school availability for the poor by offering alternative delivery options in rural areas—such as distance learning and extending FUNDEF, the subnational public finance incentives to promote efficient expansion of basic education in the poorer states to secondary education; and

---

40. This is the case when the inequality of labor income is measured by $var (log\, y)$. Then $var (log\, y) = \beta^2 var (E) + var (\mu)$, where β is the return to education in a simplified linear Mincerian equation and μ is the error term.

41. Decreasing inequality within cohorts is dominated by increasing inequality between cohorts.

3. Family incentive programs subsidizing school supplies for the poor in addition to cash transfers for the poor, which are more affordable for rich states. This battery of interventions would address the findings of the model of educational attainment that shows clear links between school attendance and within-school organization, school availability, and the opportunity cost of studying (income sacrificed).[42]

Policies aimed at improving the efficacy of schools are fundamental to addressing Brazil's shortcomings in the supply of education. They should contribute to increasing the value of attendance for those already in school by ensuring that time spent at school actually translates into learning. As a number of studies indicate, the optimal policies for bettering the quality of schools are not always gender- and race-blind. Albernaz, Ferreira, and Franco (forthcoming) find that nonwhite children perform less well at standardized tests in Brazil than whites do, even after controlling for their socioeconomic level and for school characteristics. Another worrying finding is that although girls leave school later than boys, on average, they appear to perform worse at standardized tests in most subjects. The implication is that teacher training programs and curriculum development cannot ignore racial and gender issues.

Another policy that contributes to the overall rate of human capital accumulation, while simultaneously reducing inequalities in educational attainment, is the targeted school attendance subsidy known as *Bolsa Escola*. Following the success of pilot programs in Campinas and Brasília in 1995, *Bolsa Escola* was expanded into a federal program by a law passed in April 2001. The federal program is designed to transfer R$15 per child,[43] aged 6 to 15 living in a household with per capita monthly income below R$90, provided the child is enrolled in school and attends at least 85 percent of classes. The federal program is too recent to have been evaluated after the fact, but an ex ante simulation of its impact found encouraging results regarding impact on enrollment. Bourguignon, Ferreira, and Leite (2002b) estimated that under its present design, the program could induce between one-quarter and one-third of all 10- to 15-year-olds currently out of school to enroll. Among poor households, the figure was between one-third and one-half of all children not currently enrolled.

The study was less optimistic regarding the impact of *Bolsa Escola* on current poverty and inequality. Because of the small size of the transfers, even if the program were perfectly targeted and covered the whole country, it would only reduce the incidence of poverty by one to two percentage points. This turned out to depend much more on the size of the transfer (R$15 per child) than on the level of the means test (R$90). Simulating the impact of a larger transfer program, Camargo and Ferreira (2001) found that it would in principle be possible to reduce the incidence of poverty by some 20 percentage points of the population. However, this would require substantially expanding the coverage of the program and having access to a budget of some 1.2 percent of GDP, net of administrative costs.

High Wage Differentials by Skill Create Additional Difficulties in Reducing Labor Income Inequality while Education Expands Significantly

It is important to note, however, that both theory and evidence suggest that the short- and medium-term impact of an educational expansion on income inequality would be small. It is frustrating to have to report that (a) most of Brazil's inequality is, in some way or other, ultimately related to the distribution of education, and, at the same time. (b) the one thing that one should

---

42. The importance of the quality of a school's physical infrastructure, as well as of its teachers, for standardized test scores in Brazil was documented by Albernaz, Ferreira, and Franco (forthcoming). In a study that controls for individual and family characteristics, the authors found a statistically significant link between physical conditions at schools, the schooling level of teachers, staff evaluation of the financial constraints faced by the school, and student performance at the *Sistema de Avaliação do Ensino Básico* (SAEB) 1999 exams.

43. Up to a ceiling of R$45.

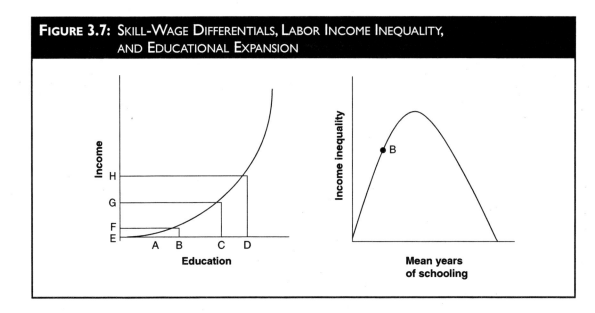

FIGURE 3.7: SKILL-WAGE DIFFERENTIALS, LABOR INCOME INEQUALITY, AND EDUCATIONAL EXPANSION

therefore be certain to do—expand education—will not have a great impact in terms of reducing income inequality in the short run. Yet this appears to be the case.

Nonetheless there are multiple ways to explain this effect (Lam 1999, Barros etal. 2002, Velez etal. 2002), the central mechanism is that individual labor income increase exponentially with educational attainment, so that the increasing dispersion of income is consistent with a higher mean of education, even when the dispersion of the latter is falling. Consider Figure 3.7, where the distribution of education is uniform (or a truncated normal) between A and B. This maps onto an income distribution of some shape between E and F. Now consider an expansion in education, so that the underlying distribution of education has the same shape and dispersion as before, but now between C and D. This leads to a distribution of income with the same class of functional form as before, but a greater dispersion, between G and H.

Because the distribution of years of schooling behaves as if it were bounded above, this process is not infinite. Eventually, the evidence suggests that educational expansions lead to a compression of the distribution of years of schooling (as if C eventually grew faster than D, compressing the distribution at high levels). See Bourguignon, et. al. (2001a) for some evidence that this has already happened in the United States. Because of this, researchers sometimes postulate a Kuznets-like curve for the relationship between the mean of the distribution of education and income inequality.

Some empirical backing for this conjecture was recently provided by Ferreira and Leite (2002), who simulated different educational expansion policies for the state of Ceará, in the Brazilian Northeast (using PNAD microdata), under different scenarios for the evolution of wage differentials by skill. They found that even substantial increases in mean years of schooling had a relatively muted impact on measures of income inequality. The main result, however, was that the impact on poverty was much more substantial and was due as much to induced changes in fertility and labor force participation behavior (both responding largely to more education for women) as it was to greater endowments of human capital to sell in the labor market.

As it was drawn, Figure 3.7 assumes a stable structure of wage differentials. The effect on inequality might be more favorable if the expansion in supply leads to a flatter wage-schooling schedule. It is unsafe to assume so, however, since this structure is also being affected by the demand for skills. The continuing tension between the supply side dynamics (for example, more education tends to lead to a flatter earnings-education profile) and the demand dynamics (for example, skill-biased technological progress tends to lead to a steeper curve) has long been known, and is usually referred to as Tinbergen's Race (Tinbergen 1975). Whether demand or supply is winning this race is an empirical issue.

Increasing Skill Premium: Excess Demand and Insufficient Supply

As we saw in the previous chapter, in explaining Brazilian inequality the joint effect of unequal endowments of education and excessive wage differentials by skill was even more fundamental than state transfers. Recent evidence suggests that the pattern of increasing wage sill premium in Brazil has responded to a shift of supply of workers towards middling ranges of the skill distribution (6–10 years), while the demand for skills at the upper reaches continued to outpace supply. This effect appears to have led to the intensification of a "kink" in the earnings-education profile, with wages for medium-skilled workers falling relative to those of both unskilled and highly skilled workers.

How has the educational policy affecting the composition of the labor force affected the skill-wage differential and overall wage inequality in Brazil? In the 1990s a number of countries in the region have, to different extents, experienced rising wage differentials by schooling, especially with respect to tertiary education with regressive effects on wage and household income inequality.[44] The most often cited factors behind alterations in skill-wage differentials are labor *demand* shifts toward higher skills via technological progress, trade liberalization, and sectoral shifts in the economy toward production of more skill-intensive goods. Apart from important demand factors, recent research has shown that *supply* factors—namely, changes in the educational composition of the labor force—are also an important factor behind the observed changes.

In Brazil, large shifts in the educational composition have taken place in the last two decades. The primary and secondary education system expanded substantially. Consequently, the workforce gained in schooling and the distribution of schooling became more equitable. The average years of schooling increased from 4.8 in 1981 to 6.9 in 1999. In the same period, the Gini coefficient of years of schooling dropped from 0.49 to 0.37. However, the tertiary education system lagged behind. This asymmetric push in education altered remuneration of education in the labor market in two ways. First, as illustrated in Figure 3.8, it increased the relative supply of medium-skilled workers compared with workers without schooling, and consequently the wages of the latter experienced a relative increase. Second, as depicted in the same figure, the relative supply of highly skilled to medium-skilled workers is falling, and, as a result, the wages of the former increased noticeably throughout the last two decades. In 1999, a worker with tertiary education earned on average 270 percent of the wages of a worker with an upper secondary education.[45]

Blom and Vélez (2002) estimate that around 60 percent of the increase of the skill premium to tertiary education can be attributed to supply shortage. The remaining 40 percent is due to a shift in labor demand toward highly skilled labor. The shift in labor demand exhibited no structural breaks during the last two last decades and therefore appears not to have been caused by the trade liberalization process of the early 1990s.

What is the impact of those changes in wage differentials for highly skilled workers on labor income inequality? The overall impact of wage differential across skills is reducing labor income inequality by approximately 2 Gini percentage points, between 1976 and 1996. In fact, the reduction of wage differentials of medium skilled to completely unskilled workers dominates the

---

44. These include the four largest countries Brazil, Mexico, Colombia and Argentina. For evidence see Blom, Verner, Holm-Nielsen (2001), Cragg and Epelbaum (1996), Santamaria (2000), and Galiani and Sanguinetti (2000).

45. These trends also hold when controlling for the changes in demographic composition of the labor force, such as female participation and age.

FIGURE 3.8: RELATIVE WAGES AND RELATIVE NET SUPPLY OF TERTIARY
TO HIGH SCHOOL GRADUATES

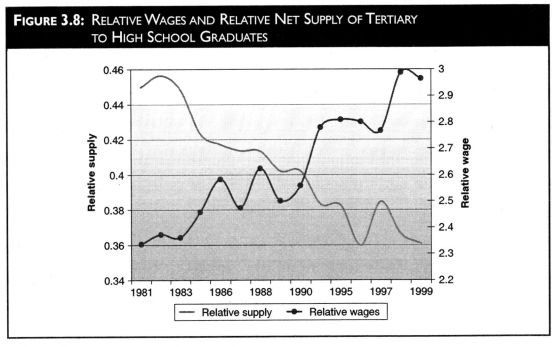

Source: PNAD. Calculations by Bloom and Velez (2002).

opposite effect produced by the increase in wage premium for the highly skilled. However, if the returns to tertiary education had remained at the 1976 level (19 instead of 23.9 percent) the total reduction of wage inequality due to changes in wage differentials by skill would have been another two percentage points of the Gini. In order to maintain the wage differentials prevalent in 1976 the supply of workers with post-secondary education should have grown much faster (5 percentage points above the observed annual rate). Finally, the equalizing effect of larger and more equally distributed endowments of education should be added.[46]

Rural Land Use: Equity May Not Improve without Improving Efficiency

As explained in the previous section, inefficiency and inequity of land use are both associated to missing markets of credit and insurance. For example, land prices remain too high, reflecting agricultural and nonagricultural benefits from land titles, in addition to uncovered property risks in land-leasing contracts. Therefore, because market imperfections have been producing an unequal distribution of land and relative inefficiency in the agricultural use of large landholdings, a land reform might be not fully effective. Even after reform, the structural mechanism creating demand for nonagricultural use of land would still subsist, and if the rental market does not work efficiently, there more large landholdings will be idle.[47]

In view of these results, Assunção (2002) analyzed the potential impact of four major federal government programs on land use and land inequality—the land tax (*Imposto Territorial Rural* [ITR]), the National Program of Land Reform, the Land Bank, and the National Program to Strengthen Family Farming (*Programa Nacional de Fortalecimento da Agricultura Familiar* [PRONAF]). First, although these programs constitute alternative ways to combat causes and

---

46. Although simulated estimates are not available for Brazil, Vélez and others (2002) have shown that this effect is substantial in the case of Colombia.

47. Nevertheless, those incentives for non-agricultural land holdings have been partially weakened with the end of inflation and the phase out of many agricultural subsidies.

effects of agricultural inefficiency, many issues of implementation still appear to compromise their effectiveness. Second, policy priorities should privilege and target reduction of inefficiencies in land use and the land rental market: (a) reformulate the ITR scheme to create disincentives for the nonagricultural use of land, (b) expand access to land via improvements in the land rental market, and (c) create incentives for cooperative formation, strengthening small farms, improving their competitiveness in the land market, and facilitating the implementation of group liability programs such as the Land Bank and microlending. The latter approaches are being pursued through a Bank-financed program "*Credito Fundiario.*"

Public Social Expenditure and Taxation

If an expansion of educational endowments is necessary for both long-term development and poverty reduction, but it is not sufficient for short- or medium-term reductions in inequality, the implications are twofold: (1) Such an educational reform must be pursued with determination. The exact manner in which it is pursued; the balance of spending across primary, secondary, and tertiary levels; the balance of finance between the private and public sectors; and the allocation of resources across educational inputs, so as to generate the most learning, all matter tremendously. (2) This is not enough to reduce inequality in the short and medium terms. What is required in the immediate future are profound reforms to improve both the effectiveness and the incidence of public social spending.

Public Social Expenditure: Sufficient but Misallocated across Sectors

Brazil devotes more resources to pension provision than would appear to be warranted either by its GDP or its demographic structure. Figure 3.9 illustrates the sectoral disaggregation of public social expenditure (PSE) across a group of comparison countries. The pattern of social

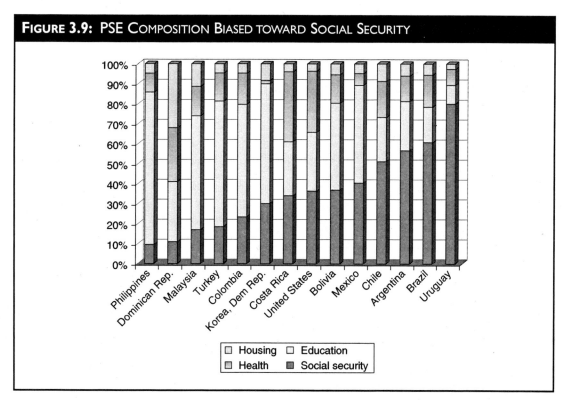

FIGURE 3.9: PSE COMPOSITION BIASED TOWARD SOCIAL SECURITY

Source: Vélez and Foster (1999).

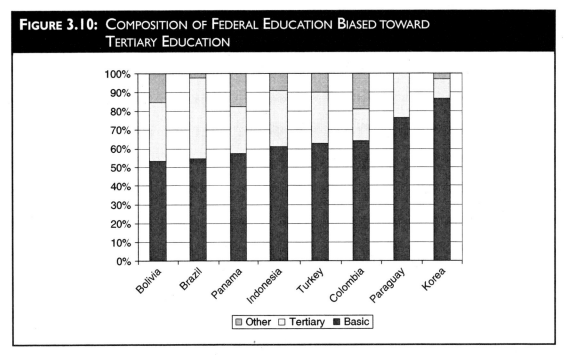

FIGURE 3.10: COMPOSITION OF FEDERAL EDUCATION BIASED TOWARD
TERTIARY EDUCATION

Source: Vélez and Foster 2000.

expenditure in Brazil is typical of that for the *Mercado Común del Sur* (Mercosur) countries; in that social security accounts for a very high proportion of total expenditure at 68 percent, a level exceeded only by Uruguay. Among other Latin American countries (outside Mercosur), the share of social security and welfare expenditure is closer to 30 percent (see, for example, Bolivia, Colombia, Costa Rica, and Panama in Figure 3.9), and in the newly industrializing Far Eastern economies, it is as low as 20 percent. Conditional comparisons by Vélez and Foster (2000), controlling for both the level of development and the demographic structure (the proportion of the population older than 65 years), show that public pension overspending is about 35 to 78 percent.[48]

Within the federal educational budget, Brazil's public social expenditure has been heavily skewed toward the tertiary tier.[49] A similar comparison of the allocation of education spending between the basic level (primary and secondary) and the tertiary level (Figure 3.10) shows that Brazil assigns a relatively low proportion of its social budget to basic education (primary and secondary levels)—55 percent—and a correspondingly high proportion—43 percent—to tertiary education. No other country in the study set allocates so much of its educational expenditure to the tertiary level. Given that access to tertiary education tends to be confined to the higher-income classes, these results provide some preliminary indication that education expenditure in Brazil may not be very equitably distributed.

---

48. An important reason for this is probably the fact that many beneficiaries of Brazilian public pensions are younger than retirement age. Indeed, about 10 percent of the population receive state pensions, although fewer than 5 percent of the population is older than 65. As noted by the World Bank (2001), it is particularly striking that "in a country as young as Brazil with five times as many people below 20 years of age as there are above 60 years of age," public expenditure on pensions should exceed that on education.
49. The reader must be aware that this comparison is complicated by the fact that a considerable proportion of public expenditure in education is non-federal (subnational) and comparator countries do not display the same degree of descentralization.

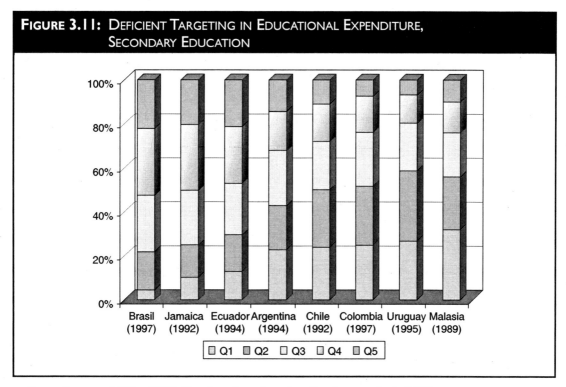

FIGURE 3.11: DEFICIENT TARGETING IN EDUCATIONAL EXPENDITURE, SECONDARY EDUCATION

Source: Foster and Vélez (1999). Data from Inter-American Development Bank (1999).

According to international comparisons, targeting of expenditures in secondary and tertiary education toward the poor could certainly be improved to reach Latin America and the Caribbean (LAC) regional average levels. According to Vélez and Foster (2000), comparing Brazil with other developing countries shows that Brazil has the lowest ranking in the targeting of secondary education expenditure toward low-income groups (Figure 3.11). Barely 5 percent of expenditure benefits the first income quintile, compared with more than 20 percent in countries such as Uruguay. As noted by the World Bank and the Inter-American Development Bank (2000) report, these figures reflect the extremely high levels of repetition in Brazilian primary education, which mean that many young people do not succeed in graduating from primary school until they have reached adulthood. Despite having high gross enrollment in primary education—significantly above the Latin American average of 110, secondary school gross enrollment in Brazil drops to a mere 45 percent, well below the regional average of 61 percent. The situation is even more extreme in tertiary education. Figure 3.12 illustrates the situation particularly clearly: 95 percent of expenditure on tertiary education in Brazil goes to benefit only the top two income quintiles. No other country comes close to this position. In the next worst case—Argentina—the proportion of expenditure devoted to the top two income quintiles falls to 70 percent, and in Jamaica, it is as low as 45 percent.

Despite rapid recent progress, Brazil's performance on basic social indicators, such as infant mortality, average schooling, and youth literacy, is still not commensurate with its level of economic development. Potential explanations of this outcome could be insufficient resources, inappropriate intersectoral allocation of funds, poor targeting across income strata, and/or global inefficiency of social programs. Vélez and Foster (2000) show that underspending on PSE is certainly not the root of the problem. Rather, the most plausible explanations are misallocation of PSE across program areas: overspending on social security (specifically state pensions) and tertiary education at the expense of basic education and

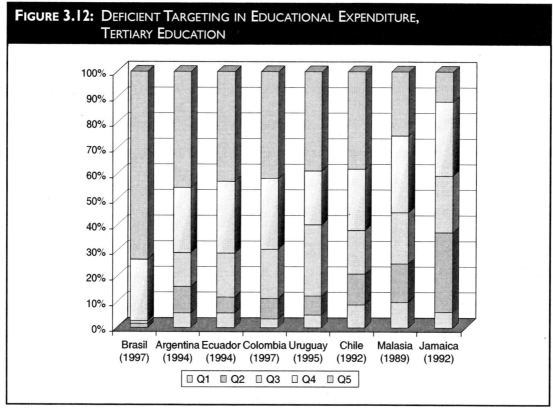

FIGURE 3.12: DEFICIENT TARGETING IN EDUCATIONAL EXPENDITURE, TERTIARY EDUCATION

Source: Foster and Vélez (1999). Data from Inter-American Development Bank (1999).

health; and deficiencies in the targeting of PSE in both pension and education across income deciles.

The high level of resources dedicated to social security is becoming an increasing constraint to what is left over for more progressive PSE, namely education and health. This situation is particularly worrisome if one takes into account the likelihood of it worsening over. A World Bank report on Brazil's pensions (2001) found that the accounting deficit associated with Brazil's state pension system is set to double in the next five years and triple in the next decade, leading to substantial expenditures to finance the associated public debt. This suggests that other, already underfunded areas of PSE, such as health and education, could come under increasing budgetary pressure over time.

Public Pension Subsidies: RJU Contravenes Vertical and Horizontal Equity Principles
The World Bank report on social security in Brazil (2000b) has already examined the fairness of the different pension programs and has indicated significant differences be among them. Although programs such as the Old Age Program are well targeted to mostly rural and female-headed households, and the RGPS improved after the reform of 1997, the Federal Government Pensions program (RJU) remains the most problematic. According to the Bank's report, the RJU absorbs excessive funds and violates basic principles of fairness of public expenditure, namely vertical, horizontal, and intergenerational equity. Vertical inequity is evident because benefits to federal employees are disproportionately concentrated in the high-income group: Half of the benefits go to the wealthiest 10 percent. Horizontal inequity follows from the fact that the average federal judiciary retiree receives 26 times more subsidy per beneficiary than the RGPS's beneficiaries. Not surprisingly, RJU concentrates benefits in a rather small population—3 million versus 19 million

retirees receiving benefits from the RGPS. (Intergenerational inequity was discussed in a previous subsection.)[50]

Other undesirable properties of the RJU program are high opportunity cost public funds, higher efficiency cost of taxation, and induced labor market inefficiencies. Public funds demanded for inequitable and inefficient (excessive) pensions could be used for public investment in human assets—mainly education for the younger Brazilian population—with higher economic productivity. Additional taxes necessary to finance excessive pensions raise the tax burden on the Brazilian economy. Because federal employees are better paid and have a more stable source of income, the RJU pension does not play any compensatory role. Therefore, RJU pensions distort labor mobility between the public and the private sector.

According to the social security report (World Bank 2000b), it seems imperative to implement reforms of the RJU. First, to reduce replacement rates by increasing time of contribution and the minimum retirement age, and modifying benefit indexation to maintain purchasing power— allowing more flexibility in wage negotiations with current employees. Second step would be to enlarge the reference period for pension calculation to abate excessive inequities of retirement pensions.

Social Sector Priorities: Education, Housing, and Health with Some Rural-Urban Discrepancies

Given the current levels of poverty and inequality in Brazil, too many households are unable to obtain basic social services through market means. Hence, for both equity and efficiency purposes, public provision of social services will inevitably continue to be significant in the decades to come. In the absence of market signals, the government policy should search for sector priority indicators to achieve an efficient intersectoral allocation of social expenditure—that is, expand services in sectors that generate the highest utility for the poor per unit of expenditure. As discussed above, incidence analysis of social expenditure is useful in estimating potential impacts on inequality of changes in specific benefits per beneficiary.[51]

Obviously, sectors where welfare gains would be the greatest should be given priority to expand. The marginal welfare gains of expansion of services for a specific social sector depend particularly on two aspects: the share of the poor—who are presumed to be more deserving—among that population *not currently served* by the public or the private sector and the sector in which there is more urgency for additional supply—that is, where the relative value of marginal provision is higher. Vélez (1998) has shown that the government might use the consumption behavior of middle- and high-income households to asses the relative value of marginal provision in one of two sectors. Because private provision is more prevalent among the nonpoor, their intersectoral allocation of consumption of (or investment in) social services is closer to economic efficiency than the allocation of poor households, which are subject to liquidity constraints and credit market imperfections.[52] To identify sectors where the welfare gain of marginal provision is the largest, the key criterion is the

---

50. Previous comparisons showed a considerable disproportion of 1 to 12 in the benefits of the young (up to 17 years old) relative to those received by the population beyond 55 (a total of 12 million people). However intergenerational inequities would look much worst if the comparison was to be made with beneficiaries of RJU—with only 3 million people.

51. See, for example, Lerman and Yitzhaki (1985) and Wodon and Yitzhaki (2002). Moreover, methods of marginal incidence, as discussed by Ravallion and Lanjouw (1998) and Wodon (2000a), provide positive, but not normative, instruments about the most likely outcome of marginal incidence. However, when public services are poorly targeted, governments have the option of attempting selective cost recovery to reduce the expenditure item bill and improve targeting at the same time.

52. For example, in their choices of access to secondary education and/or health, middle-income households incorporate relative price information and the expected wage skill premium of each of those investments in human capital. Hence, their behavior provides a consumption-efficiency signal for the intersectoral allocation of social services among lower-income groups. Obviously, if relative prices vary across regions, sector priority analysis should remain within a region, and that could imply different priorities between the urban and the rural sectors.

magnitude of the gap in probability of access between poor and middle-income households, which is a proxy for the income elasticity and the marginal utility of income.

Vélez and Paes de Barros (2002) establish sector priorities for a set of basic goods and social services, including housing and urban facilities, health services, prenatal care and nutrition, education (access, quality of education, quality inputs at school), and access to credit. Appendix table A.1 shows the priorities for rural and urban Brazil, according to the ranking-based on access gaps of the poor relative to middle-income households (the fourth quintile). According to that criterion, the top priorities for coverage expansion have the following characteristics:[53] In basic education, the problem appears to be more of quality than quantity, namely a need for policies to reduce the attainment lag of students from low-income households who suffer an increasing differential lag of educational attainment (longer than two years).[54] This is the case among the students aged 11 to 17. In access to education, priorities are kindergarten and childcare. Increasing access to postsecondary education also seems to be a new demand among the poorest 40 percent of urban households (but not for rural households). This means that although current targeting of tertiary education has been deficient in the past, the rising rate of high school completion among the poor is increasing the chances that marginal expansion could better benefit them.

While education seems to be a higher priority in urban areas, housing and infrastructure improvements are the most urgent needs in rural areas, both inside and outside the dwellings. In urban areas, expansion of access to telephones is high priority, but in rural areas piped water, sewerage, and garbage collection also appear to be vital. Improvements within dwellings are especially important in terms of improving quality of floors and walls, as well as increasing the number of rooms to lessen the excessive number of households in which three or more people are crowded into a single room. Health services for the chronically ill, infant and child diarrhea treatment, and prenatal care programs also seem to be a higher priorities in rural areas. Finally, extending fringe benefits in terms of daily transportation subsidies to poor urban workers and offering more access to credit in the rural areas are other sectors where actions seem to be promising.

Not all of the sectors that are priorities for the poor are necessarily ideal for direct public provision. Certainly, in the case of childcare and improvement of sewerage and piped water access for the poor, public provision or subsidies would be appropriate. However, in cases such as telephone access or credit in rural areas, the key response seems to be regulatory changes to remove obstacles to enlarging the sphere of action of the private sector. In the case of tertiary education, the excessive unit cost of public universities makes such expansion financially difficult to achieve. Hence, a mixture of financial support to poor students (for example, credit programs with minimal subsidy) and gradually starting cost recovery among middle- and high-income students in public universities should be considered. Moreover, expanding secondary education is key requirement for reducing regressivity of tertiary, as is enlarges the share of high school graduates from poor households demanding post-secondary education.

Indirect Tax Reform: Clear Opportunities for Welfare Improvements

The impact of the actions of the state on people's lives comes not only from what it spends on, but also from how it chooses to raise the revenue it uses to finance those expenditures. Should Brazil reform indirect taxation? The considerable magnitude of the burden of Brazilian indirect taxation (three times that of direct taxation), its dominant regressive effect on income inequality, and the inefficiency generated by the heterogeneity of tax rates across goods and services justify the examination of the best options for indirect tax reform. If both equity and efficiency criteria guide tax reform, the best candidates for tax increase (reduction) are those goods and services that the

---

53. 15 sectors and subsectors' out of a total 59.

54. This is consistent with the findings of the paper on inequality of opportunity by Bourguignon, Ferreira, and Menendez (2002).

TABLE 3.1: EQUITY AND EFFICIENCY OF INDIRECT TAXATION

	Equity		Efficiency	
	Concentration Coefficient	**Gini Income Elasticity**	**Tax Rates**	**MECF[1]**
Vehicle	0.719	1.25	18%	1.23
Leisure	0.544	0.94	30%	
Transportation	0.440	0.76	17%	1.19
Clothing	0.418	0.72	26%	1.33
Housing	0.400	0.69	4%	1.04
Pers. expenses	0.367	0.63	33%	1.51
Medications	0.331	0.57	22%	1.27
Food	0.311	0.54	18%	1.20
Tobacco	0.186	0.32	88%	1.75

Notes: 1 Indirect taxation includes: Imposto sobre Circulação de Mercadorias e Serviços [ICMS], Imposto sobre Produtos Industrializados [IPI] and Contribução para o Program do Integração Social [PIS]. 2 MECF: Marginal efficiency cost of funds.

Source: Pesquisa de Orçamentos Familiares, POF 1995/96. (Income -Expenditure Survey). IBGE, Authors' calculations Vélez and others [2002a].

poor tend to consume less (more) than is proportional and that show low (high) efficiency cost. In Brazil, tax *incidence* is also quite heterogeneous across goods and services. Table 3.1 lists the concentration coefficients for consumption expenses on all goods and shows that although taxes on tobacco and food are the most regressive (the lowest value on the concentration coefficient the higher expenditure shares for the poor), tax on vehicles is clearly progressive because expenditure shares for the rich are larger than for income, and consequently Gini income elasticity for vehicles is greater than unity.[55] Taxes on public transportation, leisure, and clothing are intermediate cases: moderately progressive because their Gini income elasticities are some of the largest, but still below unity.

At the same time, the heterogeneity of indirect tax rates in Brazil generates strong variability in efficiency costs or the so called marginal efficiency cost of funds (MECF) across alternative revenue sources. Table 3.1 shows how tax rates go from a minimum of 4 percent on housing to 26 percent on clothing and 30 percent on leisure activities, up to 88 percent on tobacco. The MECF always exceeds unity because it measures the cost of taxing one dollar plus the welfare loss—or excess burden—induced by price distortions. Not surprisingly, the MECF tends to be larger for higher tax rates. However, excess burden of taxation tends to be larger for goods with larger price elasticities, as well. For example, the MECF is larger for vehicles than for food, despite the two types of goods being taxed at the same rate. The least inefficient taxes seem to be those on housing, vehicles, and transportation, and the most inefficient are on tobacco, personal expenses, and medications. One of most inefficient taxes is the one on the group of Personal Expense goods. The 33 percent tax induces a R$1.5 for every R$1 of tax collection, hence the excess burden of taxation is of 50 cents.

Figure 3.13 simultaneously displays the efficiency and equity criteria for each good and service: Efficiency increases toward the top of the vertical axis as the MECF falls, and equity

---

55. Goods with a larger share of consumption for the rich correspond to larger concentration coefficients and Gini income elasticities.

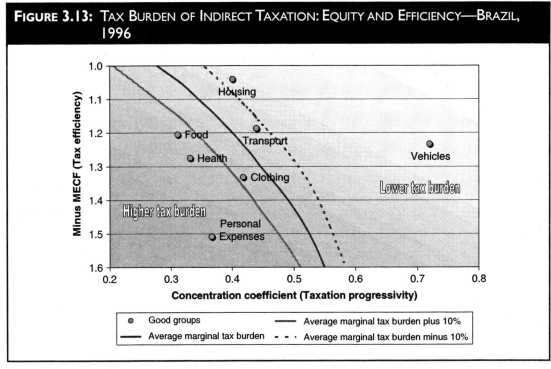

FIGURE 3.13: TAX BURDEN OF INDIRECT TAXATION: EQUITY AND EFFICIENCY—BRAZIL, 1996

Source: Vélez and others (2002a).

increases to the right along the horizontal axis. The three curves in the graph represent different combinations of tax efficiency and tax equity that produce the same tax burden.[56] Because tax burden increases toward the origin—more inefficiency and less equity—the red curve represents the combinations that produce the higher tax burden (10 percent above average), the green curve plots combinations that produce the average marginal tax burden, and the blue curve represents combinations that bring 10 percent additional tax burden. Goods below the red line (e.g., personal expenses, medications, and food) are associated with the highest tax burden and, consequently, are the candidates for tax reduction. On the contrary, goods above the blue line (housing and vehicles) produce the lowest tax burden and are the candidates for raising taxes.[57]

Vélez and others (2002a) determined the set indirect tax changes that can improve Brazilians' welfare and found multiple opportunities for improvement.[58] Out of a total of 21 potential pairs of tax reform, 6 benefit every income percentiles and 13 are welfare improvements to the Brazilian society as a whole relative to the status quo–provided some minimal and widely acceptable value judgments on equity, so called Dalton Improvements.[59] Table 3.2 displays those reforms in terms of tax rise and tax reduction pairs: housing–personal expenses, transport–personal expenses, and so forth. Accordingly, taxes should be *increased* for housing, vehicles, and transport and *reduced* for

56. The iso-welfare combinations are constructed for a Sen Welfare Index, equal to mean income times the difference between one and the Gini coefficient.

57. According to this criterion tobacco tax would be an obvious candidate for reduction because it satisfies both criteria, however there are other cost in terms of individual and public health that justify their very high level of taxation despite the regressive effects on income distribution.

58. Maintaining tax revenue constant and applying the "Dalton-Improving Tax Reforms" –DITAR-criterion proposed by Yitzhaki and Slemrod (1991), Mayshar and Yitzhaki (1995), Yitzhaki and Lewis (1996).

59. Twenty-one is the total number of pair combinations of seven taxes: personal expenses, housing, transport, vehicles, medications, food, and clothing. 6 reforms are "First-Order Dominant" and 13 are Dalton Improvements (Second-Order Dominant) relative to the status quo.

TABLE 3.2: TAX RATES CHANGE AND WELFARE EFFECTS FOR ALTERNATIVE PAIRS OF DALTON-IMPROVING INDIRECT TAX REFORMS, BRAZIL

Tax Reform Pair	Tax Rate Changes by Goods and Services							Efficiency Gain[a]		Winners[a]
	Food	Personal Expenses	Medication	Housing	Clothing	Transport	Vehicles	All	Bottom 50%	
Housing vs. personal expenses		-6.4%		0.6%				46%	14%	100%
Transport vs. personal expenses		-6.4%				1.2%		32%	13%	100%
Vehicle vs. personal expenses		-6.4%					1.1%	29%	32%	91%
Vehicle vs. clothing					-1.8%		1.1%	12%	24%	91%
Housing vs. medications			-3.5%	0.6%				23%	10%	100%
Housing vs. clothing				0.6%	-1.8%			29%	5%	100%
Vehicle vs. medications			-3.5%				1.1%	35%	34%	91%
Housing vs. food	-0.5%			0.6%				17%	11%	91%
Clothing vs. personal expenses		-6.4%			1.8%			18%	8%	91%
Transport vs. food	-0.5%					1.2%		2%	10%	81%
Transport vs. clothing					-1.8%	1.2%		14%	4%	100%
Medication vs. personal expenses		-6.4%	3.5%					23%	3%	100%
Transport vs. medications			-3.3%			1.1%		9%	9%	81%
Direction of Tax Change Initial Conditions	D	D	D/U	U	U/D	U/D	U			
Tax rate	18%	33%	22%	4%	26%	17%	20%			
Tax revenue R$ (billion)	6.3	0.9	1.2	1.2	2.7	2.7	3.5			

Note: Maximum change in revenue of any indirect tax was limited to 1% of total tax revenue; 100% means the first-order stochastic dominance relative to the status quo. a. As percentage of the revenue shift (1% of total indirect tax revenue). D = Decrease in tax rate from the initial level. U = Increase in tax rate from the initial level. U/D = Increase or decrease in the tax rate.

Source: Velez and others [2002a].

personal expenses and food. For a total shift of 1 percent of total tax revenue, the magnitude of those changes varies across goods—increased by 0.6 percent for housing, 1.1 percent for vehicles, and 1.2 percent for transport—and tax should be reduced by 6.4 percent for personal expenses and 0.5 percent for food. The bigger increase is for transport (1.2 percent), and the bigger reduction is for personal expenses (6.4 percent).[60]

These ex-ante evaluation of pair-wise indirect tax reforms should not be interpreted as specific policy proposals. They are useful to show that in the current situation of Brazil there is room for a tax reform can improve efficiency and equity without reducing revenues. Indirect tax reforms can produce significant efficiency gains relative to the status quo. However, their rankings vary with the distribution of those gains. From the average Brazilian household's point of view (table 3.2), the four largest gains happen with the tax reform involving housing and personal expenses (46 percent), followed closely by a second group of four reforms that includes vehicle-medications (35 percent), transport–personal expenses (32 percent), vehicle–personal expenses (29 percent), and housing-clothing (29 percent).[61] However, from the point of view of the poorest 50 percent, priorities are different. Their maximum benefits (32 percent) are produced by the vehicle–personal expenses tax reform. Best tax reforms for the poor should involve raising taxes on vehicles in exchange for tax reductions on personal expenses, medications, or clothing.

In summary, the considerable magnitude and the pro-poor distribution of the potential gains of possible indirect tax reforms suggests that Brazil should give serious consideration to this issue. Although different distributional perspectives make a difference in choosing the preferred goods to tax *more,* they do not make a difference in picking the preferred goods to tax *less.* Personal expenses are unambiguously the best candidate for tax reduction.

*   *   *

This section has shown that to reduce inequality, public policy must be active on four fronts. First, inequities must be reduced and the level of educational attainment must be raised—that is, it is necessary to take advantage of temporary demographic opportunities to push up the level of education of the whole Brazilian labor force and diminish the educational gap of Brazil relative to middle-income countries. Measures of the gap in access to basic services for the urban poor relative to the nonpoor showed two clear priorities in this area for education: reducing repetition and dropout rates in basic education among the poor and raising their access to childcare and preschool education. Second, the wage-skill premium of post-secondary education should be reduced by promoting its expansion. Expanding access to credit markets in order to stimulate demand for higher education should be preferred to more subsidies of education at public universities with excessive unit costs. Additional benefits in terms of social mobility—breaking persistent inequality—would follow from raising promotion rates of poor students to help them complete high school and reach postsecondary education. Third, reallocating taxes and monetary transfers would improve equity and reduce inefficiency—for example, this would involve reallocating public expenditure away from excessive and regressive transfers, such as RJU pensions. It is important to take advantage of the opportunity to implement a welfare improving reform of taxation that can reduce the inequity of indirect taxation without additional efficiency costs. Fourth, PSE should be reallocated to sectors where demand is more urgent and equitable, reducing inequality of secondary income. Finally, an integral approach to the reduction of rural land inequality is needed, taking into account the imbedded market inefficiencies that induce nonagricultural use of large landholdings.

---

60. Tax changes for medications and clothing are irrelevant because they increase for some reforms and decrease for others.

61. The efficiency gain as a percentage of the revenue shift, 1 percent.

CHAPTER 4

CONCLUSIONS

T his report has drawn on a range of preexisting published research, as well as on some original work, to document some features of inequality in Brazil, register some of its consequences for Brazilian society, and investigate policy alternatives to address it.

The distribution of income in Brazil is one of the world's most unequal, and this has been remarkably persistent over time. The Gini coefficient of household per capita income has hovered just under 0.6 for the quarter-century or so for which comparable data have been available. Although problems with the measurement of incomes—particularly in rural areas—appear to have led to overestimates of the absolute levels of inequality in Brazil, the country remains very unequal in terms of its (imputed) distribution of household expenditures as well. Also, the spatial profile of the distribution appears to have been reasonably robust to the adjustments undertaken for this report.

Brazil's inequality is not restricted to income. It extends to—or originates from—the distributions of educational attainment, agricultural land, health status, and political influence. Although we had less to say about the last two of these, we did provide some comparative evidence on the former two. In international terms, both for years of schooling and for agricultural land, Brazil is also characterized by high levels of inequality.

Along the income dimension, on which we focused, Brazil's inequality has an important color and gender dimension. Brazilian blacks (those recorded in surveys as *pretos* or *pardos*) earn salaries that are on average about half of those earned by people of other races. Eighty percent of this difference appears to be due to differences in other personal characteristics. Most of this relates to an educational gap of more than two years of schooling between blacks and whites, which has shown little tendency to decline over time—in contrast, for instance, to South Africa. Indigenous populations, which are smaller in number, have not been surveyed to an extent that permits reliable statistical analysis, but the indications are that they fare no better than blacks. Asian descendents are generally considerably better off than people from other races, including the average white.

Brazilian women earn much less than men, even when their greater endowments of education are taken into account. However, evidence on job market experience in Brazil is not sufficiently detailed to enable us to ascertain whether that is due to differences in actual experience (presumably due to time taken off for childbirth and childcare) or due to discrimination. It is not possible to rule either of these out.

However, discrimination and labor market segmentation, which are both inefficient and undesirable in themselves, are not the primary causes of Brazil's egregious inequalities. These originate primarily in very unequal distributions of assets, broadly defined, and in the fact that price differentials—notably wage differentials by skill are excessive. We investigated three types of assets in particular: agricultural land, years of schooling, and entitlements to public transfers. In the case of agricultural land, the evidence we found suggests that imbedded inefficiencies in the markets of credit and insurance explain the existence of a substantial sector of very large, low-productivity farms lowers the country's overall aggregate land productivity.

In the case of education, this report found that levels of years of schooling were low in absolute terms, that dispersion was high, and that up to the early 1990s the speed of improvement was slower than in most other Latin American countries. Despite the significant acceleration in the pace of improvements in educational attainment in the mid- and late 1990s, Brazil remains behind in the level of education of its citizens and workers in both global and in regional terms. As a result, income distribution simulations indicate that if Brazil's distribution of education was replaced by that of other countries, this would contribute substantially to a closure of the inequality gap between Brazil and those countries. This was true, for instance, of countries as different as Mexico and the United States.

Finally, public transfers in Brazil, although less unequally distributed in that country than primary incomes, are still positively correlated with household income and do not contribute to a reduction in inequality. We found, for instance, that the greater inequality in the distribution of retirement pensions in Brazil than in the United States was responsible on its own for more than a third of the difference in the overall level of inequality between the two countries.

Brazil's high levels of inequality do have costs in terms of poverty. Most obviously, the unequal nature of claims on income flows implies that a given rate of growth in GNP reduces poverty more slowly than it otherwise would. The cumulative effect of this is that Brazil has an incidence of extreme poverty (with respect to a daily per capita line of U$1) that is some 17 percentage points greater than the average country with the same level of GDP per capita. This corresponds to some 29 million people added to the extreme poor.

Other costs refer to problems of social justice. Many Brazilians would place value on equality of opportunities for the country's children. We have found quantitative evidence that opportunities are not equal in this country. They differ with one's place of birth, with the color of one's skin, and first and foremost, with the educational attainment of one's parents. This evidence merely confirms features that have long been described in a more qualitative manner. Finally, there is evidence—both across countries and within Brazil—that rising crime rates are associated with the persistence of high levels of inequality, even when low income levels or the incidence of poverty are controlled for.

The implications of this for policy fall into three broad categories: land policies, education policies, and the design of public finances and expenditures more generally.

Chapter 3 showed that the extent of inequality in the size of landholdings in Brazil is suboptimally high, probably because macroeconomic instability in the past had created a portfolio motive for the demand of land which distorts the ownership pattern form the technically efficient. In consequence, a redistribution of land from very large to medium and small holdings could contribute to greater productivity, and hence to rural output and incomes. Policy priorities should include: (a) reduction of any remaining inefficiencies that lead to excessive demand for non-agricultural use of land, (b) efficient approaches to improve access to land for small farmers, (c) reduction of inefficiencies in land use and land rental markets using the land tax and other regulatory instruments, and (d) other measures to stimulate the activities of the subset of medium and small efficient farmers.

Education is probably the key area for public action in Brazil—and not only for reducing poverty and inequality. We do not think that Brazil needs to spend more on social policies, but we do think that it needs to spend more on education. In particular, it needs to redirect public resources toward preschool (public crèches and kindergartens) and primary schools, which the best targeted to the poor among public education sectors. An additional effort should also be undertaken to expand the supply and improve the quality of secondary schooling, which is the phase in which evasion is highest. In view of the finding that education inequality is quite persistent across generations (or "inherited"), particular attention should be given to establishing mechanisms that allocate more than proportional teaching resources to students coming from poor households, who tend to lag behind and drop out more often. Recent studies of the determinants of learning, based on standardized test scores across Brazil, are available to guide the government's efforts in allocating resources to the right inputs.

Complementarily, smart transfer instruments such as *Bolsa Escola* are effective in reducing the opportunity costs of schooling for poor children and adolescents, and can thus play an important role in quality improvements on the supply side. There is some evidence, however, that the amounts currently being planned under the *Alvorada* program are too low to achieve the desired poverty reduction impact.[62]

Pensions and tertiary education are the sectors of public spending that have the worst targeting record, and from which public funds should be redirected toward education and targeted conditional cash transfers.

Although changes to the pattern of public expenditure are probably the most crucial step the Brazilian government could take to reduce poverty and inequality, there is also evidence that equity and efficiency would both benefit from tax reforms. In particular, the predominantly regressive nature of the country's indirect taxes could be vastly ameliorated by a number of specific reforms outlined in this report.

The short-term political costs of attempting a reallocation of public resources from well-off pensioners and public university students to poor farm and city dwellers and their children are likely to be considerable. The long-term benefits, however, are likely to be faster growth, less poverty, less crime, and a fairer society.

---

62. The Alvorada's program supports social sector and infrastructure initiatives to reduce poverty and to improve the quality of life in extremely poor municipalities with Human Development Index below 0.5. The program started in 2000 and is administered by the Secretariat of Social Assistance (linked to the Ministry of Welfare). For a detailed description see http://www.presidencia.gov.br/projetoalvorada.

APPENDIX

TABLE A.1: SOCIAL SECTOR PRIORITIES ACCORDING TO ACCESS GAPS OF THE POOR RELATIVE TO THE FOURTH QUINTILE. BRAZIL, URBAN AND RURAL, 1997

Basic Goods and Services (15 Highest Ranking out of 59)	Relative Access Gap*			Ranking by Access Gap		
	Brazil	Urban	Rural	Brazil	Urban	Rural
Housing and Urban Facilities						
Water			222%			4
Sewage	83%		387%	9		2
Garbage collection	63%		197%	13		8
Durable construction materials	165%	111%	202%	5	8	7
Room crowding /1	78%	78%	78%	10	11	10
Electricity			65%			14
Telephone	379%	225%	1080%	3	5	1
Health Service						
Suffers chronic illness			74%			11
Periodical exams	52%			15		
Education						
Access						
Daycare and preschool (Individuals 0–6 yrs)	68%			11		
Higher education (19–25 yrs with complete secondary)	418%	674%		1	1	
Attainment lag ** (Students 11–14 yrs)	88%	105%	127%	8	10	9
Attainment lag ** (Students 15–17 yrs)	152%	168%		6	6	
Attainment lag ** (Students 7–17 yrs)		52%			15	
Quality-Inputs at school						
Computer (1st–4th grade)	382%	319%		2	3	
Computer (5th–8th grade)	259%	255%		4	4	
Computer (Secondary)	124%	415%		7	2	
Lab (All grades)	61%	109%		14	9	
Textbooks (5th-8th grade)		58%			14	
Pregnancy, Fertility and Nutrition						
Suffered diarrhea		130%			7	
Medical attention in diarrehea case		59%			13	
Took oral re-hydration in diarrhea case			72%			12
Prenatal are			56%			15
Quality of Employment and Exposure to Risk						
If employed, receives fringe transport benefits	68%	70%	65%	12	12	13
Credit						
Access to productive credit			213%			5
Access to consumer durable credit			17%			10
Obtaining credit (Credit Solicitors)			213%			5

Note: *Relative access gap is the shortage of the average coverage rate for all the population with income below the target quintile relative to the coverage of that quintile. 1/ Defined as rooms with three or more persons per room. ** Two years or more.

TABLE A.2: RESULTS FROM ANALYSIS OF DISTRIBUTIONAL INCIDENCE OF PUBLIC SOCIAL EXPENDITURE, BRAZIL NE AND SE 1997

| | Subsidy Size | | Targeting Share by Quintile (%) | | | | | Concent.[1] | Gini[2] | Subsidy Redistributive Effect Gini-Coeff-Reduction | | |
	Value (R$ billions)	Share	Q1	Q2	Q3	Q4	Q5	Coefficient	Income Elasticity	Change in Gini (x)[3]	%	RRE[4]
Education	**19.8**	**16.3%**										
Creche	0.1	0.1%	24%	33%	14%	23%	7%	-0.17	-0.29	-0.01	0%	2.1
Kindergarten	1.0	0.8%	42%	24%	16%	12%	6%	-0.33	-0.55	-0.11	2%	2.5
Basic (Primary) education	11.6	9.6%	26%	27%	23%	17%	8%	-0.19	-0.30	-1.13	20%	2.1
Secondary education	1.7	1.4%	7%	12%	28%	33%	19%	0.18	0.29	-0.09	2%	1.1
University education	5.1	4.2%	0%	0%	3%	22%	76%	0.69	1.13	0.05	-1%	-0.2
Adult education/training	0.4	0.3%	5%	15%	30%	23%	28%	0.22	0.36	-0.02	0%	1.0
Health care	**21.8**	**18.0%**										
Universal public health care	21.8	18.0%	16%	20%	22%	23%	19%	0.03	0.05	-1.54	27%	1.5
Urban investments	**8.1**	**6.7%**										
Water connection	0.4	0.3%	12%	17%	21%	24%	26%	0.14	0.23	-0.02	0%	1.2
Sewer conneciton	1.1	0.9%	4%	14%	22%	28%	32%	0.28	0.46	-0.04	1%	0.9
Urban public transport	2.6	2.1%	9%	15%	25%	28%	24%	0.17	0.28	-0.14	3%	1.2
Housing (Carta de credito)	0.4	0.3%	0%	0%	28%	63%	9%	0.33	0.53	-0.01	0%	0.8
Fevela upgrading	3.7	3.0%	34%	27%	17%	18%	4%	-0.28	-0.45	-0.40	7%	2.3
Pension and related programs	**67.6**	**55.7%**										
Pensions	67.6	55.7%	7%	8%	15%	19%	51%	0.39	0.63	-1.85	33%	0.6
Social assistennce services	**0.2**	**0.2%**										
Child services	0.2	0.2%	42%	24%	16%	12%	6%	-0.33	-0.55	-0.02	0%	2.5
Nutrition programs	**0.8**	**0.7%**										
School lunchs	0.7	0.6%	25%	24%	24%	18%	9%	-0.15	-0.25	-0.07	1%	2.0
Maternal nutrition (Milk programs)	0.1	0.1%	29%	33%	18%	13%	7%	-0.26	-0.43	-0.01	0%	2.3
Labor programs	**3.0**	**2.5%**										
Unemployment insurance	3.0	2.5%	13%	30%	15%	5%	38%	0.09	0.15	-0.19	3%	1.4
Summary/Total	**121.4**	**100%**						**0.2**		**-5.6**	**100%**	**1.0**

Notes: (1)Concentration Coefficient for subsidy x, $CC_x = 2*COV(x, F(quantile of income)) / mean(x)$. (2)Gini Income Elasticity for subsidy x, $GIE_x = CC_x / Gini (income)$, (3) Change in Gini (x):Sector x's contribution to redistribution as change in Gini Coefficient. (4) RRE (x): Relative Redistributive Effectiveness of sector x, redirbutive power per unit of expenditure. $RRE(x)$ is equal to the ratio of the sector x's share in contribution to Gini change to the sector x's share in total expenditure. Note that $RRE(x) = [GIE(x) - 1]/[GIE$ (total subsidies)$-1]$.

Source: "Attacking Brazil's Poverty" (World Bank, 2000), Authors calculations.

BIBLIOGRAPHY

Background Papers (in Part II)

Blom, A., and C. E. Vélez. 2002. "The Dynamics of the Skill-Premium in Brazil: Growing Demand and Insufficient Supply?" Washington D.C.: World Bank. Processed.

Bourguignon, F., F. Ferreira, and P. Leite. 2002a. "Beyond Oaxaca-Blinder: Accounting for Differences in Household Income Distributions across Countries." Washington D.C.: World Bank. Processed.

———. 2002b. "Ex-Ante Evaluation of Conditional Cash Transfer Programs: The Case of Bolsa Escola." Washington D.C.: World Bank. Processed.

Bourguignon, F., F. Ferreira, and M. Menendez. 2002. "Inequality of Outcomes, Inequality of Opportunities and Intergenerational Education Mobility In Brazil." Washington D.C.: World Bank. Processed.

Elbers, C., J. O. Lanjouw, P. Lanjouw, and P. G. Leite. 2002. "Poverty and Inequality in Brazil: New Estimates from Combined PPV-PNAD Data." Washington D.C.: World Bank. Processed.

Vélez, C. E, S. Soares, and M. Medeiros. 2002. "Schooling Expansion In Demographic Transition: A Transient Opportunity For Inequality Reduction In Brazil." Washington D.C.: World Bank. Processed.

Vélez, C. E., S. Vianna, F. G. Silveira, and C. Magalhães. 2002a. "Indirect Taxation Reform: Searching for Dalton-Improvements In Brazil." Washington D.C.: World Bank. Processed.

Other References

Aghion, P., and P. Bolton. 1997. "A Theory of Trickle-Down Growth and Development." *Review of Economic Studies* 64:151–72.

Aghion, Philippe, Eve Caroli, and C. Garcia-Peñalosa. 1999. "Inequality and Economic Growth: The Perspective of the New Growth Theories." *Journal of Economic Literature* 37(4):1615–60.

Ahluwalia, M. 1976. "Inequality, Poverty and Development," *Journal of Development Economics* 3:307–42.

Albernaz, A., F. H. G. Ferreira, and C. Franco. Forthcoming. "Qualidade e Eqüidade na Educação Fundamental Brasileira." *Pesquisa e Planejamento Econômico*.

Alesina, A., and D. Rodrik. 1994. "Distributive Politics and Economic Growth." *Quarterly Journal of Economics* 108:465–90.

Almeida dos Reis, José G., and Ricardo Paes de Barros. 1991. "Wage Inequality and the Distribution of Education: A Study of the Evolution of Regional Differences in Inequality in Metropolitan Brazil." *Journal of Development Economics* 36:117–43.

Anand, S., and S. Kanbur. 1993. "Inequality and Development: A Critique." *Journal of Development Economics* 41:19–43.

Arbache, J. S., F. Green, and A. Dickerson. 2000. "A Picture of Wage Inequality and the Allocation of Labor in a Period of Trade Liberalization: The Case of Brazil." Universidade de Brasilia.

Arias, O., K. F. Hollack, and W. Sosa. 1999. "Individual Heterogeneity in the Returns to Schooling: Instrumental Variables Quantile Regression Using Twins Data." University of Illinois. Processed.

Arnott, R. J., and J. E. Stiglitz. 1979. "Aggregate Land Rents, Expenditure on Public Goods, and Optimal City Size." *Quarterly Journal of Economics* 93(4):471–500.

Asano, S and E. Fiuza. 2001. "Estimation of the Brazilian Consumer Demand System." Testo para Discussão. Instituto de Pesquisa Econômica Aplicada.

Assunção, J. J., and H. Moreira. 2000. "ITR sem mentiras: um comentário sobre a taxação de terras com informação assimétrica." Departamento de Economia, Catholic University of Rio de Janeiro (PUC-Rio). Processed.

Assunção, J. J. 2002. "Distribuição De Terra E As Políticas Públicas Voltadas Ao Meio Rural Brasileiro." Washington D.C.: World Bank. Processed.

Atkinson, Anthony B. 1970. "On the Measurement of Inequality." *Journal of Economic Theory* 2:244–63.

Atkinson, A., and F. Bourguignon. 1991. "Tax-Benefit Models for Developing Countries: Lessons from Developed Countries." In J. Khalilzadeh-Shirazi and A. Shah, eds., *Tax Policy in Developing Countries*. Washington, D.C.: World Bank.

Atkinson, A.B. and J.E. Stiglitz 1980. "Lectures on Public Economics." Maidenhead, UK.

Ávila, A. F. D., and R. Evenson. 1998. "Total Factor Productivity Growth in Brazilian Agriculture and the Role of Agricultural Research *Economia Aplicada* 2(2):317–56.

Baland, J.M., and J. Robinson. 2000. "Is Child Labor Inefficient?" *Journal of Political Economy* 108(4): 663–79.

Banerjee, A. V., and A. F. Newman. 1993. "Occupational Choice and the Process of Development." *Journal of Political Economy* 101(2):274–98.

Banerjee, A., D. Mookherjee, K. Munshi, and D. Ray. 2001. "Inequality, Control Rights, and Rent Seeking: Sugar Cooperatives in Maharashtra." *Journal of Political Economy* 109(1):138–90.

Barros, R.P. 2002. "Inequality in Brazil: Causes and Consequences." Slide presention. Rio de Janeiro: Instituto de Pesquisa Econômica Aplicada.

Barros, R.P. and Ramos, L. 1996. "Temporal Evolution of the Relationship between Wages and Educational of Brazilian Men." In N. Birdsall and R. H. Sabot, eds., *Opportunity Forgone; Education in Brazil*. Washington, D.C.: Inter-American Development Bank.

Barros, R.P, and D. Lam. 1996. "Income and Education Inequality and Children's Schooling Attainment in Brazil." In N. Birdsall and R. Sabot, eds., *Opportunity Forgone: Education in Brazil*. Washington, D.C.: Inter-American Development Bank.

Barros, R.P, C. H. Corseuil, and P.G. Leite. 2000. "Mercado de trabalho e pobreza no Brasil." In Ricardo Henriques, ed., *Desigualdade e Pobreza no Brasil*. Rio de Janeiro: Instituto de Pesquisa Econômica Aplicada.

Barros, R.P, R. Henriques, and R. Mendonça. 2000. "Pelo fim das décadas perdidas: educação e desenvolvimento sustentado no Brasil." In Ricardo Henriques, ed., *Desigualdade e Pobreza no Brasil*. Rio de Janeiro: Instituto de Pesquisa Econômica Aplicada.

Barros, R. P., Rosane Mendonça, Priscila Pereira Deliberalli, and Cristiana Lopes. 2000. "Impactos da distribuição da terra sobre a eficiência agrícola e a pobreza no Nordeste." In Ricardo Henriques, ed., *Desigualdade e Pobreza no Brasil*. Rio de Janeiro: Instituto de Pesquisa Econômica Aplicada.

Basu, K. 1999., "Child Labor: Causes, Consequences and Cure with Remarks on International Labor Standards." *Journal of Economic Literature* 37(3):1083–119.

Behrman, J. R., N. Birdsall, and R. Kaplan. 1996. "The Quality of Schooling and Labor Markets Outcomes." In N. Birdsall and R. H. Sabot, eds., *Opportunity Forgone; Education in Brazil*. Washington, D.C.: Inter-American Development Bank.

Behrman, J.R., Nancy Birdsall, and M. Szekely. 2000. "Intergenerational Mobility in Latin America: Deeper Markets and Better Schools Make the Difference." In N. Birdsall and C. Graham, eds., *New Markets, New Opportunities*. Washington, D.C.: Brookings Institution.

Bénabou, R. 2000. "Unequal Societies: Income Distribution and the Social Contract." *American Economic Review* 90(1):96–129.

Bhalotra, S. 2001. "Is Child Work Necessary?" Cambridge University, U.K. Processed.

Bianchini, Z. M., and S. Albieri. 1998. "A Review of Major Household Sample Survey Designs Used in Brazil." Proceedings of the Joint IASS/IAOS Conference, Statistics for Economic and Social Development, Mexico, September 1998.

Birdsall, N., and R.H. Sabot, eds. 1996. *Opportunity Forgone; Education in Brazil*. Washington, D.C.: Inter-American Development Bank.

Bittencourt, G. A.; D. S. B. Castilhos; V. Bianchini, and H. B. C. Silva. 1999. "Principais fatores que afetam o desenvolvimento dos assentamentos de reforma agrária no Brasil." Projeto de Coperação Técnica Organização das Nações Unidas para a Agricultura e Alimentação—Instituto Nacional de Colonização e Reforma Agrária. INCRA/FAO, Brasília.

Blau, Francine, and Lawrence Khan. 1996. "International Differences in Male Wage Inequality: Institutions versus Market Forces." *Journal of Political Economy* 104(4):791–837.

Blinder, Alan S. 1973. "Wage Discrimination: Reduced Form and Structural Estimates." *Journal of Human Resources* 8:436–45.

Blom, A., L. Holm-Nielsen, and D. Verner., 2001. "Education , Earnings and Inequality in Brazil, 1928–98: Implications for Education Policy." Policy Research working Paper. Washington, D.C.: World Bank.

Bloom, D. and Williamson, J. 1998. "Demographic Transitions and Economic Miracles in Emerging Asia." *World Bank Economic Review* 12:419–55.

Bound, J., and Johnson, G. "Changes in the Structure of Wages in the 1980's: An Evaluation of Alternative Explanations." *The American Economic Review* 82(3):371–92.

Bourguignon, F. 1979 "Decomposable Income Inequality Measures." *Econometrica* 47:901–20.

Bourguignon, F., and F. Ferreira. 2002. "Understanding Inequality In Brazil, A Conceptual Overview." Washington D.C.: World Bank. Processed.

Bourguignon, F., F. H. G. Ferreira, and N. Lustig. 1998. "The Microeconomics of Income Distribution Dynamics in East Asia and Latin America." Development Economics and Chief Economist (DEC), World Bank, Washington, D.C. Processed.

Bowles, S. 1972. "Schooling and Inequality from Generation to Generation." *Journal of Political Economy* 80(3):S219–51.

Brandão, A. S. P., and G. C. Rezende. 1992. "Credit Subsidies, Inflation and the Land Market in Brazil: A Theoretical and Empirical Analysis." World Bank, Washington, D.C. Processed.

Buainain, A. M.; J. M. Silveira, and E. Teófilo. 1999. "Reforma agrária, desenvolvimento e participação: uma discussão das transformações necessárias e possíveis." Núcleo de Educação a Distância, (NEAD), Brasília. Processed.

Buhmann, B., L. Rainwater, G. Schmaus, and T. Smeeding. 1988. "Equivalence Scales, Well-Being, Inequality and Poverty: Sensitivity Estimates across Ten Countries Using the Luxembourg Income Study Database." *Review of Income and Wealth* 34:115–42.

Burkhauser R., D. Holtz-Eakin, and S. Rhody. 1998. "Mobility and Inequality in the 1980s: A Cross-National Comparison of the United States and Germany." In S. Jenkins, A. Kapteyn, and B. M. S. van Praag, eds., *The Distribution of Welfare and Household Production: International Perspectives.* Cambridge, U.K.: Cambridge University Press.

Camargo, J. M., and F. H. G. Ferreira. 1999. "A Poverty Reduction Strategy of the Government of Brazil: A Rapid Appraisal." Catholic University of Rio de Janeiro, Department of Economics. Processed.

———. 2001. "O Benefício Social Único: Uma Proposta de Reforma da Política Social no Brasil." Texto para Discussão 443, Departamento de Economia, PUC, Rio de Janeiro.

Card, D. 1998. "The Causal Effect of Education on Earnings." In O. Ashenfelter and D. Card, eds., *Handbook of Labor Economics.* Vol. 3. Elsevier Science Pub. Co. New York.

Cardoso, F. H. 1975. "Dos Governos Militares a Prudente-Campos Sales In B. Fausto, ed., *O Brasil Republicano.* São Paulo: Difel.

Carter, M. R., and D. Mesbah. 1993. "Can Land Market Reform Mitigate the Exclusionary Aspects of Rapid Agroexport Growth?" *World Development* 21(7):1085–1100.

Case, A., and A. Deaton. 1999. "School Inputs and Education Outcomes in South Africa." *Quarterly Journal of Economics* 114(3): 1047:84.

Caselli, F., and W. J. Coleman. 2001. "Cross-Country Technology Diffusion: The Case of Computers." NBER Working Paper 8130. National Bureau of Economic Research, Cambridge, Mass.

Castro, P. F., and L. C. Magalhães. 1998. "Recebimento e dispêndio das famílias brasileiras: evidências recentes da pesquisa de orçamentos familiares (POF)—1995/1996." Texto para Discussão Interna 614. IPEA, Brasília.

Checchi, D., A. Ichino, and A. Rustichini. 1999. "More Equal but Less Mobile? Education Financing and Intergenerational Mobility in Italy and in the US." *Journal of Public Economics* 74(3):351–93.

Cowell, Frank A. 1980. "On the Structure of Additive Inequality Measures." *Review of Economic Studies* 47:521–31.

Cowell, Frank A., and Stephen P. Jenkins. 1995. "How Much Inequality Can We Explain? A Methodology and an Application to the USA." *Economic Journal* 105:421–30.

Cragg, M. and M. Epelbaum. 1996. "Why has Dispersion Grown in Mexico? Is it the incidence of Reforms or the Growing Demand for Skills." *Journal of Development Economics* 51:99–116.

Creedy, J. 1997. "Are Consumption Taxes Regressive?" Melbourne Institute Working Paper Series WP 20/97. University of Melbourne, Australia.

Dalton, H. [1920]1949. "The Measurement of the Inequality of Income." In *The Inequality of Income.* London: Routledge and Kegan Paul, Ltd.

Deaton, A. 1997. *The Analysis of Household Surveys—A Microeconometric Approach to Development Policy.* Baltimore: Johns Hopkins University Press.

Deaton, A., and C. Paxson. 1997. "The Effects of Economic and Population Growth on National Saving and Inequality." *Demography* 34(1):97–115.

Decoster, A., E. Schokkaert, and G. Van Camp. 1997. "Is Redistribution through Indirect Taxes Equitable?" *European Economic Review* 41:599–608.

Deininger, Klaus, and G. Feder. 1998. "Land Institutions and Land Markets." Policy Research Working Paper 2930. World Bank, Washington, D.C.

Deininger, Klaus, and P. Olinto. 2000. "Asset Distribution, Inequality, and Growth." Working Paper 2375. World Bank, Washington, D.C. Processed.

Deininger, Klaus, and Lyn Squire. 1996. "A New Data Set Measuring Income Inequality." *World Bank Economic Review* 10(3):565–91.

DiNardo, John, Nicole Fortin, and Thomas Lemieux. 1996. "Labor Market Institutions and the Distribution of Wages, 1973–1992: A Semi-Parametric Approach." *Econometrica* 64(5):1001–44.

Donald, Stephen, David Green, and Harry Paarsch. 2000. "Differences in Wage Distributions between Canada and the United States: An Application of a Flexible Estimator of Distribution Functions in the Presence of Covariates." *Review of Economic Studies* 67:609–33.

Duryea, S., and M. Székely. 1999. "Decomposing Schooling Differences in Latin America." Inter-American Development Bank. Washington, D.C. Processed.

Elbers, C., J. O. Lanjouw, and P. Lanjouw. 2001. "Welfare in Villages and Towns: Micro-Level Estimation of Poverty and Inequality." Development Economics Research Group, World Bank, Washington, D.C. Processed.

Elbers, C., J.O. Lanjouw, P. Lanjouw, and P.G. Leite. 2001. "Poverty and Inequality in Brazil: New Estimates from Combined PPV-PNAD Data." Development Economics and Chief Economist (DEC), World Bank, Washington, D.C. Processed.

Eswaran, M., and A. Kotwal. 1985. "A Theory of Contractual Structure in Agriculture." *The American Economic Review* 75(3):352–67.

Fajnzylber, P., D. Lederman, and N. Loayza. 1998. "Determinants of Crime Rates in Latin-America: An Empirical Assessment." World Bank. Washington, D.C. Processed.

Feenberg, D., A. W. Mitrusi, and J. M. Poterba. 1997. "Distributional Effects of Adopting a National Retail Sales Tax." NBER Working Paper 5885 National Bureau of Economic Research, Cambridge, Mass.

Feenstra, R., and G. Hanson. 1997. "Productivity Measurement and the Impact of Trade and Technology on Wages." NBER Working Paper 6052. National Bureau of Economic Research, Cambridge, Mass.

Feldstein, Martin. 1972. "Distributional Equity and the Optimal Structure of Public Spending." *American Economic Review* 62(1):32–36.

———. 1980. "Inflation, Portfolio Choice and the Prices of Land and Corporate Stock." *American Journal of Agricultural Economics* 62:910–916.

Ferreira, F. H. G. 2001. "Education for the Masses? The Interaction between Wealth, Educational and Political Inequalities." *Economics of Transition* 9(2):533–52.

Ferreira, F. H. G., and P. Lanjouw. 2001. "Rural Nonfarm Activities and Poverty in the Brazilian Northeast." *World Development* 29(3):509–28.

Ferreira, F. H. G., P. Lanjouw, and M. Neri. 2002. "A Robust Poverty Profile for Brazil Using Multiple Data Sources." *Revista Brasileira de Economia*.44:1-

Ferreira, F. H. G. and P.G. Leite. 2001. "The Effects of Expanding Education on the distribution Income in Ceará." World Institute for Development Economics Research, United Nations University. Wider Discussion Paper. 88:1–29.

Ferreira, F. H. G., and J. Litchfield. 1996. "Growing Apart: Inequality and Poverty Trends in Brazil in the 1980s." London School of Economics and Political Science. Suntory and Toyota International Centres for Economic and Related Disciplines. Distributional Analysis and Research Program. Discussion Paper 23, London.

Ferreira, F. H. G., and R. Paes de Barros. 1999. "The Slippery Slope: Explaining the Increase in Extreme Poverty in Urban Brazil, 1976–1996." *Brazilian Review of Econometrics* 19(2):211–96.

Fishlow, Albert. 1972. "Brazilian Size Distribution of Income." *American Economic Review* 62(2):391–410.

Foster, J., J. Greer, and E. Thorbecke. 1984. "A Class of Decomposable Poverty Measures." *Econometrica* 52:761–65.

Freije, S., and L. Lopez-Calva. 2000. "Child Labor and Poverty in Venezuela and Mexico" El Colegio de Mexico, Mexico D.F. and Cornell University, Ithaca.

Sanguinetti, P. and S. Galiani. 2000. "Wage Inequality and Trade Liberalization: Evidence from Argentina." *Journal of Development Economics.* Forthcoming.

Galor, O., and J. Zeira. 1993. "Income Distribution and Macroeconomics." *Review of Economic Studies* 60:35–52.

Gertler, P., and P. Glewwe. 1990. "The Willingness to Pay for Education in Developing Countries: Evidence from Rural Peru." *Journal of Public Economics* 45:251–71.

Ghatak, M., and P. Pandey. 2000. "Contract Choice in Agriculture with Joint Moral Hazard in Effort and Risk." *Journal of Development Economics* 63(2):303–26.

Goldin, I., and G. C. Rezende. 1993. "A agricultura brasileira na década de 80: crescimento numa economia em crise." Série IPEA 138. Instituto de Pesquisas Ecologicas Aplicada, Rio de Janeiro.

Gonzaga, M. G. 1996. "The Effect of Openness on Industrial Employment in Brazil." Série Seminarios 27/96. Instituto de Pesquisas Ecologicas Aplicada, Rio de Janeiro.

Goux, D., and E. Maurin. 2001. "La Mobilité sociale et son évolution: le rôle des anticipations réexaminé." *Annales d'Economie et de Statistique* 62: 49–71.

Griliches, Z., and W. Mason. 1972. "Education, Income and Ability." *Journal of Political Economy* 80(3):S74–103.

Grootaert, C., and H. Patrinos, eds. 1999. *Policy Analysis of Child Labor: A Comparative Study.* New York: St. Martin's Press.

Guanziroli, C. E., and S. E. C. S. Cardim. 2000. "Novo retrato da agricultura familiar: o Brasil redescoberto." Projeto de Coperação Técnica Organização das Nações Unidas para a Agricultura e Alimentação—Instituto Nacional de Colonização e Reforma Agrária. INCRA/FAO, Brazilia., Processed.

Harding, A., ed. 1996. *Microsimulation and Public Policy.* Amsterdam and New York: Elsevier.

Hauptman, A. 1998. "Accommodating the Growing Demand for Higher Education in Brazil: A Role for the Federal Universities?" Discussion Paper. World Bank, Latin America and the Caribbean Regional Office, Washington, D.C.

Heckman, J., and E. Leamer, eds. 2002. *Handbook of Econometrics.* Vol. 5. Amsterdam: North-Holland.

Heckman, J., E. Vytlacil, and J. Abbring. 2002. "Econometric Evaluation of Social Programs." In *Handbook of Econometrics.* Vol. 5. Amsterdam: North-Holland.

Henriques, Ricardo. 2000. *Desigualdade e Pobreza no Brasil.* Rio de Janeiro: Instituto de Pesquisa Econômica Aplicada.

Higgins, Matthew, and Jeffrey G. Williamson. 1999. "Explaining Inequality the World Round: Cohort Size, Kuznets Curves, and Openness." NBER Working Paper 7224. National Bureau of Economic Research, Cambridge, Mass.

Hoff, K. 1991. "Land Taxes, Output Taxes, and Sharecropping: Was Henry George Right?" *World Bank Economic Review* 5(1):93–111.

Hoff, K., A. Braverman, and J. E. Stiglitz, eds. 1993. *The Economics of Rural Organization: Theory, Practice and Policy.* New York: Oxford University Press.

Hoffman, Rodolfo. 1998. *Distribuição de Renda: medidas de desigualdade e pobreza.* São Paulo: Editora da Universidade de São Paulo.

———. 2001. "Desigualdade no Brasil: A Contribuição das Aposentadorias." Universidade Estadual de Campinas—UNICAMP, Instituto de Economia, São Paulo. Processed.

Howes, Stephen, and J. O. Lanjouw. 1998. "Does Sample Design Matter for Poverty Comparisons?" *Review of Income and Wealth* 44(1):99–109.

Instituto Brasileiro de Geografia e Estatística. 1998. "Pesquisa de Orçamentos Familiares, POF 1995/96." (Income-Expenditure Survey) IBGE, Rio de Janeiro. Digital Media.

———. 1999. *Pesquisa de Orçamentos Familiares 1995/96. Vol. 1. Despesas, recebimentos e características das famílias, domicílios, pessoas e locais de compra.* Rio de Janeiro: IBGE, Departamento de Índices de Preços.

Inter-American Development Bank. 1998–99. "América Latina Frente a la Desigualdad". Progreso Económico y Social en América Latina. Washington, D.C.

Juhn, Chinhui, Kevin Murphy, and Brooks Pierce. 1993. "Wage Inequality and the Rise in Returns to Skill." *Journal of Political Economy* 101(3):410–42.

Kakwani, Nanak C. 1977. "Applications of Lorenz Curve in Economic Analysis." *Econometrica* 45(3):719–27.

Katz, L., and K. Murphy. 1992. "Changes in Relative Wages, 1963–1987: Supply and Demand Factors." *Quarterly Journal of Economics* 107:35–78.

Kremer, M., and D. Chen. 2002. "Income Distribution Dynamics with Endogenous Fertility." *Journal of Economic Growth* 7(3):227–58.

Kuznets, S. 1979. *Growth, Population and Income Distribution: Selected Essays.* New York; Norton.

Lächler, U. 1998. "Education and Earnings Inequality in Mexico." Policy Research Working Paper 1949. World Bank, Washington, D.C.

Lam, David. 1986. "The Dynamics of Population Growth, Differential Fertility and Inequality." *Economic Review* 76(5):1103–16.

———. 1999. "Generating Extreme Inequality: Schooling, Earnings, and Intergenerational Transmission of Human Capital in South Africa and Brazil." Research Report 99–439. University of Michigan, Population Studies Center at the Institute For Social Research, Ann Arbor.

Lam, David, and Deborah Levison. 1992. "Age, Experience, and Schooling: Decomposing Earnings Inequality in the United States and Brazil." *Sociological Inquiry* 62(2):118–145.

Lam, David, and R. Schoeni. 1993. "The Effects of Family Background on Earnings and Returns to Schooling: Evidence from Brazil." *Journal of Political Economy* 101(4):710–40.

Lambert, Peter, and Shlomo Yitzhaki. 1995. "Equity, Equality and Welfare." *European Economic Review* 39:674–82.

Langoni, Carlos G. 1973. *Distribuição da Renda e Desenvolvimento Econômico do Brasil* Rio de Janeiro: Expressão e Cultura.

Lee, J. 2001. "Education for Technology Readiness: Prospects for Developing Countries." Journal of Human Development 2(1):115–51.

Legovini, Arianna, César Bouillon, and Nora Lustig. 2001. "Can Education Explain Income Inequality Changes in Mexico?" Inter-American Development Bank, Poverty and Inequality Unit, Washington, D.C. Processed.

Lerman, Robert, and Shlomo Yitzhaki. 1985. "Income Inequality Effects by Income Source: A New Approach and Application to the U.S." *Review of Economics and Statistics* 67:151–56.

———. 1994. "The Effect of Marginal Changes in Income Sources on U.S. Income Inequality." *Public Finance Quarterly* 22(4):403–17.

Levey, F., and R. J. Murnane. 1992. "U.S. Earnings Levels and Earnings Inequality: A Review of Recent Trends and Proposed Explanations." *Journal of Economic Literature* 30:1333–81.

Levison, D., and D. Lam. 1991. "Declining Inequality in Schooling in Brazil and Its Effects on Inequality in Earnings." *Journal of Development Economics* 37:199–225.

Lisboa, M.D.B., and M.A.Viegas, 2000. "Desesperança de Vida: Homicidio em Minas Gerais,Rio de Janeiro e São Paulo, 1981–1997." Escola de Pos-Graduacao em Economia da Fundacao Getulio Vargas.

Rio de Janeiro. *Ensaios Economicos* 383:1–53. Machado, José A. F., and José Mata. 2001. "Earning Functions in Portugal 1982–1994: Evidence from Quantile Regressions." *Empirical Economics* 26(1):115–34.

Mankiw, N.G., D. Romer, and D. N. Weil. 1992. "A Contribution to the Empirics of Economic Growth." *Quarterly Journal of Economics* 107(2):407–37.

Mayshar, Joram, and Shlomo Yitzhaki. 1995. "Dalton-Improving Indirect Tax Reforms." *American Economic Review* 84(4):793–808.

Mincer, J. 1974. "Schooling, Experience and Earnings." National Bureau of Economic Research. New York.

Ministério da Política Fundiária e do Desenvolvimento Agrário. 1999a. *Banco da Terra*. Brasília.

———. 1999b. "O futuro nasce da terra: balanço da reforma agrária e da agricultura familiar." Brasília. Processed.

———. 1999c. *O livro branco das superindenizações: como dar fim a essa indústria*. Brasília: Assessoria de Comunicação Social.

Mirrlees, J. A. 1971. "An Exploration in the Theory of Optimum Income Taxation." *Review of Economic Studies* 38:175–208.

———. 1986. "The Theory of Optimal Taxation." In K. J. Arrow and M. D. Intriligator, eds., *Handbook of Mathematical Economics*. Vol. 3. Amsterdam: North-Holland.

Mookherjee, D., and A. Shorrocks. 1982."A Decomposition Analysis of the Trend in UK Income Inequality." *Economic Journal* 92(368):886–902.

Murphy, K. M., W. C. Riddle, and P. M. Romer. 1998. "Wages, Skills, and Technology in the United States and Canada." NBER Working Paper 6638. National Bureau of Economic Research, New York.

Navarro, Z. 1998. "O projeto-piloto Cédula da Terra—comentário sobre as condições sociais e político-institucionais de seu desenvolvimento recente." Research Report. World Bank, Washington D.C. Processed.

Neri, M. C., and Camargo, C. M. 1999. "Distributive Effects of Brazilian Structural ReformsTexto para Discussão 406. Departamento de Economia, PUC, Rio de Janeiro.

Oaxaca, Ronald. 1973. "Male-Female Wage Differentials in Urban Labor Markets." *International Economic Review* 14:673–709.

Oliveira, J. T. 1983. "O imposto sobre a propriedade territorial rural 1964–1992." *Estudos Econômicos* 23:209–24.

Oliveira, J. T., and I. N. Costa. 1979. "O Imposto Territorial Rural—Avaliação Econômica" Relatório de Pesquisa 2. Instituto de Pesquisas Econômica, Universidad de São Paulo. São Paulo.

Otsuka, K., H. Chuma, and Y. Hayami. 1992. "Land and Labor Contracts in Agrarian Economies: Theories and Facts." *Journal of Economic Literature* 30:1965–2018.

Otsuka, K., and Y. Hayami. 1988. "Theories of Share Tenancy: A Critical Survey." *Economic Development and Cultural Change* 37:31–68.

Person, T., and G. Tabellini. 1994. "Is Inequality Harmful to Growth?" *American Economic Review* 84(3):600–21.

Petti, R. H. V. 1993. "ICMS e agricultura: da reforma tributária de 1965/67 à sistemática atual." Master's Thesis. Universidade Federal Rural do Rio de Janeiro, Instituto de Ciência Humanas e Sociais.

PNAD. "*Pesquisa Nacional por Amostra de Domicilios.*" Instituto Brasileiro de Geografia E Estatistica, Brazil, IBGE.

Prichett, L. 2000. "An Economist's Midnight Thoughts on Education: The Puzzle of Government Production." Harvard University, Kennedy School of Government Cambridge, Mass.

Ram, R. 1990. "Educational Expansion and Schooling Inequality: International Evidence and Some Implications." The *Review of Economics and Statistics* 72(2):266–74.

Ravallion, M. 1994. *Poverty Comparison*. Chur, Switzerland: Harwood Press.

———. 1997. "Can High-Inequality Developing Countries Escape Poverty?" *Economic Letters* 56(1):51–57.

Ravallion, M. and P. Lanjouw, 1998. "Benefit Incidence and the Timing of Program Capture." Policy Research Working Paper 1956. World Bank, Washington D.C.

Reydon, B. P., and L. A. Plata. 2000. "Evolução recente do preço da terra rural no Brasil e os impactos do Programa da Cédula da Terra." Núcleo de Educação a Distância, (NEAD), Brasília. Processed.

Reydon, B. P., A. R. Romeiro, and L. A. Plata. 2000. "Aspectos da questão agrária brasileira: lições à luz do mercado de terras." Projeto de Coperação Técnica Organização das Nações Unidas para a Agricultura e Alimentação—Instituto Nacional de Colonização e Reforma Agrária. INCRA/FAO, Brasília.

Rezende, F. 1991. "O peso dos impostos no custo da alimentação: análise do problema e propostas de redução." Rio de Janeiro. Processed.

Rezende, G. C. 1999. "Programa de crédito especial para reforma agrária (Procera): institucionalidade, subsídio e eficácia." Técnica Organização das Nações Unidas para a Agricultura e Alimentação—Instituto Nacional de Colonização e Reforma Agrária. INCRA/FAO, Brasília.

Robbins, D, and T.H. Gindling. 1999. "Trade Liberalization and the Relative Wages for More-Skilled Workers in Costa Rica." *Review of Development Economics* 3(2):155–69.

Rodriguez, A., and C.A. Herrán. 2000. *Secondary Education in Brazil.* Inter-American Development Bank, Washington, D.C.

Rodrigues, J. J. 1998. "Carga tributária sobre os salários"—Secretaria da Receita Federal: Coordenação Geral de Estudos Econômico e Tributário." Texto para Discussão 1. Brasília.

Roemer, J. E. 1998. *Equality of Opportunity.* Cambridge, Mass.: Harvard University Press.

Romeiro, A. R., B. P. Reydon, and L. A. Plata. 2000. "Impacto do ITR nos preços da terra na concentração fundiária." Projeto Projeto de Coperação Técnica Organização das Nações Unidas para a Agricultura e Alimentação—Instituto Nacional de Colonização e Reforma Agrária. INCRA/FAO, Brasília.

Rosembaum, D. T. 2000. "Ability, Educational Ranks, and Labor Market Trends: The Effects of Shifts in the Skill Composition of the Educational Groups." University of North Carolina at Greensboro, Department of Economics.

Sacconato, André L., and Naércio Menezes Filho. 2001. "A Diferença Salarial entre os Trabalhadores Americanos e Brasileiros: uma Análise com Micro Dados." Texto para Discussão 25/2001. Universidade de São Paulo, Instituto de Pesquisas Econômicas.

Sachs, J. D., and Shartz, H. J. 1996. "U.S. Trade with Developing Countries and Wage Inequality." *AEA Papers and Proceedings* 86(2):234–39.

Santamaria, M. 2000. "External Trade, Skill, Technology and the Recent Increase of Income Inequality in Colombia." Ph.D. dissertation, Department of Economics, Georgetown University, Washington, D.C.

Sayad, J. 1992. "Especulação em terras rurais, efeitos sobre a produção agrícola e o novo ITR." *Pesquisa e Planejamento Econômico* 12(1):87–108.

Schultz, T. P. 2000. "The Impact of Progresa on School Enrollments, IFPRI Final Report on Progresa." IFPRI, Washington, D.C.

Secretaria de Comunicação de Governo da Presidência da República. 1997. "Reforma agrária: compromisso de todos." www.planalto.gov.br/secom/colecao/refagr8.htm.

Sedlacek, Guilherme. 1999. "An Assessment of the Bolsa Escola Program in Brazil." Washington, D.C.: World Bank. Processed.

Shorrocks, Anthony F. 1980. "The Class of Additive Decomposable Inequality Measures." *Econometrica* 48(3):613–25.

———. 1999. "Decomposition Procedures for Distributional Analysis: A Unified Framework Based on the Shapley Value." University of Essex, Department of Economics, Colchester, UK. Processed.

Silva, E. R. A. 1999. "Programa nacional de fortalecimento da agricultura familiar—relatório técnico das ações desenvolvidas no período 1995/1998." Texto para Discussão 664. IPEA, Brasília.

Silva, M.C. and S. Wajnman. 2000. "Tendências de coorte nos diferenciais de rendimentos por sexo." In *Desigualdade e Pobreza no Brasil*. Rio de Janeiro: Instituto de Pesquisa Econômica Aplicada.

Siqueira, R. B., J. R. Nogueira, and E. S. Souza. 1999. "Imposto sobre consumo no Brasil: a questão da regressividade reconsiderada." Universidade de Pernambuco, Departamento de Economia, Recife.

———. 1998. "Uma análise da incidência final dos impostos indiretos no Brasil." Universidade de Pernambuco, Departamento de Economia, Recife. Processed.

Skinner, J. 1991a. "If Agricultural land Taxation Is So Efficient, Why Is It So Rarely Used?" *World Bank Economic Review* 5(1):113–33.

———. 1991b. "Prospects for Agricultural Land Taxation in Developing Countries." *World Bank Economic Review* 5(3):493–511.

Soares de Freitas, M., R. Nogueira Duarte, D. Carneiro Pessoa, S. Albieri, and P. do Naschimento Silva. 1997. "Comparando Distribuições Etárias em Pesquisas por Amostragem: PNAD 1995 e PPV 96/97." Fundação Instituto Brasileiro de Geografia e Estatística, Rio de Janeiro. Processed.

Souza, M. C. S. 1996. "Tributação indireta no Brasil: eficiência versus eqüidade." *Revista Brasileira de Economia* 50(1):3–20.

Stiglitz, J. 1974. "Incentives and Risk-Sharing in Sharecropping." *Review of Economic Studies* 41:219–55.

Stiglitz, V. L., and A. Weiss. 1981. "Credit Rationing in Markets with Imperfect Information." *American Economic Review* 71(3):393–410.

Stock, J. H., and M. W. Watson. 1988. "Testing for Common Trends." *Journal of the American Statistical Association* 83:1097–1107.

Székely, Miguel. 1998. *The Economics of Poverty, Inequality and Wealth Accumulation in Mexico*. New York: St. Martin's Press.

Tinbergen, J. 1975. *Income Distribution Analysis and Policies*. Amsterdam: North-Holland Pub. Co.

Thomas, Vinod. "Differences in Income and Poverty across Brazil." *World Development*, Vol 15, No 2, 1987.

Vélez, C. E. 1998. "Public Social Spending: Efficiency, Equity and Sectorial Restructuring." Banco de la República, Bogotá.

Vélez, C. E., and V. Foster. 2000. "Public Social Expenditure in Brazil: An International Comparison." In World Bank, ed., *Brazil: Selected Issues in Social Protection*, Volume 2. World Bank , Washington, D.C.

Vélez, C. E., J. Leibovich, A. Kugler, C. Bouillon, and J. Núñez. 2001. "The Reversal of Inequality Gains in Colombia, 1978–1995: A Combination of Persistent and Fluctuating Forces." World Bank, Washington, D.C. Processed.

Vélez, C.E., L. Rawlings, V. Paqueo, and J. Riaño. 2002b. "Shared Growth, Poverty and Inequality." Colombia, the Economic Foundation of Peace, World Bank, Washington, D.C.

Verner, D. 2000a. "The Dynamics of Poverty and Its Determinants: The Case of Pernambuco and the Northeast Brazil." World Bank, Washington D.C.

———. (2000b) "Wage Determination in Pernambuco, Bahia, Ceará, and the Northeast: An Application of Quantile Regressions." Policy Working Paper. World Bank, Washington, D.C.

Varsano, R., E.P. Pessoa, N.L.C. Silva, J.R.R. Afonso, E.A. Araújo, and J.C.M. Ramundo, 1998. "Uma Análise da Carga Tributária do Brasil." Texto Para Discussão Interna 583, IPEA, Rio de Janeiro.

Vianna, S. T. W. 2000. "Tributação sobre renda e consumo das famílias no Brasil: avaliação de sua incidência nas grandes regiões urbanas—1996." Ph.D. diss. Universidade Federal do Rio de Janeiro, Instituto de Economia.

Wodon, T. Q. 2000. "Poverty and Policy in the Latin America and the Caribbean." World Bank Technical Paper 467. Washington, D.C.

Wodon, T. Q., and I. Ajwad. 2001. "Marginal Benefit Incidence Analysis: An alternative approach." World Bank, Washington, DC. Processed.

Wodon, T. Q., and S. Yitzhaki. 2002. "Inequality and Social Welfare." In J. Klugman, ed., *Poverty Reduction Strategies Sourcebook*. Washington, D.C.: World Bank.

Wood, A. 2000. "Globalization and Wage Inequalities: A Synthesis of Three Theories." Department for International Development, London.

World Bank and Inter-American Development Bank. 2000. "Brazil, Secondary Education in Brazil." Report 1940. World Bank, Washington, D.C.

World Bank. 2000a. "Higher Education in Brazil." Country Study. World Bank, Washington, D.C.

———. 2000b. "Brazil, Selected Issues in Social Protection". Report 20054-BR. World Bank, Washington, D.C.

———. 2001a. "Attacking Brazil's Poverty: A Poverty Report with a Focus on Urban Poverty Reduction Policies." Washington D.C.

———. 2001b. "Brazil: An Assessment of the Bolsa Escola programs." Report 20208BR. Washington, D.C.

———. 2002a. "World Development Indicators", World Bank, Washington D.C.

———. 2002b. *Building Institutions for a Market Economy: World Development Report, 2002*. New York: Oxford University Press.

———. 2002c. "Brazil, Jobs Report". Report 24408-BR. World Bank, Washington, D.C.

———. 2003. "Brazil, Strategies for Poverty Reduction in Ceará". Report 24500-BR. World Bank, Washington, D.C.

Yitzhaki, Shlomo, and Joel Slemrod. 1991. "Welfare Dominance: An Application to Commodity Taxation." *American Economic Review* 81(3):480–89.

Yitzhaki, Shlomo, and J. Mayshar. 1996. "Dalton-Improving Tax Reforms When Households Differ in Ability and Needs." *Journal of Public Economics* 62(3): 399–412.

Yitzhaki, Shlomo, and J. Lewis. 1996. "Guidelines on Searching for a Dalton-Improving Tax Reform: An Illustratio with Data from Indonesia." *World Bank Economic Review (International)* 10:541–62. Washington, D.C.: World Bank.

PART II

BACKGROUND PAPERS

CHAPTER 5

POVERTY AND INEQUALITY IN BRAZIL: NEW ESTIMATES FROM COMBINED PPV-PNAD DATA[63]

By Chris Elbers (*Vrije* Universiteit, Amsterdam), Jean Olson Lanjouw (Yale University and Brookings Institution), Peter Lanjouw (World Bank), and Phillippe George Leite (Pontificia Universidade Católica do Rio de Janeiro)

Inequality and poverty occupy a prominent place in debates surrounding the recent development experience of Brazil, its future prospects and available policy options. There is an extensive literature on the distribution of wellbeing in Brazil—describing levels and dynamics of poverty and inequality outcomes; scrutinizing regional and sectoral disparities; studying the links to labour markets, human capital outcomes, public spending patterns; and so on.[64] An important stylized fact that emerges from this body of research is that, compared to other countries, Brazil is a clear outlier in terms of inequality and also accounts for a dominant share of the total number of poor in Latin America.

Conclusions regarding measured poverty and inequality levels, and trends, depend crucially on the underlying empirical foundations that support such analysis. Almost all of what is known about the distribution of economic welfare in Brazil, at the level of the country as a whole, comes from the well-known PNAD (*Pesquisa Nacional por Amostra de Domicílios*) household surveys. These are large surveys, fielded on an annual basis since the late 1960s, covering virtually all of Brazil (except the sparsely populated north of the country). The PNAD survey permits the

---

63. We are grateful to Francois Bourguignon, Francisco Ferreira, Pedro Luis do Nascimento Silva, Ricardo Paes de Barrros, and Martin Ravallion for useful discussions. Financial support was gratefully received from to the Bank-Netherlands Partnership program and the World Bank PREM Inequality Thematic Group. The views presented in this paper are those of the authors only and should not be taken to reflect the views of the World Bank or any affiliated institution.

64. The literature is very large. Useful recent contributions include Camargo and Ferreira (1999), Ferreira and Litchfield (1996), Ferreira and Paes de Barros (1999) and World Bank (2001a, 2001b).

construction of a measure of household income, and this indicator of economic welfare underpins much of the subsequent analysis of well-being that has drawn on PNAD data.

A recent study by Ferreira, Lanjouw and Neri (2000) suggests that there are at least some reasons for concern regarding the welfare indicator available in the PNAD surveys. Because the survey is essentially an earnings survey, it is oriented towards formal sector employment. As a result income data from households engaged in self-employment activities are only cursorily collected. These problems may result in inaccurate measures of income from two groups of particular importance in distributional analyses: self-employed informal sector and cultivating households. The question thus arises whether the limitations of the PNAD income figures are driving some of the conclusions about welfare outcomes in Brazil—with respect to both levels and patterns across population subgroups.

In 1996 a pilot household survey was fielded in Brazil's northeast and southeast regions. This survey, known as the *Pesquisa sobre Padrões de Vida* (PPV), is modelled after the World Bank Living Standard Measurement Survey (LSMS). The PPV is a multi-module integrated survey which collects, in addition to information on incomes, data on household consumption. Fairly detailed information on consumption expenditures are collected and it is also possible to impute values of consumption streams from items such as housing and home-produced food products.

In addition to being more detailed and comprehensive in construction, a consumption measure is generally perceived to provide a more reliable indicator of economic wellbeing than income, even when there are no clear biases in the income measure. This is particularly so when the purpose of the analysis is to study poverty. Essentially it is argued that it is easier to collect reliable and reasonably complete information on consumption than on income. In addition, there are theoretical arguments in favor of using consumption as a measure of welfare because consumption is thought to better proxy long term living standards than current income.[65]

Despite this surface appeal, the PPV also has clear limitations. Compared to the PNAD survey, the PPV sample is tiny. In addition, the PPV is not designed to be representative of the country as a whole—its coverage extends only to the northeast and southeast of Brazil (covering roughly three quarters of the national population).

The purpose of this paper is to report on the results of an attempt to exploit the best features of the two datasets described above, so as to produce consumption-based estimates of poverty and inequality, but in the large PNAD sample. We employ a recently developed methodology which permits the analyst to impute a welfare indicator from one survey, the PPV in our case, into another survey, the PNAD.

Imputing consumption into the much larger PNAD survey allows us then to estimate summary measures of poverty and inequality at levels of regional disaggregation significantly lower than what would have been possible in the PPV survey. An additional feature of the methodology is that we are able to assess the statistical precision of the welfare measures we estimate. One of our concerns in this paper will be to determine whether the imputation methodology comes at an unacceptably high price in terms of statistical significance of the estimates.

Aside from demonstrating the feasibility of imputing consumption from the PPV into the PNAD survey, we also aim in this paper to ask whether the picture of poverty and inequality that derives via this approach differs significantly from that which obtains from standard analysis based on the conventional PNAD income measure. In that sense we are interested to use our approach as a means to gauge the robustness of the conventional picture of poverty and inequality in Brazil.

It is clear that we cannot directly assess the reliability of the PNAD income measure by simply comparing the conventional results against those we obtain following our approach: the welfare *concepts* of income and consumption are different and could not be expected to yield identical quantitative estimates of poverty and inequality. However it may perhaps be arguable that if the

---

65. See Ravallion (1994) for further discussion.

two welfare measures were sound, their *qualitative* implications, in terms of the profile of poverty they yield, would be broadly similar. To that end we compare the spatial profile of poverty and inequality across these two approaches on the basis of simple cross tabulations and decompositions.

The structure of the remainder of this paper is as follows. In the next section we describe in greater detail the two data sources we draw on in this analysis. The third section turns to an overview of the methodology we employ. The fourth section describes how we implement the methodology in this particular setting. The fifth section presents results at the level of the PPV's representative region. We ask whether our estimates of poverty and inequality accord with those of the PPV, we assess the statistical precision of our estimates, and we compare our consumption based estimates against the estimates that would obtain had we used the income measure that is conventionally analyzed using the PNAD survey. The sixth section produces further consumption-based estimates, at levels of disaggregation which the PPV survey could not support. Once again we compare findings against the PNAD income concept in order to develop a further sense of whether, and where, the two approaches part company. In the seventh section we report some basic inequality decomposition results, again in turn based on the PNAD income measure and the PNAD imputed consumption measure. We ask whether qualitative conclusions regarding the relative contribution to overall inequality from certain population subgroups are robust to the welfare measure that is employed. The eight section summarizes our findings and discusses directions for future enquiry.

Data

As described above, the analysis in this paper draws on two sources of household survey of data: the combined 1996 and the 1997 rounds of the *Pesquisa Nacional por Amostra de Domicílios* (PNAD); and the *Pesquisa sobre Padrões de Vida* (PPV) of 1996.

The PNAD, implemented by the national statistical organization IBGE (*Instituto Brasileiro de Geografia e Estatística*), has been the main staple of country-wide (as opposed to metropolitan) distributional analysis in Brazil since the mid-1970s. It is an annual survey covering both urban and rural areas (except in the Northern region), and is representative at the level of the state and all metropolitan areas. Its sample size, currently around 105,000 dwellings per survey-round, is generally viewed as ample to produce reliable estimates of poverty or inequality at the regional, state, or possibly even lower, level. However, for such a large survey, and one which is fielded so often, some of the PNAD questionnaire shortcomings are remarkable. The questionnaire has evolved a great deal between the mid-1970s and 1996, generally much for the better. Nevertheless, there is one aspect, crucial for poverty and income distribution analysis, which has remained rather problematic: the income questions for any income source other than wage employment are insufficiently disaggregated and detailed.[66]

In principle, the nonsampling errors likely to arise from the absence of these more detailed questions could bias income measurement in either direction. Too few questions about in-kind benefits or the values of different types of production for own consumption are likely to lead to an underestimate of welfare, through forgetfulness. On the other hand, the absence of detailed questions about expenditure on inputs is likely to lead to an overestimate of net incomes from home production. In practice, the international evidence suggests that the first effect often predominates, and the absence of such detailed questions can lead to income under-reporting by categories of workers which, as it happens, are quite likely to be poor. Ferreira, Lanjouw and Neri (2000) examine these issues for the case of Brazil in some detail and suggest not only that under-reporting of income in the PNAD may well be significant, but that the degree is likely to vary considerably significantly across population subgroups.

---

66. The data issues addressed in this section are more thoroughly discussed in Ferreira, Lanjouw and Neri (2000).

As mentioned earlier, our second data source, the PPV, is a household survey modeled on the Living Standard Measurement Survey. It was fielded in 1996–97 by IBGE to assess the poverty targeting of Government social spending in Brazil. The aim of the PPV was to supplement the information already available through the PNAD, in order to improve the data available for poverty monitoring and policy analysis in Brazil.

The PPV was designed to fill some of the data gaps left by the PNAD. It provides a much more detailed picture of household expenditures and consumption, as well as utilization of various publicly subsidized services, particularly education, health, and transportation. The questionnaire is much longer, and requires multiple visits to each household. This richer information comes at a price. To keep survey expenses within reason, the sample size is much smaller (just under 5000 households in total) and the survey only covers the two most populous of Brazil's five regions, the Northeast and Southeast. These two regions together account for 73 percent of Brazil's population. The PPV is representative for ten spatial units (the metropolitan areas of São Paulo, Rio de Janeiro, Belo Horizonte, Salvador, Recife, and Fortaleza; the non-metropolitan urban Northeast; the non-metropolitan urban Southeast; the rural Northeast; and the rural Southeast). However, as we shall see below, even at the representative region level, estimates of poverty and other welfare indicators may be rather imprecisely estimated.

The purpose of this paper is to report on the application of a technique to combine the PPV and the PNAD datasets, seeking to complement their respective strengths and to compensate for their weaknesses. Because a maintained hypothesis of the imputation is that the consumption models estimated on the PPV data apply to PNAD households, it is most tenable to implement our method with reference to the Northeast and Southeast of Brazil only (that part of the country which the PPV is representative of). All results presented in this paper, including those based on the PNAD, thus pertain to these two regions only.[67]

A final word on the data concerns the comparability of the PPV and the PNAD surveys. It is imperative for the successful implementation of our methodology, that the two data sources we draw on be closely comparable. The methodologies underlying sampling, data collection methods, questionnaire design, etc., across these two datasets are quite different. Nonetheless, Soares de Freitas, et al (1997) find little evidence, in a comparison of the PPV with the 1995 PNAD survey, that these basic methodological differences introduce major discrepancies across the two data sources in terms of population characteristics.[68] The PPV survey was fielded during a period of one year spanning 1996 and 1997. The annual PNAD surveys are fielded on or around a given date, usually in September, in their respective survey years. In a further attempt to ensure that the two data sources we work with are as comparable as possible, and also in order to maximize the sample size of the database into which consumption is imputed, we have merged the 1996 and 1997 rounds of the PNAD on the grounds that these two neatly bridge the period covered by the PPV survey. Although the geographic coverage of this combined dataset is confined to the Northeast and Southeast of Brazil only, the size of the sample is sufficiently large (around 111,000 households) to permit considerable disaggregation.

Methodology

The methodology we implement here has been described in detail in Elbers, Lanjouw and Lanjouw (2001). The basic idea is straightforward. We estimate poverty and inequality based on a household per-capita measure of consumption expenditure, y_h. A model of y_h is estimated using the PPV survey data, restricting explanatory variables to those that can be linked to households in

---

67. We return in the concluding secton to a discussion of the feasibility of extending this analysis to areas not covered by the PPV, such as the South and Center-West of Brazil.

68. Bianchini and Albieri (1998) provide further details on the survey designs of all of Brazil's major household surveys.

both sets of data.[69] Then, letting W represent an indicator of poverty or inequality, we estimate the expected level of W given the PNAD-based observable characteristics of the area of interest using parameter estimates from the 'first-stage' model of y. The same approach could be used with other household measures of well-being, such as per-capita expenditure adjusted by equivalence scales, or to estimate inequalities in the distribution of household characteristics other than expenditures, such as assets or income.

Definitions

The basis of the approach is that per-capita household expenditure, y_h, is related to a set of observable characteristics, x_h, that can be linked to households in both the PPV and PNAD sample surveys[70]:

$$\ln y_h = E[\ln y_h \mid x_h] + u_h. \tag{1}$$

Using a linear approximation to the conditional expectation, we model the observed log per-capita expenditure for household h as:

$$\ln y_h = x_h \beta + u_h, \tag{2}$$

where β is a vector of k parameters and u_h is a disturbance term satisfying $E[u_h|x_h] = 0$. The vector of disturbances in the population is distributed $u \sim \Im(0, \Sigma)$.

The model in (2) is estimated using the PPV data. We are interested in using these estimates to calculate the welfare of an area or group for which we do not have any, or insufficient, expenditure information. Although the disaggregation may be along any dimension—not necessarily geographic—for convenience we will refer to our target population as a 'UF' (union federação). There are M_v households in UF v, M_v^s households in the PNAD sample from UF v, and household h has m_h family members.

While the unit of observation for expenditure in these data is the household, we are more often interested in poverty and inequality measures based on individuals. Thus we write $W(m, X, \beta, u_v)$, where m is a vector of household sizes, X is a matrix of observable characteristics and u is a vector of disturbances.

Because the disturbances for households in the target population are always unknown, we consider estimating the expected value of the indicator given the PNAD households' observable characteristics and the model of expenditure in (2).[71] We denote this expectation as

$$\mu_v^s = E[W \mid m_v^s, X_v^s, \xi], \tag{3}$$

where ξ is the vector of model parameters, including those which describe the distribution of the disturbances, and the superscript 's' indicates that the expectation is conditional on the sample of PNAD households from UF v rather than a census of households.

In constructing an estimator of μ_v^s we replace the unknown vector ξ with consistent estimators, $\hat{\xi}$, from the first-stage expenditure regression. This yields $\hat{\mu}_v^s = E[W \mid m_v^s, X_v^s, \hat{\xi}]$. This expectation is generally analytically intractable so we use simulation to obtain our estimator, $\bar{\mu}_v^s$.

---

69. Elbers et al (2001) describe the case when we impute expenditure from a household survey into the population census.

70. The explanatory variables are observed values and thus need to have the same degree of accuracy in addition to the same definitions across data sources. From the point of view of our methodology it does not matter whether these variables are exogeneous.

71. If the target population includes PPV households then some information is known. As a practical matter we do not use these few pieces of direct information on y.

Properties

The difference between $\tilde{\mu}_v^s$, our estimator of the expected value of W for the UF, and the *actual* level of welfare for the UF may be written (suppressing the index v):

$$W - \tilde{\mu}^s = (W - \mu) + (\mu - \mu^s) + (\mu^s - \hat{\mu}^s) + (\hat{\mu}^s - \tilde{\mu}^s). \tag{4}$$

Thus the prediction error has four components: the first due to the presence of a disturbance term in the first stage model which implies that households' actual expenditures deviate from their expected values (*idiosyncratic error*); the second due to the fact that we are imputing into a sample rather than a census of households (*sampling error*); the third due to variance in the first-stage estimates of the parameters of the expenditure model (*model error*); and the forth due to using an inexact method to compute $\hat{\mu}$ (*computation error*). Elbers, Lanjouw and Lanjouw (2001) provide a detailed description of the properties of the first and last two components of the prediction error.

To summarize, the variance in our estimator due to idiosyncratic error falls approximately proportionately in M_v, the size of the actual population of households in the UF. In other words, the smaller the target population, the greater is this component of the prediction error, and there is thus a practical limit to the degree of disaggregation possible. At what population size this error becomes unacceptably large depends on the explanatory power of the x variables in the expenditure model and, correspondingly, the importance of the remaining idiosyncratic component of the expenditure.

We calculate *sampling errors* on our poverty estimates taking into account the fact that the PNAD surveys are complex samples which involve stratification and multi-stage clustering (see Howes and Lanjouw, 1998, Deaton, 1997) .

We employ the delta method to calculate the variance due to *model error*: $V_M \approx \nabla^T V(\hat{\xi}) \nabla$, where $\nabla = [\partial_i^{-s} / \partial \xi] / \hat{\xi}$ and $V(\hat{\xi})$ is the asymptotic variance covariance matrix of the first-stage parameter estimators. Because this component of the prediction error is determined by the properties of the first-stage estimators, it does not increase or fall systematically as the size of the target population changes. Its magnitude depends, in general, only on the precision of the first-stage coefficients and the sensitivity of the indicator to deviations in household expenditure. For a given UF its magnitude will also depend on the distance of the explanatory variables for households in that UF from the levels of those variables in the sample data.

The variance in our estimator due to *computation error* depends on the method of computation used. As our calculations of the idiosyncratic and models errors are based on simulations, we can make the computation error become as small as desired by choosing a large enough number of simulation draws (at the cost of computational resources and time).

We use Monte Carlo simulations to calculate: $\hat{\mu}^s$, the expected value of the poverty or inequality measure conditional on the first stage model of expenditure; V_p, the variance in W due to the idiosyncratic component of household expenditures; and, for use in determining the model variance, the gradient vector $\nabla = [\partial_i^{-s} / \partial \xi] / \hat{\xi}$.

Let the vector $\hat{\mathbf{u}}^r$ be the rth draw from our estimated disturbance distribution—a random draw from an M_v-variate standard normal or t distribution, pre-multiplied by a matrix T, defined such that $TT^T = \hat{\Sigma}_v$, where $\hat{\Sigma}_v$ is the estimated disturbance covariance matrix for the population of households in UF v. With each vector of simulated disturbances we construct a value for the indicator, $\hat{W}_r = W(m, X, \hat{\xi}, \hat{u}^r)$, where m and X represent numbers of households and observable characteristics of PNAD households, respectively, each repeated in accordance with its expansion factor so as to have rows equal to the census number of households, M_v. The simulated expected value for the indicator is the mean over R replications:

$$\tilde{\mu}^s = \frac{1}{R} \sum_{r=1}^{R} \hat{W}_r. \tag{5}$$

Having estimated μ using the population number of households, the variance of W around its expected value due to the idiosyncratic component of expenditures can be estimated in a straightforward manner using the same simulated values:

$$\hat{V}_I = \frac{1}{R}\sum_{r=1}^{R}(\hat{W}_r - \tilde{\mu}^s)^2. \tag{6}$$

Simulated numerical gradient estimators are constructed as follows: We make a positive perturbation to a parameter estimate, say $\hat{\beta}_k$, by adding $\delta\,|\,\hat{\beta}_k\,|$, and then calculate $\tilde{\mu}^{s+}$. A negative perturbation of the same size is used to obtain $\tilde{\mu}^{s-}$. The simulated central distance estimator of the derivative $\partial_i^{-s}/\partial\beta\,|_\xi$ is $(\tilde{\mu}^{s+} - \tilde{\mu}^{s-})/(2\delta\,|\,\hat{\beta}_k\,|)$. Having thus derived an estimate of the gradient vector, we can calculate $\hat{V}_M = \nabla^T V(\hat{\xi})\nabla$.

Implementation

The first-stage estimation is carried out using the PPV survey. As described in section II this survey is stratified into ten regions and is intended to be representative at that level. Within each region there are several levels of clustering. At the final level, 8 households are randomly selected from a census enumeration area. Such groups we call a 'cluster' and denote with a subscript c. Expansion factors, l_{ch}, allow the calculation of regional totals.

Our first concern is to develop an accurate empirical model of household consumption. Consider the following model:

$$\ln y_{ch} = E[\ln y_{ch}\,|\,x_{ch}^T] + u_{ch} = x_{ch}^T\beta + \eta_c + \varepsilon_{ch} \tag{9}$$

where η and ε are independent of each other and uncorrelated with observables, x_{ch}. This specification allows for an intra-cluster correlation in the disturbances. One expects location to be related to household income and consumption, and it is certainly plausible that some of the effect of location might remain unexplained even with a rich set of regressors. For any given disturbance variance, σ_{ch}^2, the greater the fraction due to the common component η_c the less one enjoys the benefits of aggregating over more households within a UF. Welfare estimates become less precise. Further, the greater the part of the disturbance which is common, the lower will be inequality. Thus, failing to take account of spatial correlation in the disturbances would result in underestimated standard errors on welfare estimates, and upward biased estimates of inequality.

Because unexplained location effects reduce the precision of poverty estimates, the first goal is to explain the variation in consumption due to location as far as possible with the choice and construction of x_{ch} variables. We try to tackle this in four ways. First, we estimate different models for each of the ten regions in the PPV. Second, we include in our specification household level indicators of connection to various networked infrastructure services, such as connection to electricity, piped water, telephone. To the extent that all or most households within a given neighborhood or community are likely to enjoy similar levels of access to such infrastructure, these variables might capture unobserved latent location effects. Third, we calculate in the PPV and PNAD dataset cluster-mean values of household level variables, such as the average level of education of household heads per cluster, and also consider these variables for inclusion in the first-stage regression specification. These cluster-level variables might also serve to proxy location-specific correlates of expenditure. Finally, we have merged both the PPV and the PNAD datasets with an independently compiled municipio-level database (BIM) of variables (such as employment rates, school attendance rates, etc.) and also consider these variables as candidate variables for inclusion in our household expenditure models.[72]

---

72. A municipio represents a higher level of aggregation than the census EA, and as such BIM variables are intended to capture loactional effects at this higher level, rather than the more local cluster-level means.

We apply a selection criterion when deciding on our final specification requiring a significance level of 5 percent of all household-level regressors. To select location variables cluster means and BIM variables), we estimate a regression of the total residuals, $\hat{u}$, on cluster fixed effects. We then regress the cluster fixed-effect parameter estimates on our location variables and select those five that best explain the variation in the cluster fixed-effects estimates. These five location variables are then added to our household level variables in the first-stage regression model.

We apply a Hausman test described in Deaton (1997) to determine whether each regression should be estimated with household weights. In seven out of ten regions we find that weighting has no significant effect on the coefficients, and these first-stage regressions are thus estimated without weights. $\bar{R}^2$'s on our models are generally high, ranging between 0.45 and 0.77.[73]

We next model the variance of the idiosyncratic part of the disturbance, $\sigma^2_{\varepsilon,ch}$. Note that the total first-stage residual can be decomposed into uncorrelated components as follows:

$$\hat{u} = \hat{u}_{c.} + (\hat{u}_{ch} - \hat{u}_{c.}) = \hat{\eta}_c + e_{ch} \tag{10}$$

where a subscript '.' indicates an average over that index. To model heteroskedasticity in the household-specific part of the residual, we choose the twenty variables, z_{ch}, that best explain variation in e^2_{ch} out of all potential explanatory variables, their squares, and interactions.[74] We estimate a logistic model of the variance of ε_{ch} conditional on z_{ch}, bounding the prediction between zero and a maximum, A, set equal to $(1.05)^* \max\{e^2_{ch}\}$:

$$\ln\left[\frac{e^2_{ch}}{A - e^2_{ch}}\right] = z^T_{ch}\hat{\alpha} + r_{ch}. \tag{11}$$

Letting $\exp\{z^T_{ch}\hat{\alpha}\} = B$ and using the delta method, the model implies a household specific variance estimator for ε_{ch} of

$$\hat{\sigma}^2_{\varepsilon,ch} = \left[\frac{AB}{1+B}\right] + \frac{1}{2}Var(r)\left[\frac{AB(1-B)}{(1+B)^3}\right]. \tag{12}$$

Finally, we check whether η and ε are distributed normally, based on the cluster residuals $\hat{\eta}_c$ and standardized household residuals $e^*_{ch} = (e_{ch} / \hat{\sigma}_{\varepsilon,ch}) - [\frac{1}{H}\Sigma_{ch}(e_{ch} / \hat{\sigma}_{\varepsilon,ch})]$, respectively where H is the number of households in the survey. The second term in e^*_{ch} is not needed when first stage regressions are not weighted. In many cases normality is rejected, although the standard normal does occasionally appear to be the better approximation even if formally rejected. Elsewhere we use t distributions with varying degrees of freedom (usually 5), as the better approximation.

Before proceeding to simulation, the estimated variance-covariance matrix, $\hat{\Sigma}$, is used to obtain GLS estimates of the first-stage parameters, $\hat{\beta}_{GLS}$, and their variance, $Var(\hat{\beta}_{GLS})$.

Poverty and Inequality at the Regional Level

We begin our examination of empirical results at the level of the representative region in the PPV survey. Table 5.1 reports estimates of the incidence of poverty for the ten representative regions of the PPV. We report poverty estimates based on the three possible combinations of welfare concept and data-source that are available. In the first column we present estimates of the incidence of poverty in the combined 1996–97 PNAD survey based on the PNAD income measure of welfare. Column two provides our calculation of the standard error on this income-based poverty measure.

---

73. For reasons of space we do not reproduce here the parameter estimates and full set of diagnostics for all ten regression models. These can be furnished upon request.

74. We limit the number of explanatory variables to twenty to be cautious about overfitting.

TABLE 5.1: POVERTY MEASURES BY REGION FOR DIFFERENT DATA SETS HEADCOUNT

Region	PNAD Income[1]		PPV Consumption		PNAD Imputed Consumption	
	FGT0	S.E.	FGT0	S.E.	FGT0	Total S.E.
RM Fortaleza	0.350	0.015	0.188	0.039	0.176	0.029
RM Recife	0.344	0.013	0.222	0.034	0.136	0.020
RM Salvador	0.359	0.015	0.195	0.033	0.212	0.036
Urban NE	0.483	0.010	0.378	0.038	0.393	0.018
Rural NE	0.709	0.009	0.499	0.049	0.517	0.027
RM B. Horizonte	0.151	0.009	0.079	0.029	0.090	0.022
RM Rio de Janeiro	0.111	0.005	0.031	0.011	0.039	0.028
RM São Paulo	0.069	0.004	0.038	0.017	0.031	0.009
Urban SE	0.117	0.005	0.047	0.014	0.053	0.006
Rural SE	0.383	0.015	0.261	0.045	0.274	0.026

Note:
1. PNAD per capita income, PPV per capita consumption and PNAD imputed per capita consumption have been adjusted for spatial price variation (see Ferreira, Lanjouw and Neri, 2000).
2. Sampling errors incorporate adjustments for complex survey design (see text and also Howes and Lanjouw, 1998).
3. Poverty Line of R$65.07 in 1996 São Paulo reais (see Ferreira, Lanjouw, and Neri, 2000).

Source: PNAD 1996 and 1997, and PPV 1995.

This standard error comprises the *sampling error* described earlier, and our calculations of this have taken into account the complex sample design of the PNAD survey. The second set of poverty estimates and standard errors (columns 3 and 4) are based on the PPV survey and the per capita consumption aggregate that can be constructed from that survey. The standard errors are once again sampling errors incorporating the complex sample design of the PPV. Finally, columns 5 and 6, provide estimates of poverty from the PNAD using the consumption indicator of welfare that we have imputed into the PNAD. The standard errors on these poverty estimates comprise both a *sampling error* as well as the *model error* described in sections III and IV. The *idiosyncratic error* is vanishingly small at the levels of disaggregation that we are concerned with in this paper, and is therefore not reported.[75] *Computational error* has been pushed close to zero by employing at least 100 simulations in all our calculations.

We use the same poverty line to measure the incidence of poverty across all three cases. We employ the poverty line of R$65.07 in 1996 São Paulo reais which was derived in Ferreira, Lanjouw, and Neri (2000) as an extreme poverty line, sufficient to permit consumption of a minimum bundle of food items only. Both the income and consumption measures of welfare have been adjusted to capture spatial price variation (see Ferreira et al, 2000).

75. Calculation of this component is very computationally intensive as it requires using expansion factors to explode the PNAD sample up to a meta-census level, and then carrying out simulations to estimate the idiosyncratic error on the point estimate of poverty. Elbers et al (2001) document that that idiosyncratic error becomes negligible when welfare estimates are for populations of 10,000 households or more. In no case do we estimate welfare measures for populations below this size. (Note that the criterion is *population* not sample size).

Considering first a comparison of poverty based on PNAD income versus PPV consumption we are immediately struck by the much higher levels of measured poverty in the PNAD. This point has already been discussed at length by Ferreira, et al (2000) and it is perhaps useful to add only that the differences in measured poverty between PNAD income and PPV consumption are generally statistically significant. It is important to note that even though the PPV is designed to be representative at the level of these ten regions, the standard errors on the poverty estimates at this level are generally higher than 10 percent of the point estimate—indicating that confidence bounds around these point estimates are quite wide.[76] Even so, measured poverty in the PNAD is so much higher than in the PPV that one can generally rule out that they are statistically indistinct.

While levels of poverty across the two surveys and welfare concepts are clearly different, qualitative conclusions between the PNAD-income poverty profile and the PPV-consumption profile, are much more similar. Both approaches find clear evidence that rural poverty in the northeast is highest of all ten regions, followed by poverty in the urban northeast and then the rural southeast. Poverty in the metropolitan areas of the southeast is clearly lowest.

These conclusions are echoed when we return to the PNAD data but base our poverty estimates on consumption imputed according to the method described above. The ranking of poverty across regions is identical to that obtained with the PNAD-income approach, but point estimates of poverty are now virtually the same as those obtained in the PPV. The method we have employed seems to work in that it provides us with estimates of poverty in the large PNAD dataset that are in close accordance with the PPV survey. An indirect implication is that the two data sources are reasonably good samples of, and are describing, the same underlying population. Without that strict comparability of the surveys we could not have expected to obtain such close agreement between the PPV and the PNAD consumption-based estimates.

Although the standard errors for the imputed-consumption based PNAD profile incorporate several error components that do not affect the PPV estimates, the precision of the PNAD consumption estimates is generally greater than that of the PPV estimates, even at this high level of aggregation. This is because the PNAD consumption estimates are calculated over the much larger PNAD dataset and sampling errors are thus commensurately smaller. Although the model errors on the PNAD consumption estimates are not negligible (as reflected in the higher total standard errors for these estimates than for the PNAD income estimates), it appears that they are not so large as to invalidate the exercise.[77]

In Table 5.2 we turn to a similar examination of the three alternatives, but consider measured inequality. The inequality measure we employ for this purpose is the General Entropy class measure, with a parameter value of $c = 0.5$

$$GE_c = \frac{1}{c(1-c)}\left\{1 - \frac{1}{N}\sum_{h \in H_p} m_h \left(\frac{y_h}{\bar{y}}\right)^c\right\} \tag{13}$$

This class of inequality measures has the attractive feature of being sub-group decomposable, and the choice of c allows the analyst to weight changes in inequality differently depending on which segments of the income distribution are affected (see Bourguignon 1979, Cowell 1980, and Shorrocks 1980). We employ here a value for c of 0.5 which corresponds to a fairly high weighting to changes in inequality amongst the lower tail of the distribution.[78]

---

76. For this reason one would be very reluctant to disaggregate the PPV down below this level.

77. Note efforts are ongoing to reduce these model errors further by returning to the first-stage specification of the consumption models in the PPV. The estimates, and errors, reported here should thus be viewed as preliminary.

78. In future work we will be replicating the analysis here for other values of c, as well as other measures of inequality.

TABLE 5.2: INEQUALITY MEASURES BY REGION FOR DIFFERENT DATA SETS: GENERAL ENTROPY CLASS c = 0.5

Region	PNAD Income	PPV Consumption	PNAD Imputed Consumption	
	GE 0.5	GE 0.5	G.E. 0.5	Model S.E.
RM Fortaleza	0.646	0.397	0.324	0.020
RM Recife	0.622	0.419	0.346	0.026
RM Salvador	0.724	0.364	0.397	0.094
Urban NE	0.619	0.373	0.504	0.031
Rural NE	0.476	0.303	0.244	0.015
RM B. Horizonte	0.588	0.339	0.333	0.027
RM Rio de Janeiro	0.578	0.380	0.328	0.025
RM São Paulo	0.496	0.378	0.316	0.044
Urban SE	0.479	0.277	0.295	0.011
Rural SE	0.490	0.240	0.443	0.061

Note: PNAD per capita income, PPV per capita consumption and PNAD imputed per capita consumption have been adjusted for spatial price variation (see Ferreira, Lanjouw and Neri, 2000).

Source: PNAD 1996 and 1997, and PPV 1996.

The first conclusion is that, as with poverty measurement, measured inequality is much higher with the PNAD income concept than based on consumption. Consumption based estimates in both the PPV and PNAD are much lower than those in the first column. We are unable to state at this point whether these differences are statistically significant because we have not yet been able to calculate sampling errors on inequality measures which properly take into account the complex design of both the PNAD and PPV surveys. This means also that we are only able to report model errors on the PNAD consumption-based inequality estimates. Future work will address this concern.

There is considerable disagreement between all three data-source/welfare-concept combinations in terms of the relative ranking of inequality across regions. We do note that the range of values of the inequality estimates is more compressed than the values of poverty estimates in Table 5.1, and that it is therefore quite possible that rankings would not be statistically significant if we had information on sampling errors. We will find below that inequality differences at lower levels of disaggregation are more pronounced.

The PNAD consumption-based estimates are generally of the same order of magnitude as those estimated in the PPV, and are similarly lower than the PNAD income-based estimates. The only outlier in this regard is inequality in the rural southeast which is estimated at 0.443 with the PNAD consumption criterion and 0.240 with the PPV. The model error on the PNAD consumption-based estimate is very high however, 0.06, suggesting that perhaps the large difference in estimates is not statistically significant. Certainly, the large model error on the estimate with the PNAD consumption criterion suggests that it may be worth returning to the imputation exercise to see whether a better first stage model can be estimated.[79]

---

79. Indeed, the large model error for the RSE estimate is attributable to the parameter estimates on the heterskedasticity model and it may be possible to obtain a specification of this model which is more successful.

The broad conclusion on which all three alternatives agree is that inequality in the rural northeast tends to be particularly low compared to urban areas as a whole. A similar uniform finding is that metropolitan areas in the southeast tend to be more unequal than other urban areas in the southeast.

Poverty and Inequality at Lower Levels of Disaggregation

The discussion in the preceding section indicated that our methodology appears to allow us to impute consumption into the PNAD survey and obtain estimates of poverty and inequality that are not out of line with what we would expect (based on analysis at the representative region in the PPV). The next step is to produce PNAD consumption-based estimates at levels of disaggregation that are below what we would be able to produce with the PPV. This step represents the actual goal of the whole exercise: to employ a concept of welfare we are more comfortable with in a dataset which offers much more scope for disaggregation than the PPV.

In Table 5.3 we produce estimates of poverty at the level of the Union Federação, breaking these states up, in turn, into metropolitan, other urban, and rural areas. Once again, in order to compare broad qualitative conclusions, we produce both PNAD income estimates as well as estimates in the PNAD based on our imputed consumption measure. A first point to note is that there is considerable heterogeneity of estimated poverty rates across states, in total as well as within urban and rural areas. The two approaches both clearly identify the Maranhão and Piauí as the two poorest states in total. The high poverty in these two states is attributable to both high rates in rural areas as well as in urban areas. Our two approaches to measuring poverty also agree that Céara, Alagoas and Bahia are among the next poorest group of four states; although the precise ranking within this group is not the same for the two approaches.

Considering rural areas only, the two approaches reach some common conclusions (on the high poverty in Ceara and Piauí) but they also indicate some clear differences (rural Paraiba is least poor according to the PNAD consumption criterion, but is the third poorest state according to the PNAD income criterion). Considering non-metropolitan urban areas only, Maranhao stands out as most poor according to both criteria.

Metropolitan areas are clearly less poor than both other urban and rural areas in the northeast, but this is less markedly the case in the Southeast, according to both the income and consumption criteria. In the southeast other urban areas are particularly low in the UF of Sao Paulo. This finding is also common to both criteria.

It is important to note that, at this level of disaggregation, the sampling error has become sufficiently large that standard errors on the PNAD income-based measures are generally only slightly smaller than the PNAD consumption-based measures. The model error affecting the consumption based measures does not vary systematically with level of disaggregation, but sampling errors clearly rise. Eventually, at even lower levels of disaggregation, these would come to dominate in the overall standard errors of the consumption-based estimates as well, and the two approaches would become similarly (im)precise.[80]

It is useful to ask, given the size on the standard errors observed at this level of disaggregation, whether one is clearly doing better in using the PNAD consumption-based estimates than one would have been able to with the PPV. If one restricted oneself to working only with the PPV data, then one's best estimate of poverty or inequality at the UF level would be the region level PPV estimate within which the UF is located. The question thus arises whether the point estimates in our PNAD consumption-based approach are sufficiently precise at the UF level to infer that the UF's do not all have the same regional average poverty rate. Figures 5.1–5.4 indicate (in turn for the rural northeast, other urban northeast, rural southeast and other urban

---

80. Of course, as mentioned earlier, at very much lower levels of disaggregation idiosyncratic errors would also kick in, and the consumption based standard errors would explode.

TABLE 5.3: POVERTY ESTIMATES BY UF IN THE NORTHEAST: HEADCOUNT

State/Sector	PNAD Income		PNAD Imputed Consumption	
	FGT0	S.E.	FGT0	S.E.
Maranhão (21)				
Urban	0.583	0.039	0.481	0.047
Rural	0.684	0.036	0.534	0.037
Total	0.639	0.027	0.510	0.042
Paiuí (22)				
Urban	0.496	0.040	0.383	0.043
Rural	0.781	0.026	0.550	0.026
Total	0.611	0.030	0.502	0.037
Ceará (23)				
Metropolitan region	0.350	0.015	0.176	0.029
Other urban	0.551	0.033	0.434	0.041
Rural	0.777	0.014	0.612	0.015
Total	0.551	0.016	0.393	0.030
Rio Grande do Norte (24)				
Urban	0.359	0.032	0.301	0.041
Rural	0.636	0.048	0.504	0.048
Total	0.456	0.029	0.367	0.043
Paraíba (25)				
Urban	0.377	0.027	0.298	0.031
Rural	0.745	0.024	0.422	0.025
Total	0.504	0.026	0.337	0.029
Pernambuco (26)				
Metropolitan region	0.344	0.013	0.136	0.020
Other urban	0.501	0.024	0.399	0.035
Rural	0.717	0.018	0.518	0.020
Total	0.488	0.013	0.314	0.027
Alagoas (27)				
Urban	0.450	0.035	0.331	0.046
Rural	0.701	0.035	0.515	0.037
Total	0.539	0.029	0.394	0.043
Sergipe (28)				
Urban	0.406	0.036	0.356	0.039
Rural	0.687	0.033	0.532	0.033
Total	0.484	0.031	0.406	0.037
Bahia (29)				
Metropolitan region	0.359	0.015	0.212	0.036
Other urban	0.513	0.021	0.436	0.026
Rural	0.679	0.014	0.476	0.015
Total	0.539	0.012	0.402	0.025
Northeast				
Urban	0.446	0.007	0.329	0.035
Rural	0.709	0.008	0.516	0.027
Total	0.540	0.004	0.393	0.032

(Continued)

TABLE 5.3: POVERTY ESTIMATES BY UF IN THE NORTHEAST: HEADCOUNT (CONTINUED)

State/Sector	PNAD Income		PNAD Imputed Consumption	
	FGT0	S.E.	FGT0	S.E.
Minas Gerais (31)				
Metropolitan region	0.151	0.009	0.090	0.021
Other urban	0.190	0.011	0.081	0.012
Rural	0.495	0.019	0.394	0.021
Total	0.245	0.008	0.146	0.016
Espirito Santo (32)				
Urban	0.184	0.018	0.067	0.019
Rural	0.415	0.028	0.257	0.030
Total	0.243	0.018	0.112	0.022
Rio de Janeiro (33)				
Metropolitan region	0.111	0.005	0.039	0.028
Other urban	0.128	0.010	0.052	0.011
Rural	0.374	0.034	0.283	0.035
Total	0.127	0.005	0.051	0.026
Sao Paulo (35)				
Metropolitan region	0.069	0.004	0.031	0.009
Other urban	0.063	0.005	0.035	0.006
Rural	0.193	0.024	0.076	0.028
Total	0.074	0.004	0.035	0.010
Southeast				
Urban	0.105	0.015	0.046	0.015
Rural	0.383	0.003	0.271	0.026
Total	0.134	0.004	0.068	0.017

Source: PNAD 1996 and 1997.
1. PNAD per capita income, PPV per capita consumption and PNAD imputed per capita consumption have been adjusted for spatial price variation (see Ferreira, Lanjouw and Neri, 2000).
2. Sampling errors incorporate adjustments for complex survey design (see text and also Howes and Lanjouw, 1998).
3. Poverty Line of R$65.07 in 1996 São Paulo reais (see Ferreira, Lanjouw, and Neri, 2000).

southeast) that the point estimates from our PNAD consumption-based approach are often significantly different from the PPV-estimate for the region as a whole. Two-fifths to one half of UF-level poverty rates are significantly above or below the PPV estimate for their respective region as a whole. This indicates that the approach proposed here does offer a perspective on the spatial distribution of poverty that would not be achievable with only the PPV.[81]

Table 5.4 reports UF-level point estimates of inequality from the PNAD based on the income and imputed consumption criteria. Within the Northeast, both approaches find that inequality is generally lower in rural areas than in metropolitan or other urban areas. This pattern is not found, with either approach, in the Southeast. A difference between the two approaches is

81. Note that although only 40-50 percent of UF's are significantly different from the PPV regional—estimate, depending on representative region, this is an understatement of the number of pairwise comparisons across UFs that are significant.

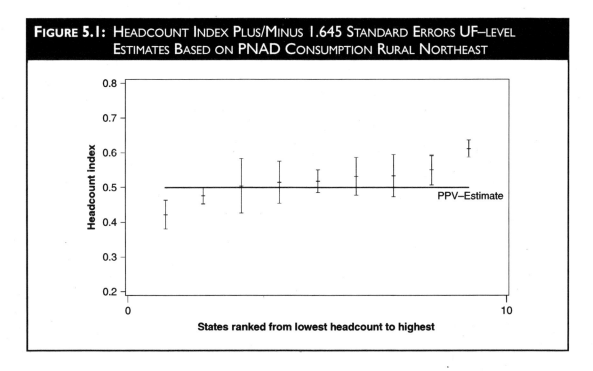

FIGURE 5.1: HEADCOUNT INDEX PLUS/MINUS 1.645 STANDARD ERRORS UF–LEVEL ESTIMATES BASED ON PNAD CONSUMPTION RURAL NORTHEAST

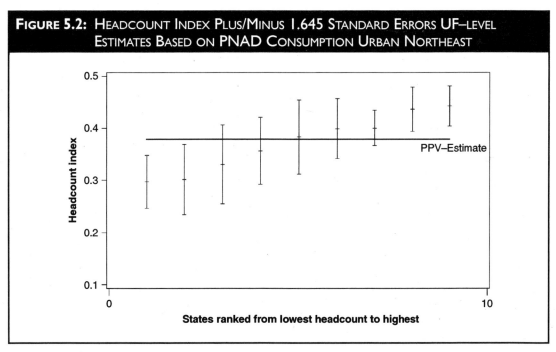

FIGURE 5.2: HEADCOUNT INDEX PLUS/MINUS 1.645 STANDARD ERRORS UF–LEVEL ESTIMATES BASED ON PNAD CONSUMPTION URBAN NORTHEAST

that according to the PNAD consumption-based inequality estimates, inequality in metropolitan areas of the northeast is clearly lower than in other urban areas. The reverse is found in the PNAD income-based estimates. In the southeast both approaches find higher inequality in metropolitan areas. Once again, although levels of measured inequality are markedly different, broad qualitative conclusions across the two approaches tend to be broadly similar, with only a few subtle differences.

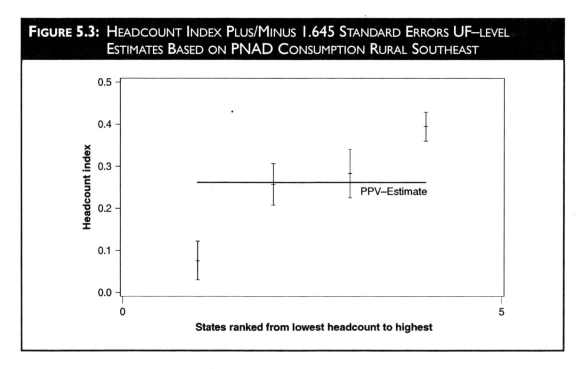

FIGURE 5.3: HEADCOUNT INDEX PLUS/MINUS 1.645 STANDARD ERRORS UF–LEVEL ESTIMATES BASED ON PNAD CONSUMPTION RURAL SOUTHEAST

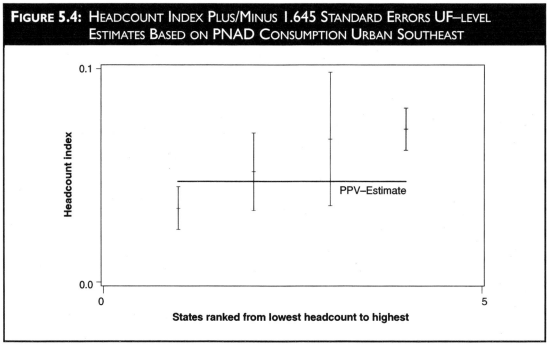

FIGURE 5.4: HEADCOUNT INDEX PLUS/MINUS 1.645 STANDARD ERRORS UF–LEVEL ESTIMATES BASED ON PNAD CONSUMPTION URBAN SOUTHEAST

We briefly report, in Table 5.5, a further attempt at disaggregation. Here we confine ourselves only to poverty rates in the northeast, based on the consumption measure of welfare imputed into the PNAD. In this table we break up urban and rural areas further. In urban areas we draw a distinction between actually urbanized settlements, and those which have been delineated as urban but which may are still rather sparsely populated (a proxy for peri-urban areas). In rural areas we draw a distinction between those areas designated as rural but which are in fact somewhat built up,

TABLE 5.4: INEQUALITY ESTIMATES BY UF IN THE NORTHEAST: GENERAL ENTROPY 0.5

State/Sector	PNAD Income GE 0.5	PNAD Imputed Consumption GE 0.5
Maranhão (21)		
Urban	0.644	0.453
Rural	0.706	0.401
Total	0.681	0.426
Paiuí (22)		
Urban	0.573	0.553
Rural	0.562	0.193
Total	0.631	0.502
Ceará (23)		
Metropolitan region	0.646	0.324
Other urban	0.585	0.471
Rural	0.362	0.185
Total	0.699	0.410
Rio Grande do Norte (24)		
Urban	0.624	0.526
Rural	0.403	0.203
Total	0.634	0.519
Paraíba (25)		
Urban	0.626	0.494
Rural	0.442	0.176
Total	0.680	0.470
Pernambuco (26)		
Metropolitan region	0.623	0.346
Other urban	0.520	0.406
Rural	0.342	0.196
Total	0.616	0.406
Alagoas (27)		
Urban	0.681	0.545
Rural	0.439	0.293
Total	0.682	0.535
Sergipe (28)		
Urban	0.635	0.508
Rural	0.313	0.203
Total	0.645	0.488
Bahia (29)		
Metropolitan region	0.725	0.397
Other urban	0.582	0.467
Rural	0.355	0.185
Total	0.658	0.423
Rural Northeast		
Urban	0.650	0.467
Rural	0.476	0.241
Total	0.665	0.449

(Continued)

TABLE 5.4: INEQUALITY ESTIMATES BY UF IN THE NORTHEAST: GENERAL ENTROPY 0.5 (CONTINUED)

State/Sector	PNAD Income GE 0.5	PNAD Imputed Consumption GE 0.5
Minas Gerais (31)		
Metropolitan region	0.588	0.331
Other urban	0.511	0.288
Rural	0.512	0.270
Total	0.580	0.340
Espirito Santo (32)		
Urban	0.531	0.335
Rural	0.498	0.257
Total	0.565	0.356
Rio de Janeiro (33)		
Metropolitan region	0.578	0.328
Other urban	0.416	0.276
Rural	0.504	0.293
Total	0.566	0.327
Sao Paulo (35)		
Metropolitan region	0.496	0.316
Other urban	0.435	0.285
Rural	0.380	0.380
Total	0.475	0.309
Rural Southeast		
Urban	0.535	0.315
Rural	0.490	0.444
Total	0.538	0.334

Source: PNAD 1996 and 1997.
   1. PNAD per capita income, PPV per capita consumption and PNAD imputed per capita consumption have been adjusted for spatial price variation (see Ferreira, Lanjouw and Neri, 2000).

with certain minimal facilities and infrastructure, and those areas which are rather more remote and dispersed.[82]

Rural poverty is unambiguously highest in dispersed, remote areas. This is also where the bulk of the rural population resides. In those states which have a sizable rural population residing in built-up areas, poverty rates are generally markedly lower in those areas than in the dispersed regions. In states where the built-up rural sector is small, poverty rates are not particularly low. There is considerable variation across states in the distribution of poverty across these locations, with the unambiguous results that metropolitan areas are always least poor, followed by urbanized urban areas. The definition of peri-urban areas we have used does not appear to work terribly well, as it generally represents only a very small fraction of the urban population.

---

82. This exercise is essentially intended as a cross-check on results reported in Ferreira and Lanjouw (2001) which implemented a very basic version of the methodology employed here.

TABLE 5.5: INCIDENCE OF POVERTY IN NORTHEAST BRAZIL: BY STATE AND LOCATION TYPE

Union Federacão	Location Type	PNAD Imputed Consumption	
		Headcount	Total Population
Ceará			
	Metropolitan area	0.1757	5,200,874
	Urban area 'urbanizadas'	0.4314	3,822,943
	Other urban	0.6054	58,101
	Rural	0.6286	4,277,386
	Other rural (extensao urbana + povoado + nucleo)	0.3752	304,375
	Total	**0.3952**	**13,663,679**
Pernambuco			
	Metropolitan area	0.1363	6,143,549
	Urban area 'urbanizadas'	0.3968	5,370,770
	Other urban	0.4569	241,801
	Rural	0.5169	3,050,896
	Other rural (extensao urbana + povoado + nucleo)	0.5350	155,883
	Total	**0.3167**	**14,962,899**
Bahia			
	Metropolitan area	0.2120	5,488,158
	Urban area 'urbanizadas'	0.4363	10,506,684
	Other urban		
	Rural	0.4981	8,032,862
	Other rural (extensao urbana + povoado + nucleo)	0.3521	1,412,093
	Total	**0.4027**	**25,439,797**
Maranhão			
	Urban area 'urbanizadas'	0.4811	4,664,666
	Other urban		
	Rural	0.6426	3,427,483
	Other rural (extensao urbana + povoado + nucleo)	0.3826	2,468,407
	Total	**0.5105**	**10,560,556**
Piauí			
	Urban area 'urbanizadas'	0.3829	3,144,276
	Other urban		
	Rural	0.5744	1,838,160
	Other rural (extensao urbana + povoado + nucleo)	0.4464	434,462
	Total	**0.4529**	**5,416,898**
Rio Grande do Norte			
	Urban area 'urbanizadas'	0.3013	3,344,104
	Other urban		
	Rural	0.5552	1,205,068
	Other rural (extensao urbana + povoado + nucleo)	0.4092	649,996
	Total	**0.3736**	**5,199,168**
Paraíba			
	Urban area 'urbanizadas'	0.2975	4,356,333
	Other urban		
	Rural	0.4471	2,068,372
	Other rural (extensao urbana + povoado + nucleo)	0.2099	248,292
	Total	**0.3406**	**6,672,997**

(Continued)

TABLE 5.5: INCIDENCE OF POVERTY IN NORTHEAST BRAZIL: BY STATE AND LOCATION TYPE (CONTINUED)

Union Federacão	Location Type	PNAD Imputed Consumption	
		Headcount	Total Population
Sergipe			
	Urban area 'urbanizadas'	0.3494	2,268,819
	Other urban	0.5542	80,481
	Rural	0.5370	697,821
	Other rural (extensao urbana + povoado + nucleo)	0.5172	230,398
	Total	**0.4062**	**3,277,519**
Alagoas			
	Urban area 'urbanizadas'	0.3264	3,359,234
	Other urban	0.5625	61,935
	Rural	0.5469	1,374,245
	Other rural (extensao urbana + povoado + nucleo)	0.4368	559,560
	Total	**0.3972**	**5,354,974**

Source: PNAD 1996 and 1997.
1. PNAD imputed per capita consumption has been adjusted for spatial price variation (see Ferreira, Lanjouw and Neri, 2000).
2. Poverty Line of R$65.07 in 1996 São Paulo reais (see Ferreira, Lanjouw, and Neri, 2000).

Inequality Decompositions

A final exercise we carry out in this study is a decomposition of inequality across different population subgroups, based on the PNAD data and our two different welfare concepts. As mentioned earlier, the General Entropy class of inequality can be readily decomposed into a within-group and between group component. With our parameter $c = 0.5$ our decomposition takes the following form:

$$W_{0.5} = 4\left\{1 - \sum_{j=1}^{J} f_j \left(\frac{y_j}{\bar{y}}\right)^{0.5}\right\} + \sum_{j=1}^{J} w_j f_j \left(\frac{\bar{y}_j}{\bar{y}}\right)^{0.5}, \tag{14}$$

where N individuals are placed in one of J groups subscripted by j, and the proportion of the population in the jth group, denoted f_j, has weighted mean per-capita expenditure (or income) $\bar{y}_j$ and inequality w_j. The first term in this expression is the inequality between groups and the second is within groups. One can think of the share of the between group inequality to total inequality as the amount of inequality that is due simply to differences in average expenditures between the groups. That portion of inequality that would remain if all differences across individuals within each group were to be eliminated.[83]

---

83. One minus this proportion can then be attributed to the share of inequality that is due to heterogeneity within the groups.

TABLE 5.6: DECOMPOSING INEQUALITY: PNAD INCOME VERSUS PNAD CONSUMPTION: GENERAL ENTROPY CLASS (0.5)

	PNAD Income	PNAD Consumption
1. National level		
Total inequality	0.6574	0.4254
% Attributable to BETWEEN Group component		
Rural vs Urban	11.8	10.6
Northeast vs Southeast	14.7	13.9
Rural NE vs Urban NE vs Rural SE vs Urban SE	20.8	19.4
Metropolitan regions vs Rest	6.4	6.1
Metropolitan regions vs Other Urban vs Rural	14.0	12.7
2. Rural Areas		
Total Inequality	0.5377	0.3781
% Attributable to BETWEEN Group Component		
Northeast vs Southeast	11.8	16.7
By State	16.3	31.4
3. Urban Areas		
Total Inequality	0.5991	0.3859
% Attributable to BETWEEN Group Component		
Northeast vs Southeast	10.0	8.7
By State	12.0	10.7

Table 5.6 reports the results from our decomposition exercise. We first take the country as a whole and ask how much of overall inequality is attributable to the between-group component in a series of settings. We observe that if one breaks Brazil down into an urban and rural sector, that only 10–12 percent of overall inequality can be attributed to the difference in average consumption or income between these two sectors. Most of inequality would remain if this difference in averages would be removed. The conclusion holds irrespective of the welfare concept that is being used. If the country were broken down into Northeast and Southeast only, then the between component rises slightly to 14–15 percent (once again remarkably similar across the two welfare concepts). When the country is divided into four—urban northeast, rural northeast, urban southeast and rural southeast—the between-group component continues to rise slowly. Again, the two approaches give essentially the same result. Turning to the question of whether inequality is largely attributable to differences between metropolitan areas and the rest of the country, we find that only 6 percent of inequality is due to the difference in average welfare across these two sectors. Adding a further subgroup, other urban, raises the between group component to 13–14 percent. At the national level, it is evident that much of overall inequality remains within the groups that have been considered here. An important point to note, given the purpose of this paper, is that the decomposition results at the national level are qualitatively the same whether we use the PNAD income measure or our imputed consumption measure.

When we look at rural areas only, we see that the two approaches to appear to give rather different results. The PNAD income approach suggests that rural inequality would fall by around 12 percent if the difference in average income between the northeast and southeast were removed. The consumption based approach in the PNAD suggests that the reduction in inequality would be higher, around 17 percent. If differences in average income across all states were removed, the PNAD income approach suggests that inequality would fall by approximately 16 percent. The consumption approach suggests that the fall in inequality would be about twice as high:

31 percent. The two approaches depart here in a quite significant way, with the consumption based approach suggesting that a much larger source of overall rural inequality is due to differences across states in average rural incomes. It seems possible that the consumption approach is capturing better the enormous distances and varied geography of the country, and the different agroclimatic conditions that is associated with this. And the PNAD income measure may be failing to capture state variation because it is more focused on formal sector earnings which might tend to be relatively homogeneous across states. It would seem worth exploring to what extent this finding is robust to alternative choices of the parameter c, and possibly other measures of inequality.

The final decompositions, within urban areas only, find again that the between group component is quite modest irrespective of the approach that is being used.

Conclusions

This paper had two objectives. The first objective has been to demonstrate a methodology to impute a measure of consumption, as defined in the PPV household survey, into the much large PNAD household survey. The purpose of this exercise has been to estimate measures of welfare, such as poverty and inequality, defined in terms of consumption, at levels of disaggregation that are permitted by PNAD dataset. Although the results are still to be finalized we have shown that the methodology works quite well. We are able to validate the exercise at the representative region level in the PPV, and find that at that level, point estimates are very similar across the PPV and the PNAD. We have also shown that standard errors on the consumption-based point estimates in the PNAD are quite reasonable—certainly compared to the standard of typical household surveys.

Our second objective has been to shed some light on the question of whether the analysis of poverty and inequality based on the PNAD income indicator yields different conclusions than an analysis based on consumption. We referred to the concern in the literature on PNAD-based distributional analysis that the income measure in the PNAD might suffer from serious biases.

We have found that poverty and inequality, estimated on the basis of consumption in the PNAD, tend to be much lower than estimates based on the income concept. This is not necessarily an indictment of income based analysis, however, as the two concepts of welfare are different and should not be expected to yield the same quantitative estimates. We demonstrated however, that differences in estimates of poverty and inequality between the PNAD and the PPV are not attributable to non-comparability of these two surveys. Our PNAD consumption-based estimates are very close to those which obtain with the PPV.

We pursued the comparability of income and consumption-based results further by examining whether there are important qualitative differences in the geographic profile of welfare across the two approaches. We found that, in fact, the two reach broadly similar findings. In only a few cases do we note differences across the two approaches that may need to pursued further. First, according to the consumption criterion, there is a clear basis for viewing metropolitan areas in the northeast as less poor than other areas. This distinction is less clear-cut according to the income criterion. Second, within rural areas in the northeast, rural Paraiba is least poor state according to the PNAD consumption criterion, but is found to be the third poorest state according to the PNAD income criterion. Third, the PNAD consumption criterion finds that metropolitan areas in the northeast are markedly more equal than other urban areas in this region. The PNAD income criterion finds the reverse. Fourth, the consumption-based approach reflects much more strongly than the income-based one the contribution of differences in average incomes across states to overall rural inequality.

Looking for differences in qualitative conclusions regarding the spatial distribution of poverty and inequality, may not be the best way to examine whether the income-based PNAD measures introduce important biases into distributional analysis in Brazil. As described in section II, the PNAD income measure is thought to be inadequately capturing income levels of certain population subgroups, notably those who are engaged in informal sector self-employment activities. A more effective direction to take might thus be to compare consumption-based estimates of poverty and inequality amongst population subgroups defined in terms of occupations and education levels, rather than along geographic lines.[84] This seems an important next step.

Still within a geographic focus, there would seem to be two promising directions for further work. First, it is important to examine whether the conclusions of Ferreira et al (2000) regarding the distribution of urban poverty across city-size is robust to the application of a consumption-based indicator of welfare. It is possible to link urban households in the PNAD to the size of conurbation in which they reside. Ferreira et al observe a much higher incidence of poverty in smaller towns relative to large cities and metropolitan areas. Second, the results presented here suggest that there may be considerable variation in poverty rates within rural areas. So far we have split rural areas up quite crudely into dispersed and built-up areas. An important additional direction to take would be to divide rural areas into agro-ecological and climatic zones, as well as areas demarcated by differences in access to facilities and infrastructure.

The analysis in this paper has concentrated on the northeast and southeast of Brazil. As a result, some 25 percent of the population have not been included in the analysis. In principle it would be possible to extend the analysis carried out here, to regions such as the south and the center west of the country. But to do so would require making some important, unverifiable, assumptions. Because there are no PPV data applicable to these regions one would have to select a set of parameter estimates from the PPV data and impose the assumption that they are applicable for these regions which lie outside the PPV sampling domain. One might, for example, assume that the appropriate model to apply to the rural center west region is a first stage model based on the combined rural northeast and southeast sample of the PPV. Similarly one might impose the rural southeast parameter estimates on the rural south PNAD data. This exercise is possible but still pending.

In the medium run there is a potential to apply the methodology reported here to the 2001 population census for Brazil. There are initiatives underway to implement a large new consumption survey in Brazil, covering both rural and urban areas. While the mooted sample size of 50,000 is very large in absolute terms, it is clear that these data will not permit disaggregations of poverty and inequality significantly below the UF level. If this new survey were to serve a basis for estimating first stage consumption models with which to impute consumption into the population census, it would then be possible to measure inequality and poverty, based on a consumption measure of welfare, at the town or village (and possibly neighborhood) level across the entire country. Such initiatives are being actively implemented and/or explored in a number countries in the last few years. Some, such as Mexico, Indonesia and China have total populations that, like Brazil, are very large.

References

Bianchini, Z. M., and S. Albieri. 1998. "A Review of Major Household Sample Survey Designs Used in Brazil." Proceedings of the Joint IASS/IAOS Conference, Statistics for Economic and Social Development, September.

Bourguignon, F. 1979. "Decomposable Income Inequality Measures." *Econometrica* 47:901:920.

Camargo, J. M., and F.H.G. Ferreira. 1999. "A Poverty Reduction Strategy of the Government of Brazil: A Rapid Appraisal." Dept. of Economics, Catholic University of Rio de Janeiro. Processed.

Cowell, F. 1980. "On the Structure of Additive Inequality Measures." *Review of Economic Studies* 47:521–531.

Deaton, A. 1997. *The Analysis of Household Surveys: A Microeconometric Approach to Development Policy.* World Bank and Johns Hopkins University Press.

---

84. Note the spatial dimension was a natural one to pursue in this paper given our interest to also validate results against the representative region level estimates in the PPV.

Elbers, C., J.O. Lanjouw, and P. Lanjouw. 2001. "Welfare in Villages and Towns: Micro-Level Estimation of Poverty and Inequality." Development Economics Research Group, the World Bank. Processed.

Ferrerira, F.H.G., P. Lanjouw, and M. Neri. 2000. "A New Poverty Profile For Brazil Using PPV, PNAD and Census Data." Departamento de Economia PUC-Rio, TD #418, March.

Ferreira, F.H.G., and P. Lanjouw. 2001. "Rural Nonfarm Activities and Poverty in the Brazilian Northeast." *World Development* 29(3):509–528.

Ferreira, F.H.G., and J. Litchfield. 1996. "Growing Apart: Inequality and Poverty Trends in Brazil in the 1980s." LSE—STICERD—DARP Discussion Paper No. 23, London. August.

Ferreira, F.H.G., and R. Paes de Barros. 1999. "The Slippery Slope: Explaining Increases in Extreme Poverty in Urban Brazil, 1976–1996." *Brazilian Review of Econometrics* 19(2).

Howes, Stephen, and J.O. Lanjouw. 1998. "Does Sample Design Matter for Poverty Comparisons?" *Review of Income and Wealth* 44(1):99–109.

Ravallion, M. 1994. *Poverty Comparison.* Chur: Harwood Press.

Shorrocks, A. 1980. "The Class of Additive Decomposable Inequality Measures." *Econometrica* 48:613–625.

Soares de Freitas, M., R. Nogueira Duarte, D. Carneiro Pessoa, S. Albieri, and P. do Naschimento Silva. 1997. "Comparando Distribuições Etárias em Pesquisas por Amostragem: PNAD 1995 e PPV 96/97." Fundação Instituto Brasileiro de Geografia e Estatística, DPE, DEMET. Processed.

World Bank. 2001a. "Attacking Brazil's Poverty: A Poverty Report with a Focus on Urban Poverty Reduction Policies." Washington D.C.

———. 2001b. "Brazil: Rural Poverty Report." Washington D.C.

CHAPTER 6

BEYOND OAXACA-BLINDER: ACCOUNTING FOR DIFFERENCES IN HOUSEHOLD INCOME DISTRIBUTIONS ACROSS COUNTRIES

By François Bourguignon, Francisco H. G. Ferreira, and Phillippe G. Leite[85]

Abstract

This paper develops a micro-econometric method to account for differences across distributions of household income. Going beyond the determination of earnings in labor markets, we also estimate statistical models for occupational choice and for the conditional distributions of education, fertility and non-labor incomes. We import combinations of estimated parameters from these models to simulate counterfactual income distributions. This allows us to decompose differences between functions of two income distributions (such as inequality or poverty measures) into shares due to differences in the structure of labor market returns (price effects); differences in the occupational structure; and differences in the underlying distribution of assets (endowment effects). We apply the method to the differences between the Brazilian income distribution and those of the United States and Mexico, and find that most of Brazil's excess income

85. Bourguignon is with DELTA, Paris, and the World Bank. Ferreira and Leite are at the Department of Economics of the Pontifícia Universidade Católica do Rio de Janeiro. We thank David Lam, Dean Jolliffe, Klara Sabirianova and seminar participants at PUC-Rio, IBMEC-Rio, the University of Michigan, the World Bank and DELTA for helpful comments; and Nora Lustig and Cesar Bouillon at the IDB for making the Mexican data available to us, ready to use. The opinions expressed here are those of the authors and do not necessarily reflect those of the World Bank, its Executive Directors or the countries they represent.

inequality is due to underlying inequalities in the distribution of two key endowments: access to education and to sources of non-labor income, mainly pensions.

JEL Classification Codes: C15, D31, I31, J13, J22
Keywords: Inequality, Distribution, Micro-simulations

Introduction

The distribution of personal welfare varies enormously across countries. The Gini coefficient for the distribution of household per capita incomes, for instance, ranges from 0.20 in the Slovak Republic to 0.63 in Sierra Leone (World Bank, 2002) and similar (or greater) international variation can be found for any alternative measure of inequality. Given that inequality levels *within* countries are generally rather stable, one would think that there ought to be considerable interest in understanding why income distributions vary so much *across* countries. Is it because the underlying distributions of wealth differ greatly, perhaps due to historical reasons? Or is it because returns to education are higher in one country than in the other? What is the role of differences in labor market institutions? Do different fertility rates and family structures play a role? And if, as is likely, differences in income distributions reflect all of these (and possibly other) factors, in what manner and to what extent does each one contribute?

Yet, applied research on differences across income distribution has not been as abundant as one might expect.[86] Increasingly, this seems to have less to do with lack of data and more to do with inadequate methodological tools. Through initiatives like the Luxembourg Income Study, the WIDER International Income Distribution Dataset and others, the availability of high-quality household-level data is growing. Methodologically, however, those seeking an understanding of why distributions are so different—and reluctant to rely exclusively on cross-country regressions with inequality measures as dependent variables—have often resorted to comparing Theil decompositions across countries.[87] We will argue below that, while these can be informative, their ability to shed light on determinants of differences across distributions is inherently limited.

Meanwhile, substantial progress has been made in our ability to understand differences in wage (or earnings) distributions. Some of this work, such as Almeida dos Reis and Paes de Barros (1991), Juhn, Murphy and Pierce (1993), Blau and Khan (1996) and Machado and Mata (2001), draws on variants of a decomposition technique based on simulating counterfactual distributions by combining data on individual characteristics (X) from one distribution, with estimated parameters (β) from another, which is due originally to Oaxaca (1973) and Blinder (1973).[88] Another strand, which includes DiNardo, Fortin and Lemieux (1996) and Donald, Green and Paarsch (2000), is based on alternative semi-parametric approaches. DiNardo et al. (1996) use weighted kernel density estimators—instead of regression coefficients—to generate counterfactual density functions that combine population attributes (or labor market institutions) from one period, with the structure of returns from another. Donald et al. (2000) adapt hazard-function estimators from the spell-duration literature to develop density-function estimators, and use these

---

86. Theoretical models of why income distributions might differ across countries have been more abundant. Banerjee and Newman (1993) and Bénabou (2000) are two well-known examples. See Aghion et al. (1999) for a survey.

87. Theil decompositions are known more formally as decompositions of Generalized Entropy inequality measures by population subgroups. They were developed independently by Bourguignon (1979), Cowell (1980) and Shorrocks (1980).

88. Some of these studies, like Juhn, Murphy and Pierce (1993) and Machado and Mata (2001) decompose changes in the wage distribution of a single country, over time. Others, like Almeida dos Reis and Paes de Barros (for metropolitan areas within Brazil) and Blau and Khan (for ten industrialized countries) decompose differences across wage distributions for different spatial units. For a less well known but also pioneering work, see Langoni (1973).

to construct counterfactual density and distribution functions (comparing the US and Canada).[89]

These approaches have been very fruitful, but they have not yet been generalized from wage distributions to those of household incomes, largely because the latter involve some additional complexities. The distribution of wages is defined over those currently employed. Taking the characteristics of these workers as given, earnings determination can be reasonably well under-stood by estimating returns to those characteristics in the labor market, through a Mincerian earnings equation: $y_i = X_i\beta + \varepsilon_i$. Most of the aforementioned recent literature on differences in wage inequality is based on simulating counterfactual distributions on the basis of equations such as this, and many further restrict their samples to include prime-age, full-time male workers only. In addition, some authors are quite clear that they are interested in wages primarily as indicators of the price of labor, rather than as measures of welfare.

Naturally, the distribution of household incomes also depends on the returns and characteristics of its employed members, and will thus draw on earnings models too. It also depends on their participation and occupational choices and on decisions concerning the size and composition of the family. In addition, changes in some personal characteristics, such as education, affect household incomes through more than one channel. Suppose we ask what the effect of "importing" the U.S. distribution of education to Mexico is on the Mexican distributions of earnings and incomes. Whereas for earnings it might very well suffice to replace the relevant vector of X with U.S. values, the distribution of household incomes will also be affected through changes in participation and fertility behavior. This greater complexity of the determinants of household income distributions seems to have prevented counterfactual simulation techniques from being applied to them, thus depriving those interested in understanding cross-country differences in the distribution of welfare from the powerful insights they can deliver.

Nevertheless, a more general version of the Oaxaca-Blinder idea—of simulating counterfactual distributions on the basis of combining models estimated for different real distributions—can fruitfully be applied to household incomes. What is required is an expansion of the set of models to be estimated, to include labor market participation, fertility behavior and educational choices. In this paper, we first propose a general statement of statistical decompositions applied to household income distributions; and then suggest a specific model of household income determination that enables us to implement the decomposition empirically. In particular, we investigate the comparative roles of three factors: the distribution of population characteristics (or endowments); the structure of returns to these endowments, and the occupational structure of the population. We apply the method to an understanding of the differences between the income distributions in Brazil, Mexico, and the United States.[90]

The paper is organized as follows. The next section summarizes what can be learned from conventional comparisons of income distributions across these three countries, and presents an empirical motivation. The second section contains a general statement of statistical decomposition analysis, which encompasses all variants currently in use as special cases. The third section proposes a specific model of household income determination and describes the estimation and

---

89. The distinction between "parametric" and "semi-parametric" methods is not terribly sharp. DiNardo et al. (1996) use a probit model to estimate one of their conditional reweighing functions. Donald et al. (2000) rely entirely on maximum likelihood estimates of parameters in a proportional-hazards model, and what is non-parametric about their method is a fine double-partitioning of the income space, allowing for considerable flexibility in both the estimation of the baseline hazard function, and in the manner in which it is shifted by the proportional-hazards estimates. Conversely, in the current paper, which follows a predominantly parametric route, some non-parametric reweighing of joint distribution functions is also used (see below). These techniques are often more complementary than substitutable.

90. This approach is a cross-country extension of a methodology previously developed to analyze the dynamics of the distribution of income within a single country. See Bourguignon, Ferreira and Lustig (1998).

simulation procedures needed for the decomposition. The results obtained in the case of the Brazil-U.S. comparison are discussed in some detail in the fourth section. The fifth section discusses the Brazil-Mexico comparison and the sixth section concludes.

Income Distribution in Brazil, Mexico, and the United States

This section compares the distributions of household income in the three most populous countries in the Western Hemisphere.[91] The comparisons are based on an analysis of the original household-level data sets: the Pesquisa Nacional por Amostra de Domicílios (PNAD) 1999 is used for Brazil; the Encuesta Nacional de Ingresos y Gastos de Hogares (ENIGH) 1994 for Mexico; and the Annual Demographic Survey in the March Supplement to the Current Population Survey (CPS) 2000, for the United States. As always with the March Supplement of the CPS, total personal income data refers to the preceding calendar year:1999. Sample sizes for each data set (actually used) are as follows: the CPS 2000 contained 50,982 households (133,649 individuals); the ENIGH 1994 contained 6,614 households (29,149 individuals); and the PNAD 1999 contained 80,972 households (294,244 individuals).

We use income, rather than consumption, data because the decompositions described in the remainder of the paper rely in part on the determination of earnings.[92] In Brazil and Mexico, the income variable used was monthly total household income per capita, available in the surveys as a constructed variable from the disaggregated income questionnaire. In the US, the variable used was the sum (across individuals in the household) of annual total personal income and other incomes, excluding disability benefits, educational assistance and child support, divided by 12.[93] All three income definitions are before tax, but include transfers. While total annual incomes are not top-coded in the CPS, some of their components might be. The US Census Bureau warns that weekly earnings, in particular, are "subject to top-coding at US$1,923," so as to censor the distribution of annual earnings from the main job at US$100,000. Inspection of our sample revealed, however, that 2.1 percent (2.5 percent) of observations had reported weekly (annual) earnings above those value. The maximum reported weekly value was US$2,884. We therefore did not correct for top-coding in the United States. Incomes are not top-coded in Brazil or Mexico either.

As usual, there are reasons to suspect that incomes may be measured with some error. In the case of Brazil, the problem is particularly severe in rural areas, to the extent that the usefulness of any estimate based on rural income data is thrown into doubt.[94] For this reason, we prefer to confine our attention to urban areas only, in Brazil and Mexico.[95] Care is taken to ensure that the distributions used are as comparable as possible, and this requires that we work with data unadjusted for misreporting, imputed rents, or for regional price level differences within countries.[96]

---

91. Our emphasis here is purely comparative. We make no attempt to present a detailed analysis of inequality or poverty in each of these countries. There is a large literature on these topics for each of our three countries, but see Henriques (2000) for a recent compilation of work on Brazil, and Székely (1998) on Mexico. For earlier studies comparing the Brazilian and US *earnings* distributions, see Lam and Levison (1992) and Sacconato and Menezes-Filho (2001).

92. And also because consumption data for Brazil is either very old (ENDEF, 1975) or incomplete in geographical coverage (POF, 1996; PPV, 1996).

93. These income sources were excluded from the analysis because non-retirement public transfers are proportionately much more important in the US than in Brazil or Mexico, and their allocation follows rules which are not modelled in our approach. When they were included, the residual term of the decomposition was slightly larger, but all of our conclusions remained qualitatively valid.

94. For evidence on the weaknesses of income data for rural Brazil, see Ferreira, Lanjouw and Neri (2000) and Elbers, Lanjouw, Lanjouw and Leite (2001).

95. For the United States, because the CPS does not disaggregate non-metropolitan areas into urban and rural, and the former dominate, we included both metropolitan and non-metropolitan areas.

96. All three datasets are well-known in their respective countries. For more detailed information about the CPS, go to www.census.gov. Information on the PNAD is available from www.ibge.gov.br. Information on the ENIGH is available from http://www.inegi.gob.mx/.

TABLE 6.1: DESCRIPTIVE STATISTICS

Country	Population (millions, 1999)	GDP Per Capita (monthly, USD)	Mean Equivalised Income (monthly, USD)	Gini Coefficient	Theil-T	Theil-L
		q = 1.0 (household income per capita)				
Brazil	168	526.42	290.34	0.587	0.693	0.646
Mexico	97	643.25	280.90	0.536	0.580	0.511
USA	273	2550.00	1691.64	0.445	0.349	0.391
			q = 0.5			
Brazil	168	526.42	551.08	0.560	0.613	0.572
Mexico	97	643.25	587.91	0.493	0.478	0.423
USA	273	2550.00	2791.78	0.415	0.298	0.344

Notes: Population and GDP per capita figures are from World Bank (2001). The other figures are from calculations by the authors from the household surveys. GDP per capita and mean equivalised income (MEY) are monthly and measured in 1999 US dollars at PPP exchange rates. Mexican survey data is for 1994; Brazilian survey data is for 1999, and US survey data is for 2000. Values of q are for the economy of scale parameter in the Buhmann et al. (1988) equivalence scale —q = 1 corresponds to income per capita.

Table 6.1 below reports some key summary statistics of the income distributions for our three countries. In addition to population, GDP per capita and mean income from the household survey, three inequality measures are computed: the Gini Coefficient, the Theil T and L indices—in what follows, the last two are sometimes labeled $E(1)$ and $E(0)$, respectively, as members of the class of generalized entropy inequality measures. Each of these statistics is presented for the distribution of household income per capita, as well as for a distribution of equivalised incomes, where the Buhmann et al. (q = 0.5) equivalence scale is used. [97] All households are weighted by the number of individuals they comprise.

Similarities between Brazil (in 1999) and Mexico (in 1994) are immediately apparent. Across those different years, the two countries had broadly similar levels of GDP per capita. Mexico's was 22 percent higher than Brazil's , which pales in comparison to the difference between the two countries and the United States: 384 percent higher than Brazil's. Brazil's inequality is ranked highest by all three measures reported, followed by Mexico and the United States. The difference between Brazil's and Mexico's Ginis, at approximately five points, is not too large, while there are a full fourteen points between Brazil and the US. It is interesting to note that the effect of allowing for (a good deal) of scale economies in household consumption differs across both countries and measures. Focusing on the Gini coefficient, the reduction in inequality in Mexico from reducing q from 1.0 to 0.5 is larger than either in the United States or Brazil.

The considerable differences in both mean incomes and inequality across these three countries must translate into different poverty levels as well. Table 6.2 below presents the three standard FGT poverty measures[98] for each country, based on the distribution of per capita household incomes. The first panel shows poverty rates for the entire countries, whereas the second panel shows them for urban areas only, which is the universe for the analysis carried out in the next sections of the paper. In both cases, we use two alternative poverty thresholds. The first block in each panel employs an absolute poverty line, originally calculated as a strict indigence line for Brazil by Ferreira, Lanjouw, and Neri (2000). Translated to 1999 values, it was set at R$74.48,

---

97. According to that method, the equivalised income of a household with income y and size N is taken to be y/N^θ. This definition coincides with income per capita when q = 1.

98. Foster, Greer and Thorbecke (1984). In what follows, we use the three common measures of that family of poverty indices : $P(0)$, the headcount, $P(1)$, the poverty gap and $P(2)$, the cumulated squared gap.

TABLE 6.2: FGT MEASURES

FGT(α) Measures for Urban and Rural Areas					FGT(α) Measures for Urban Areas				
	P(0)	P(1)	P(2)	Poverty Line[1]		P(0)	P(1)	P(2)	Poverty Line[1]
Brazil	29,18	12,10	6,74	83,69	Brazil	22,33	8,40	4,37	83,69
Mexico	23,29	8,02	3,84	83,69	Mexico	6,66	1,52	0,51	83,69
USA	1,41	0,75	0,54	83,69					
Brazil	30,02	12,22	6,82	84,27	Brazil	26,74	10,42	5,55	95,51
Mexico	17,86	5,59	2,57	70,11	Mexico	14,98	3,73	1,39	110,46
USA	25,02	10,19	5,92	687,70					

or US$83.69 at PPP exchange rates. Having the lowest mean and the highest inequality of the three countries, Brazil has the most poverty by all three measures, in urban areas and overall. The United States has, by this ungenerous developing country standards, only traces of poverty. As for Mexico, it is striking how much of its poverty is rural: poverty incidence falls from 23 percent nationally, to less than 7 percent in urban areas. While being mindful that urban-rural definitions vary across countries, it would seem that poverty has an even more predominantly rural profile in Mexico than in Brazil.

Yet, when one considers welfare across countries at such different levels of development and per capita income as these three countries, a strong argument can be made that a relative poverty concept might be more appropriate. For this reason we also present the same poverty measures, in the same distributions, calculated with respect to a line set at half the median income in each distribution, in the second block of each panel. By these more relative standards, poverty in the US reaches a full quarter of the population, which happens to be quite similar to Brazil's urban incidence. Mexico's P(0) also rises to 15 percent in urban areas.

Figure 6.1, which contains the Lorenz curves for the urban household income distributions for Brazil, Mexico and the US, is a useful complement to the indices presented so far. Brazil is Lorenz dominated by both Mexico and the United States, whereas those two countries, at least with only urban Mexico being considered, can not be Lorenz ranked. The Atkinson Theorem (1970)—which establishes the link between normalized second-order stochastic dominance and unambiguous inequality ranking—makes Lorenz Curves very useful diagrammatic tools to compare income distributions. Nevertheless, because they are two levels of integration above a density function, we can do even better in terms of picturing the distribution. Figure 6.2 below plots kernel estimates of the (mean normalized) density functions for the distribution of (the logarithm of) household per capita income in our three countries. The greater dispersion of the Brazilian distribution is noticeable with respect to the Mexican, as is the greater skewness of the Brazilian and Mexican distributions, vis-à-vis that of the United States.

Finally, Table 6.3 reports on standard decompositions of E(0), E(1) and E(2) by population subgroups,[99] computing the R_B statistic developed by Cowell and Jenkins (1995). This statistic is an indicator of the relative importance of each attribute used to partition the population, in the process of "accounting for" the inequality. The idea is that the larger the share of dispersion which is between groups defined by some attribute—rather than within those groups—the more likely it is that something about the distribution of or returns to that attribute are causally related to the observed inequality. The attributes to be used include education of the household head (or main earner for the distribution of household incomes); his or her age; his or her race or ethnic group; his or her gender; as well as the location of the household (both regional and rural/urban) and its size or type.

---

99. See Bourguignon (1979), Cowell (1980) and Shorrocks (1980).

FIGURE 6.1: URBAN LORENZ CURVE FOR BRAZIL, MEXICO AND THE U.S.

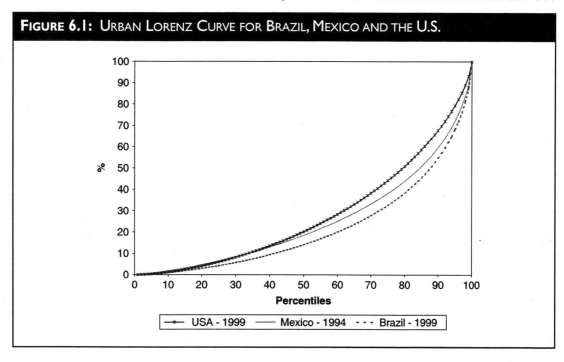

FIGURE 6.2: INCOME DISTRIBUTIONS FOR BRAZIL, MEXICOAND THE UNITED STATES

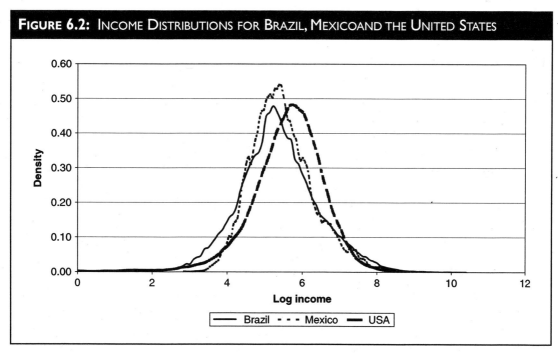

Note: Gaussian Kernel Estimates (with optimal window width) of the density functions for the distributions of the logarithms of household per capita incomes. The distribution were scaled so as to have the Brazilian mean. Brazil and Mexico are urban areas only. Incomes were converted to US dollar at PPP exchange rates.

Sources: PNAD/IBGE 1999, CPS/ADS 2000, ENIGH 1994.

The results are suggestive. In Brazil, education of the head is clearly the most important partitioning characteristic, followed by race and family type. In the United States, family type dominates, with education a surprisingly low second, and age of head third. In Mexico, education and urban/rural vie for first place, with family type third. It is clear that education accounts for more

TABLE 6.3: THEIL DECOMPOSITIONS OF INEQUALITY BY POPULATION CHARACTERISTICS

	Brasil			USA			Mexico		
	RB(0)	**RB(1)**	**RB(2)**	**RB(0)**	**RB(1)**	**RB(2)**	**RB(0)**	**RB(1)**	**RB(2)**
Region	0,092	0,076	0,031	0,003	0,004	0,003	0,113	0,103	0,050
Household type	0,126	0,121	0,060	0,192	0,210	0,155	0,194	0,180	0,092
Urban / rural	0,101	0,073	0,026	—	—	—	0,253	0,194	0,079
Gender of the head	0,000	0,000	0,000	0,002	0,002	0,002	0,000	0,000	0,000
Race of the head	0,137	0,119	0,051	0,024	0,024	0,016	—	—	—
Education level	0,266	0,316	0,213	0,129	0,133	0,093	0,247	0,255	0,150
Age group	0,051	0,047	0,021	0,082	0,091	0,066	0,042	0,037	0,017

Note: Entries reflect share of overall inequality which is between subgroups for each partition. See Cowell and Jenkins (1995).

inequality in Brazil (and Mexico) than in the United States, although this technique can not tell us whether this is due predominantly to different returns or different endowments of education—i.e. a different distribution of the population across educational levels. The greater role of the urban/rural partition in Mexico is in line with our findings regarding total and urban poverty rates there. Strikingly little of overall U.S. inequality is between different regions of the country, reinforcing the widespread perception of a well-integrated economy. This is in contrast to the two Latin American countries, where some 10 percent of the Theil-L is accounted for by the regional partition.[100] Finally, it is interesting to note that inequality between households headed by people of different races—which one would expect to be prominent in the United States—is five to six times as large in Brazil.

Yet, although this is a useful preliminary exercise, there are at least three reasons why one would wish to go further. First, none of these decompositions control for any of the others: some of the inequality between regions in Mexico is also between individuals with different races, and there is no way of telling how much. Second, the decompositions are of scalar measures, and therefore "waste" information on how the entire distributions differ (along their support). Although some information can be recovered from knowledge of the different sensitivities of each measure, this is at best a hazardous and imprecise route. Finally, even to the extent that one is prepared to treat inequality between subgroups defined by age or education, say, as being driven by those attributes—rather than by correlates—the share of total inequality attributed to that partition tells us nothing of whether it is the distribution of the characteristic (or asset), or the structure of its returns that matters. In the next section, we propose an alternative approach, which suffers from none of these shortcomings.

A General Statement of Statistical Decomposition Analysis

In order to understand the differences between two distributions of household incomes, $f^A(y)$ and $f^B(y)$, it seems natural to depart from the joint distributions $\varphi^C(y, T)$, where T is a vector of observed household characteristics, such as family size, the age, gender, race, education and occupation of each individual member of the household, etc. The superscript C (= A, B) denotes the

---

100. The regional breakdowns used in this decomposition were standard for each country. Brazil was divided up into five regions: North, Northeast, Centre-West, Southeast and South. Mexico was divided up into nine regions: "Noroeste", "Noreste", "Norte", "Centro Occidente", "Centro", "Sur", "Sureste", "Suroeste" and "Distrito Federal". The US was broken down into four regions: Northeast, Midwest, South and West. For a much more detailed analysis of the importance of regional effects in Mexican inequality, see Legovini, Bouillon and Lustig (2000).

country. Because a number (but not all) of the characteristics in T clearly depend on others (e.g. family size, via the number of children, will vary with the age and education of the parents), it will prove helpful to partition $T = [V, W]$ where, for any given household h in C, each element of V_h may be thought of as logically depending on W_h, and possibly on some other elements of V_h, but W_h is to be considered as fully exogenous to the household.

The distribution of household incomes, $f^C(y)$, is of course the marginal distribution of the joint distribution $\varphi^C(y, T) : f^C(y) = \iiint \varphi^C(y,T)dT$. It can therefore be rewritten as $f^C(y) = \iiint g^C(y|V,W)\phi^C(V, W)dVdW$, where $g^C(y \mid V,W)$ denotes the distribution of y conditional on V and W, and $\phi^C(V, W)$ is the joint distribution on all elements of T in country C. Given the distinction made above between the "semi-exogenous"[101] household characteristics V and the "truly exogenous" characteristics W, this can be further rewritten as:

$$f^C(y) = \iiint g^C(y|V,W)h_1^C(v_1|V_{-1},W)h_2^C(v_2|V_{-1,2},W)\dots h_\upsilon^C(v_\upsilon|W)\psi^C(W)dW \qquad (1)$$

In (1), the joint distribution of all elements of $T = [V,W]$ has been replaced by the product of υ conditional distributions and the joint distribution of all elements in W, $\psi^C(W)$. Each conditional distribution h_n is for an element of V, conditioning on the υ-n elements of V not yet conditioned on, and on W. The order $n = \{1,\dots\upsilon\}$ obviously does not matter for the product of the conditional distributions. (1) is an identity, invariant in that ordering. However, the order does matter for the definition of each individual conditional distribution $h_n(v_n|V_{-1,\dots,n}, W)$, and therefore for the interpretation of each decomposition defined below.[102]

Once we have written the distributions of household incomes for countries $C = A$, B as in (1), one could investigate how $f^B(y)$ differs from $f^A(y)$ by replacing some of the observed conditional distributions in the ordered set $k^A = \{g^A, h^A\}$ by the corresponding conditional distributions in the ordered set $k^B = \{g^B, \boldsymbol{h}^B\}$. Each such replacement generates a counterfactual (ordered) set of conditional distributions k^s, the dimension of which is $\upsilon + 1$, (like k^A and k^B) whose elements are drawn either from k^A or k^B. It is now possible to define a counterfactual distribution $f^s_{A \to B}(y, k^s, \psi^A)$ as the marginal distribution that arises from the integration of the product of the conditional distributions in k^s and the joint distribution function $\psi^A(W)$, with respect to all elements of W. As an example, the counterfactual distribution $f^s_{A \to B}(y, g^A, h_1{}^B, \boldsymbol{h}_{-1}{}^A, \psi^A)$ is given by: $f^s_{A \to B}(y) = \iiint g^A(y|V,W)h_1^B(v_1|V_{-1},W)h_2^A(v_2|V_{-1,2},W)\dots h_\upsilon^A(v_\upsilon|W)\psi^A(W)dW$.

The number of possible such counterfactual distributions is the number of possible combinations of elements of the set k, i.e. the dimension of its sigma-algebra.[103]

For each counterfactual distribution, it is possible to decompose the observed difference in the income distributions for countries A and B as follows:

$$f^B(y) - f^A(y) = \left[f^s(y) - f^A(y)\right] + \left[f^B(y) - f^s(y)\right] \qquad (2)$$

---

101. This terminology is motivated by the fact that we do not pretend that our models of V should be interpreted causally, and make no claims to be endogenizing these variables in a behavioural sense.

102. Shorrocks (1999) proposes an algorithm based on the Shapley Value in order to calculate the correct "average" contribution of a particular $h_n()$ or of $g()$, over the set of possible orderings, to the overall difference across the distributions. Rather than constructing these values in this paper, we present our results by showing a number of different orderings explicitly in Sections 5 and 6 below.

103. When we turn to the empirical implementation of these counterfactual distributions, we will see that is also possible, of course, to simulate replacing the joint distribution $\psi^A(y)$ by a non-parametric approximation of $\psi^B(y)$. Depending on how each specific conditional distribution is modelled, it is also possible to have more than one counterfactual distribution per element of k. These matters pertain more properly to a discussion of the empirical application of the approach, however, and we return to them later.

where the first term on the right-hand side measures the "explanatory power" of decomposition s, and the second term measures the "residual" of decomposition s.[104] Since these are differences in densities, they can be evaluated for all values of y. Furthermore, any functional of a density function can be evaluated for f^A, f^B or f^s, and similarly decomposed, according to its own metric.

So, we have the same decomposition relationship as (2) for the cumulative distribution. $F^C(y) = \int_0^y f^C(x)dx$. Likewise, for the mean income of quantile q: $\mu_q^C(y) = 1/Q \int_{F_C^{-1}(q)}^{F_C^{-1}(q+1)} y f^C(y)dy$, we have:

$$\mu_q^B(y) - \mu_q^A(y) = [\mu_q^s(y) - \mu_q^A(y)] + [\mu_q^B(y) - \mu_q^s(y)] \tag{3}$$

And we have analogous decompositions for any inequality measure $I(f(y))$ or poverty measure $P(f(y); z)$. In the applications discussed in Sections 5 and 6, the results are presented exactly in this form: Tables 5 and 7 contain inequality and poverty measures, evaluated for $f^A(y)$, $f^B(y)$ and for a set of counterfactual distributions $f^s(y)$, so that the reader can make his own subtractions. Figures 4–8 and 10–14 plot the differences in the (log) mean income of "hundredths" $q \in [1, 100]$, in a graphical representation of Equation (3). In recognition of their parentage, we call these the Generalized Oaxaca-Blinder decompositions.

The Decompositions in Practice: A Specific Model

The essence of the approach outlined above is to compare two actual income distributions, by means of a sequence of "intermediate" counterfactual distributions. These are constructed by replacing one or more of the underlying conditional distributions of A by those imported from B. In practice, this requires generating statistical approximations to the true conditional distributions. This may be done either through parametric models—following the tradition of Oaxaca (1973), Blinder (1973) and Almeida dos Reis and Paes de Barros (1991)—or through non-parametric techniques, as in DiNardo, Fortin and Lemieux (1996).[105] Because of the direct economic interpretations of the parameter estimates in our approximated distributions, we find it convenient in this paper to follow (mainly) the parametric route, by approximating each of the true conditional distributions through a set of standard econometric models, with pre-imposed functional forms.[106]

In particular, we will find it convenient to propose two (sets of) models:

(4) $y = G(V, W, \varepsilon; \Omega)$ and
(5) $V = H(W, \eta; \Phi)$,

where Ω and Φ are sets of parameters and ε and η stand for vectors of random variables, with $\varepsilon \perp (\{V, W\}$, and $\eta \perp W$, by construction. G and H have pre-imposed functional forms. We can then write an approximation $f^*(y)$ to the true marginal distribution $f^C(y)$ in Equation (1) as:

$$f^{*C}(y) = \int_{G(V,W,\varepsilon;\Omega)=y} \pi^y(\varepsilon)d\varepsilon \left[\int_{H(W,\eta;\Phi)=V} \pi^v(\eta)d\eta \right] \Psi^C(W)dW \tag{1'}$$

where $\pi^y(\varepsilon)$ is the joint probability distribution function of ε and $\pi^v(\eta)$ is the joint probability distribution function of η.

---

104. A decomposition is defined (by (2)) with respect to a unique counterfactual distribution s, and is thus also indexed by s.

105. Although, as noted earlier, these authors too rely on parametric approximations to some conditional distributions, such as the probit for the conditional distribution of union status on individual characteristics.

106. This is an advantage of our approach vis-à-vis, for instance, the hazard-function estimators of Donald et al. (2000), who "note that the estimates of the hazard function for wages, earnings or incomes are difficult to interpret" (p.616).

Just as an exact decomposition was defined by (2) for each true counterfactual distribution, we can now define the (actually operational) decomposition s in terms of the approximated distributions f*(y), as follows:

$$f^B(y) - f^A(y) = \left[f^{*s}(y) - f^A(y)\right] + \left[f^B(y) - f^s(y)\right] + \left[f^s(y) - f^{*s}(y)\right]. \tag{2'}$$

Recall that a counterfactual distribution s is conceptually given by $f^s_{A \to B}(y, k^s, \psi^A)$, and is thus defined by (ψ^A and) the simulated sequence of conditional distributions k^s, which consists of some original distributions from A, and some imported from B. Analogously, an approximated distribution $f^{*s}_{A \to B}(y; \Omega^s; \Phi^s, \psi^A)$ is defined with respect to (ψ^A and) the two sets of simulated parameters Ω^s and Φ^s, which consist of some original parameters from the models estimated for country A, and some imported from the models estimated for country B.

The last term in (2') gives the difference between the approximated and the true counterfactual distribution We therefore call it the approximation error and denote it by R_A. Clearly, how useful this decomposition methodology is in gauging differences between income distributions depends to some extent on the relative size of the approximation error. The applications in the next two sections illustrate that it can be surprisingly small.

Following from (1'), our statistical model of household incomes has three levels. The first corresponds to model G ($V, W, \varepsilon; \Omega$), which seeks to approximate the conditional distribution of household incomes on observed characteristics: $g(y| V, W)$. This level generates estimates for the parameter set Ω, which we associate with the structure of returns in the labor markets and with the determination of the occupational structure in the economy. The second level corresponds to model H ($W, \eta; \Phi$) which seeks to approximate the conditional distributions $h_n(v_n|V_{-1}, \ldots, n, W)$, for V ={number of children in the household (n_{ch}); years of schooling of individual i (E_{ih}); and total household non-labor income (y_{0h})} In the third level, we investigate the effects of replacing $\psi^A(W)$ with a (non-parametric) estimate of $\psi^B(W)$. This largely corresponds to the racial and demographic make-up of the population.

First-level model G ($V, W, \varepsilon; \Omega$) is given by equations (6–8) below. Household incomes are an aggregation of individual earnings y_{hi}, and of additional, unearned income such as transfers or capital income, y_0. Per capita household income for household h is given by:

$$y_h = \frac{1}{n_h} \left[\sum_{i=1}^{n_h} \sum_{j=1}^{J} I^j_{hi} y^j_{hi} + y_0 \right] \tag{6}$$

where I^j_{hi} is an indicator variable that takes the value 1 if individual i in household h participates in earning activity j, and 0 otherwise. The allocation of individuals across activities (i.e. labor force participation and the occupational structure of the economy) is modeled through a multinomial logit of the form:

$$\Pr\{j=s\} = P^s(Z_{hi}, \lambda) = \frac{e^{Z_{hi}\lambda_s}}{e^{Z_{hi}\lambda_s} + \sum_{j \neq s} e^{Z_{hi}\lambda_j}} \tag{7}$$

where $P^s(\ )$ is the probability of individual i in household h being in occupational category s, which could be: inactivity, formal employment in industry, informal employment in industry, formal employment in services or informal employment in services. Separate but identically specified models are estimated for males and females. The vector of characteristics $Z \subset T$ is given by $Z = \{1, \text{age, age squared, education dummies, age interacted with education, race, and region for the individual in question; average endowments of age and education among adults in his or her household; numbers of adults and children in the household; whether the individual is the head or not; and if not whether the head is active}\}$.

As is well known, the multinomial logit model may be interpreted as a utility-maximizing discrete choice model where the utility associated with choice j is given by $U_{hi}^{j} = Z_{hi} \cdot \lambda_j + \varepsilon_{hi}^{Uj}$. The last term stands for unobserved choice determinants of individual i, and it is assumed to be distributed according to a double exponential law in the population. We prefer, however, not to insist on this utility-maximizing interpretation of the multi-logit and to treat it merely as a building block of the statistical model G, defined in equation (4).

Turning to the labor market determination of earnings, y_{hi}^{j} in (6) is assumed to be log-linear in α_j and β_j, and the individual earnings equation is estimated separately for males and females, as follows:

$$\log y_{hi}^{j} = \alpha_j + \mathbf{x}_{hi} \beta_j + \varepsilon_i \tag{8}$$

where $\mathbf{x} \subset T$ is given by $\mathbf{x} = \{$education dummies, age, age squared, age $*$ education, and intercept dummies for region, race, sector of activity and formality status$\}$. In the absence of specific information on experience, the education and age variables are the standard Becker—Mincer human capital terms. The racial and regional intercept dummies allow for a simple level effect of possible spatial segmentation of the labor markets, as well as for the possibility of racial discrimination. Earning activities are defined by sector and formality status. To simplify, it is assumed that earnings functions across activities also differ only through the intercepts, so that the sets of coefficients β_j are the same across activities ($\beta_j = \beta$). We interpret these β coefficients in the usual manner: as estimates of the labor market rates of return on the corresponding individual characteristics.

This first level of the methodology generates estimates for the set Ω, comprising occupational choice parameters λ, and (random) estimates of the residual terms ε_{hi}^{Us}[107], as well as for α_j and β and for the variance of the residual terms, $\sigma_{\varepsilon m}^2$, $\sigma_{\varepsilon f}^2$.

In the second level of the model, H (W, η; Φ), we estimate the conditional distributions of $V = \{$number of children in the household (n_{ch}); years of schooling of individual i (E_{ih}); and total household non-labor income (y_{0h})$\}$ on $W = \{$number of adults in the household (n_{ah}), its regional location (r_h), individual age (A_{ih}), race (R_{ih}) and gender (g_{ih})$\}$. This is done by imposing the functional form associated with the multinomial logit (such as the one in Equation 7) on both the conditional distribution of E_{ih} on W: ML_E ($E|A, R, r, g, n_{ah}$) and on the conditional distribution of the number of children in the household on $\{E, W\}$: ML_C ($n_{ch}|E, A, R, r, g, n_{ah}$).

Unlike Equation (7), these models are estimated jointly for men and women. The educational choice multilogit ML_E has as choice categories 1–4; 5–6; 7–8; 9–12; and 13 and more years of schooling, with 0 as the omitted category. Estimation of this model generates estimates for the educational endowment parameters, γ. The demographic multilogit ML_C has as choice categories the number of children in the household: 1, 2, 3, 4 and 5 and more, with 0 as the omitted category. Estimation of this model generates estimates for the demographic endowment parameters, ψ. Finally, the conditional distribution of total household non-labor incomes on $\{E, W\}$ is modelled as a Tobit: T ($y|E, A, R, r, g, n_{ah}$).[108] Estimation of this model generates estimates for the non-human asset endowment parameters, ξ. These three vectors constitute the set of parameters $\Phi = \{\gamma, \psi, \xi\}$.

---

107. For details on how the latter may be determined, see Bourguignon, Ferreira and Lustig (1998).

108. We also experimented with an alternative approximation for the conditional distribution of non-labor incomes. This was a (non-parametric) rank-preserving transformation of the observed distribution of y_0, conditional on earned incomes in each country. In practical terms, we ranked the two distributions by per capita household earned income $y_e = y_h - y_0 / n_h$. If $p = F_B(y_e)$ was the rank of household with income y_e in country B, then we replaced y_0^B with the unearned income of the household with the same rank (by earned income) in country A, after normalizing by mean unearned incomes: $y_{op}^A[\mu_B(y_0) / \mu_A(y_0)]$. The results, which are available from the authors on request, were similar in direction and magnitude to those of the parametric exercise reported in the text.

After each of these reduced-form models has been estimated for two countries (Brazil and a comparator nation), the approximate decompositions in (2') can be carried out. Each decomposition is based on the construction of one approximated counterfactual distribution $f_{A \to B}^{*s}(y; \Omega^s, \Phi^s, \Psi^A)$, defined largely by which set of parameters in Ω^A and Φ^A is replaced by their counterparts in Ω^B and Φ^B. All of our results in the next two sections are presented in this manner. Tables 5 and 7, for example, list mean incomes, four inequality measures and three poverty measures for a set of approximated counterfactual distributions, denoted by the vectors of parameters which were replaced with their counterparts from B. Similarly, Figures 4–8 and 10–14 draw differences in log mean quantile incomes between actual and approximated counterfactual distributions, where these are denoted by the vectors of parameters which were replaced with their counterparts from B to generate them.

As an example, consider line 4 of Table 5 (denoted "α, β, and σ^2"). It lists the mean income and the inequality and poverty measures calculated for the distribution obtained by replacing the Brazilian α and β in equation (8), with those estimated for the US; scaling up the variance of the residual terms ε_i by the ratio of the estimated variance in the US to that of Brazil; and then predicting values of y_{ih} for all individuals in the Brazilian income distribution, given their original characteristics (Ψ^A). The density function defined over this vector of predicted incomes is $f_{A \to B}^{*s}(y; \Omega^s, \Phi^s, \Psi^A)$ for $\Omega^s = \{\alpha^B, \beta^B, \sigma^{2B}, \lambda^A, \eta^A\}$ and $\Phi^s = \Phi^A$.

Whenever $\lambda^B \in \Omega^s$, individuals may be reallocated across occupations. This involves drawing counterfactual ε^U's from censored double exponential distributions with the relevant empirically observed variances.[109] The labor income ascribed to the individuals who change occupation (to a remunerated one) is the predicted value by equation (8), with the relevant vector of parameters, and with ε's drawn from a Normal distribution with mean zero and the relevant variance. When $\Phi^s \neq \Phi^A$, so that the values of the years of schooling variable and/or the number of children in households may change, these changes are incorporated into the vector V, and counterfactual distributions are recomputed for the new (counterfactual) household characteristics. As the discussion in the next two sections will show, the interactions between these various simulations are often qualitatively and quantitatively important. The ability to shed light on them directly and the ease with which they can be interpreted are two of the main advantages of this methodology.

The third and final level of the model consists of altering the joint distribution of the truly exogenous household characteristics, $\psi^C(W)$. The set W is given by the age (A), race (R), gender (g) of each adult individual in the household, as well as by adult household size (n_{ab}) and the region where the household is located (r). Since these variables do not depend on other exogenous variables in the model, this estimation is carried out simply by re-calibrating the population by the weights corresponding to the joint distribution of these attributes in the target country.[110]

In practice, this is done by partitioning the two populations by the numbers of adults in the household. To remain manageable, the partition is in three groups: households with a single adult; households with two adults; and households with more than two adults. Each of these groups is then further partitioned by the race (whites and non-whites) and age category (six groups) of each adult.[111] The number of household in each of these subgroups can be denoted $M_{a,r}^{n,C}$, where a stands for the age category of the group, r for the race of the group, n for the

---

109. The censoring of the distribution from which the unobserved choice determinants are drawn is designed to ensure that they are consistent with observed behaviour under the alternative vector λ. See Bourguignon, Ferreira and Lustig (1998) for details.

110. The spirit of this procedure is very much the same as in DiNardo et al. (1996).

111. In the case of households with more than two adults, this is done for two adults only: the head and a randomly drawn other adult. In this manner, the group of single adult households is partitioned into 12 sub-groups, and the other two groups into 144 sub-groups each.

TABLE 6.4: SIMULATED POVERTY AND INEQUALITY FOR BRAZILIAN EARNINGS IN 1999, USING 2000 USA COEFFICIENTS

	Men						Women					
	Mean p/c Income	Inequality					Mean p/c Income	Inequality				
		Gini	E(U)	E(1)	E(2)	V(log)		Gini	E(U)	E(1)	E(2)	V(log)
Brazil	636.3	0.517	0.467	0.510	0.902	0.837	411.1	0.507	0.450	0.488	0.838	0.819
USA	636.3	0.427	0.355	0.325	0.441	0.820	411.1	0.409	0.336	0.288	0.362	0.814
α, β												
i. Intercept	636.3	0.517	0.467	0.510	0.902	0.837	411.1	0.507	0.450	0.488	0.838	0.819
ii. Education	636.3	0.513	0.479	0.485	0.783	0.948	411.1	0.479	0.401	0.423	0.674	0.761
iii. Experience	636.3	0.575	0.609	0.644	1.244	1.120	411.1	0.535	0.506	0.549	0.986	0.914
iv. Race	636.3	0.515	0.463	0.507	0.893	0.830	411.1	0.497	0.430	0.467	0.791	0.783
v. Interaction: Age/education	636.3	0.439	0.332	0.344	0.504	0.642	411.1	0.461	0.374	0.386	0.586	0.731
vi. Sector of activity	636.3	0.513	0.457	0.502	0.884	0.817	411.1	0.508	0.451	0.489	0.839	0.823
vii. Formal/Informal	636.3	0.517	0.476	0.509	0.900	0.887	411.1	0.517	0.484	0.506	0.876	0.929
viii. All betas	636.3	0.460	0.379	0.376	0.545	0.767	411.1	0.453	0.371	0.368	0.544	0.761
α, β, σ^2												
i. Intercept	636.3	0.540	0.516	0.562	1.039	0.927	411.1	0.545	0.533	0.578	1.084	0.971
ii. Education	636.3	0.536	0.528	0.536	0.910	1.038	411.1	0.519	0.483	0.510	0.888	0.913
iii. Experience	636.3	0.594	0.659	0.697	1.415	1.210	411.1	0.570	0.590	0.640	1.260	1.066
iv. Race	636.3	0.538	0.512	0.559	1.030	0.920	411.1	0.535	0.512	0.556	1.028	0.935
v. Interaction: Age/education	636.3	0.465	0.379	0.392	0.600	0.733	411.1	0.503	0.454	0.470	0.779	0.883
vi. Sector of activity	636.3	0.536	0.506	0.554	1.020	0.907	411.1	0.545	0.534	0.578	1.085	0.975
vii. Formal/Informal	636.3	0.538	0.523	0.557	1.028	0.977	411.1	0.551	0.561	0.589	1.116	1.080
viii. All betas	636.3	0.484	0.424	0.421	0.638	0.857	411.1	0.492	0.446	0.446	0.720	0.913
λ	722.9	0.502	0.434	0.475	0.803	0.772	465.4	0.503	0.439	0.471	0.781	0.800
λ, α, β	636.3	0.442	0.336	0.345	0.492	0.649	411.1	0.432	0.321	0.332	0.479	0.624
$\lambda, \alpha, \beta, \sigma^2$	636.3	0.468	0.382	0.392	0.584	0.735	411.1	0.476	0.400	0.415	0.651	0.773

γ	1210.0	0.477	0.408	0.400	0.572	0.825	705.9	0.468	0.391	0.384	0.545	0.789
λ, γ	1306.8	0.464	0.382	0.375	0.526	0.769	809.2	0.456	0.369	0.363	0.506	0.742
$\lambda, \chi\alpha, \beta$	636.3	0.428	0.322	0.315	0.421	0.654	411.1	0.415	0.300	0.297	0.396	0.608
$\lambda, \chi\alpha, \beta, \sigma^2$	636.3	0.455	0.367	0.361	0.505	0.741	411.1	0.460	0.378	0.376	0.547	0.761
ψ, γ	1235.3	0.469	0.397	0.381	0.529	0.818	732.2	0.457	0.373	0.361	0.500	0.762
$\psi, \chi\alpha, \beta$	636.4	0.441	0.346	0.333	0.447	0.717	411.1	0.431	0.328	0.319	0.425	0.674
$\psi, \chi\alpha, \beta, \sigma^2$	636.4	0.465	0.391	0.378	0.532	0.808	411.1	0.474	0.405	0.395	0.573	0.828
ψ, λ, γ	1281.8	0.463	0.385	0.369	0.506	0.796	797.2	0.449	0.361	0.348	0.477	0.743
$\psi, \lambda, \chi\alpha, \beta$	636.3	0.430	0.328	0.315	0.413	0.681	411.1	0.412	0.297	0.289	0.378	0.611
$\psi, \lambda, \chi\alpha, \beta, \sigma^2$	636.3	0.455	0.373	0.359	0.496	0.772	411.1	0.457	0.374	0.365	0.523	0.764
ϕ	818.7	0.528	0.492	0.518	0.865	0.907	508.7	0.524	0.485	0.510	0.834	0.896
$\phi, \psi, \lambda, \chi\alpha, \beta, \sigma^2$	704.3	0.448	0.362	0.349	0.484	0.751	435.3	0.454	0.369	0.362	0.520	0.752

Source: PNAD 1999 and CPS March 2000.

number of adults in the household, and C for the country. If we are importing the structure from country A (population of households P^A) to country B (population of households P^B), we then simply re-scale the household weights in the sample for country B by the factor:

$$\phi_{a,r}^{n} = \left(\frac{M_{a,r}^{n,A}}{M_{a,r}^{n,B}} \right) \frac{P^B}{P^A} \qquad (9)$$

Results for this final level of simulations are reported in Tables 5 and 7 under the letter ϕ.

The Brazil-United States Comparison

The decompositions described in the previous section were conducted for differences in distributions between Brazil in 1999 and the United States in 2000. The estimated coefficients for equations (7) and (8), as well as those for the multinomial logit models for the demographic and educational structures and the tobit model of the conditional distribution of non-labor incomes are included in Tables 6A1–6A5, in the Appendix. Table 6.4, at the end of the paper, presents the results for importing the parameters from the United States into Brazil, in terms of means and inequality measures for the individual earnings distributions, separately for men and women. Table 6.5 displays analogous results for household per capita incomes, and includes also three poverty measures.[112] Figures 4 to 8 present the full picture, by plotting differences in log incomes between the distributions simulated in various steps and the original distribution, for each percentile of the new distribution.[113]

Looking first at individual earnings, the observed differences between the Gini coefficients in Brazil and the US are nine points for men, and ten for women. Brazil's gender-specific earnings distributions have a Gini of 0.5, whereas those of the United States are around 0.4. Roughly speaking, price effects (identified by simulating Brazilian earnings with the US á and â parameters) account for half of this difference. As we shall see, this is a much greater share than that which will hold for the distribution of household incomes per capita. Among the different price effects, the coefficient on the interaction of age and education stands out as making the largest difference.

Differences in participation behavior are unimportant in isolation. Importing the U.S. participation parameters only contributes to reducing Brazilian earnings inequality when combined with importing U.S. prices, as may be seen by comparing the rows α, β (viii) and the row λ, α, β. Educational and fertility choices are more important effects. The former raises educational endowments and hence both increases and upgrades the sectoral profile of labor supply. The latter leads to increased participation rates by women. This effect accounts for nearly all of the remaining four to five Gini points. As one would expect, demographic effects are particularly important for the female distribution, where, in combination with the effect of education, it reduces the Brazilian Gini by a full five points even before any changes are made to prices. Reweighing the purely exogenous endowments—including race—has no effect.

Table 6.5, which reports on the simulations for the distribution of household incomes per capita, can be read in an analogous way. The first two lines present inequality and poverty measures for the actual distributions of household per capita income by individuals in Brazil (in 1999) and the U.S. (in 2000). In terms of the Gini coefficient, the gap we are trying to "explain" is

---

112. In order for the poverty comparisons to make sense across two countries as different as the US and Brazil, the US **earnings** distributions were scaled down so as to have the Brazilian mean. This was done by appropriately adjusting the estimate for α^{US}, as can be seen from the means reported in Tables 4 and 5. Accordingly, counterfactual poverty measures are not reported for simulations which do not include an α estimate. The same procedure was used in Section 6, to rescale the Mexican earnings distributions to have the Brazilian means.

113. Analogous figures for differences in log incomes by percentiles ranked by the original distribution—which show the re-rankings induced by each simulation—are available from the authors on request.

TABLE 6.5: SIMULATED POVERTY AND INEQUALITY FOR BRAZIL IN 1999, USING 2000 USA COEFFICIENTS

		Mean p/c Income	Inequality				Poverty Z = median/2 per month		
			Gini	E(U)	E(1)	E(2)	P(U)	P(1)	P(2)
1	Brasil	294.8	0.569	0.597	0.644	1.395	26.23	10.10	5.36
2	USA	294.8	0.445	0.391	0.349	0.485	25.02	10.19	5.92
3	α e β	294.9	0.516	0.486	0.515	1.049	20.32	7.53	3.92
4	α, β e σ^2	294.9	0.530	0.517	0.545	1.119	21.92	8.39	4.46
5	λ	277.9	0.579	0.632	0.653	1.313			
6	λ, α e β	255.4	0.535	0.536	0.542	1.022	28.06	11.58	6.46
7	λ, α, β e σ^2	255.5	0.548	0.565	0.572	1.093	29.59	12.50	7.06
8	γ	454.0	0.505	0.489	0.460	0.719			
8a	γ, α e β	283.9	0.480	0.425	0.425	0.732	18.81	7.12	3.75
8b	γ, α, β e σ^2	283.9	0.494	0.453	0.452	0.786	20.33	7.84	4.18
9	λ e γ	469.0	0.511	0.514	0.467	0.711			
10	λ, γ, α e β	274.2	0.490	0.450	0.445	0.780	21.15	8.36	4.54
11	$\lambda, \gamma, \alpha, \beta$ e σ^2	274.2	0.505	0.480	0.474	0.837	22.73	9.19	5.07
12	ψ	295.2	0.576	0.613	0.663	1.449			
13	ψ e γ	464.6	0.505	0.493	0.454	0.686			
14	ψ, γ, α e β	287.1	0.486	0.437	0.434	0.746	19.31	7.31	3.85
15	$\psi, \gamma, \alpha, \beta$ e σ^2	287.1	0.499	0.464	0.459	0.794	20.85	8.09	4.35
16	ψ, λ e γ	507.2	0.500	0.492	0.441	0.641			
17	$\psi, \lambda, \gamma, \alpha$ e β	299.2	0.481	0.433	0.423	0.709	18.14	7.00	3.75
18	$\psi, \lambda, \gamma, \alpha, \beta$ e σ^2	299.2	0.495	0.462	0.448	0.755	19.59	7.77	4.24
19	ξ^5	317.5	0.534	0.531	0.551	1.144	20.58	7.97	4.32
20	$\psi, \lambda, \gamma, \alpha, \beta$ e σ^2, ξ^5	356.3	0.428	0.353	0.315	0.416	11.17	4.33	2.38
21	ϕ	404.7	0.585	0.637	0.683	1.496			
22	$\phi, \psi, \lambda, \gamma, \alpha, \beta$ e σ^2	387.7	0.511	0.490	0.489	0.874	14.35	5.43	2.88
23	$\phi, \psi, \lambda, \gamma, \alpha, \beta$ e σ^2, ξ^5	436.4	0.432	0.359	0.325	0.448	8.14	3.11	1.71

Source: PNAD 1999 and CPS March 2000.

substantial: it is twelve and a half points higher in Brazil than in the United States. The difference is even larger when the entropy inequality measures E() are used.

The first block of simulations suggests that differences in the structure of returns to observed personal characteristics in the labor market can account for some five of these thirteen points.[114] When one disaggregates by individual âs, it turns out that returns to education, conditionally on experience—as for individual earnings—play the crucial role.

---

114. The relative importance of each effect varies across the four inequality measures presented, but the orders of magnitude are broadly the same, and the main story could be told from any of them. All are presented in Table 5, but we use the Gini for the discussion in the text.

Figure 6.3: Distribution of Education Across the Countries

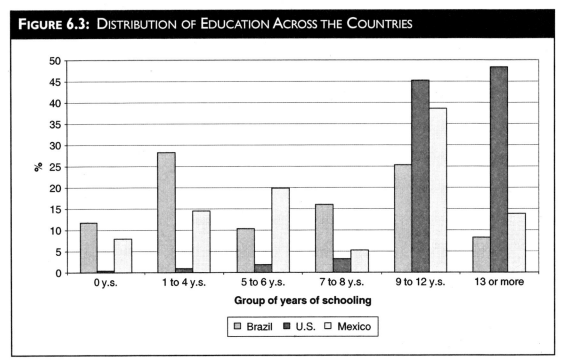

Sources: PNAD/IBGE 1999, CPS/ADS 2000, ENIGH 1994.

Overall, it can thus be said that difference in returns to schooling and experience together explain approximately 40 per cent of the difference in inequality between Brazil and the US. The order of magnitude is practically the same with E(1) and E(2) but it is higher with E(0), suggesting that the problem is not only that returns to schooling are relatively higher at the top of the Brazilian schooling scale but also that they are relatively lower at the bottom. This is confirmed by the fact that importing US prices lowers poverty in Brazil, even though (relative) poverty is initially comparable in the two countries.

Importing the U.S. variance of residuals goes in the opposite direction, contributing to an increase of almost 1.5 Gini points in Brazilian inequality.[115] Two candidate explanations suggest themselves: either there is greater heterogeneity among U.S. workers along unobserved dimensions (such as ability) than among their Brazilian counterparts, or the U.S. labor market is more efficient at observing and pricing these characteristics. This is an interesting question, which deserves further investigation. In the absence of additional information on, say, the variance of IQ test results or other measures of innate ability, orthogonal to education, we are inclined to favor the second interpretation. It may be that the lower labor market turnover and longer tenures that characterize the U.S. labor market translate into a lessened degree of asymmetric information between workers and managers in that country, with a more accurate remuneration of endowments which are unobserved to researchers. We thus consider the σ^2 effect as a price effect, which dampens the overall contribution of price effects to some 3.5 to 4 points of the Gini.

The next block shows that importing the U.S. occupational structure (λ) by itself, has almost no impact on Brazilian inequality, but lowers average incomes and raises poverty. This is a consequence of the great differences in the distribution of education across the two countries, as revealed by Figure 6.3 below. Since education is negatively correlated with inactivity, and positively

---

115. This result is in line with the earlier findings of Lam and Levinson (1992), who noted that the variance of residuals from earnings regressions such as these was considerably higher in the US than in Brazil.

FIGURE 6.4: BRAZIL—US DIFFERENCES IN THE LOGARITHM OF HOUSEHOLD INCOME PER CAPITA, ACTUAL AND SIMULATED, STEPS 1 AND 2

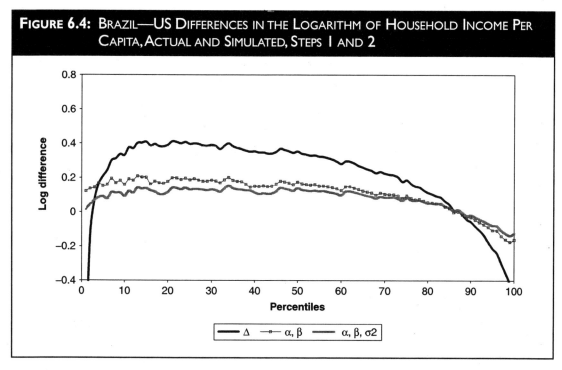

FIGURE 6.5: BRAZIL—US DIFFERENCES IN THE LOGARITHM OF HOUSEHOLD INCOME PER CAPITA, ACTUAL AND SIMULATED, STEP 4

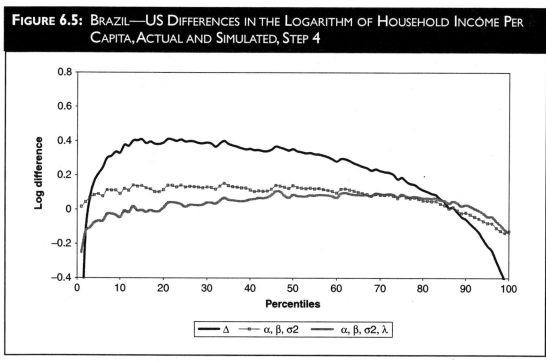

with employment in industry and with formality in the United States, when we simulate participation behavior with U.S. parameters but Brazilian levels of education, we withdraw a non-negligible number of people from the labor force, and 'downgrade' many others. Figure 6.5 shows the impoverishing effect of imposing U.S. occupational choice behavior, combined with its price effect, on Brazil's original distribution of endowments.

TABLE 6.6: SIMULATED POVERTY AND INEQUALITY FOR BRAZILIAN EARNINGS IN 1999, USING 1999 MEXICO COEFFICIENTS

	Men						Women					
	Mean p/c Income	Gini	Inequality				Mean p/c Income	Gini	Inequality			
			E(U)	E(1)	E(2)	V(log)			E(U)	E(1)	E(2)	V(log)
Brazil	636.2	0.517	0.467	0.511	0.906	0.837	410.3	0.507	0.449	0.486	0.831	0.818
Mexico	636.3	0.498	0.432	0.492	0.925	0.765	411.1	0.466	0.416	0.387	0.565	0.944
α, β												
i. Intercept	636.2	0.517	0.467	0.511	0.906	0.837	410.3	0.507	0.449	0.486	0.831	0.81
ii. Education	636.2	0.500	0.435	0.470	0.804	0.795	410.3	0.459	0.368	0.384	0.585	0.709
iii. Experience	636.2	0.516	0.463	0.509	0.904	0.827	410.3	0.516	0.466	0.508	0.891	0.840
iv. Interaction: Age/education	636.2	0.504	0.445	0.467	0.756	0.831	410.3	0.511	0.457	0.495	0.848	0.833
v. Sector of activity	636.2	0.519	0.471	0.514	0.911	0.847	410.3	0.513	0.469	0.497	0.847	0.886
vi. Formal/Informal	636.2	0.539	0.509	0.563	1.052	0.890	410.3	0.520	0.470	0.520	0.934	0.831
vii. All betas	636.2	0.500	0.431	0.469	0.794	0.776	410.3	0.490	0.421	0.449	0.745	0.793
α, β, σ^2												
i. Intercept	636.2	0.511	0.453	0.497	0.869	0.812	410.3	0.532	0.504	0.546	0.989	0.921
ii. Education	636.2	0.493	0.421	0.456	0.769	0.769	410.3	0.488	0.423	0.442	0.713	0.812
iii. Experience	636.2	0.509	0.449	0.494	0.867	0.802	410.3	0.541	0.521	0.568	1.057	0.942
iv. Interaction: Age/education	636.2	0.497	0.431	0.453	0.723	0.806	410.3	0.536	0.512	0.554	1.008	0.935
v. Sector of activity	636.2	0.512	0.457	0.499	0.873	0.822	410.3	0.538	0.524	0.556	1.006	0.988
vi. Formal/Informal	636.2	0.533	0.494	0.547	1.009	0.864	410.3	0.546	0.528	0.584	1.115	0.933
vii. All betas	636.2	0.493	0.417	0.454	0.758	0.751	410.3	0.518	0.479	0.512	0.903	0.895
λ	657.0	0.508	0.449	0.491	0.854	0.805	439.2	0.519	0.477	0.506	0.857	0.882
λ, α, β	636.2	0.478	0.392	0.421	0.675	0.718	410.3	0.481	0.399	0.425	0.673	0.738
$\lambda, \alpha, \beta, \sigma^2$	636.2	0.471	0.378	0.406	0.643	0.692	410.3	0.510	0.456	0.486	0.814	0.842

γ	912.5	0.523	0.486	0.499	0.803	0.916	615.4	0.514	0.479	0.471	0.703	0.950
λ, γ	926.6	0.525	0.493	0.501	0.794	0.940	736.0	0.516	0.495	0.467	0.673	1.022
$\lambda, \chi, \alpha, \beta$	636.2	0.493	0.426	0.439	0.686	0.809	410.3	0.487	0.421	0.421	0.623	0.830
$\lambda, \chi, \alpha, \beta, \sigma^2$	636.2	0.486	0.412	0.425	0.654	0.784	410.3	0.514	0.477	0.480	0.759	0.934
ψ, γ	922.4	0.517	0.479	0.484	0.771	0.924	628.2	0.504	0.465	0.444	0.637	0.949
$\psi, \chi, \alpha, \beta$	636.2	0.495	0.435	0.443	0.701	0.842	410.3	0.474	0.402	0.391	0.553	0.813
$\psi, \chi, \alpha, \beta, \sigma^2$	636.2	0.489	0.422	0.430	0.669	0.817	410.3	0.499	0.453	0.441	0.661	0.916
ψ, λ, γ	909.3	0.522	0.491	0.494	0.787	0.950	721.9	0.505	0.479	0.441	0.605	1.015
$\psi, \lambda, \chi, \alpha, \beta$	636.2	0.483	0.414	0.416	0.629	0.811	410.3	0.469	0.398	0.380	0.520	0.823
$\psi, \lambda, \chi, \alpha, \beta, \sigma^2$	636.2	0.477	0.401	0.404	0.600	0.786	410.3	0.494	0.449	0.429	0.624	0.926
ϕ	621.3	0.511	0.455	0.500	0.887	0.814	401.3	0.500	0.437	0.474	0.809	0.798
$\phi, \psi, \lambda, \chi, \alpha, \beta, \sigma^2$	615.8	0.476	0.398	0.403	0.602	0.777	400.0	0.495	0.448	0.431	0.630	0.921

Source: PNAD 1999 and ENIGH 1994.

Turning to the second-level model, H(W, η, Φ), we see further support for the aforementioned role of education in determining occupational choice. When U.S. educational parameters are imported by themselves, this raises education levels in Brazil substantially, thus significantly increasing incomes and reducing poverty. Education endowments increase more for the poor (as expected by the upper-bounded nature of the education distribution), and inequality also falls dramatically. The α̃ simulation alone takes six points of the Gini off the Brazilian coefficient and, crucially, takes the impoverishing effect away from the occupational structure simulation. The latter result suggests that the most important difference in the distribution of educational endowments between Brazil and the United States might actually be in the lack of minimum compulsory level in Brazil (see Figure 6.3).

At this stage, it might seem that almost all of the difference in inequality between the United States and Brazil is explained by education-related factors. Six points of the Gini are explained by the differences in the distribution of education and five points by the difference in the structure of earnings by educational level (that is, the coefficients of the earning functions). Yet, when these changes (that is, α, β and γ) are simulated together, as in row 8a in Table 6.5, it turns out that their overall effect is not the sum of the two effects (eleven points), but only eight points. The two education-related effects, distribution and earnings structure, are therefore far from being additive. The same is true of the decomposition of earnings inequality in Table 6.6.

The explanation for this non-additivity property is straight-forward. As can be seen in Figure 6.3, only a tiny minority of U.S. citizens have fewer than nine years of education, whereas practically 60 percent of the Brazilian population do. At the same time, the structure of US earnings for the few people below that minimum level of schooling is approximately flat, possibly because of minimum wage laws. In Brazil, on the contrary, earnings are strongly differentiated over that range. People with less than full primary education earn on average 70 percent of the mean earnings of people with some secondary education.[116] This proportion is 95 per cent for the few people with such a low level of schooling in the United States. Thus, importing the earnings structure from the United States to Brazil contributes to a drastic equalization of the distribution when the demographic structure of education of Brazil remains unchanged. Many people with less than secondary education are then paid at practically the same rate as people with completed secondary.

Doing the same exercise with the U.S. demographic structure of education has much less effect, because there are very few people in that country with less than secondary. This appears clearly in Table 6.5 when comparing rows 1 and 3 on the one hand, and rows 8 and 8a on the other. The basic effect of switching to U.S. earnings when the U.S. demographic educational structure is used comes from the fact that the relative earnings of college versus high school graduates is substantially higher in Brazil.

The question which remains is: how much of the excess inequality in Brazil with respect to the United States is due to the distribution of education, and how much is due to the structure of schooling returns?[117] The foregoing argument makes it tempting to place greater weight on the distribution of education effect. This is because the structure of educational returns at low schooling levels is relevant to very few people in the United States, and yet it has such an important effect when imported to Brazil. One may also hold that the structure of returns actually reflects the educational profile of both populations. There are positive returns at the bottom in Brazil because many people in the labor force have zero or a very low level of schooling, whereas this is exceptional in the United States. There are also larger returns in Brazil at the top of the schooling range because there are relatively fewer people with a college education.

---

116. These figures refer to mean earnings by educational level and differ from what may be inferred from the regression coefficients for schooling in table A2.

117. This is not a new question. In fact, it was at the heart of the public debate about the causes of increasing inequality in Brazil during the 1960s. See Fishlow (1972) and Langoni (1973) for different views on the matter at that time.

FIGURE 6.6: BRAZIL—US DIFFERENCES IN THE LOGARITHM OF HOUSEHOLD INCOME PER CAPITA, ACTUAL AND SIMULATED, STEP 6

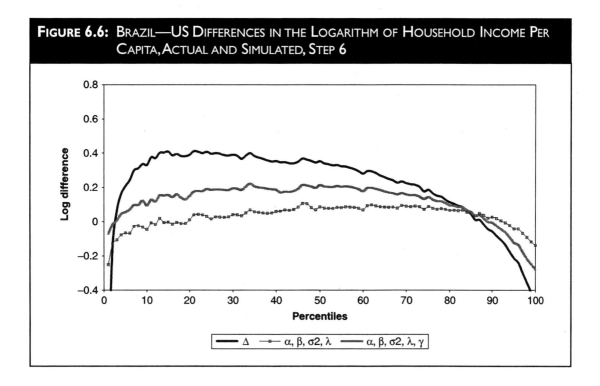

Moving on to demographic behavior, we observe a similar role for education. As with occupational structure, importing ø alone hardly changes inequality—it would even increase it slightly. However, fertility is negatively correlated with educational attainment, particularly of women. If the change in fertility were taking place in the Brazilian population with U.S. levels of schooling and participation behavior, inequality would drop by 1 percentage point of the Gini coefficient and poverty would fall. This seems to mean that fertility behavior differs between the two countries mostly for lowest educated households.

When the effects of some of the "semi-exogenous" endowments (embodied in the approximations to the educational and demographic counterfactual conditional distributions) are combined with occupational structure and price effects (as in the row for ø, ë, $\tilde{\alpha}$, á, â, ó^2), we see an overall reduction of seven points in the Gini. Most of this (around five points) seems to be associated with adopting the U.S. endowments of education, either directly or indirectly, through knock-on effects on participation and fertility. The remainder is due to the price effects.[118] This still leaves, however, some additional five Gini points—a rather substantial amount—in the difference in inequality between the two countries unexplained. Figure 6.7 illustrates the results of the combined simulations for the entire distribution: while the simulated line has moved much closer to the actual (log income percentile) differences, it is not yet a very good fit.

Of the various candidate factors we are considering, two remain: the differences in the joint distributions of exogenous observed personal endowments: $\psi^A(W)$ and $\psi^B(W)$; and non-labor incomes. The two final blocks of simulations show that it is the latter, rather than the former, that accounts for the remaining inequality differences. While reweighing the households in accordance with Equation (9) actually has an increasing effect on Brazilian inequality (see line 21)—thus

---

118. This allocation of the various effects is made difficult by the fact that their size depends on the other effects already being accounted for. The figures mentioned here are obtained as averages over the various possible configurations appearing in table 5.

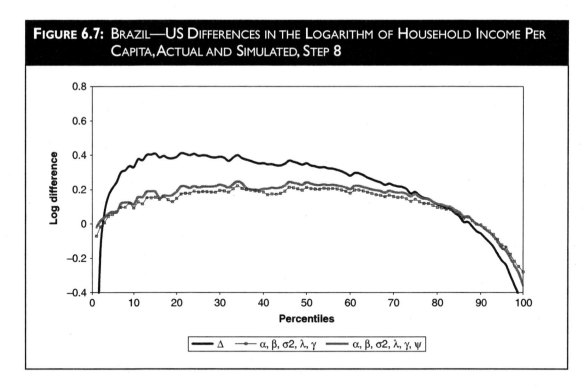

FIGURE 6.7: BRAZIL—US DIFFERENCES IN THE LOGARITHM OF HOUSEHOLD INCOME PER CAPITA, ACTUAL AND SIMULATED, STEP 8

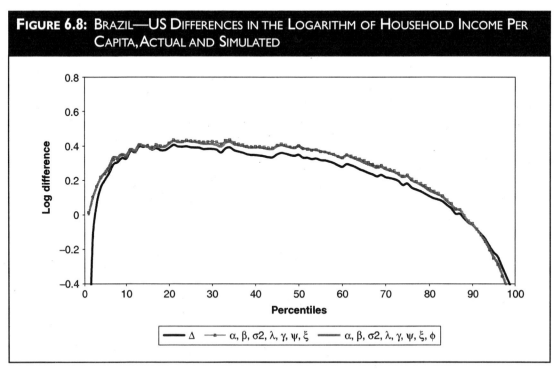

FIGURE 6.8: BRAZIL—US DIFFERENCES IN THE LOGARITHM OF HOUSEHOLD INCOME PER CAPITA, ACTUAL AND SIMULATED

weakening the explanatory power of the overall simulation by about one and half Gini points—importing the conditional distribution of non-labor incomes has a surprisingly large explanatory power. As may be seen from line 20 of Table 6.5, it actually moves the simulated Gini coefficient for Brazil to within 1.7 Gini point of the true U.S. Gini.

FIGURE 6.9: INCIDENCE OF RETIREMENT PENSIONS IN BRAZIL AND THE US

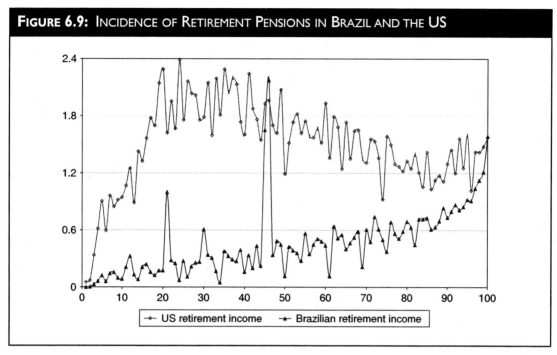

Sources: PNAD/IBGE 1999, CPS/ADS 2000.

When reweighing the joint distributions of exogenous observed personal endowments is combined with all the previous steps, in line 23, the difference is further reduced to 1.3 Gini points It also does remarkably well by all other inequality measures in Table 6.5. Figure 6.8 shows the simulated income differences for two different counterfactual distributions with non-labor incomes—one with and the other without reweighing. The fit with regard to the actual differences is clearly much improved with respect to the preceding simulations, and it is evident that reweighing the exogenous endowments has a limited effect. The fact that the curve for simulated income differences now lies much nearer the actual differences curve graphically illustrates the success of the simulated decomposition. This suggests that the approximation error R_A is very small, at least in this application.

In order to identify the relative importance of the various components of non-labor income, we considered the effect of each source separately.[119] Private transfers are responsible for a drop in the Gini coefficient equal to 0.7 percentage points, certainly not a negligible effect. However, most of the effect of unearned income is in effect due to retirement income. Retirement income is strongly inequality-increasing in Brazil, whereas it would be (mildly) equalizing in the United States. This can be seen in Figure 6.9, which shows the mean retirement pension income for each hundredth of the distribution of household income. Apart for some outliers in the middle of the distribution, retirement income clearly concentrates among the richest households in Brazil, whereas it is the largest in the deciles just below the median in the United States. The explanation of that difference is simple. Retirement income in Brazil concentrates among retirees of the formal sector who tend to be better off than the rest of the population.[120] In the United States, on the

---

119. This analysis is available from the authors on request.

120. See Hoffman (2001) for an interesting analysis of the contribution of retirement pensions to Brazilian inequality. His findings confirm the importance of this income source to the country's high levels of inequality, but he shows that this effect is particularly pronounced in the metropolitan areas of the poorer Northeastern region, as well as in the states of Rio de Janeiro, Minas Gerais and Espírito Santo. The effect appears to be much weaker in rural areas.

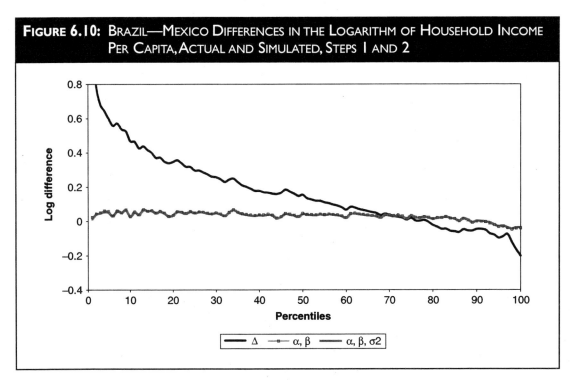

FIGURE 6.10: BRAZIL—MEXICO DIFFERENCES IN THE LOGARITHM OF HOUSEHOLD INCOME PER CAPITA, ACTUAL AND SIMULATED, STEPS 1 AND 2

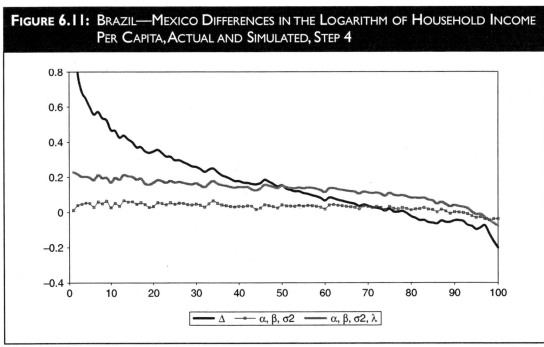

FIGURE 6.11: BRAZIL—MEXICO DIFFERENCES IN THE LOGARITHM OF HOUSEHOLD INCOME PER CAPITA, ACTUAL AND SIMULATED, STEP 4

contrary, retirees are more evenly distributed in the population. When summing up all income sources, they tend to be around the median of the distribution. Hence the switch from Brazilian to U.S. retirement income is very strongly equalizing, reflecting first of all the universality of retirement in the United States and the privilege that it may represent in Brazil.

Overall, the bottom line seems to be that differences in income inequality between Brazil and the United States are predominantly due to differences in the underlying distributions of endowments in the two countries, including among endowments the right to retirement income. Of the almost thirteen Gini points difference, almost ten can be ascribed to endowment effects. Among these, the data suggest almost equally important roles to inequalities in the Brazilian distribution of human capital (as proxied by years of schooling), and other claims on resources, measured by flows of non-labor income.

The remaining three points of the Gini are due to price effects and, in particular, steeper returns to education in Brazil than in the United States. Combined to the more unequal distribution of educational endowments themselves, this confirms the importance of education (prices and quantities) in driving Brazilian inequality, as previewed by the Theil decompositions reported above. While human capital remains firmly at the center-stage, our results suggest that it is joined there by the distribution of non-labor incomes and, in particular, of post-retirement incomes.

The Brazil-Mexico Comparison

The differences between the distributions of household income per capita in Brazil and Mexico are much smaller than those between either country and the United States. The two Latin American countries are at roughly the same level of development, and both are high inequality countries in international terms. Nevertheless, urban Brazil is much poorer than urban Mexico, and more unequal by any of the four measures reported in Table 6.7 below. The Lorenz curve for urban Brazil, in Figure 6.1, lies everywhere below Mexico's. The estimated coefficients for equations (7) and (8), run now so as to be strictly comparable between Brazil and Mexico, as well as those for the multinomial logit models for the demographic and educational structures, are included in Tables 6A.6–6A.9, in the Appendix.

In terms of the Gini coefficient, Brazil's excess inequality amounts to some seven points. Price effects account for 1.2 of these, with the variance of the residuals making no contribution at all to differences between Mexico and Brazil. Participation behavior and occupational structure also account for about a Gini point, but its interaction with the price effects is more-than-additive. The combined impact of all price and participation effects is of more than three points of the Gini.

Education alone also accounts for some three Gini points, but its interaction with occupational choice and price effects is less-than-additive. Joint simulation of Mexican $\ddot{e}$, $\tilde{a}$, $\acute{a}$, $\hat{a}$ and $\hat{o}^2$ account for some four and a half of the seven-point difference. Interacting demographic effects takes away another Gini point from Brazil's measure, but again only once the Mexican approximated conditional distribution of education has been imported too. As in the case of the United States, the educational structure of the population seems to be, either directly or indirectly, a powerful explanatory factor of the difference in household income distribution between Brazil and Mexico.

Replacing $\psi^A(W)$ by $\psi^B(W)$—in effect, reweighing the Brazilian population so that its make-up in terms of exogenous characteristics such as age, race and household type is the same as Mexico's—has a small inequality-reducing effect: the Gini coefficient falls by 0.7 percentage point. This effect is slightly bigger when these new exogenous endowments are interacted with Mexican ("semi-exogenous" endowments of) education and fertility, as well as its price and occupational choice effects. They also help subtract a Gini point.

Altogether, the preceding effects account for almost all the difference observed between Brazil and Mexico, in terms of the Gini coefficient. This is not true, however, of the other inequality measures or of poverty, as shown in table 6.7. In particular, it can be seen that very little of the excessive relative poverty in Brazil is explained by the decomposition methodology, when it is limited to price, occupational structure and endowment effects, a feature that also appears quite clearly in Figure 6.12. As in the comparison with the U. S, it may thus be expected that what is left unexplained actually corresponds to the factors behind unearned income.

TABLE 6.7: SIMULATED POVERTY AND INEQUALITY FOR BRAZIL IN 1999, USING 1994 MEXICO COEFFICIENTS

		Mean p/c Income	Inequality					Poverty Z = median/2 per month		
			Gini	E(U)	E(1)	E(2)	V(log)	P(U)	P(1)	P(2)
1	Brasil	294.8	0.569	0.597	0.644	1.395	1.101	26.23	10.10	5.36
2	Mexico	294.8	0.498	0.420	0.495	1.028	0.703	14.98	3.73	1.39
3	α, β	294.8	0.556	0.567	0.610	1.303	1.059	24.50	9.33	4.90
4	α, β, σ^2	294.8	0.557	0.570	0.613	1.314	1.063	24.62	9.39	4.94
5	λ	289.5	0.557	0.567	0.608	1.229	1.053	25.47	9.56	5.00
6	$\lambda, \alpha, \beta, \sigma^2$	281.3	0.535	0.518	0.552	1.079	0.977	23.64	8.68	4.46
7	γ	375.3	0.537	0.544	0.532	0.908	1.112	18.04	6.87	3.62
8	λ, γ	399.2	0.535	0.540	0.525	0.889	1.108	16.47	6.12	3.18
9	$\lambda, \gamma, \alpha, \beta$	285.1	0.522	0.500	0.513	0.950	0.981	22.95	8.56	4.44
10	$\lambda, \gamma, \alpha, \beta, \sigma^2$	285.1	0.524	0.502	0.516	0.957	0.985	23.09	8.61	4.46
11	ψ	275.5	0.579	0.619	0.671	1.496	1.133	29.94	11.90	6.44
12	ψ, γ	348.0	0.537	0.550	0.529	0.891	1.144	20.48	8.13	4.41
13	ψ, λ, γ	389.7	0.532	0.538	0.514	0.844	1.125	17.41	6.61	3.50
14	$\psi, \lambda, \gamma, \alpha, \beta$	282.6	0.514	0.490	0.493	0.887	0.991	22.85	8.82	4.70
15	$\psi, \lambda, \gamma, \alpha, \beta, \sigma^2$	282.6	0.515	0.491	0.494	0.888	0.992	22.88	8.81	4.69
16	ξ_0	291.9	0.529	0.488	0.554	1.216	0.848	20.6	6.3	2.8
16	$\psi, \lambda, \gamma, \alpha \, \beta, \sigma^2, \xi_0$	279.9	0.447	0.348	0.356	0.539	0.678	14.75	4.40	1.87
17	ϕ	284.5	0.562	0.579	0.625	1.330	1.074	26.51	10.17	5.39
18	$\phi, \psi, \lambda, \gamma, \alpha, \beta, \sigma^2$	269.2	0.506	0.471	0.473	0.834	0.955	23.39	8.92	4.72
19	ϕ, ξ_0	283.7	0.522	0.475	0.535	1.138	0.832	20.9	6.5	2.8
20	$\phi, \psi, \lambda, \gamma, \alpha, \beta, \sigma^2; \xi_0$	268.6	0.437	0.331	0.337	0.496	0.650	14.94	4.43	1.88

Source: PNAD 1999 and ENIGH 1994.

The conditional distribution of non-labor incomes in Mexico was approximated by a non-parametric method, described in footnote 18. As Figure 6.13 illustrates, the impact of this approximation is powerfully equalizing. By itself, it subtracts four points from the Brazilian Gini, and six points from the headcount index (see row 16: ξ_0, in Table 7). Tellingly, it almost halves the distribution-sensitive poverty measure FGT(2). At the same time, it may also be seen that, when combined with all the preceding changes, importing the structure of Mexican unearned incomes overshoots the observed difference between the two countries (see also Figure 6.13). This means that the approximation error R_A for this decomposition is negative—and larger in module than in the previous section.[121]

In any case, however, the results obtained so far suggest that the Brazilian urban poor are at a disadvantage in terms of access to non-human assets and to public or private transfers when

---

121. In addition, the Brazil–Mexico decompositions appear, on the whole, to be less additively separable than the Brazil–US ones. The sum of individual effects in Table 7 is further away from the corresponding combined effects than in Table 5.

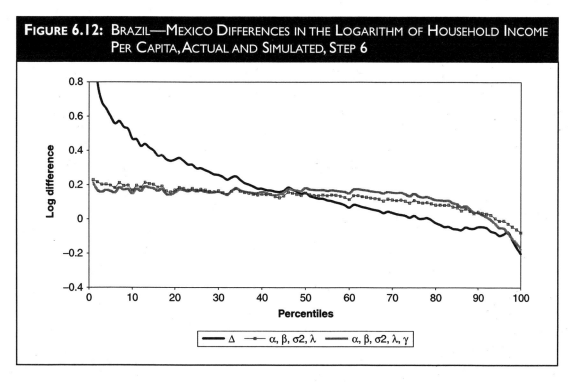

FIGURE 6.12: BRAZIL—MEXICO DIFFERENCES IN THE LOGARITHM OF HOUSEHOLD INCOME PER CAPITA, ACTUAL AND SIMULATED, STEP 6

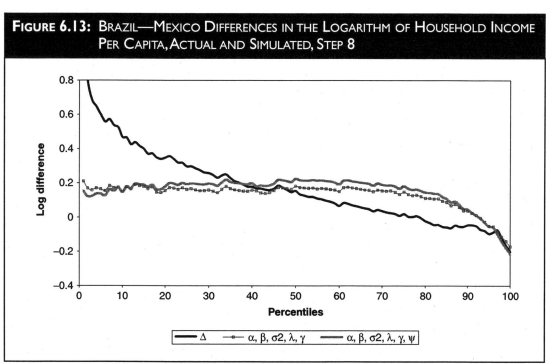

FIGURE 6.13: BRAZIL—MEXICO DIFFERENCES IN THE LOGARITHM OF HOUSEHOLD INCOME PER CAPITA, ACTUAL AND SIMULATED, STEP 8

compared not only to their U.S. counterparts—which might not be so surprising—but also when compared to the Mexican urban poor. This is an issue of clear relevance for the design of poverty-reduction policy in Brazil. Identifying more precisely the reasons of the difference with Mexico deserves further investigation.

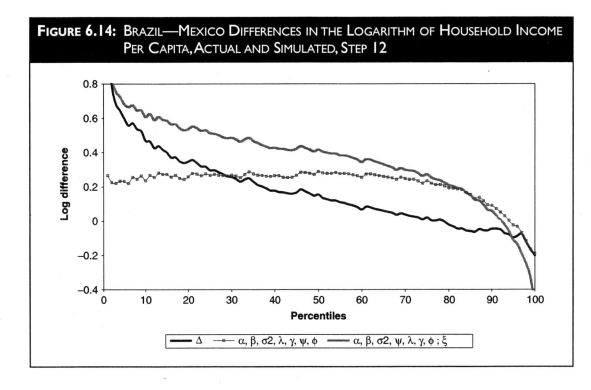

FIGURE 6.14: BRAZIL—MEXICO DIFFERENCES IN THE LOGARITHM OF HOUSEHOLD INCOME PER CAPITA, ACTUAL AND SIMULATED, STEP 12

Conclusions

This paper proposed a micro-econometric approach to investigating the nature of the differences between income distributions across countries. Because a distribution of household incomes is the marginal of the joint distribution of income and a number of other observed household attributes, simple statistical theory allows us to express it as an integral of the product of a sequence of conditional distributions and a (reduced order) joint distribution of exogenous characteristics. Our method is then to approximate these conditional distributions by pre-specified parametric models, which can be econometrically estimated in each country. We then construct counterfactual approximated income distributions, by importing sets of parameter estimates from the models of country B into country A. This allows us to decompose the difference between the density functions (evaluated at any point) of the two distributions—or any of their functionals, such as inequality or poverty indices—into a term corresponding to the effect of the imported parameters, a residual term, and an approximation error. The decomposition residual can be reduced arbitrarily by combining the sets of parameters to be imported into a given simulation. The approximation error is shown to be small for the applications considered.

The sets of counterfactual income distributions constructed in this paper were designed to decompose differences across income distributions into effects due to three broad sources: differences in the returns or pricing structure prevailing in the countries' labor markets; differences in the parameters of the occupational structure of the economy; and differences in the endowments of age, race, gender, education, fertility and non-labor assets, broadly defined. By comparing the counterfactual distributions corresponding to each of these effects and to various combinations of them, we shed light on the nature of the inter-relationships between returns, occupations, and the underlying distributions of endowments. These can lead to interesting findings, such as a quantification of the impact of educational expansion on inequality through a specific channel: its effect on women's fertility behavior and labor force participation.

We applied this approach to the question of what makes the Brazilian distribution of income so unequal. In particular, we considered the determinants of the differences between it and the distributions of two other large American nations: Mexico and the United States. We found that differences in the structure of occupations account for little in both cases. Prices were not insubstantial in explaining difference between the US and Brazil, with this being due largely to steeper returns to education in Brazil. But the most important source of Brazil's uniquely large income inequality is the underlying inequality in the distribution of its human and non-human endowments. In particular, the main causes of Brazil's inequality—and indeed of its urban poverty—seem to be poor access to education and claims on assets and transfers that potentially generate non-labor incomes.

The importance of these non-labor incomes was one of our chief findings. Income distribution in Brazil would be much improved if only the distribution of this income component was more similar to those of the US or Mexico—themselves hardly paragons of the Welfare State. If this is due to public transfers, which needs to be investigated further, it is possible that our findings would vindicate those who have argued for a speedier public approach to the reduction in inequality than that which would be available from educational policies alone.

Appendix

TABLE 6A.1: THE MULTINOMIAL LOGIT ESTIMATES FOR PARTICIPATION BEHAVIOR AND OCCUPATIONAL CHOICE: BRAZIL AND THE UNITED STATES

	Brazil (1999)							
	Men				Women			
	Formal Employment in Industry	Informal Employment in Industry	Formal Employment in Services	Informal Employment in Services	Formal Employment in Industry	Informal Employment in Industry	Formal Employment in Services	Informal Employment in Services
Age	0.281	0.352	0.288	0.326	0.389	0.263	0.306	0.316
Age2	−0.004	−0.004	−0.003	−0.004	−0.005	−0.003	−0.004	−0.003
Education								
1 to 4	1.207	1.381	1.556	1.284	1.355	0.837	1.034	1.145
5 to 6	1.082	1.107	1.735	1.017	1.957	1.661	1.318	1.463
7 to 8	0.472	0.682	1.310	0.905	2.125	1.064	0.813	1.525
9 to 12	0.020	−0.725	1.464	0.424	2.076	1.293	1.364	1.644
13 or more	−1.339	−2.139	0.627	0.085	1.773	1.225	1.228	1.973
Age * education								
1 to 4	−0.020	−0.022	−0.022	−0.018	−0.016	−0.007	−0.012	−0.011
5 to 6	−0.016	−0.016	−0.020	−0.006	−0.029	−0.030	−0.020	−0.015
7 to 8	−0.005	−0.016	−0.011	−0.008	−0.031	−0.006	−0.004	−0.013
9 to 12	0.005	0.006	−0.011	0.004	−0.028	−0.008	−0.006	−0.013
13 or more	0.035	0.036	0.014	0.013	−0.018	−0.009	0.013	−0.013
Race-White	0.040	0.059	0.076	0.409	0.105	0.237	−0.113	0.067
Average endowments of age	−0.019	−0.018	−0.014	−0.009	−0.011	0.003	−0.008	0.002
Education among adults in his or her household								
0	1.456	0.865	0.859	0.466	0.617	−0.033	0.020	−0.331
1 to 4	1.443	1.021	0.942	0.550	0.429	−0.057	−0.025	−0.232
5 to 6	1.329	0.887	0.998	0.520	0.388	−0.214	−0.058	−0.330
7 to 8	1.153	0.706	0.969	0.648	0.297	−0.172	−0.155	−0.284
9 to 12	0.969	0.720	0.888	0.715	0.033	0.135	−0.338	−0.230
13 or more	0.443	0.410	0.494	0.623	−0.271	0.115	−0.603	−0.230
Numbers of adults in the household	−0.042	−0.089	−0.089	−0.137	−0.003	0.018	−0.028	−0.047
Numbers of children in the household	0.066	0.083	0.021	0.047	−0.129	0.085	−0.080	−0.024
The individual is the head in the household	0.778	0.846	0.714	1.078	0.432	1.437	0.420	1.297
The individual is not the head in the household	−0.106	−0.125	−0.025	0.115	0.179	0.442	0.133	0.510
The individual is the spouse in the household					−0.429	0.750	−0.358	0.418
If is not then head, is the head active?	−0.157	−0.223	−0.152	0.084	0.224	0.302	0.237	0.472
Intercept	−6.242	−8.622	−6.586	−8.523	−9.976	−12.134	−6.338	−10.038
#obs	86,216				102,292			

(Continued)

TABLE 6A.1: THE MULTINOMIAL LOGIT ESTIMATES FOR PARTICIPATION BEHAVIOR AND OCCUPATIONAL CHOICE: BRAZIL AND THE UNITED STATES (CONTINUED)

	USA (2000)							
	Men				Women			
	Formal Employment in Industry	Informal Employment in Industry	Formal Employment in Services	Informal Employment in Services	Formal Employment in Industry	Informal Employment in Industry	Formal Employment in Services	Informal Employment in Services
Age	0.442	0.389	0.320	0.506	0.409	0.446	0.294	0.391
Age2	−0.005	−0.005	−0.004	−0.004	−0.005	−0.006	−0.004	−0.004
Education								
1 to 4	4.359	0.345	1.830	4.531	2.751	−18.742	−0.136	−1.308
5 to 6	5.335	−2.486	2.156	8.560	2.730	−17.430	−0.641	2.953
7 to 8	4.370	−2.548	0.902	9.238	1.309	14.725	−0.255	2.000
9 to 12	4.265	−0.430	1.433	9.354	2.001	21.015	0.888	3.796
13 or more	3.064	−2.828	1.129	8.829	1.910	19.730	0.911	3.545
Age * education								
1 to 4	−0.064	0.028	−0.020	−0.089	−0.042	0.167	0.019	0.029
5 to 6	−0.076	0.090	−0.019	−0.150	−0.042	0.142	0.030	−0.051
7 to 8	−0.058	0.086	0.005	−0.143	−0.020	0.125	0.024	−0.041
9 to 12	−0.050	0.056	0.005	−0.141	−0.023	0.031	0.016	−0.056
13 or more	−0.027	0.096	0.022	−0.120	−0.022	0.056	0.029	−0.038
Race-White	0.703	1.258	0.309	0.541	0.107	1.016	0.049	0.350
Average endowments of age	−0.028	−0.030	−0.022	−0.021	−0.010	0.012	−0.012	0.003
Education among adults in his or her household								
0	2.462	0.879	1.772	−0.005	0.429	−219.006	0.454	0.100
1 to 4	2.010	1.462	1.457	1.273	0.180	−0.968	0.281	−2.354
5 to 6	1.973	1.131	1.468	1.520	0.336	−0.222	0.146	−0.027
7 to 8	1.821	1.096	1.070	0.862	0.401	0.101	0.054	0.139
9 to 12	1.777	1.806	1.222	1.062	0.342	−0.450	0.304	−0.176
13 or more	1.569	1.789	1.340	1.252	−0.130	−0.501	0.170	0.013
Numbers of adults in the household	−0.176	−0.309	−0.183	−0.225	−0.119	−0.161	−0.081	−0.109
Numbers of children in the household	0.036	0.130	−0.006	0.096	−0.304	0.006	−0.269	−0.110
The individual is the head in the household	0.654	−0.208	0.219	1.245	0.667	2.253	0.671	2.186
The individual is not the head in the household	0.470	−0.385	0.095	1.017	0.555	1.461	0.528	1.012
The individual is the spouse in the household					0.219	0.417	0.218	1.334
If is not then head, is the head active?	0.237	−0.678	−0.176	0.708	0.278	−30.903	0.442	1.272
Intercept	−12.695	−11.357	−7.402	−20.697	−10.750	−37.000	−6.489	−15.289
#obs		45,873				51,419		

Note: Omitted category for the educational variable is 0 years of schooling.

Source: PNAD 1999 and CPS March 2000.

TABLE 6A.2: ESTIMATES FOR THE MINCERIAN EQUATION: BRAZIL (1999) AND THE UNITED STATES (1994)

| | Brazil | | | | | | | | USA | | | | | | | |
| | Men | | | | Women | | | | Men | | | | Women | | | |
	R²	Coef	Std	p-value	R²	Coef	Std	p-value	R²	Coef	Std	p-value	R²	Coef	Std	p-value
	0.499				0.485				0.368				0.286			
Intercept		3.947	0.038	0.000		4.055	0.058	0.000		2.983	0.297	0.000		3.826	0.454	0.000
Education																
1 to 4		-0.073	0.031	0.019		-0.166	0.049	0.001		0.778	0.330	0.018		0.347	0.523	0.506
5 to 6		0.009	0.038	0.813		0.023	0.057	0.686		0.878	0.306	0.004		0.287	0.477	0.547
7 to 8		0.063	0.034	0.067		-0.008	0.052	0.885		0.638	0.306	0.037		0.029	0.472	0.951
9 to 12		0.067	0.033	0.040		0.202	0.049	0.000		0.925	0.295	0.002		0.453	0.452	0.317
13 or more		0.680	0.041	0.000		0.891	0.055	0.000		1.243	0.295	0.000		0.928	0.452	0.040
Age		0.079	0.001	0.000		0.046	0.002	0.000		0.150	0.007	0.000		0.100	0.010	0.000
Age²		-0.001	0.000	0.000		-0.001	0.000	0.000		-0.001	0.000	0.000		-0.001	0.000	0.000
Age * education																
1 to 4		0.008	0.001	0.000		0.007	0.001	0.000		-0.015	0.007	0.031		-0.012	0.011	0.308
5 to 6		0.009	0.001	0.000		0.005	0.001	0.000		-0.018	0.007	0.008		-0.005	0.010	0.649
7 to 8		0.012	0.001	0.000		0.012	0.001	0.000		-0.009	0.007	0.188		0.002	0.010	0.811
9 to 12		0.022	0.001	0.000		0.018	0.001	0.000		-0.009	0.006	0.150		0.000	0.010	0.978
13 or more		0.026	0.001	0.000		0.022	0.001	0.000		-0.006	0.006	0.338		0.000	0.010	0.970
Race–White		0.188	0.006	0.000		0.159	0.007	0.000		0.164	0.012	0.000		-0.008	0.013	0.504
Sector of activity																
Agriculture		-0.352	0.010	0.000		-0.213	0.028	0.000		-0.180	0.024	0.000		-0.253	0.044	0.000
Industry		0.018	0.006	0.002		0.103	0.010	0.000		0.099	0.009	0.000		0.221	0.014	0.000
Employees		-0.035	0.005	0.000		0.098	0.007	0.000		0.454	0.013	0.000		0.666	0.016	0.000
#obs	65,110				44,376				32,397				28,963			

Note: Omitted category for the educational variable is 0 years of schooling; for the sector of activity it is services; and for occupational status it is self-employed.

Source: PNAD 1999 and CPS March 2000.

TABLE 6A.3: THE MULTINOMIAL LOGIT ESTIMATES FOR DEMOGRAPHIC CHOICE: BRAZIL AND THE UNITED STATES

| | Brazil (1999) | | | | | USA (2000) | | | | |
| | Number of Children | | | | | Number of Children | | | | |
	0	1	2	3	4	0	1	2	3	4
Race–White	-0.574	-0.262	-0.324	-0.280	-0.155	-0.784	-0.160	-0.202	-0.212	-0.121
Numbers of adults in the household	0.865	0.779	0.730	0.501	0.283	0.979	0.644	0.802	0.776	0.407
Age	0.094	0.036	0.022	0.013	0.005	0.091	0.027	0.014	0.009	0.005
Education										
1 to 4	0.627	0.403	0.468	0.386	0.103	-0.286	-0.198	-0.382	-0.338	-0.461
5 to 6	1.023	0.926	1.110	0.890	0.383	-0.017	0.072	-0.268	-0.115	-0.450
7 to 8	1.825	1.690	1.766	1.362	0.686	0.449	0.347	-0.004	0.008	0.034
9 to 12	2.688	2.467	2.432	1.798	0.813	1.719	1.474	1.224	0.796	0.269
13 or more	4.125	3.645	3.679	2.950	0.844	2.357	2.022	1.865	1.217	0.580
Intercept	-0.723	0.874	1.307	1.026	0.440	0.310	1.043	1.472	1.198	0.668
#obs	80,931					52,091				

Note: Omitted category for the educational variable is 0 years of schooling.

Source: PNAD 1999 and CPS March 2000.

TABLE 6A.4: THE MULTINOMIAL LOGIT ESTIMATES FOR EDUCATIONAL STRUCTURE: BRAZIL AND THE UNITED STATES

	Brazil (1999)					USA (2000)				
	Years of Schooling					Years of Schooling				
	0	1 to 4	5 to 6	7 to 8	9 to 12	0	1 to 4	5 to 6	7 to 8	9 to 12
Gender–male	-0.041	0.070	0.112	0.071	-0.134	0.051	0.183	0.106	0.161	-0.041
Age	0.047	0.009	-0.040	-0.037	-0.038	0.047	0.047	0.034	0.045	0.007
Race–white	-2.221	-1.723	-1.622	-1.324	-0.889	-0.781	-0.417	-0.184	-0.223	-0.185
Cohort										
1931 to 1940	-4.224	-3.706	-4.715	-4.282	-3.969	-1.969	-0.685	-1.484	-3.969	-1.985
1941 to 1950	-5.020	-4.462	-5.442	-5.177	-4.719	-2.308	-0.946	-1.927	-4.837	-2.453
1951 to 1960	-5.535	-4.957	-5.493	-5.399	-4.902	-1.735	-0.962	-1.920	-4.902	-2.473
1961 to 1970	-5.486	-5.280	-5.292	-5.508	-4.913	-1.965	-0.585	-1.507	-4.653	-2.354
1971 to 1980	-5.173	-5.216	-5.271	-5.489	-4.630	-1.927	-0.574	-1.266	-4.126	-2.293
Intercept	4.287	6.675	7.745	8.133	7.794	-4.363	-5.101	-3.037	-0.387	2.058
#obs	209,949					103,174				

Note: Omitted category for the cohort variable is 1981 to 1990.

Source: PNAD 1999 and CPS March 2000.

TABLE 6A.5: TOBIT MODEL ESTIMATES FOR NON LABOUR INCOMES: BRAZIL AND THE UNITED STATES

	Brazil (1999)			USA (2000)		
	Coef	Std	P-value	Coef	Std	P-value
Gender–male	–239.38	7.77	0.000	173.88	7.87	0.000
Race–white	88.19	7.12	0.000	225.24	11.37	0.000
Age	28.65	1.11	0.000	10.78	1.17	0.000
Age^2	0.12	0.01	0.000	0.29	0.01	0.000
Education						
1 to 4	116.39	10.63	0.000	–99.07	69.60	0.155
5 to 6	236.22	16.47	0.000	–68.14	65.17	0.296
7 to 8	277.86	13.81	0.000	91.34	62.61	0.145
9 to 12	456.68	12.45	0.000	435.98	59.33	0.000
13 or more	902.82	13.96	0.000	863.07	59.35	0.000
The individual is the head in the household	557.85	8.24	0.000	184.05	8.11	0.000
Intercept	–2925.83	29.39	0.000	–2103.24	65.68	0.000
Standard deviations of residual	953.36			1088.00		
Left-censored observation (< = 0)	153,143	79%		35,300	36%	
Uncensored observations	39,972	21%		61,894	64%	
Total	193,115			97,194		
R^2	0.07			0.03		

Note: Omitted category for the educational variable is 0 years of schooling.

Source: PNAD 1999 and CPS March 2000.

Table 6A.6: The Multinomial Logit Estimates for Participation Behavior and Occupational Choice: Brazil and Mexico

| | Brazil (1999) | | | | | | | |
| | Men | | | | Women | | | |
	Formal Employment in Industry	Informal Employment in Industry	Formal Employment in Services	Informal Employment in Services	Formal Employment in Industry	Informal Employment in Industry	Formal Employment in Services	Informal Employment in Services
Age	0.281	0.352	0.287	0.324	−0.388	−0.262	−0.307	−0.316
Age2	−0.004	−0.004	−0.003	−0.004	0.005	0.003	0.004	0.003
Education								
1 to 4	1.205	1.376	1.551	1.263	−1.345	−0.830	−1.043	−1.142
5 to 6	1.080	1.104	1.731	1.002	−1.943	−1.647	−1.331	−1.458
7 to 8	0.470	0.679	1.308	0.909	−2.120	−1.064	−0.816	−1.524
9 to 12	0.021	−0.722	1.468	0.455	−2.076	−1.304	−1.361	−1.646
13 or more	−1.329	−2.125	0.644	0.184	−1.786	−1.261	−1.210	−1.983
Age * education								
1 to 4	−0.020	−0.022	−0.022	−0.017	0.016	0.007	0.012	0.011
5 to 6	−0.016	−0.015	−0.020	−0.005	0.028	0.029	0.020	0.014
7 to 8	−0.005	−0.016	−0.011	−0.007	0.031	0.005	0.004	0.013
9 to 12	0.005	0.006	−0.011	0.004	0.028	0.007	0.006	0.013
13 or more	0.035	0.036	0.014	0.013	0.018	0.009	−0.013	0.013
Average endowments of age	−0.019	−0.018	−0.014	−0.008	0.011	−0.003	0.008	−0.002
Education among adults in his or her household								
0	1.445	0.850	0.844	0.420	−0.593	0.076	−0.043	0.344
1 to 4	1.437	1.013	0.935	0.539	−0.415	0.088	0.010	0.241
5 to 6	1.324	0.879	0.992	0.508	−0.376	0.243	0.044	0.339
7 to 8	1.149	0.701	0.967	0.652	−0.288	0.191	0.146	0.290
9 to 12	0.968	0.719	0.890	0.738	−0.031	−0.131	0.337	0.232
13 or more	0.449	0.416	0.506	0.680	0.266	−0.128	0.611	0.227
Numbers of adults in the household	−0.042	−0.089	−0.090	−0.141	0.004	−0.016	0.027	0.047
Numbers of children in the household	0.065	0.082	0.019	0.039	0.132	−0.079	0.077	0.026
The individual is the head in the household	0.779	0.848	0.716	1.089	−0.436	−1.437	−0.419	−1.297
The individual is not the head in the household	−0.106	−0.124	−0.023	0.122	−0.183	−0.447	−0.130	−0.511
The individual is the spouse in the household					0.425	−0.757	0.362	−0.421
If is not then head, is the head active?	−0.157	−0.223	−0.153	0.084	−0.225	−0.304	−0.236	−0.473
Intercept	−6.213	−8.581	−6.538	−8.263	9.900	11.961	6.417	9.989
#obs		86,216				102,292		

(Continued)

TABLE 6A.6: THE MULTINOMIAL LOGIT ESTIMATES FOR PARTICIPATION BEHAVIOR AND OCCUPATIONAL CHOICE: BRAZIL AND MEXICO (CONTINUED)

	USA (2000)							
	Men				Women			
	Formal Employment in Industry	Informal Employment in Industry	Formal Employment in Services	Informal Employment in Services	Formal Employment in Industry	Informal Employment in Industry	Formal Employment in Services	Informal Employment in Services
Age	−0.212	−0.223	−0.227	−0.222	−0.141	−0.127	−0.300	−0.244
Age2	0.003	0.003	0.003	0.003	0.002	0.002	0.004	0.002
Education								
1 to 4	−2.609	−0.436	−1.253	−2.010	−1.166	0.125	−1.490	−0.676
5 to 6	−2.479	−0.835	−1.823	−1.585	−1.259	0.232	−1.592	−1.883
7 to 8	−2.133	−0.337	−1.236	−1.503	−2.458	−0.375	−2.433	−1.571
9 to 12	−0.709	0.490	−0.614	−0.371	−0.943	1.415	−1.643	−1.866
13 or more	1.101	2.550	0.158	−0.190	1.118	5.322	−0.884	−0.675
Age * education								
1 to 4	0.043	−0.010	0.009	0.024	0.018	−0.004	0.029	0.010
5 to 6	0.041	0.009	0.023	0.018	−0.001	−0.005	0.033	0.035
7 to 8	0.035	0.016	0.011	0.021	0.040	0.002	0.042	0.020
9 to 12	0.000	−0.003	−0.014	−0.015	−0.019	−0.029	0.000	0.033
13 or more	−0.048	−0.038	−0.047	−0.015	−0.089	−0.123	−0.044	−0.003
Average endowments of age	0.027	0.031	0.019	0.015	0.019	0.001	0.004	−0.005
Education among adults in his or her household								
0	−1.508	−1.110	−0.733	0.019	0.055	−0.094	0.616	0.281
1 to 4	−1.340	−0.820	−0.870	−0.002	−0.724	0.062	0.333	0.230
5 to 6	−0.925	−0.542	−0.671	0.034	−0.328	0.442	0.435	0.320
7 to 8	−1.097	−0.294	−1.209	−0.287	−0.877	0.409	0.155	0.310
9 to 12	−0.660	−0.185	−0.587	0.186	−0.253	0.145	0.373	0.447
13 or more	0.296	1.748	0.174	1.114	0.311	1.190	0.609	0.891
Numbers of adults in the household	0.060	0.121	0.094	0.176	0.012	0.024	0.035	0.150
Numbers of children in the household	−0.123	−0.134	−0.061	−0.067	0.062	0.018	0.052	0.008
The individual is the head in the household	−0.969	−1.447	−0.848	−1.509	0.035	−0.700	−0.548	−0.878
The individual is not the head in the household	0.854	−0.256	0.938	−0.127	0.443	−0.370	0.244	0.309
The individual is the spouse in the household					1.394	0.421	1.369	0.221
If is not then head, is the head active?	0.196	0.332	0.461	−0.090	−0.013	0.547	0.250	0.303
Intercept	3.858	5.123	3.233	4.702	4.151	6.300	6.017	7.122
#obs		11,517				16,542		

Note: Omitted category for the educational variable is 0 years of schooling.

Source: PNAD 1999 and ENIGH 1994.

TABLE 6A.7: ESTIMATES FOR THE MINCERIAN EQUATION: BRAZIL (1999) AND MEXICO (1994)

| | Brazil | | | | | | | Mexico (1994) | | | | | | |
| | Men | | | | Women | | | Men | | | | Women | | |
	R²	Coef	Std	p-value	R²	Coef	Std	p-value	R²	Coef	Std	p-value	R²	Coef	Std	p-value
	0.491				0.480				0.430				0.432			
Intercept		4.052	0.038	0.000		4.141	0.058	0.000		5.110	0.140	0.000		4.668	0.243	0.000
Education																
1 to 4		-0.089	0.032	0.005		-0.169	0.050	0.001		0.256	0.127	0.044		0.157	0.205	0.444
5 to 6		0.004	0.038	0.913		0.022	0.058	0.707		0.044	0.125	0.727		0.359	0.203	0.077
7 to 8		0.064	0.035	0.065		-0.002	0.052	0.967		-0.104	0.150	0.488		0.290	0.266	0.276
9 to 12		0.083	0.033	0.012		0.223	0.049	0.000		-0.038	0.123	0.758		0.413	0.198	0.037
13 or more		0.736	0.041	0.000		0.934	0.055	0.000		0.657	0.132	0.000		0.778	0.231	0.001
Age		0.079	0.001	0.000		0.046	0.002	0.000		0.070	0.004	0.000		0.054	0.008	0.000
Age²		-0.001	0.000	0.000		-0.001	0.000	0.000		-0.001	0.000	0.000		-0.001	0.000	0.000
Age * education																
1 to 4		0.008	0.001	0.000		0.007	0.001	0.000		-0.001	0.003	0.585		-0.001	0.004	0.875
5 to 6		0.010	0.001	0.000		0.006	0.001	0.000		0.008	0.003	0.004		-0.001	0.004	0.747
7 to 8		0.013	0.001	0.000		0.012	0.001	0.000		0.017	0.004	0.000		0.008	0.007	0.262
9 to 12		0.023	0.001	0.000		0.019	0.001	0.000		0.020	0.003	0.000		0.013	0.004	0.003
13 or more		0.026	0.001	0.000		0.022	0.001	0.000		0.021	0.003	0.000		0.019	0.006	0.001
Sector of activity																
Agriculture		-0.355	0.010	0.000		-0.219	0.028	0.000		-0.406	0.045	0.000		-1.746	0.109	0.000
Industry		0.011	0.006	0.054		0.108	0.010	0.000		0.012	0.017	0.478		-0.107	0.033	0.001
Employees		-0.042	0.005	0.000		0.090	0.007	0.000		0.115	0.020	0.000		0.512	0.031	0.000
#obs		65,110				44,376				6,695				3,596		

Note: Omitted category for the educational variable is 0 years of schooling; for the sector of activity it is services; and for occupational status it is self-employed.

Source: PNAD 1999 and ENIGH 1994.

TABLE 6A.8: THE MULTINOMIAL LOGIT ESTIMATES FOR DEMOGRAPHIC CHOICE: BRAZIL AND THE MEXICO

	Brazil (1999)					Mexico (1994)				
	Number of Children					Number of Children				
	0	1	2	3	4	0	1	2	3	4
Numbers of adults in the household	-0.578	-0.265	-0.328	-0.284	-0.158	-0.459	-0.135	-0.193	-0.176	-0.097
Age	0.096	0.037	0.024	0.014	0.006	0.115	0.046	0.034	0.020	0.015
Education										
1 to 4	0.703	0.466	0.525	0.422	0.122	0.467	0.321	0.325	0.383	0.465
5 to 6	1.114	1.003	1.180	0.935	0.407	0.552	1.278	1.567	1.306	1.053
7 to 8	1.965	1.810	1.878	1.435	0.724	2.618	2.380	2.178	1.946	1.537
9 to 12	2.892	2.645	2.598	1.906	0.871	3.032	2.743	2.766	2.077	1.480
13 or more	4.459	3.944	3.959	3.141	0.950	5.013	4.284	4.395	3.512	1.086
Intercept	-0.419	1.151	1.565	1.197	0.533	-2.373	-0.433	0.081	0.396	-0.374
#obs	80,931					12,800				

Note: Omitted category for the educational variable is 0 years of schooling.

Source: PNAD 1999 and ENIGH 1994.

TABLE 6A.9: THE MULTINOMIAL LOGIT ESTIMATES FOR EDUCATIONAL STRUCTURE: BRAZIL AND THE MEXICO

| | Brazil (1999) | | | | | Mexico (1994) | | | | |
| | Years of Schooling | | | | | Years of Schooling | | | | |
	0	1 to 4	5 to 6	7 to 8	9 to 12	0	1 to 4	5 to 6	7 to 8	9 to 12
Gender–male	-0.014	0.092	0.133	0.087	-0.126	-1.011	-0.573	-0.627	-0.214	-0.626
Age	0.041	0.005	-0.044	-0.040	-0.040	0.041	0.011	-0.006	-0.109	-0.046
Cohort										
1931 to 1940	-4.216	-3.720	-4.734	-4.299	-3.979	—	—	—	—	—
1941 to 1950	-4.973	-4.447	-5.432	-5.172	-4.717	-1.041	-0.928	-0.838	-1.783	-0.852
1951 to 1960	-5.462	-4.919	-5.462	-5.377	-4.889	-1.758	-1.671	-1.418	-2.551	-1.504
1961 to 1970	-5.410	-5.232	-5.249	-5.477	-4.895	-2.491	-2.216	-1.764	-3.606	-1.604
1971 to 1980	-5.110	-5.171	-5.230	-5.459	-4.611	-1.758	-1.730	-1.155	-3.020	-0.900
Intercept	2.912	5.504	6.621	7.174	7.112	-1.776	0.566	1.564	5.021	3.767
#obs	209,949					37,324				

Note: Omitted category for the cohort variable is 1981 to 1990.

Source: PNAD 1999 and ENIGH 1994.

References

Aghion, Philippe, Eve Caroli, and C. Garcia-Peñalosa. 1999. "Inequality and Economic Growth: The Perspective of the New Growth Theories." *Journal of Economic Literature* XXXVII(4):1615–1660.

Almeida dos Reis, José G., and Ricardo Paes de Barros. 1991. "Wage Inequality and the Distribution of Education: A Study of the Evolution of Regional Differences in Inequality in Metropolitan Brazil." *Journal of Development Economics* 36:117–143.

Atkinson, Anthony B. 1970. "On the Measurement of Inequality." *Journal of Economic Theory* 2:244–263.

Banerjee, Abhijit, and Andrew Newman. 1993. "Occupational Choice and the Process of Development." *Journal of Political Economy* 101(2):274–298.

Bénabou, Roland. 2000. "Unequal Societies: Income Distribution and the Social Contract." *American Economic Review* 90(1):96–129.

Blau, Francine, and Lawrence Khan. 1996. "International Differences in Male Wage Inequality: Institutions versus Market Forces." *Journal of Political Economy* 104(4):791–837.

Blinder, Alan S. 1973. "Wage Discrimination: Reduced Form and Structural Estimates" *Journal of Human Resources* 8:436–455.

Bourguignon, François. 1979. "Decomposable Income Inequality Measures." *Econometrica* 47:901–20.

Bourguignon, François, Francisco H.G. Ferreira, and Nora Lustig. 1998. "The Microeconomics of Income Distribution Dynamics in East Asia and Latin America." DECRA, World Bank. Processed.

Buhmann, B., L. Rainwater, G. Schmaus, and T. Smeeding. 1988. "Equivalence Scales, Well-being, Inequality and Poverty: Sensitivity Estimates Across Ten Countries using the Luxembourg Income Study database." *Review of Income and Wealth* 34:115–42.

Cowell, Frank A. 1980. "On the Structure of Additive Inequality Measures," *Review of Economic Studies* 47:521–31.

Cowell, Frank A., and Stephen P. Jenkins. 1995. "How much inequality can we explain? A methodology and an application to the USA." *Economic Journal* 105:421–430.

DiNardo, John, Nicole Fortin, and Thomas Lemieux. 1996. "Labor Market Institutions and the Distribution of Wages, 1973–1992: A Semi-Parametric Approach." *Econometrica* 64(5):1001–1044.

Donald, Stephen, David Green, and Harry Paarsch. 2000. "Differences in Wage Distributions between Canada and the United States: An Application of a Flexible Estimator of Distribution Functions in the Presence of Covariates." *Review of Economic Studies* 67:609–633.

Elbers, Chris, Jean O. Lanjouw, Peter Lanjouw, and Phillippe G. Leite. 2001. "Poverty and Inequality in Brazil: New Estimates from Combined PPV-PNAD Data." DECRG, World Bank. Processed.

Ferreira, Francisco H.G., Peter Lanjouw, and Marcelo Neri. 2000. "A New Poverty Profile for Brazil using PPV, PNAD and census data." PUC-Rio, Department of Economics, TD#418.

Fishlow, Albert. 1972. "Brazilian Size Distribution of Income." *American Economic Review* 62(2):391–410.

Foster, J., J. Greer, and E. Thorbecke. 1984. "A class of decomposable poverty measures." *Econometrica*, 52:761–65.

Henriques, Ricardo. 2000. *Desigualdade e Pobreza no Brasil.* Rio de Janeiro: IPEA.

Hoffman, Rodolfo. 2001. "Desigualdade no Brasil: A Contribuição das Aposentadorias." UNICAMP, Instituto de Economia. Processed.

Juhn, Chinhui, Kevin Murphy and Brooks Pierce. 1993. "Wage Inequality and the Rise in Returns to Skill." *Journal of Political Economy* 101(3):410–442.

Lam, David, and Deborah Levinson. 1992. "Age, Experience, and Schooling: Decomposing Earnings Inequality in the United States and Brazil." *Sociological Inquiry* 62(2):218–145.

Langoni, Carlos G. 1973. *Distribuição da Renda e Desenvolvimento Econômico do Brasil.* Rio de Janeiro: Expressão e Cultura.

Legovini, Arianna, César Bouillon, and Nora Lustig. 2001. "Can Education Explain Income Inequality Changes in Mexico." IADB Poverty and Inequality Unit. Processed.

Machado, José A.F., and José Mata. 2001. "Earning Functions in Portugal 1982–1994: Evidence from Quantile Regressions." *Empirical Economics* 26(1):115–134.

Oaxaca, Ronald. 1973. "Male-Female Wage Differentials in Urban Labor Markets." *International Economic Review* 14:673–709.

Sacconato, André L., and Naércio Menezes Filho. 2001. "A Diferença Salarial entre os Trabalhadores Americanos e Brasileiros: Uma Análise com Micro Dados." Universidade de São Paulo, Instituto de Pesquisas Econômicas, TD No. 25/2001.

Shorrocks, Anthony F. 1980. "The Class of Additively Decomposable Inequality Measures." *Econometrica* 48:613–25.

———. 1999. "Decomposition Procedures for Distributional Analysis: A Unified Framework Based on the Shapley Value." University of Essex, Department of Economics. Processed.

Székely, Miguel. 1998. *The Economics of Poverty, Inequality and Wealth Accumulation in Mexico*. New York: St. Martin's Press.

World Bank. 2002. *Building Institutions for a Market Economy: World Development Report, 2002*. New York: Oxford University Press.

CHAPTER 7

INEQUALITY OF OUTCOMES, INEQUALITY OF OPPORTUNITIES AND INTERGENERATIONAL EDUCATION MOBILITY IN BRAZIL

By François Bourguignon,[*] Francisco Ferreira,[**] and Marta Menéndez[***]

Abstract

This paper departs from Roemer's (1998) theoretical formulations of the concept of equal opportunity and analyzes, for the Brazilian case, the general relationship between inequality of outcomes, inequality of opportunities and intergenerational educational mobility. Our main purpose is to study, both in a regression framework and through a micro-simulation decomposition technique, what part of observed (outcome) inequality may be attributed to "circumstances," or family background, and what is due to the 'effort' of individuals, given the variables available in our data set. In particular we focus on intergenerational educational mobility and the way in which parents' education affects, directly or indirectly, the earnings of their offspring. Data are from the 1996 Brazilian household survey (PNAD), where information about parental education is available. The analysis is conducted by five-year cohorts, which permits following the long-run evolution of the inequality of opportunity and intergenerational mobility over time. Results show that among observed variables, parental education proves to be the major source of inequality of opportunities in Brazil. It is not only a powerful determinant of the education of the children, but also an important independent determinant of individual earnings. The same conclusion applies to household income per capita, though now observed circumstances do not operate only through the individual earnings, but also through other channels: fertility in particular, and to a lesser extent, labor-force participation, non-labor income and matching behavior. We also observe that intergenerational

---

*. Worldbank and DELTA, Paris.
**. PUC, Rio de Janeiro.
***. DELTA, Paris. 48, Bd Jourdan, Paris, France. Tel: (0)-1-4313-6311. Fax: (0)-1-4313-6310. E-mail: menendez@delta.ens.fr.

educational mobility has increased over time, especially at the bottom of the distribution. However, even after correcting for the inequality of observed opportunities, Brazilian inequality remains at high levels by international standards, which means that observed opportunities may not be enough to explain the excessive inequality observed in Brazil in comparison with other countries in the world.

JEL classification code: C13, D31, D63, I21, J31, O15

Introduction

Inequality of "outcomes" and inequality of "opportunities" (or chances) have long been considered as corresponding to very different views on social justice in the literature on economic inequality. The first definition refers to the distribution of the joint product of the *efforts* of a person and the particular *circumstances* under which this effort was or is made. It is mostly concerned with income inequality. The second definition refers to the heterogeneity in those circumstances that are out of individuals' control but that nevertheless significantly affect the results of their efforts, and possibly the efforts themselves. This distinction, the formulation of which is borrowed from Roemer (1998), building on earlier work by John Rawls, Amartya Sen and others, is well illustrated by the standard opposition between *inequality* and *mobility*. The United States are often presented as more unequal than European societies but at the same time more mobile from a generation to the next. The latter feature is sometimes taken as the sign of a more equal distribution of chances or opportunities in the United States.[122]

Despite the obvious relevance of the concept of inequality of opportunities and implicitly of the question of social mobility, limited empirical work has been done in this area in comparison with the huge literature on the inequality of outcomes.[123] The main reason for this is probably to be found in the conceptual difficulty of separating out "circumstances" and "efforts" in the limited availability of variables that could satisfactorily describe "circumstances" or in scarce data sources on mobility. All these problems are still more acute in developing countries. Yet, knowing what part of observed outcome inequality may be attributed to circumstances, and in particular to family background, is as important there as in richer countries. Such knowledge should help define the actual scope for redistribution policies and in particular the choice between redistributing current income or expanding the opportunities of the poor through making the accumulation of human capital among children less dependent on parents.

In view of the very high level of (outcome) inequality in Brazil, the question arises of the proportion that is due to opportunities that individuals inherit from their parents and the proportion that is due to the heterogeneity in their efforts and in the results of these efforts. There are various ways to estimate these proportions. The first one consists of studying how much parents do invest in their children conditionally on the characteristics of the parents. That part of the schooling inequality that is explained by parents' characteristics corresponds to the inequality of opportunities, whereas the remainder may be attributed to heterogeneous individual efforts. The latter may also be interpreted as an index of mobility across generations as in the study of Behrman, Birdsall, and Szekely (2000) for Latin American countries. In the case of Brazil, this line of analysis has been followed by Lam (1999). Because it is based on observed *current* schooling decision, a problem with that approach is that it only permits to study future social mobility, that is, the relation between the education of children, when they will be adults, and that of their parents. Because the (future) income of the children is not observed, this kind of analysis does not permit to disentangle the actual contribution of the inequality of opportunities to overall (outcome) inequality.

---

122. For comparisons of mobility between the US and European countries, see Burkhauser et al. (1998), or Checchi et al. (1999).

123. By contrast, social mobility has always been a leading theme of the sociological literature. However, it is not clear whether that literature translates easily into standard economic inequality concepts.

The approach taken in the present paper is of a different nature. It is based on direct information given by survey respondents about the education and occupational position of their parents in the 1996 Brazilian household survey (PNAD). That information permits measuring not only the extent of intergenerational educational mobility but also the way in which parents' characteristics and other circumstance variables may affect the earnings or income of their children, directly rather than indirectly through the education of the children. Also, by controlling for the year of birth, it is possible to see how this influence of parents and background changed over time and whether opportunities account for an increasing or decreasing proportion of total inequality.

This analysis reveals a sizeable inequality of opportunities in Brazil. On the one hand, parents' education proves to be a powerful independent determinant of individual earnings, besides the schooling of respondents. On the other hand, parent education is a strong predictor of children's schooling. Estimated coefficients suggest that for older cohorts the relationship between the number of years of schooling of the parents and that of the children is very high (coefficients close to 0.8). In other words, the distribution of schooling is close to be fully reproduced—up to some increase in average schooling—across generations. There are signs that this situation is changing for the youngest cohorts, but the evolution is very slow.

The paper is organized as follows. The next section shortly discusses the theoretical background for the estimation work undertaken in this paper, that is, the general relationship between inequality of outcomes, inequality of opportunities and intergenerational educational mobility, given the variables available in the database being used. The second section discusses the regression results used to measure the preceding concepts. The third section analyzes the inequality measures associated with the concepts discussed above for the distribution of individual earnings. It also shows how the proportion of income inequality that may be attributed to opportunities has changed over time. The fourth section generalizes this analysis to the case of household income per capita. The concluding section draws the implications of these results for our understanding of anti-inequality policy in Brazil.

Opportunities discussed in this paper focus mostly on those related to the education of the parents. There are other dimensions in the space of opportunities. We are able to capture some of them while others are unobserved in the data. Race and regions of origin are in the first group and are of obvious importance in the case of Brazil.

Theoretical Background

Among the determinants of the earnings of an active individual at some point of time, one may distinguish characteristics that are independent of the individual's will, which we shall call circumstances, following Roemer (1998), and characteristics that, on the contrary, reflect the "efforts" made by the individual to increase his/her productivity and earnings. Let denote C the first set of variables and E the second set. C typically includes fixed socio-demographic attributes like race, region of origin, and the individual's family background. E corresponds essentially to the human capital accumulated by the individual once free to make decisions for himself/herself. This may include the last part of formal schooling, but also on the job training, past decisions to change job or region of residence, or current efforts at work.

Formally, let the following simple equation represent the interaction between circumstances, efforts and current (log) hourly earnings, w, for an individual i:

$$\ln(w_i) = C_i.\alpha + E_i.\beta + u_i \tag{1}$$

where α and β are two vectors of coefficients and u_i is a residual term that accounts for unobserved circumstance and effort variables, sheer luck, measurement errors, and temporary departures from the permanent level of income. All these factors are assumed to be independent of the variables actually included in C and E. They are also assumed to have zero mean and to be identically and independently distributed across individuals.

If inequality were to be measured by the variance of the logarithm of earning, and if it were justified to assume that circumstances and efforts are mutually independent, then we would have the following simple decomposition of total inequality:

$$v(Lnw) = \alpha'.V(C).\alpha + \beta'V(E)\beta + v(u) \qquad (2)$$

where $v(\ )$ stands for the variance of the variable in bracket and $V(\ )$ for the covariance matrix of all the variables in bracket. In other words, total inequality could be explained simply as the sum of the inequality of observed opportunities (first term on the RHS), the inequality of observed efforts (second term) and the inequality due to unobserved earning determinants. A more general description of the role of these various components in shaping the distribution of individual earnings may be obtained by simulating the effects of equalizing C or E across individuals. Such a decomposition is shown for Brazil in the empirical part of this paper.

Complications arise in the preceding framework if one assumes that there is no independence between circumstances and efforts, or between unobservables and observable wage determinants. Consider first that efforts are partly determined by circumstances. For instance, formal schooling is supposed to be partly determined by family background. Assuming reasonably that unobserved effort determinants, v_i, are orthogonal to observed circumstances, this is equivalent to specifying a second model for efforts. Let that model be:

$$E_i = C_i.b + v_i \qquad (3)$$

where b is a matrix of coefficients and v_i stands for a vector of unobserved effort determinants—one component for each component of the vector E_i. As usual the v_i's are supposed to be *iid* across individuals and with zero mean. Substituting in (1) yields:

$$\ln(w_i) = C_i.(\alpha + \beta.b) + (E_i - C_i.b).\ \beta + u_i \qquad (4)$$

In this expression, it may be seen that circumstances now have a double effect on the wage rate. They affect it directly, for given efforts, through the set of coefficients α. They also affect it indirectly through their influence on efforts, the size of this second effect being given by the scalar product $\beta.b$. This restatement of the original model modifies the variance decomposition formula (2) and more generally any decomposition of the distribution of individual wages into components associated with observable circumstances and efforts. Accounting for the possible correlation between observed efforts and circumstances and relying on the joint estimation of the earning and effort equations (1) and (3) is therefore important.

The preceding decomposition is easy to implement, provided that one can rely on unbiased estimators of the various sets of coefficients, α, β and b. Some precaution must be taken when the required assumption that u in equation (1) is orthogonal to C and E is open to doubt. The problem is not too serious for the circumstance variables. One may not be so much interested in the "true" effect of the variables included in C but in their overall impact once their correlation with unobservable circumstances are taken into account. For instance, say that C include parents education but not their wealth. Then estimating (1) through standard regression techniques will lead to a bias in the estimation of the coefficient of parental education that will depend on the unobserved correlation between parents' education and parents' wealth, and on the effect of the latter on children's earnings. The coefficients α will be biased in the corresponding direction and there will be a doubt in the decomposition of total inequality as to what is the actual role of parental education. It is simply a matter of being aware of it.

Things are more serious when unobservables in the earning equations cannot be assumed to be independent of the effort variable. Again, imagine that the wealth of parents is important to determine both the schooling and the current earnings of their children, independently of their own education. This correlation between u and E, or equivalently between u and v, is introducing some bias in the estimation of the β coefficients and therefore in the decomposition of the total inequality into circumstance and effort components.

One way out of this difficulty would be to observe instrumental variables, Z that would influence efforts but not earnings. Equation (3) would then be replaced by:

$$E_i = C_{i.}b + Z_{i.}d + v_i \qquad (5)$$

with the vector Z_i being orthogonal to u_i. Then instrumenting the effort variables in (1) through (5) would yield an unbiased estimator of β and then an unbiased decomposition of total inequality into inequality of observed opportunities, or circumstances, and inequality of efforts. Models of this type have been extensively used in the return to education literature. In the standard Mincerian equation, for instance, it was thought that instrumenting education by family background would correct for obvious endogeneity biases of education. It was checked in a few countries that this was indeed the case. Then family background was considered as an independent earning determinant too, which required using additional instruments. Ability tests taken while attending school often played that role. Few data sets come with all that information, however, this problem being still more acute in developing countries.[124]

In the absence of adequate instrumental variables, Z, the only solution is simply to explore the likely effect of the potential bias in the estimation of β due to the correlation between u and v, and then to decide on that basis what is the most reasonable range of estimates. This is what we shall do in the case of Brazil.

When circumstance variables include characteristics of parents, very much of the preceding analysis has to do with intergenerational mobility. A direct measure of income mobility would be provided by the preceding model if parents' income was among the variables C. But other types of mobility may be behind equations (3). For instance, if parental education is among variables C and individuals' schooling is among the effort variables E, then part of system (3) actually describes intergenerational educational mobility. The schooling of observed individuals is simply explained by that of their parents and the corresponding coefficient b gives an indication of the extent of intergenerational mobility. For example, if education is measured in number of years of schooling for both parents and children, then the extent to which b is less than unity would describe how fast differences in education tend to systematically lessen across generations. It can be seen on equation (4) that the degree of intergenerational mobility determines at the same time the extent of the share of current earning inequality due to individuals' circumstances or opportunities, provided of course that schooling has a positive effect on earnings—that is, the first term in bracket on the *RHS* of (4) is an increasing function of b when β is positive.

Another source of intergenerational educational mobility could be found in the residual term, v. It corresponds to the non-systematic part of mobility and is orthogonal to the concept of inequality of opportunities. As a matter of fact, if this residual is taken to represent the role of individual efforts in schooling achievements, equation (4) shows that it contributes to increasing the share of earning inequality not due to the inequality of observed or unobserved opportunities. The problem, however, is that, by definition, nothing is known of the phenomena behind this residual term, v. Because of this, it is of lesser interest in the present context.[125]

Opportunities and the Distribution of Individual Wages

The preceding methodology to decompose the inequality of outcomes into various components due to the inequality of observed opportunities and that due to other factors is now applied to Brazilian data. This section first describes the data and the nature of the variables being used.

---

124. Earlier contributions include Bowles (1972), Griliches (1972), Taubman (1976). For a survey of all models of returns to schooling based on this kind of instrumentation see Card (2001).

125. Note that this term is the focus of the analysis in Behrman, Birdsall and Szekely (2000), which interpret its contribution to the variance of individuals' schooling as a measure of intergenerational educational mobility.

It then discusses the various estimates obtained for the earning equations and for the equation describing intergenerational educational mobility.

Data and Variables

Data are from the 1996 wave of the Pesquisa Nacional por Amostragem a Domicilio (PNAD), the Brazilian Household Surveys conducted by the Instituto Brasileiro de Geografia e Estadistica (IBGE).[126] For that year, information about parental education of all surveyed household heads and spouses is available. Information is also available on the occupation of the parents. The analysis is restricted to urban areas because of the general imprecision of earning and income measurement in rural areas. It is also restricted to individuals 26 to 60 years old, in an effort to concentrate on individuals having finished schooling and potentially active in the labor market.

The analysis described in the preceding section is conducted by five-year cohorts—from individuals born between 1936–40 up to those born between 1966–70. This permits not only to measure the role of the inequality of opportunities in shaping the inequality of observed earnings at a point of time, but also to study how this role may have changed over time. An important question is indeed whether the increase in the educational level of successive cohorts was accompanied by more or less educational mobility and a reduction in the inequality of opportunities or whether it corresponded to a uniform upward shift in schooling achievements with constant inequality of opportunities. Comparing various cohorts observed at a single point of time permits to answer this question in a simple way.

We shall first focus on individual earnings, measured as "all jobs real hourly earnings," in agreement with most of the intergenerational mobility literature. This might not be the most satisfactory concept to use if one is interested in the contribution of the inequality of individual opportunities to the inequality of individual "welfare," though. This is the reason why the analysis will be conducted at a second stage on the income per capita in the households where observed individuals belong to. This clearly makes more prominent the role of labor supply behavior and fertility as a channel for the intergenerational transmission of inequality.

The vector of circumstance variables, C, includes race dummies, parental education expressed in numbers of years of schooling[127]—using the mean schooling achievement of the father and the mother and the difference between them—the occupational position of the father (a nine-level occupational status variable), and dummies for the regions of origin.[128] The vector of effort variables is restricted to the schooling achievement of the individual, measured in years of schooling[129], squared-years of schooling, to capture possible non-linearities, and a migration dummy, defined as whether the observed municipality of residence was different from the one where born. Note, however, that this migration might have been done by the individual him/herself when adult or by his/her parents when he/she was a child. It should be taken as a circumstance variable in the second case and as an effort variable in the first case.

---

126. The same information is available in both the 1982 and the 1988 surveys. Serious biases seem to plague the observation of earnings in the former survey however. The latter was used to check the robustness of some of the results reported in the present paper.

127. Parental education is given in discrete levels. They were converted into years of schooling (here in brackets) using the following rule. No school or incomplete 1st grade (0); incomplete elementary (2); complete elementary, or complete 4th grade (4); incomplete 1st cycle of secondary or 5th to 7th grade (6); complete 1st cycle of secondary or complete 8th grade (8); incomplete 2nd cycle (9.5); complete 2nd cycle of secondary (11); incomplete superior (13); complete superior (15); master or doctorate (17).

128. A variable that was used in a first stage as a 'circumstance' variable was whether the individual was forced to work as a child—i.e. before 14—or not. This variable proved to be too closely related to the number of years of schooling to be of very much independent interest.

129. The number of years of schooling directly provided in the PNAD is bounded at 15. For consistency with the scale used for parents' schooling, this variable was changed to 17 for individuals reporting a master or a doctorate degree.

TABLE 7.1: DESCRIPTIVE STATISTICS

Cohort	b1936_40	b1941_45	b1946_50	b1951_55	b1956_60	b1961_65	b1966_70
Mean monthly earnings (Reais, all jobs)	559.8	762.5	848.9	823.7	753.7	682.1	553.2
Mean number of years of schooling	4.7	5.7	6.6	7.2	7.7	8	7.8
Mean father's number of years of schooling	2.5	2.7	2.8	2.9	3	3.2	3.2
Mean mother's number of years of schooling	2.2	2.4	2.6	2.7	2.9	3	3.1
Race (Percents)							
Branca (Whites)	61.5	60.4	61.1	61.1	60.3	61.1	59.6
Preta (Blacks)	6	5.9	5.9	6	5.1	4.8	5.1
Amarela (Asians)	0.5	0.8	0.6	0.5	0.4	0.3	0.3
Parda (MR)	32.1	32.3	32.4	32.5	34.2	33.8	35
Regions (Percents)							
North	5.8	6.7	6.3	7.3	7.6	7.4	7.6
North East	24.9	26.3	24.4	22.2	22.9	23.3	24.3
South East	39.7	37.5	39	38.5	37	36.5	33.8
South	21.1	20.3	20.7	22	21.8	21.7	21.5
Center-West	8.5	9.2	9.6	10	10.7	11.2	12.9
Migrants (Percents)	69.4	68.4	68.4	65.5	63.1	58.9	57.5
Agricultural workers	16.4	12.8	8.5	6.5	5.9	5.4	5.6
Number of individuals	2300	3378	5256	7132	8080	8192	6401

Unfortunately, there was no way this distinction could be made. Results obtained are more consistent with the effort interpretation of that variable.

In addition to the preceding list of variables, a labor force participation equation has been estimated for married women in order to correct for the well-known selection bias in estimating the earning equation (1). The standard Heckman 2-stage procedure was used with the composition of the family, the number of children and household income per capita—excluding own earnings—as instrumental variables in the first stage. Summary statistics for all variables used in the analysis are shown in Table 7.1.

Earning Equation

Earning equations were estimated separately for men and women, and by cohort, using simple OLS for men and using the two-stage selection bias correction procedure for women [130]. Results are shown in Tables 7.2a and 7.2b. Note that, unlike with the standard Mincerian specification, age or imputed experience does not appear among the regressors. This is because cohorts are homogeneous at this respect.

---

130. The Heckman correction was initially applied to men as well, but available instruments proved unsatisfactory.

TABLE 7.2A: WAGE EQUATIONS BY COHORT USING OLS, FOR MEN

	b1936_40	b1941_45	b1946_50	b1951_55	b1956_60	b1961_65	b1966_70
Race							
Branca (omitted)							
Preta	−0.449**	−0.305**	−0.293**	−0.301**	−0.265**	−0.185**	−0.250**
	(0.09)	(0.08)	(0.06)	(0.06)	(0.06)	(0.05)	(0.05)
Amarela	0.009	0.600**	0.677**	0.054	0.341*	0.153	−0.333
	(0.32)	(0.20)	(0.18)	(0.17)	(0.17)	(0.19)	(0.24)
Parda	−0.224**	−0.294**	−0.278**	−0.243**	−0.191**	−0.199**	−0.237**
	(0.05)	(0.04)	(0.04)	(0.03)	(0.03)	(0.03)	(0.03)
Parental schooling							
Mean parental sch.	0.039**	0.037**	0.051**	0.034**	0.033**	0.033**	0.035**
	(0.01)	(0.01)	(0.01)	(0.01)	(0.01)	(0.00)	(0.01)
Diff. Parental sch.	0.005	0.018*	0.005	0.005	0.000	−0.001	0.007
	(0.01)	(0.01)	(0.01)	(0.01)	(0.00)	(0.00)	(0.00)
Region dummies							
South East (omitted)							
North	−0.223	−0.078	−0.099	−0.052	−0.191**	−0.113	−0.131*
	(0.14)	(0.12)	(0.09)	(0.08)	(0.06)	(0.06)	(0.07)
North East	−0.202**	−0.142	−0.096**	−0.209**	−0.169**	−0.234**	−0.175**
	(0.05)	(0.05)	(0.04)	(0.03)	(0.03)	(0.03)	(0.03)
South	−0.194**	−0.155**	−0.068	−0.035	−0.044	−0.103**	−0.073*
	(0.07)	(0.06)	(0.04)	(0.03)	(0.03)	(0.03)	(0.03)
Center-West	−0.206	−0.129	0.015	−0.207**	−0.090	−0.128*	0.009
	(0.16)	(0.10)	(0.09)	(0.07)	(0.06)	(0.05)	(0.05)
Years of schooling	0.087**	0.069**	0.083**	0.073**	0.051**	0.027**	0.029**
	(0.02)	(0.01)	(0.01)	(0.01)	(0.01)	(0.01)	(0.01)
Years of schooling squared	0.002*	0.003**	0.002**	0.003**	0.004**	0.005**	0.004**
	(0.00)	(0.00)	(0.00)	(0.00)	(0.00)	(0.00)	(0.00)
Migrant dummy	0.010	0.190**	0.140**	0.085**	0.114**	0.124**	0.160**
	(0.05)	(0.04)	(0.03)	(0.03)	(0.02)	(0.02)	(0.02)
Father's occupational status							
Status 1 (omitted)							
Status 2	0.056	−0.021	0.034	−0.016	−0.044	−0.011	−0.082*
	(0.05)	(0.05)	(0.04)	(0.04)	(0.03)	(0.03)	(0.04)
Status 3	0.008	0.071	0.121*	0.011	0.040	0.055	0.093*
	(0.09)	(0.08)	(0.06)	(0.05)	(0.04)	(0.04)	(0.04)
Status 4	−0.042	0.060	−0.017	0.088	0.082	0.043	0.129**
	(0.10)	(0.09)	(0.07)	(0.06)	(0.05)	(0.04)	(0.05)
Status 5	0.337**	0.050	0.095	0.093	0.116*	0.115**	0.112*
	(0.10)	(0.09)	(0.06)	(0.05)	(0.05)	(0.04)	(0.04)
Status 6	0.099	0.177*	0.132*	0.158**	0.252**	0.125**	0.140*
	(0.11)	(0.09)	(0.07)	(0.06)	(0.05)	(0.05)	(0.06)
Status 7	0.183	0.111	0.046	−0.004	0.069	0.082	0.148**
	(0.13)	(0.11)	(0.07)	(0.06)	(0.05)	(0.05)	(0.06)
Status 8	0.079	0.165	0.126	0.191**	0.173**	0.206**	0.131
	(0.11)	(0.10)	(0.08)	(0.07)	(0.06)	(0.06)	(0.07)

(Continued)

	b1936_40	b1941_45	b1946_50	b1951_55	b1956_60	b1961_65	b1966_70
Status 9	0.176	0.235	0.261*	0.143	0.036	0.211**	0.219**
	(0.22)	(0.14)	(0.10)	(0.09)	(0.08)	(0.07)	(0.08)
Constant	0.210**	0.236**	0.182**	0.321**	0.274**	0.238**	0.162**
	(0.06)	(0.06)	(0.05)	(0.05)	(0.04)	(0.04)	(0.05)
Sample size	1520	2158	3200	4192	4635	4807	3846
F-test	52.91	80.87	143.7	158.86	167.45	190.4	116.94
R-squared	0.414	0.431	0.475	0.432	0.421	0.443	0.379
Adj R-squared	0.406	0.426	0.472	0.430	0.418	0.441	0.376

TABLE 7.2A: WAGE EQUATIONS BY COHORT USING OLS, FOR MEN (CONTINUED)

Source: OLS estimates, standard errors in brackets; * = significant at the 5% prob. Level; ** = significant at the 1% prob. Level.

The first part of these two tables refers to circumstance variables. They all have the expected effect on earnings. Racial discrimination coefficients are significant and negative for black and "pardo." They are generally positive, but not always significant for people with an Asian origin. For women, however, it is interesting that discrimination is strong and significant for the first group (black) only in two cohorts. The extent of discrimination is also less pronounced than for men. Regional differences are also important. Compared to the omitted region (South East), being born in any other region has a negative effect for men, though not always significant; note that part of this effect might be captured by the migration variable. For women this negative effect is also present though less often significant. The region with the worst effect on earnings, other things being equal, is the North East.

The estimated effect of parental education on individual earnings is always positive, significant, and relatively stable across cohorts. It is also sizable since it amounts to 3 to 6 per cent earning difference for each year of schooling of the parents. The difference in the education of the father and the mother is meant to detect a possible asymmetry in the role of the two parents. But no such asymmetry seems to be systematically present.

Turning now to the vector of "effort" variables, individuals' own education has the usual positive and significant effect on earnings for men. This effect is decreasing as one considers younger male cohorts. This is consistent with the negative coefficient generally found for the squared imputed experience term—that is, age minus number of years of schooling minus first schooling age—in the standard Mincerian specification. In effect, this implies that the return to schooling increases with age. This is exactly what is found here.[131] Note also that the coefficient of schooling is sometimes insignificant—it is almost always the case for women. The reason why is that the overall education effect is captured by the squared of the number of years of schooling variable, which is positive and significant both for men and women.

It is interesting that the order of magnitude obtained for the return to schooling in the preceding equations seems to fall slightly below what was obtained in comparable studies for Brazil. For instance, Ferreira and Paes de Barros (2000) found that the marginal return on a year

131. The conventional Mincerian specification is such that: $Lnw = a.S + b.Exp - c.Exp^2$ where $Exp = Age - S - 6$. Expanding the Exp term leads to: $Lnw = (a - b - 12c).S + 2cAge.S - c.S^2 +$ terms in Age or Age squared. If this equation is estimated within groups with constant age, one should indeed observe that the coefficient of S is higher in older cohorts. Note that the present specification also includes an independent S^2. term.

TABLE 7.2B: WAGE EQUATIONS BY COHORT USING HECKMAN CORRECTION (2SLS), FOR WOMEN

	b1936_40	b1941_45	b1946_50	b1951_55	b1956_60	b1961_65	b1966_70
Race							
Branca (omitted)							
Preta	0.119	−0.080	−0.145	−0.192**	−0.200**	−0.124	0.001
	(0.17)	(0.10)	(0.09)	(0.07)	(0.08)	(0.08)	(0.08)
Amarela	0.296	−0.259	−0.077	0.193	0.390	0.191	−0.026
	(0.50)	(0.31)	(0.25)	(0.25)	(0.24)	(0.31)	(0.30)
Parda	−0.140	−0.165**	−0.196**	−0.246**	−0.105*	−0.097**	−0.129**
	(0.09)	(0.06)	(0.05)	(0.04)	(0.04)	(0.04)	(0.04)
Parental schooling							
Mean parental sch.	0.052**	0.057**	0.057**	0.033**	0.045**	0.049**	0.040**
	(0.02)	(0.01)	(0.01)	(0.01)	(0.01)	(0.01)	(0.01)
Diff. Parental sch.	0.018	−0.009	0.004	−0.002	0.009	−0.003	0.002
	(0.01)	(0.01)	(0.01)	(0.01)	(0.01)	(0.00)	(0.01)
Region dummies							
South East (omitted)							
North	−0.253	−0.062	0.012	−0.017	−0.088	−0.073	−0.094
	(0.25)	(0.11)	(0.10)	(0.07)	(0.08)	(0.07)	(0.08)
North East	−0.156	−0.267**	−0.231**	−0.215**	−0.284**	−0.265**	−0.243**
	(0.10)	(0.06)	(0.05)	(0.04)	(0.04)	(0.04)	(0.05)
South	−0.188	−0.068	−0.034	−0.068	−0.068	−0.015	−0.027
	(0.11)	(0.07)	(0.06)	(0.05)	(0.05)	(0.04)	(0.05)
Center–West	−0.365	−0.281*	−0.232*	−0.183*	−0.081	−0.122	−0.129
	(0.20)	(0.12)	(0.10)	(0.08)	(0.07)	(0.06)	(0.07)
Years of schooling	0.053	0.056**	0.018	−0.002	0.020	−0.012	−0.007
	(0.04)	(0.02)	(0.02)	(0.01)	(0.02)	(0.01)	(0.02)
Years of schooling-squared	0.003	0.004**	0.007**	0.007**	0.007**	0.008**	0.008**
	(0.00)	(0.00)	(0.00)	(0.00)	(0.00)	(0.00)	(0.00)
Migrant dummy	0.120	0.134*	0.143**	0.103	0.093**	0.100**	0.143**
	(0.08)	(0.05)	(0.04)	(0.03)	(0.03)	(0.03)	(0.03)
Father's occupational status							
status 1 (omitted)							
status 2	0.018	0.013	−0.004	−0.049	0.037	0.037	−0.015
	(0.10)	(0.07)	(0.06)	(0.05)	(0.04)	(0.04)	(0.06)
status 3	−0.010	0.111	−0.065	0.004	0.079	0.092	0.047
	(0.15)	(0.10)	(0.08)	(0.07)	(0.06)	(0.06)	(0.07)
status 4	0.146	0.018	0.083	0.070	0.079	0.208**	0.078
	(0.17)	(0.12)	(0.09)	(0.07)	(0.06)	(0.06)	(0.07)
status 5	−0.010	−0.232*	−0.049	0.034	0.119*	0.107	0.078
	(0.16)	(0.12)	(0.08)	(0.06)	(0.06)	(0.06)	(0.07)
status 6	0.083	0.240*	−0.004	0.251**	0.182**	0.204**	0.140
	(0.17)	(0.10)	(0.09)	(0.07)	(0.06)	(0.06)	(0.08)
status 7	0.294	−0.058	−0.136	0.054	0.023	0.136*	0.101
	(0.17)	(0.13)	(0.10)	(0.07)	(0.07)	(0.07)	(0.08)

(Continued)

TABLE 7.2B: WAGE EQUATIONS BY COHORT USING HECKMAN CORRECTION (2SLS), FOR WOMEN (CONTINUED)

	b1936_40	b1941_45	b1946_50	b1951_55	b1956_60	b1961_65	b1966_70
status 8	0.138	0.113	0.272**	0.126	0.177	0.230**	0.250**
	(0.18)	(0.12)	(0.11)	(0.08)	(0.08)	(0.08)	(0.10)
status 9	0.292	−0.003	0.012	0.102	0.217*	0.249**	0.402**
	(0.26)	(0.17)	(0.12)	(0.10)	(0.09)	(0.08)	(0.11)
Constant	−0.330	−0.175	−0.088	0.135	−0.440**	−0.408**	−0.413**
	(0.24)	(0.15)	(0.13)	(0.10)	(0.12)	(0.09)	(0.13)
Mills lambda	0.539	0.105	0.203	−0.206	0.940	0.703	0.496
Rho	0.617	0.144	0.260	−0.269	1.023	0.855	0.636
Sigma	0.874	0.729	0.781	0.767	0.919	0.822	0.780
Number of obs	870	1341	2233	3149	3723	3737	2988
Censored obs	675	1097	1888	2748	3251	3212	2424
Uncensored obs	195	244	345	401	472	525	564

Source: Two-stage Heckman estimates, standard errors in brackets; * = significant at the 5% prob. Level; ** = significant at the 1% prob. level.

of schooling is in the range 12 to 15 per cent for both men and women in 1999. In table 2, marginal returns at 5 years of schooling range from 7 to 11 per cent for men and from 11 to 13 for 10 years of schooling A possible explanation of that difference may again lie in the specification being used here, which is not strictly comparable to the Mincerian model. More fundamentally, however, this difference is consistent with the probable over-estimation of the returns to schooling in an earnings equation that does not include family background variables. Indeed, excluding positive earnings determinants which are themselves positively correlated with the number of years of schooling leads standard OLS estimation to over-estimate the role of schooling.

The preceding intuition is fully confirmed by the data used in this study. In unreported regressions, though available from the authors upon request, we have re-estimated the preceding wage equation with years of schooling instrumented by parents' schooling achievements and the other exogenous variables of the model, and with parents' education excluded from the regressors. The coefficients of the number of years of schooling turn out to be substantially higher than in the previous case because they now partly account for the direct influence of parental education on individual earnings. Their order of magnitude is also comparable to what has been found in other earnings equations estimated for Brazil (see, for example, Ferreira and Paes de Barros, 1999).

Migration has a significant and positive effect on earnings, both for men and women. This sign would be consistent with a human capital interpretation of migration. Because the coefficient is rather large, amounting to a 10/20 per cent increase in earnings, it is tempting to consider that variable among effort variables. Yet, it may also reflect the decision of parents to move to an area with better income opportunities when the surveyed individual was still a child, in which case this variable should be taken as indicative of circumstances. If this were true, however, the size of the estimated coefficients would suggest very much persistence in the earnings differential that might have motivated the migration of the parents.[132]

---

132. Note that we are considering migration across municipalities.

TABLE 7.3: YEARS OF SCHOOLING, BY PARENTAL EDUCATION LEVELS

Individual's Birth Cohort	By Father's Education Level				By Mother's Education Level			
	None	Low	Medium	High	None	Low	Medium	High
1936–40	2.1	4.62	7.48	11.18	2.27	4.48	7.83	11.23
1941–45	2.55	5.46	8.37	12.32	2.8	5.46	8.7	12.28
1946–50	3.3	5.98	9.01	12.66	3.3	5.85	9.28	12.64
1951–55	3.99	6.66	9.23	12.52	4.05	6.55	9.41	12.61
1956–60	4.35	7.02	9.33	12.52	4.3	6.84	9.4	12.45
1961–65	4.53	7.17	9.47	12.31	4.68	6.94	9.35	12.28
1966–70	4.78	7.03	8.97	11.57	4.84	6.82	8.85	11.62

Effort Equations: Intergenerational Educational Mobility

The analysis now moves one step forward by examining the effort equations (schooling, schooling-squared and migration). Because no significant model for migration was found, we concentrate here on schooling. In particular, we will concentrate on the relationship between schooling of individuals and that of their parents, so as to be able to measure the extent to which that variable results from circumstances or true efforts. As noted above, this is partially equivalent with measuring the degree of intergenerational educational mobility.

Table 7.3 gives, for each cohort, the mean number of years of schooling for various levels of the education of the father or the mother. It was seen in table 1 that the mean schooling of the Brazilian society increased steadily over time up to the youngest cohorts. In this respect, note that the apparent drop in schooling achievement for that cohort is artificial. It is due to the fact that some people in that cohort are still going to university. More interestingly, the mean number of years of schooling by parental schooling levels across cohorts shown in table 3 suggests some progressive increase in intergenerational educational mobility. Indeed, it may be noticed that the number of years of schooling of those individuals with low educated parents increased much more over the four last cohorts than that of individuals whose parents had a medium or high level of education, as if there were some kind of saturation effect among the latter.

A more direct evaluation of intergenerational educational mobility is provided by a regression of type (3) where individuals schooling achievement is explained by all circumstance variables, including the number of years of schooling of the parents. Regressions for the various cohorts are shown in Tables 7.4a and 7.4b separately for men and women. They call for several interesting remarks.

Intergenerational educational mobility is measured, negatively, by the coefficient of the number of years of schooling of parents. The higher that coefficient, the stronger is parental education in determining the schooling of their children, and therefore the less mobility there is. Because education is measured for both parents and children in years of schooling, a unit value for that coefficient is a convenient reference. It would correspond to the perpetuation of differences in years of schooling across generations—thus, being consistent with an increase in mean schooling. On the contrary, a coefficient less than unity means that educational differences tend to diminish across generations. From that point of view, a striking feature in Tables 7.4a and 7.4b is that intergenerational mobility has been increasing monotonically across cohorts—with the exclusion of the oldest cohort, where sample selection might be biasing results. Overall the gain is substantial. For people born in the early 1940s, a one-year difference in the schooling of their parents resulted in a difference of 0.7 years in their own schooling. For those born in the late

TABLE 7.4A: EDUCATIONAL MOBILITY OLS REGRESSIONS BY COHORT: MEN'S YEARS OF SCHOOLING

	b1936_40	b1941_45	b1946_50	b1951_55	b1956_60	b1961_65	b1966_70
Race							
Branca (omitted)							
Preta	−1.078**	−1.208**	−1.145**	−1.298**	−1.690**	−1.538**	−0.761**
	(0.37)	(0.32)	(0.28)	(0.24)	(0.24)	(0.22)	(0.24)
Amarela	4.972**	2.079**	2.136**	2.433**	1.350	2.971**	−0.057
	(1.26)	(0.75)	(0.77)	(0.72)	(0.74)	(0.86)	(1.03)
Parda	−0.787**	−1.303**	−1.113**	−1.111**	−1.165**	−1.269**	−0.767**
	(0.21)	(0.18)	(0.16)	(0.13)	(0.12)	(0.11)	(0.12)
Parental schooling							
Mean parental sch.	0.740**	0.777**	0.741**	0.673**	0.615**	0.586**	0.526**
	(0.05)	(0.04)	(0.03)	(0.02)	(0.02)	(0.02)	(0.02)
Diff. Parental sch.	0.093*	0.027	0.067*	0.010	−0.004	0.018	0.006
	(0.04)	(0.04)	(0.03)	(0.02)	(0.02)	(0.02)	(0.02)
Region dummies							
South East (omitted)							
North	−1.629**	−0.858	−0.657	−0.382	−0.252	−0.374	−0.307
	(0.55)	(0.49)	(0.39)	(0.33)	(0.28)	(0.28)	(0.29)
North East	−0.973**	−0.895**	−0.651**	−1.087**	−0.959**	−0.764**	−0.967**
	(0.21)	(0.18)	(0.16)	(0.14)	(0.13)	(0.12)	(0.13)
South	0.313	−0.458*	−0.641**	−0.505**	−0.329*	−0.148	−0.289*
	(0.26)	(0.23)	(0.18)	(0.15)	(0.13)	(0.13)	(0.14)
Center–West	0.298	0.437	−0.356	0.303	−0.291	0.317	−0.208
	(0.65)	(0.43)	(0.37)	(0.31)	(0.25)	(0.23)	(0.22)
Father's occupational status							
status 1 (omitted)							
status 2	0.513*	0.348	0.407*	0.705**	0.801**	0.925**	0.552**
	(0.22)	(0.19)	(0.17)	(0.15)	(0.14)	(0.15)	(0.16)
status 3	2.101**	1.598**	1.826**	1.560**	1.578**	1.377**	1.347**
	(0.37)	(0.34)	(0.26)	(0.21)	(0.19)	(0.18)	(0.19)
status 4	2.057**	2.059**	2.732**	2.456**	2.483**	1.976**	2.077**
	(0.39)	(0.35)	(0.29)	(0.24)	(0.20)	(0.19)	(0.21)
status 5	2.398**	2.528**	2.629**	2.767**	3.143**	2.484**	1.707**
	(0.41)	(0.35)	(0.26)	(0.22)	(0.19)	(0.18)	(0.19)
status 6	4.290**	3.355**	4.015**	3.388**	3.426**	3.071**	2.667**
	(0.42)	(0.34)	(0.28)	(0.24)	(0.23)	(0.21)	(0.25)
status 7	4.196**	2.723**	3.768**	2.951**	3.094**	2.509**	1.954**
	(0.52)	(0.43)	(0.32)	(0.27)	(0.23)	(0.22)	(0.25)
status 8	2.185**	2.725**	2.324**	2.754**	2.511**	2.017**	1.735**
	(0.44)	(0.39)	(0.33)	(0.29)	(0.27)	(0.28)	(0.31)
status 9	3.640**	2.546**	2.515**	2.705**	2.421**	2.091**	1.878**
	(0.86)	(0.57)	(0.45)	(0.39)	(0.34)	(0.32)	(0.36)
Constant	2.782**	3.581**	3.872**	4.518**	4.712**	4.937**	5.080**
	(0.19)	(0.18)	(0.15)	(0.14)	(0.13)	(0.14)	(0.15)

(Continued)

TABLE 7.4A: EDUCATIONAL MOBILITY OLS REGRESSIONS BY COHORT: MEN'S YEARS OF SCHOOLING (CONTINUED)

	b1936_40	b1941_45	b1946_50	b1951_55	b1956_60	b1961_65	b1966_70
Sample size	1557	2199	3253	4253	4682	4859	3877
F-test	76.73**	114.92**	164.12**	188.93**	232.72**	221.87**	131.47**
R-squared	0.459	0.473	0.463	0.431	0.459	0.438	0.367
Adj R-squared	0.453	0.468	0.460	0.429	0.457	0.436	0.364

Source: OLS estimates, standard errors in brackets; * = significant at the 5% prob. Level; ** = significant at the 1% prob. level.

1960s, the same initial difference in parental education resulted in a little less than half year of schooling. From an educational point of view, these results suggest that the inequality of opportunities may thus have decreased significantly in Brazil over time.

Seeing in the preceding evolution essentially a mere image of the general spreading of education over time would not be totally justified. If most children are now going to school for 5 years whereas they were going to school only for 3 years 20 years ago, it may seem natural that the influence of parental education declined with time. This is not necessarily true, however. This two-year addition to schooling achievement might very well hold for the whole population, whatever their family background. If this were the whole story, then only the constant in the regressions reported in Tables 7.4a and 7.4b would be increasing across successive cohorts, and the coefficients of all variables would remain approximately constant. This is clearly true of race for which no clear trend seems to be present. Black people have the same quantitative disadvantage in education in the 1960s—1 to 2 years of schooling—as they had in the 1940s or the 1950s. Likewise, the disadvantage of being born in the North East for men has remained approximately constant, the same being true of the father being a farmer. Somewhat surprisingly, only the coefficient reflecting the disadvantage of being born from parent with a low level of schooling seems to have been falling regularly over time. In other words, the *equality of educational opportunities seems to have remained approximately constant over time except with respect to educational family background.* For a given race, region of birth and occupation of the father, the schooling gap between children of families with high and low schooling achievements has narrowed substantially between 1940 and 1970.

Another view at educational mobility consists of examining the relative importance of unobservables, including personal efforts and sheer luck, in determining educational attainments. This may be measured by the complement of the familiar R^2 statistic to unity. Indeed, the higher the variance of the residual term, the more mobility there is (Behrman, Birdsall, and Szekely 2000). Tables 7.4a and 7.4b that a slight upward trend when one moves from older to younger cohorts—even when one downplays the sudden drop in the R^2 for the youngest cohort, which, as seen before, may be due to people still studying in that cohort. This trend seems to be rather irregular, though.

Finally, an interesting feature of intergenerational educational mobility is that it seems to be influenced by intra-household decision mechanisms for women but not for men. In the case of women, the transmission of education from parents to children is higher when the relative schooling advantage of the mother with respect to the father is high. This effect is significant and persistent across cohorts. This is not true for men, however. Mothers' education seems to weigh more than fathers' but the difference is significant only for a single cohort. In both cases, it is difficult to find a trend in the evolution across cohorts. If any, it would seem to be negative.

TABLE 7.4B: EDUCATIONAL MOBILITY OLS REGRESSIONS BY COHORT: WOMEN'S YEARS OF SCHOOLING

	b1936_40	b1941_45	b1946_50	b1951_55	b1956_60	b1961_65	b1966_70
Race							
Branca (omitted)							
Preta	0.482	−1.289**	−1.866**	−0.870**	−1.577**	−1.425**	−1.360**
	(0.46)	(0.42)	(0.34)	(0.29)	(0.27)	(0.29)	(0.29)
Amarela	2.603*	0.979	3.372**	1.034	2.600**	2.081*	1.523
	(1.12)	(1.01)	(0.80)	(0.95)	(0.84)	(0.88)	(1.22)
Parda	−0.437**	−0.696**	−1.290**	−1.309**	−0.757**	−0.987**	−1.027**
	(0.26)	(0.26)	(0.19)	(0.16)	(0.14)	(0.14)	(0.15)
Parental schooling							
Mean parental sch.	0.787**	0.789**	0.759**	0.658**	0.628**	0.548**	0.499**
	(0.05)	(0.05)	(0.04)	(0.03)	(0.02)	(0.02)	(0.02)
Diff. Parental sch.	0.107*	−0.024	0.084*	0.088**	0.094**	0.048*	0.074**
	(0.05)	(0.05)	(0.03)	(0.03)	(0.02)	(0.02)	(0.02)
Region dummies							
South East (omitted)							
North	0.162	−0.421	−0.142	0.550	0.363	−0.219	0.054
	(0.69)	(0.59)	(0.45)	(0.35)	(0.33)	(0.31)	(0.34)
North East	−0.277	−0.235	−0.145	0.000	−0.557**	−0.225	−0.703**
	(0.26)	(0.26)	(0.19)	(0.17)	(0.15)	(0.15)	(0.16)
South	0.051	−0.094	−0.469*	−0.366*	−0.399*	−0.540**	−0.735**
	(0.31)	(0.30)	(0.22)	(0.18)	(0.16)	(0.15)	(0.16)
Center–West	0.065	−0.192	−0.398	1.086**	0.233	0.177	−0.142
	(0.61)	(0.61)	(0.43)	(0.36)	(0.29)	(0.27)	(0.26)
Father's occupational status							
status 1 (omitted)							
status 2	0.510	0.679*	0.827**	0.859**	0.985**	1.194**	1.048**
	(0.27)	(0.27)	(0.21)	(0.18)	(0.17)	(0.17)	(0.19)
status 3	1.707**	2.598**	2.295**	2.059**	1.699**	2.098**	1.836**
	(0.47)	(0.43)	(0.33)	(0.28)	(0.23)	(0.22)	(0.23)
status 4	1.656**	2.360**	3.119**	2.843**	2.275**	2.510**	2.098**
	(0.47)	(0.46)	(0.35)	(0.29)	(0.26)	(0.24)	(0.25)
status 5	3.536**	3.332**	3.365**	2.737**	3.204**	3.114**	2.736**
	(0.50)	(0.48)	(0.32)	(0.26)	(0.23)	(0.22)	(0.23)
status 6	4.670**	3.354**	4.691**	4.088**	4.142**	4.109**	3.323**
	(0.50)	(0.44)	(0.34)	(0.29)	(0.25)	(0.25)	(0.27)
status 7	2.066**	2.577**	3.237**	3.161**	3.198**	3.152**	2.694**
	(0.57)	(0.61)	(0.39)	(0.32)	(0.28)	(0.27)	(0.28)
status 8	2.242**	2.420**	3.229**	2.881**	2.710**	3.007**	2.991**
	(0.55)	(0.60)	(0.43)	(0.36)	(0.32)	(0.32)	(0.37)
status 9	3.626**	3.364**	3.000**	2.862**	2.679**	2.680**	2.106**
	(0.84)	(0.81)	(0.52)	(0.44)	(0.37)	(0.35)	(0.42)
Constant	1.809**	2.942**	3.597**	4.309**	4.725**	4.929**	5.600**
	(0.24)	(0.25)	(0.19)	(0.17)	(0.15)	(0.16)	(0.18)

(Continued)

TABLE 7.4B: EDUCATIONAL MOBILITY OLS REGRESSIONS BY COHORT: WOMEN'S YEARS OF SCHOOLING (CONTINUED)

	b1936_40	b1941_45	b1946_50	b1951_55	b1956_60	b1961_65	b1966_70
Sample size	905	1396	2310	3229	3805	3813	3035
F-test	52.35**	54.22**	116.3**	133.01**	159.73**	158.85**	108.82**
R-squared	0.501	0.401	0.463	0.413	0.418	0.416	0.380
Adj R-squared	0.491	0.393	0.459	0.410	0.415	0.413	0.377

Source: OLS estimates, standard errors in brackets; * = significant at the 5% prob. Level; ** = significant at the 1% prob. level.

TABLE 7.5A: INTERGENERATIONAL EDUCATIONAL MOBILITY: COHORT 1936–1940

Parental Years of Schooling, in Deviations from the Mean (mean of two parents)	Individuals' Years of Schooling, in Deviations from the Mean			
	−2 or less	Between 2 and −2	2 or more	Total
−2 or less	92.75	4.16	3.10	100.00
	37.90	1.70	1.27	40.87
Between 2 and −2	66.61	13.78	19.61	100.00
	32.98	6.82	9.71	49.52
2 or more	15.57	15.38	69.05	100.00
	1.50	1.48	6.64	9.62
Total	72.39	10.00	17.61	100.00

Another way of looking at intergenerational educational mobility is through the usual transition matrices. Matrices for four cohorts are shown in Tables 7.5a–d, where the number of years of education is expressed as deviations from the mean, in order to correct for the general increase in the number of years of schooling across generations—and across cohorts. Intergenerational educational mobility has clearly increased for the less educated individuals. For the older cohorts, around 80 percent of those individuals whose parents had two or less years of education less than the mean, stayed at a similar position with respect to their own mean, while for the youngest cohort this percentage has fallen up to 55 percent. For the higher-educated people, however, mobility first decreased and then remained more or less constant. Based on transition matrices, it would thus seem that the increase in intergenerational educational mobility depends very much on the weight given to the various educational groups. Another interesting feature in Tables 7.5a–d is the fact that a significant intergenerational downward mobility (with respect to the cohort mean) is observed for any cohort, though at a decreasing rate. These transition matrices strongly suggest that there exist important non-linearities in the relation between parental education and that of the sons.

To understand intergenerational educational mobility in Brazil well would require a much more detailed analysis. In particular, very much of the preceding discussion is based on measuring education in terms of the number of years of schooling. One might prefer a more general approach where "human capital" is what matters in intergenerational transmission mechanisms, human capital being measured by the cost of education, including foregone earnings, or possibly by the earnings that a given schooling level actually commands. The two approaches are equivalent

TABLE 7.5B: INTERGENERATIONAL EDUCATIONAL MOBILITY: COHORT 1946–1950

Parental Years of Schooling, in Deviations from the Mean (mean of two parents)	Individuals' Years of Schooling, in Deviations from the Mean			
	−2 or less	Between 2 and −2	2 or more	Total
−2 or less	85.13	7.88	6.99	100.00
	25.76	2.39	2.11	30.26
Between 2 and −2	53.30	15.19	31.50	100.00
	29.95	8.54	17.70	56.19
2 or more	6.80	10.17	83.03	100.00
	0.92	1.38	11.25	13.55
Total	56.63	12.30	31.07	100.00

TABLE 7.5C: INTERGENERATIONAL EDUCATIONAL MOBILITY: COHORT 1956–1960

Parental Years of Schooling, in Deviations from the Mean (mean of two parents)	Individuals' Years of Schooling, in Deviations from the Mean			
	−2 or less	Between 2 and −2	2 or more	Total
−2 or less	74.46	15.42	10.13	100.00
	17.35	3.59	2.36	23.31
Between 2 and −2	38.73	24.91	36.36	100.00
	22.65	14.57	21.27	58.49
2 or more	5.06	12.26	82.68	100.00
	0.92	2.23	15.05	18.20
Total	40.93	20.39	38.68	100.00

TABLE 7.5D: INTERGENERATIONAL EDUCATIONAL MOBILITY: COHORT 1966–1970

Parental Years of Schooling, in Deviations from the Mean (mean of two parents)	Individuals' Years of Schooling, in Deviations from the Mean			
	−2 or less	Between 2 and −2	2 or more	Total
−2 or less	64.83	22.44	12.73	100.00
	12.11	4.19	2.38	18.67
Between 2 and −2	32.59	34.30	33.11	100.00
	19.42	20.44	19.74	59.60
2 or more	6.89	17.93	75.18	100.00
	1.50	3.89	16.33	21.72
Total	33.03	28.53	38.45	100.00

when it is assumed that the rate of return to the number of years of schooling is constant. They are not if the marginal rate of return to an additional year of schooling depends on the level of schooling, as done in the earning equations above. Also, the quality of schooling is totally ignored in the preceding description of intergenerational educational mobility. But it cannot be ruled out that taking into account the quality of education so as to get closer again to a concept of human capital would modify the preceding conclusion of an increasing educational mobility in Brazil.[133] These conclusions must thus be taken with very much care.

The Issue of the Endogeneity Bias

Before putting together the preceding wage and effort equations to measure the inequality of opportunities and its evolution across cohorts, it is necessary to discuss the implications of the bias in the earning equation that could arise from the endogeneity of the effort variables, that is their correlation with unobserved earnings determinants. As said above, there is no variable in the data source being used for Brazil that permits instrumenting satisfactorily the effort variables in equation (1) so as to test for the existence of such a bias and to correct for it. Instead, various experiments were made on the basis of the preceding models, which permitted defining useful benchmarks for the rest of the analysis.

Practically, the problem comes from a possible correlation between the variables which are behind the residual, u_i, of equation (1) and the variables, schooling (S_i), schooling-squared ($S2_i$) and migration (M_i) included in E_i. Let ρ_{uS}, ρ_{uS2} and ρ_{uM} be the coefficients of correlation between the residual and these three effort variables, and assume reasonably that the residual term, u_i, is orthogonal to all other circumstance variables in the earning equation (1)[13]. Let ρ_{MS}, ρ_{MS2} be the known correlations between the effort variables and σ_x the standard deviation of any variable X. Consider the covariance matrix Σ between circumstance variables (C), effort variables (E) and the residual term, u, after normalizing all variables.

$$\Sigma = \begin{bmatrix} C'C & E'C & 0 \\ C'E & E'E & E'u \\ 0 & u'E & u'u \end{bmatrix}$$

This matrix must be definite positive. Given that $E'u$ in Σ is not zero, OLS estimates of the regression of w on $V = (C,E)$ is biased. This bias writes:

$$b = (V'V)^{-1} Exp[(C,E)'u] = N(V'V)^{-1}(0, \rho_{uS} \cdot \sigma_S, \rho_{uS2} \cdot \sigma_{S2}, \rho_{uS} \cdot \sigma_M)' \sigma_u \qquad (6)$$

where N is the number of observations and Exp is the expected value operator. The problem is that ρ_{uS}, ρ_{uS2}, ρ_{uM} and σ_u are unknown. Let us concentrate on σ_u for a moment. OLS gives a biased estimate of it. By definition:

$$\sigma_u^2 = \frac{1}{N}[w - V(\hat{\beta} + b)]'[w - V(\hat{\beta} + b)]$$

where $\hat{\beta}$ is the vector of OLS estimates of the regression coefficients of w on V. Expanding this expression yields:

$$\sigma_u^2 = \hat{\sigma}_u^2 + \frac{1}{N} b'V'Vb \qquad (7)$$

where $\hat{\sigma}_u^2$ is the variance of the OLS residuals.

---

133. For some references to the role of educational quality in shaping inequalities in Brazil see the motivation of the theoretical model in Ferreira (2000).

Substituting the definition of the bias b in (6) into (7) leads to :

$$\sigma_u^2 = \hat{\sigma}_u^2 + K\sigma_u^2$$

where K is given by:

$$K = (0, \rho_{uS} \cdot \sigma_S, \rho_{uS2} \cdot \sigma_{S2}, \rho_{uM} \cdot \sigma_M) N(V'V)^{-1} (0, \rho_{uS} \cdot \sigma_S, \rho_{uS2} \cdot \sigma_{S2}, \rho_{uM} \cdot \sigma_M)'$$

It follows that the whole bias vector, b, and σ_u are perfectly known, once the correlation coefficients ρ_{uS}, ρ_{uS2} and ρ_{uM}, are known. As these coefficients are not known, the idea is to do a Monte-Carlo analysis of the bias they imply by drawing them from uniform distributions over an arbitrary range. Of course, these drawings cannot be independent, since they must satisfy that the matrix Σ is positive definite.[134] The resulting conditions imply in particular that the coefficient K above is less than unity. Thus we may write:

$$\sigma_u^2 = \frac{\hat{\sigma}_u^2}{1 - K}$$

This is of course what one expects. The true σ_u is larger than the OLS estimate, which has the property of minimizing the sum of squared residuals.

The preceding method essentially is sensitivity analysis. Practically, 300 drawings were made and the inequality of opportunities evaluated for each permissible drawing. Calculations reported in the next section involve the mean of all these values and extreme values as intervals of confidence.

Simulating the Effects of the Inequality of Opportunities on Earnings

The preceding models provide a simple way of measuring the effect of the inequality of observed opportunities upon the inequality of current earnings. To see how this may be done, the two basic equations (1) and (3) above are first rewritten with all circumstance and effort variables now being made explicit:

$$Ln(w_i) = \alpha_0 + R_i\alpha_R + GR_i.\alpha_G + MPE_i.\alpha_P + DPE_i.\alpha_D + FO_i.\alpha_F + S_i.\beta_S$$
$$+ S2_i.\beta_{S2} + M_i.\beta_M + u_i \tag{8}$$

$$E_i = a_0 + R_i a_R + GR_i.a_G + MPE_i.a_P + DPE_i.a_D + FO_i.a_F + v_i \tag{9}$$

where E is the vector $\{S, S2, M\}$ and R, GR, MPE, DPE and FO stand respectively for the race dummies, the regional dummies, mean parental schooling, the mother/father difference in schooling, and father occupation, whereas S is the number of years of schooling of the surveyed individual, $S2$ is the squared number of years of schooling and M his/her migrant status. α_R, α_G, a_R, and a_G are vectors of coefficients whereas other parameters are scalars.

An appealing way of measuring the role of inequality of opportunities in generating earnings inequality consists of evaluating what would be the distribution of earnings with the preceding system of equations if all the inequality due to the circumstance variables had been eliminated.

---

134. Analitically, coefficients ρ_{uS}, ρ_{uS2} and ρ_{uM} are drawn in three uniform distributions and drawings that do not satisfy the condition that Σ I positive definite are simply discarded. ρ_{uS2} will be directly estimated from ρ_{uS}, since $\rho_{s2u} = \frac{2.\bar{S}.\rho_{Su}}{\sigma_{S2}/\sigma_S} + \varepsilon$, where ε will also be drawn from a uniform distribution. In particular, we have imposed that own schooling, parental schooling and migration must not have a negative effect on wages.

Thus one may simply equalize all the circumstance variables across all the population and then, use (8) and (9) to figure out what the distribution of earnings would then be. Comparing with the actual distribution permits then evaluating the role of opportunities. Yet, a decision must still be taken with respect to the two residual terms u_i and v_i. If they are both interpreted as pure circumstance variables, inequality with respect to the effort variables should be considered as pure inequality of opportunities. Thus, equalizing opportunities would be equivalent to equalizing earnings. On the contrary, if the two residual terms were taken to reflect pure efforts, they must be retained when evaluating the inequality of opportunities.

There clearly is something arbitrary in deciding that the residual terms reflect inequality of opportunities or inequality of efforts, or some combination of both. Because of this ambiguity, measuring the "total" contribution of the inequality of opportunities to observed inequality might simply be impossible or totally arbitrary. Only the inequality of observed opportunities may actually be evaluated. This is done in what follows through three different types of simulations:

(i) Equalizing all circumstance variables, as well as the effort variables schooling and migration. The residual v_i of the effort equations is then considered to be full circumstance, but u_i as pure efforts.
(ii) Equalizing all circumstance variables in (8) and (9). Schooling and migration are now considered partially as circumstances. In other words, both u_i and v_i are taken to be efforts.
(iii) Equalizing all circumstance variables with schooling and migration considered as pure efforts. Thus, equations (9) are in (8) ignored and u_i taken as pure effort.

Comparing with the actual distribution of earnings, (i) is equivalent to considering that all earnings determinants are circumstances; (ii) assumes that schooling and migration are only partly circumstances; (iii) postulates that there are no circumstances behind the effort variables. In all cases the residual ui term is taken as pure effort. It is in that sense that evaluation of what follows refers to "observed" opportunities. It must also be clear that the preceding scenarios are mostly aimed at fixing some 'bounds' for the role of this specific set of opportunities in shaping the actual distribution of earnings.

Results are shown in Figures 7.1a–b and 7.2a–b. Figure 7.1a presents the contribution of inequality of opportunity to the total inequality of male earnings under the preceding scenarios using the Gini inequality measure. The top line represents observed total inequality for the various cohorts. Mean Ginis (as well as the minimum and maximum) resulting from the permissible Monte-Carlo simulations are then provided for the three scenarios above. When schooling and migration are considered pure efforts, the Gini coefficient drops by around 5 percentage points on average. When schooling and migration are considered partially circumstances, the Gini drops by around 10 points. When they are considered fully circumstances, the fall is of 12–15 points. Interpreting the scenarios as providing bounds, it can thus be said that the inequality of observed opportunities represents *at least* 5 percentage points of the actual Gini, but most probably around 10 points as in the intermediate case and 12–15 if one is ready to accept that there is no effort nor chance in observed schooling. Of course, it could be more if other opportunity variables were observed (income and wealth of parents, land ownership, . . .). Figure 1b gives the results using the Theil inequality measure, instead of the Gini. The Theil measure is more sensible to the upper tail of the distribution. Equalizing circumstance variables then implies larger drops of total inequality (around 25–30 point). Results for women (see figures 2a and 2b) show larger inequality drops. Dotted curves associated with the 3 scenarios correspond to the extreme values generated by the Monte-Carlo experiment described above. It may be seen that the eventuality of a bias due to endogeneity of effort variables does not modify radically the conclusions derived from observing mean estimates, although estimated intervals of confidence are slightly higher for women.

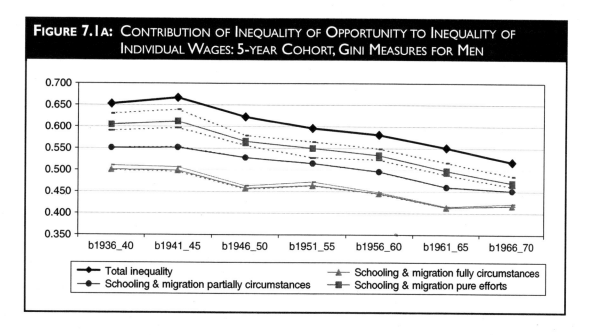

FIGURE 7.1A: CONTRIBUTION OF INEQUALITY OF OPPORTUNITY TO INEQUALITY OF INDIVIDUAL WAGES: 5-YEAR COHORT, GINI MEASURES FOR MEN

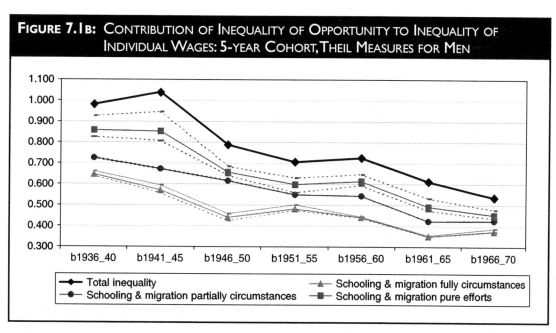

FIGURE 7.1B: CONTRIBUTION OF INEQUALITY OF OPPORTUNITY TO INEQUALITY OF INDIVIDUAL WAGES: 5-YEAR COHORT, THEIL MEASURES FOR MEN

What do we conclude from these experiments? Essentially that, even after discounting for inequality of observed opportunities, inequality in Brazilian earnings remains extremely high, that is, with a Gini of around 0.40 and a Theil of 0.35 in the most extreme of all scenarios. Two interpretations are possible. First, observed circumstance variables (parents' education, father's occupation, region of origin, race) actually are a limited part of actual circumstance variables. Presumably, parents' income and wealth could explain much more of actual inequality. This is an empirical issue which could be solved only by observing more circumstance variables or by getting an estimate of what those particular variables observed in Brazil actually represent with respect to other variables as observed in other countries. Unfortunately, we could not come up with the right

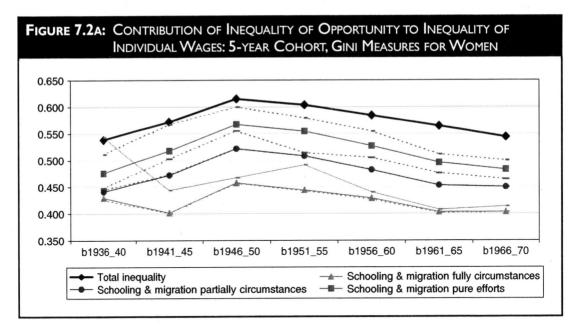

FIGURE 7.2A: CONTRIBUTION OF INEQUALITY OF OPPORTUNITY TO INEQUALITY OF INDIVIDUAL WAGES: 5-YEAR COHORT, GINI MEASURES FOR WOMEN

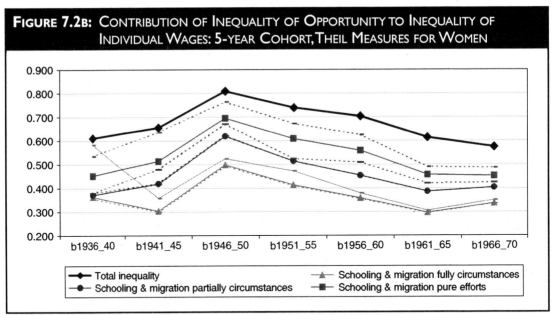

FIGURE 7.2B: CONTRIBUTION OF INEQUALITY OF OPPORTUNITY TO INEQUALITY OF INDIVIDUAL WAGES: 5-YEAR COHORT, THEIL MEASURES FOR WOMEN

comparison Brazil needs, that is, a country where a wider set of circumstance variables would be available, that would include the variables observed in Brazil. The second interpretation would be that non-opportunity related earning inequality in Brazil is very high, and presumably higher than in other countries, because of structural circumstances in the labor market, which remain to be identified. Another important conclusion is that the proportion of inequality due to observed opportunities in actual inequality seems rather stable over cohorts, that is over time, whether we look at Ginis or at Theils. Unfortunately, this conclusion may not be fully consistent with the two explanations given above.

We have also analyzed isolated effect of each particular observed circumstance variable, for the intermediate case where schooling and migration are considered partially circumstances.

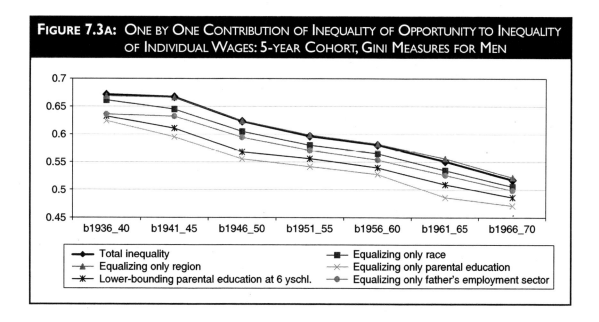

FIGURE 7.3A: ONE BY ONE CONTRIBUTION OF INEQUALITY OF OPPORTUNITY TO INEQUALITY OF INDIVIDUAL WAGES: 5-YEAR COHORT, GINI MEASURES FOR MEN

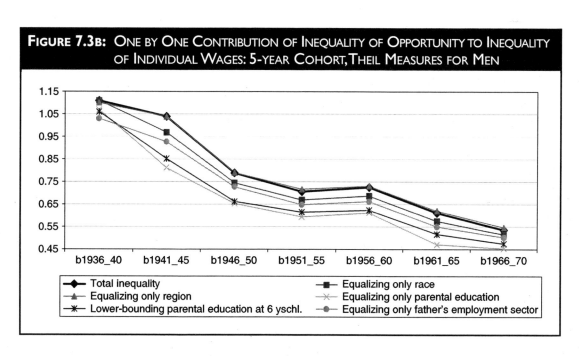

FIGURE 7.3B: ONE BY ONE CONTRIBUTION OF INEQUALITY OF OPPORTUNITY TO INEQUALITY OF INDIVIDUAL WAGES: 5-YEAR COHORT, THEIL MEASURES FOR MEN

Results with Gini and Theil measures are shown in Figures 7.3a–b for men and 7.4a–b for women. Of all circumstance variables, parental education is the one that plays the most important role in determining inequality. In this respect, it may be underlined that results are not very different when parents' schooling is not equalized as above but a lower bound is imposed as if schooling were compulsory until a certain age. In other words, it is the inequality of education at bottom of the distribution that really matters. Interestingly enough, race alone seems to account for very little, when parental occupation and education are already controlled for. These results suggest that the most efficient policies for reducing inequality of opportunities in Brazil are those that may weaken the role of parents' education in own schooling and earnings.

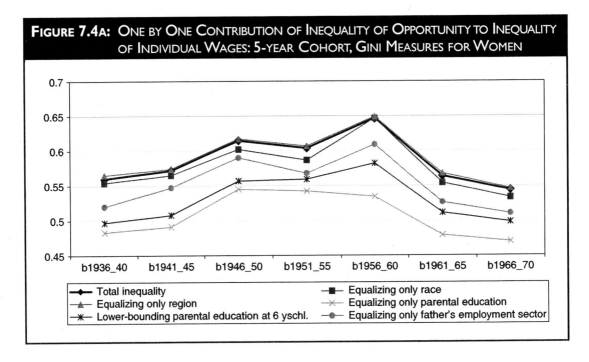

FIGURE 7.4A: ONE BY ONE CONTRIBUTION OF INEQUALITY OF OPPORTUNITY TO INEQUALITY OF INDIVIDUAL WAGES: 5-YEAR COHORT, GINI MEASURES FOR WOMEN

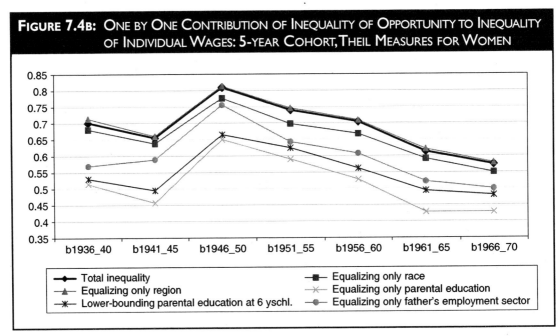

FIGURE 7.4B: ONE BY ONE CONTRIBUTION OF INEQUALITY OF OPPORTUNITY TO INEQUALITY OF INDIVIDUAL WAGES: 5-YEAR COHORT, THEIL MEASURES FOR WOMEN

The Effects of the Inequality of Opportunities on the Distribution of Household Income

The previous analysis refers to earnings and active individuals. The same type of analysis may also be conducted with exactly the same logic on households. The idea is then to measure the effect of the inequality of opportunities faced in the past by household heads and spouses on today's distribution of welfare within the whole population. The welfare measure used in this section is the monetary household income per capita and the current distribution of welfare is estimated by weighing all households by their size. Thus, the distribution of welfare is defined over all living individuals. With this new definition, the inequality of opportunities faced by the parents now passes not only through their earnings as before, but also through participation behavior, fertility, non-labor income, and, of course, the matching of individuals within couples.

In an effort to capture these effects the previous earning model was re-estimated using household per capita income (hpcy) as the main left-hand side variable. In effect, three models were estimated. In all cases, income per capita in household is given by the identity:

$$Y_i = \frac{y_{hi} + y_{si} + y_{0i}}{n_i} \tag{10}$$

where y_j stands for earnings of member j (=h for household head, s for spouse), y_0 is non-labor income and n is the number of persons in the household.

In the first model, household per capita income in household i is specified as a function of the characteristics of both the head (h) and the spouse (s):

$$\log(Y_i) = C_{hi}\beta_h + C_{si}\beta_s + E_{hi}\gamma_h + E_{si}\gamma_s + \varepsilon_i \tag{i}$$

As before, effort variables, E are taken to be functions of circumstances, C:

$$E_{ji} = C_{ji}\alpha_j + v_i \text{ with } j = h, s \tag{11}$$

In the second model, individual earnings for each main earner in the same household—head and spouse—are specified separately as a function of the same variables as in model (I).

$$\log(y_{ji}) = C_{hi}\beta'_h + C_{si}\beta'_s + E_{hi}\gamma'_h + E_{si}\gamma'_s + \varepsilon'_i \tag{ii}$$

In simulations, household income per capita Y_i is then computed using identity (0) with family size n being taken as exogenous.

In the third model, the family size itself is being made endogenous. It is specified according to the multi-logit model:

$$\Pr\{n_i = k\} = \frac{e^{Z_i\lambda_k}}{\sum_m e^{Z_i\lambda_m}}. \tag{12}$$

with $Z_i = \{C_{hi}, C_{si}, E_{hi}, E_{si}\}$ and k = $\{2, 3, \ldots, 7 \text{ and more}\}$. Then household income Y_i is simulated considering changes in both earnings and family size.

Based on these models, the effect of equalizing circumstances of household heads and spouses on household income per capita may be simulated in various ways. Comparing these ways permit identifying the role of circumstances on the following determinants of household income: individual earnings, participation and fertility.

Consider the three following simulations:

i. $y_i^* := y_i^I$

ii. $y_i^{**} := (y_{mi}^{II} + y_{fi}^{II} + y_{0i}) / n_i$

iii. $y_i^{**} := (y_{mi}^{II} + y_{fi}^{II} + y_{0i}) / n_i^{III}$

where the left-hand side variable is household income per capita simulated by equalizing circumstance variables according to model (I), y^*, (II), y^{**}, or model (III), that is (II) and (12), y^{***}. y^* is simulated household per capita income obtained from equalizing circumstances simultaneously in all possible household income determinants. In other words, model (I) is a reduced form where the role of circumstances of both household heads and spouses in fertility, non-labor income, participation and the earnings of participants is simultaneously taken into account. y^{**} is obtained from equalizing circumstances only insofar as the earnings of participants is concerned. In other words, participation behavior, fertility and non-labor income are maintained constant. Comparing the distribution of y^* and y^{**} thus indicates the role of circumstances in the determinants of household income per capita other than individual earnings. Comparing y^{***} and y^{**} clearly permits identifying the role of circumstances in household income per capita inequality that goes through fertility.

Tables 7.6a–c present the simulations for the household per capita income models, considering schooling and migration respectively as fully circumstances (Table 7.6a), partially circumstances (Table 7.6b), and pure efforts (Table 7.6c). In all these tables, cohorts are defined by the age of the household head.

The drop of inequality that can be attributed to the inequality of observed opportunities is roughly of the same order of magnitude for household income as for individual earnings. In terms of the Gini coefficient, inequality falls by some 14 to 18 percentage points when circumstances are equalized and both schooling and the migration status of the household heads and spouses are taken as fully circumstances. As before the remaining inequality is still high by international standards, amounting to a Gini coefficient around .44. What is more interesting is that the comparison between the y^* and y^{**} simulation suggests that *it is not only through the earnings of labor-force participants* that the inequality of observed opportunities affect the inequality of current welfare levels but also through the other determinants of household income—that is, non-labor income, participation, fertility, and matching. Thus concluding from the similarity of overall effects that the inequality of opportunities plays the same role among individual earnings and individual welfare levels would seem erroneous. To be sure, comparing the first two rows in Tables 7.6a–c to the fifth and sixth row, show that equalizing the role of observed circumstances in individual earnings would have an effect on the overall inequality of household income per capita that amounts to 7/13 percentage points of the Gini, that is roughly 5 points below the effect obtained with all household income determinants.

The second interesting result is the important role played by fertility. Comparing the third and fourth blocks of Table 7.6a shows that the role of the observed inequality of opportunities that goes through fertility behavior may account for 3/5 percentage points of the Gini in actual household income per capita inequality. It must be noted, however, that this effect is purely mechanical in the sense that the induced effects of fertility on labor-force participation is not taken into account. Thus, the fertility effect shown in Table 7.6a may probably be considered as a lower bound for the role of inequality of opportunities that goes through family size and simultaneously participation decision. The overall effect of fertility would be bigger if this induced effect were accounted for. However, one can see by comparing the fourth and the second block in Table 7.6a that not so much is really to be gained in including these additional effects. In effect, the inequality of opportunities that goes through participation and non-labor income is extremely limited, except for the two older cohorts.

The comparison between Tables 7.6a and 7.6c shows that circumstances remain an important determinant of current inequality, even in the case where schooling and migration are considered as partially or completely as the result of individual efforts. The drop in the Gini coefficient coming from equalizing opportunities is around 10 percentage points when all household income determinants are taken into account. in Table 7.6c. Another interesting finding is that circumstances affect fertility directly rather than indirectly throught the schooling variable. In Table 7.6c where the equalizing of circumstances has no effect on schooling, their differential

TABLE 7.6A: CONTRIBUTION OF INEQUALITY OF OPPORTUNITY TO INEQUALITY OF FAMILY PER CAPITA INCOME: 5-YEAR COHORT. SCHOOLING AND MIGRATION AS FULLY CIRCUMSTANCES

		b1936_40	b1941_45	b1946_50	b1951_55	b1956_60	b1961_65	b1966_70
Total inequality	Gini	0.62	0.626	0.614	0.613	0.618	0.616	0.591
	Theil	0.803	0.805	0.75	0.779	0.767	0.753	0.684
Joint earnings, non-labor income, fertility & participation effects	Gini	0.428	0.451	0.445	0.451	0.444	0.439	0.438
	Theil	0.329	0.388	0.37	0.394	0.381	0.365	0.353
Earnings effects (non-labor income, participation & fertility kept constant)	Gini	0.507	0.504	0.489	0.48	0.48	0.475	0.469
	Theil	0.484	0.472	0.454	0.449	0.459	0.431	0.409
Joint earnings & fertility effects (non-labor income & participation kept constant)	Gini	0.487	0.478	0.457	0.445	0.442	0.433	0.427
	Theil	0.432	0.41	0.389	0.37	0.378	0.357	0.343

TABLE 7.6B: CONTRIBUTION OF INEQUALITY OF OPPORTUNITY TO INEQUALITY OF FAMILY PER CAPITA INCOME: 5-YEAR COHORT. SCHOOLING AND MIGRATION AS PARTIALLY CIRCUMSTANCES

		b1936_40	b1941_45	b1946_50	b1951_55	b1956_60	b1961_65	b1966_70
Total inequality	Gini	0.62	0.626	0.614	0.613	0.618	0.616	0.591
	Theil	0.803	0.805	0.75	0.779	0.767	0.753	0.684
Earnings, non-labor income, fertility & participation effects	Gini	0.479	0.508	0.499	0.505	0.501	0.491	0.49
	Theil	0.44	0.511	0.489	0.499	0.489	0.459	0.455
Earnings effects (non-labor income, participation & fertility kept constant)	Gini	0.54	0.542	0.522	0.518	0.52	0.514	0.508
	Theil	0.572	0.561	0.526	0.52	0.534	0.507	0.487
Earnings & fertility effects (non-labor income & participation kept constant)	Gini	0.532	0.524	0.497	0.483	0.48	0.469	0.462
	Theil	0.549	0.514	0.463	0.431	0.442	0.422	0.403

TABLE 7.6c: CONTRIBUTION OF INEQUALITY OF OPPORTUNITY TO INEQUALITY OF FAMILY PER CAPITA INCOME: 5-YEAR COHORT. SCHOOLING AND MIGRATION AS PURE EFFORTS.

		b1936_40	b1941_45	b1946_50	b1951_55	b1956_60	b1961_65	b1966_70
Total inequality	Gini	0.62	0.626	0.614	0.613	0.618	0.616	0.591
	Theil	0.803	0.805	0.75	0.779	0.767	0.753	0.684
Earnings, non-labor income fertility & participation effects	Gini	0.507	0.516	0.507	0.525	0.518	0.51	0.501
	Theil	0.513	0.511	0.497	0.561	0.537	0.503	0.478
Earnings effects (non-labor income, participation & fertility kept constant)	Gini	0.592	0.583	0.56	0.567	0.564	0.561	0.537
	Theil	0.726	0.655	0.601	0.638	0.627	0.607	0.544
Earnings & fertility effects (non-labor income & participation kept constant)	Gini	0.603	0.58	0.549	0.536	0.528	0.518	0.486
	Theil	0.75	0.645	0.572	0.537	0.543	0.514	0.446

effect on fertility remains as high as in Table 7.6a where schooling is equalized at the same time as all circumstances. The same remark can be done for the role of opportunities' inequality that goes through individual earnings. It is certainly less important than when schooling is taken as pure or partial circumstance but it still amounts to approximately 5 points in the Gini coefficient. The same conclusion holds with the *direct* role of circumstances on the inequality of household income due to labor-force participation, non-labor income and matching.

In summary, the picture one gets from considering the role of observed opportunities on household income rather than individual earnings inequality is quantitatively comparable but qualitatively very different. In particular, it seems to be the case that the proportion of the inequality of opportunities of household heads and spouses that is transmitted to actual household income per capita through individual earnings is important, but not exclusive More seems to go through other channels, fertility in particular, but also labor force participation, non-labor income, matching and particularly, fertility. For all these additional channels, the evidence reported in this section suggest that circumstances play an important direct role in transmitting inequalities, even though the indirect effect through schooling is far from negligible.

Summary and Conclusion

In this paper, we tried to quantify the role of the inequality in observed opportunities of individuals—as summarized by their race, their region of origin, the education and the occupation of their parents—in generating inequality in current earnings or household income per capita in Brazil. There may be some biases in the econometric technique being used, essentially due to the lack of adequate instruments for correcting for the endogeneity of some income determinants. Yet, a simple sensitivity analysis reveals some strong conclusions.

Altogether, the inequality of opportunities that go through parents' schooling may be responsible for a very substantial proportion of total inequality in Brazil. Parents' schooling and/or own schooling are jointly responsible for 12 percentage points in the Gini coefficient of individual earnings, on average across cohorts and genders. This percentage is higher for older cohorts and for women. Out of this, 60 to 80 per cent may be attributed to parents' schooling alone. The same conclusion applies, although for other reasons, to household income per capita. In particular, it turns out that the role of the inequality of observed opportunities in shaping the distribution of household income per capita is not only through the individual earnings of household heads or spouses but also through other channels : fertility in particular, and to a lesser extent, labor force participation, non-labor income and matching behavior.

Even though the role of the inequality of observed opportunities in shaping the inequality of current earnings or income is a major one, what they leave unexplained remains very substantial. In effect, correcting for observed disparities in opportunities would leave the Gini coefficient of individual earnings or household income per capita certainly above .42. To the extent that no strictly comparable figure is available in other countries, it may be difficult to see the bearing of such conclusion. Yet, one thing is sure. Even after correcting for the inequality of opportunities, Brazil would still be high in an international ranking of inequality. In particular, it would necessarily be above all the countries with a Gini coefficient for actual incomes at .42 or below. On that basis, it is tempting to conclude that the inequality of observed opportunities may not be enough to explain the excessive inequality observed in Brazil in comparison with other countries in the world.

Parents' education was shown to be the major source of inequality of opportunities in Brazil. It affects earnings either directly or indirectly through own schooling. The exercise undertaken in this paper suggests that the latter effect represents at least 60 per cent of the overall effect of parents' schooling. Eliminating the influence of parents' schooling on the schooling of their children could have reduced the Gini coefficient of individual earnings by at least 3 percentage points on average across past cohorts and gender. Ignoring possible general equilibrium effects, this would clearly leave inequality in Brazil at a very high level.

Successive cohorts faced different situations in terms of inequality of opportunities. Intergenerational educational mobility has increased over time, especially at the bottom of the distribution. Equivalently, the education of the parents became a less powerful predictor of the education of their children. For the moment, this evolution does not reflect itself completely in the evolution of earning inequality across cohorts. This is because the rate of return to schooling and therefore the inequality of earnings is strongly age dependent. Yet, it is to be expected that because of that evolution earnings inequality along the life cycle will be smaller for younger cohorts. This point has to be checked by comparing different cohorts at the same age and at different points of time, which requires using additional data.

References

Bowles, S. 1972. "Schooling and inequality from generation to generation." *Journal of Political Economy* 80(3):S219–S51.

Burkhauser R., D. Holtz-Eakin, and S. Rhody. 1998. "Mobility and Inequality in the 1980s: A Cross-National Comparison of the United States and Germany." In S. Jenkins, A. Kapteyn, and B. M. S van Praag, eds., *The distribution of welfare and household production: International perspectives.* Cambridge University Press.

Checchi, D., A. Ichino, and A. Rustichini. 1999. "More Equal but Less Mobile? Education Financing and Intergenerational Mobility in Italy and in the US." *Journal of Public Economics* 74(3):351–93.

Ferreira, F. 2000. "Education for the masses? The interaction between wealth, educational and political inequalities." PUC. Processed.

Ferreira, F.H.G., and R. Paes de Barros. 1999. "The Slippery Slope: Explaining the Increase in Extreme Poverty in Urban Brazil, 1976–1996." *Brazilian Review of Econometrics* 19(2):211–296.

Goux, D., and E. Maurin. 2001. "La Mobilité Sociale et son évolution: le rôle des anticipations réexaminé." *Annales d'Economie et de Statistique* 62(forthcoming).

Griliches, Z., and W. Mason. 1972. "Education, Income and Ability." *Journal of Political Economy* 80(3):S74–S103.

J. R. Behrman, N. Birdsall, and M. Szekely. 2000. "Intergenerational mobility in Latin America : deeper markets and better schools make the difference." In Birdsall, N. and C. Graham, eds., *New Markets, New Opportunities.* Washington, D.C.: Brookings.

Lam, D. 1999. "Generating extreme inequality: schooling, earnings, and intergenerational transmission of human capital in South Africa and Brazil." Population Studies Center, University of Michigan, Report 99–439.

Roemer, J. E. 1998. *Equality of Opportunity.* Cambridge, MA: Harvard University Press.

CHAPTER 8

INDIRECT TAXATION REFORM: SEARCHING FOR DALTON-IMPROVEMENTS IN BRAZIL

By Carlos EduardoVélez, Salvador Werneck Vianna,
Fernando Gaiger Silveira, and Luís Carlos Magalães[*]

Abstract

Should Brazil reform indirect taxation? The considerable magnitude of the burden of Brazilian indirect taxation (three times that of direct taxation), its dominant regressive effect on after-tax-income inequality, and the heterogeneity of tax rates across goods and services justify the consideration of indirect tax reform. This paper determines the set indirect tax changes that can improve Brazilian's welfare. It uses the "Dalton-Improving Tax Reforms" (DITAR) criterion proposed by Yitzhaki and Slemrod (1991), Mayshar and Yitzhaki (1995), Yitzhaki and Lewis (1996). Dalton Improving Tax Reform simulations for Brazil reveal considerable room for improvement to move indirect taxation towards less regressivity and lower efficiency cost. Out of 21 potential pairs of tax changes, 13 are found to be DITAR. One of the two "best" tax reforms (vehicles and personal expenses) concentrates the benefits on the lowest quartile, while the other (housing and personal expenses) spreads the benefits more evenly across all income groups. This suggests that a tax reform trio (raising taxes for housing and vehicles, and lowering them for personal expenses) would dominate any other tax reform combination.

JEL classification code: D31, D63, H22, H23, H24
Keywords: Iindirect taxation, inequality, tax reform.

*. C. E. Vélez from World Bank and S.W. Vianna, F. G. Silveira and L.C. Magalhães from IPEA, Brazil. Special acknowledgement to Schlomo Yitzhaki (Hebrew University) and Rosane Siqueira (FGV-Brazil) for valuable comments. We thank the helpful comments from participants in the seminar "*A Desigualdade no Brasil: Dimensoes, Peculiaridades e Politicas Publicas*" in Rio de Janeiro (August 2001). Valuable research assistantship was provided by Taizo Takeno and Juanita Riaño.

Introduction

Should Brazil reform indirect taxation? There is relative consensus about the necessity of reforming, or at least revising indirect taxation in Brazil. Well known arguments for such consensus are on one hand, the lost of competitiveness of national firms due to extremely high and inefficient taxation, and, on the other hand, federative issues, such as the "fiscal competition" among Brazilian states, coming from specific legal matters of taxation in sub-national levels. This paper shows that there is a third important reason: reducing significant consumption-efficiency costs and moderating the regressive effects that characterize the current Brazilian tax system.

The tax burden in Brazil has risen significantly along the 1990s, mainly because of the creation of cumulative indirect taxation; mostly at the federal level. The Constitution of 1988 had delegated to states and local administrations great autonomy on several issues, including fiscal issues.[136] In addition to rising state shares in federal tax revenues—Income Tax and federal VAT (IPI, tax on industrial products, therefore called Federal VAT). They were allowed to set their own tax policy. Their most important tax instrument became the state VAT (ICMS, tax on goods and services, therefore State VAT). Although the state VAT existed before 1988, its tax base was more restricted, excluding services, and tax rates were determined at the federal level.

During the last decade, Brazil had to increase tax revenue vigorously in order to reduce the fiscal deficit associated to economic stagnation and hyperinflation. Simultaneously, with the weakening of Federal Government revenue sources produced by fiscal decentralization during the 1990s, Brazil was facing a severe macroeconomic crisis. The most accepted explanation was the persistent public sector deficit, which was associated to the national development process carried out since the 1950s, mostly through considerable public investments and incentives. Hence, the correction of public sector imbalance, specially at the federal level required two steps: imposing heavy controls on public expenditures, and raising public revenues. Therefore, new taxes were created in order to increase public revenues and in most cases the preferred taxes were those which could generate great revenues with the lowest administrative costs.

Efficiency and equity concerns were not the guiding principles for public administrators; because their most immediate goal was to raise public revenues promptly. Year after year, since the beginning of the 1990's, and in fact until today, new changes have been introduced into the national tax system, sometimes altering the rules of Income Tax (for households and firms) sometimes raising the rates of payroll taxes and contributions, other times just introducing new taxes, such as CPMF (tax on financial transactions). The common feature of this process was the following: the legal changes of the tax system always aimed to increase (federal) public revenues.

This paper shows that Brazilians could improve their welfare with a Dalton improving reform of indirect taxation. The best tax reform should combine a *reduction of taxes* on personal expenses while *raising* them for private vehicles and housing. Moreover, the potential gains from such tax reform are significant when compared to the total tax burden.

This paper is organized as follows. The next section characterizes Brazilian tax structure, its composition and magnitude with respect to the economy. The second section presents the incidence of taxation on the distribution of secondary income of the population: first, total incidence of direct and indirect taxation on income distribution; second, it presents the separate redistributive effect of direct and indirect taxation; and third, it presents redistributive effects of indirect taxation decomposed by types of goods and services. The bias of decomposition is evaluated by re-ranking households in the after tax income distribution. The third section presents the methodology and the fourth section pre-identifies the best candidates for reducing and raising taxes according to efficiency and equity considerations. The fifth section simulates the DITAR

---

136. The vigorous decentralization movement present in the Constitution of 88 has been interpreted as a natural reaction to more than 20 years of strong power concentration in the federal government, during 1964–1985 military dictatorship period in Brazil. For more details of the discussions of tax reform in that context see Werneck Vianna (2000) and Varsano (1996).

TABLE 8.1: TAX BURDEN IN BRAZIL, 1996–2000 AS PERCENT OF GDP AND OF TOTAL REVENUES (TR), BY ITS MAIN TAXES AND CONTRIBUTIONS

Taxes and Contributions	1996		1997		1998		1999		2000	
	% to GDP	% to TR	% to GDP	% to TR	% to GDP	% to TR	% to GDP	% to TR	% to GDP	% to TR
Indirect (a)	12,3	42,2	11,7	39,4	11,1	37,5	13,0	40,7	13,6	41,7
St.VAT	7,3	24,9	6,9	23,2	6,7	22,5	7,1	22,3	7,6	23,2
Fd.VAT	1,9	6,6	1,9	6,3	1,7	5,8	1,7	5,2	1,6	4,9
PIS[1]	0,9	3,1	0,8	2,8	0,8	2,6	1,0	3,1	0,9	2,7
Cofins[1]	2,2	7,6	2,1	7,1	1,9	6,6	3,2	10,1	3,5	10,9
Direct (b)	10,0	34,3	9,8	33,0	10,6	35,5	10,8	33,8	10,4	31,7
Income tax	4,0	13,6	3,8	12,7	4,5	15,1	4,7	14,8	4,4	13,5
Pensions	5,2	17,8	5,1	17,2	5,1	17,2	5,1	16,0	5,0	15,2
IPTU[2]	0,4	1,5	0,4	1,4	0,5	1,6	0,5	1,5	0,5	1,5
IPVA[3]	0,4	1,4	0,5	1,7	0,5	1,6	0,5	1,5	0,5	1,5
Subtotal (a+b)	22,3	76,5	21,5	72,4	21,7	73,0	23,8	74,5	24,0	73,4
Other taxes[4]	6,8	23,5	8,1	27,6	7,9	27,0	7,8	25,5	8,6	26,6
Total	29,1	100,0	29,6	100,0	29,6	100,0	31,6	100,0	32,6	100,0

Notes: 1. Contributions to social funds. Cofins specifically finances Social Security.
2. Tax on urban area property; local level.
3. Tax on vehicles property; state level.
4. Constituted mostly by indirect taxes.

Source: Araújo (2001), and Varsano et al. (1998).

reforms, explores the properties of the DITAR set, and ranks them according to first and second dominance criteria.

Taxation in Brazil: Recent Evolution, Trends and Issues
Increasing Burden of Indirect Taxation in the 1990s
In the 2000 year, national tax burden reached its historical record, almost 33 percent of GDP.[137] Two macroeconomic programs were successful in rising tax collection in Brazil. The first one was the Tax Reform of 1967. It was implemented in the initial years of military dictatorship period (which started in 1964 and lasted 21 years) and conceived in the context of radical transformations of the economy as a whole. This tax reform raised dramatically tax collection after no more than three years of implemented: the country's tax burden jumped from 20.5 percent of GDP in 1967 to 26 percent in 1970, when it stabilized until the beginning of the 1990s (Araújo 2001, Varsano et al. 1998).

The second one was the Real Plan implemented in 1994, which produced considerate expansion of the tax burden by nearly 3.5 percentage points of GDP. Economic stabilization provided by the Real Plan along with the intensification of tax collection on good and services raised total tax revenue almost 30 percent of GDP in that year, from 26 in 1993 and 25 percent in 1992, respectively. Since 1994, total tax burden has been nearly 30 percent of GDP, until 1999, when it reached 31.6 percent, to hit a year after, the historical record mentioned above of 32.6 percent.

Most of the raise of tax revenues in the 1990s was produced by indirect taxation. Table 8.1 shows that in last two years there was a persistent growth of indirect taxation *vis-à-vis* direct

---

137. According to our calculations using the IBGE's national accounts (still a preliminary result).

TABLE 8.2: TAX BURDEN IN BRAZIL, 1996–2000 AS PERCENTAGE OF TOTAL REVENUES, BY LEVELS OF GOVERNMENT

Taxes	1996	1997	1998	1999	2000
Federal level					
Federal VAT	6,6	6,3	5,8	5,2	4,9
PIS	3,1	2,8	2,6	3,1	2,7
Cofins	7,6	7,1	6,6	10,1	10,9
Income tax	13,6	12,7	15,1	14,8	13,5
Pensions	17,8	17,2	17,2	16,0	15,2
IOF[1]	1,3	1,5	1,3	1,6	1,9
Import Tax	1,8	2,0	2,4	2,6	2,4
CPMF[2]		2,7	3,0	2,6	4,1
CSLL[3]	2,7	2,8	2,4	2,2	2,4
Subtotal	**54,5**	**55,1**	**56,4**	**58,2**	**58,0**
State level					
State VAT	24,9	23,2	22,5	22,3	23,2
IPVA	1,4	1,7	1,6	1,5	1,5
Subtotal	**26,3**	**24,9**	**24,1**	**23,8**	**24,7**
Local level					
IPTU	1,5	1,4	1,6	1,5	1,5
ISS[4]	1,9	1,9	2,0	1,8	1,8
Subtotal	**3,4**	**3,3**	**3,6**	**3,3**	**3,3**
Other taxes	15,8	16,7	15,9	14,7	14,0

Notes: 1. Tax on Finance Operations. 2. Tax on Finance Transactions. 3. Social Contribution on net profits. 4. Tax on services of any nature.

Source: Araújo (2001) and Varsano *et al.* (1998).

taxation; in fact, almost the whole increase of tax burden in this period was due to that. The main explanation for this, is the implementation in 1998 of a higher tax rate for Cofins (3 percent), which finances Social Security. Created in the Constitution of 1988, its initial rate was 0.5 percent. Then, in 1990 it was increased to 2 percent, until 1998, when the raise of public revenues became imperative for the government to face the effects of the Russian crisis. Regardless its apparent low tax rate, Cofins is a cumulative tax, with its incidence occurring at all stages of production chain. Hence, its final effective rate can get much higher, depending on the product. That is why it represented last year 3.5 percent of GDP and almost 11 percent of total public revenues.[138]

Federal Government Tax Collection is Predominant, and It Has Been Increasing in Recent Years

Table 8.2 shows that in recent years the federal share in total tax revenue increased *pari passu* with reductions in the share of state and local governments. From 1996 to 2000, federal tax collection as share of the total tax collection, increased 3.5 percentage points. This rise is explained almost entirely for the rise in *Cofins* tax collection, 3.3 percentage points. Since its creation, collection of

---

138. Cofins is an example of the *modus operandi* of the government for tax policy, in which financial objectives matter the most while distortions and inequality issues remain ignored. (According to calculations of Araújo (2001), nearly 20% of total tax revenue comes from cumulative taxation).

TABLE 8.3: INDIRECT TAXATION IN BRAZIL, RATES AND REVENUES, 1999

	Magnitude (R $ bill)	Share	Tax Rates
Goods and services			
Vehicles	3.5	16%	18%
Leisure	1.8	8%	30%
Transportation	2.7	12%	17%
Clothing	2.7	12%	26%
Housing	1.2	5%	4%
Personal expenses	0.9	4%	33%
Medication	1.2	5%	22%
Food	6.3	28%	18%
Tobacco	1.8	8%	88%

Source: Araújo (2001) and Varsano *et al.* (1998) Income Expenditure Service 1996, Authors' Calculations.

the tax on financial transactions (CPMF) has rapidly increased, 1.4 percentage points during three years. It is worth noticing that during this period, revenues of the federal VAT declined almost two percentage points. At the state level, tax collection decreased almost 2 percentage points during the same period. Local tax collection remained almost unchanged.

Tax Competition Across States Ignores Constitutional Mandates and Produces Tax Heterogeneity Across States

According to the Constitution, Brazilian states could only change their VAT rates throughout unanimous decisions at a special forum created exclusively with this purpose.[139] In practice, this Council has lost its original function and, specially in recent years, states have been competing among themselves using this tax to attract new firms and investments, in a process known as "fiscal war." Effective rates of state VAT may differ from its nominal rates because of several kind of tax benefits and pure exceptions for specific goods.

There are about 30 different taxes and contributions and some of them are not considered in the tax reform simulations of this paper because of the difficulties in calculating its impact over households. Such is the case of import taxes and local level Tax on Services. For the first one the problem is that Income-Expenditure Survey does not report about purchases of import goods, except for cars, and for the second one, the problem is the vast number of rules applied in each city.

Indirect Taxes are Quite Heterogeneous Across Goods Due to Accumulation of Taxes at Different Levels of Government

In Brazil, indirect taxation rates are quite heterogeneous. As Table 8.3 shows, indirect tax rates by types of goods diverge from 88 percent for tobacco to 4 percent for housing. After tobacco, personal expenses are the items most heavily taxed (33 percent), followed by leisure activities (30 percent), clothing (26 percent), as well as medication and health expenses (22 percent). Among goods and services with lower tax rates are vehicles (18 percent), food items (18 percent), and transportation services (17 percent). In terms of tax revenues, taxation of food items provides the biggest contribution to total tax revenues (28 percent), followed by vehicles (16 percent),

---

139. The National Council of Finance Policy (CONFAZ), which is constituted by all state finance secretaries, plus the Ministry of Finance.

transportation (12 percent), and clothing (12 percent). On the contrary, taxation of personal expenses produces the smaller contribution to tax revenues (4 percent), followed by medications and health expenses (5 percent), housing (5 percent), leisure activities (8 percent) and tobacco (8 percent).

Issues of Taxation in Brazil: Tax Competition Among States, International Competitiveness, Equity, and Efficiency

As mentioned before, the main aspects that have been regarded in Brazilian tax reform debate rest on two concerns: the lost of international competitiveness of Brazilian firms, which results from high and inefficient taxation, and federative issues, such as the fiscal competition among states. However, up to now, issues of equity and consumption efficiency at national level have had not the required attention for a more efficient tax policy.

Some recent studies examine distributive incidence of taxation in Brazil, all of them using IBGE's Income-Expenditure Survey of 1995–96. Magalhães etal. (2001a and 2001b) are pure empirical studies which present estimations of indirect taxation on food products and medications, respectively. The results obtained point to a high regressivity of this kind of taxation, and to a promising social range to tax policies that give exemptions or subsidies to products which have great importance in the expenditures of low income households. Barbosa (2001), applying an Almost Ideal Demand System (estimated by Asano and Fiuza, 2001), to a Ramsey model of optimal indirect taxation.

What is the Impact of Taxation on the Distribution of Secondary Income?

Total Taxation has a Regressive Impact on the Poor and It is Directly Associated to Indirect Taxation

Figure 8.1 presents tax incidence as percentage of household income. Although income taxation has a moderate progressive effect on income distribution, its effect is quite modest as compared

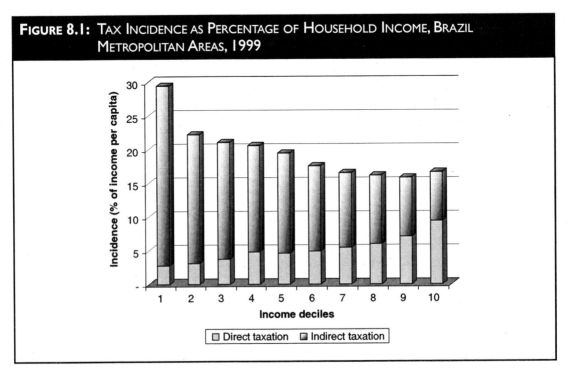

FIGURE 8.1: TAX INCIDENCE AS PERCENTAGE OF HOUSEHOLD INCOME, BRAZIL METROPOLITAN AREAS, 1999

Source: Werneck Vianna et al. (2001).

with the regressive effect of indirect taxation. Thus, the regressive incidence of indirect taxation though small, dominates the progressive impact of direct taxation making total taxation regressive. While individuals in the lowest decile spend 30 percent of their income in taxes, individuals in the top decile, spend 17 percent. As Figure 8.1 shows, the regressive impact of indirect taxation is evident: in the lowest decile, the tax burden associated to direct taxation is 2.8 percent, while the tax burden associated to indirect taxation is 10 times larger (29 percent). In contrast, in the top decile, tax burden is almost equally distributed, 9 percent associated to direct taxation and 7 percent to indirect taxation.

Total Taxation Has a Moderate Regressive Effect on Income Distribution

Table 8.4 presents the redistributive impact of direct and direct taxation by components in Metropolitan areas of Brazil. The distributive effect of total taxation on income distribution in metropolitan areas in Brazil is equal to 0.7 percentage points of the Gini coefficient (or after re-ranking household by after tax income). Applying Kakwani's (1975, 1976, 1983 and 1986) additive decomposition, we found the redistributive impact of taxation in the following way:[140] Indirect taxation is regressive and it increases the Gini coefficient by 1.6 percentage points, while direct taxation is progressive and it reduces the Gini coefficient by 1 percentage point. Table 8.4 also shows tax collection by type of tax. While indirect taxation represents almost two thirds of total collection, direct taxation only represents one third.

Components of indirect taxation by levels of government are relatively similar in terms of regressiveness. ICMS, PIS and IPI have similar concentration coefficients and GIEs. The progressive effect of direct taxation is explained almost entirely by the Income Tax. Components of direct taxation are not homogeneous in their redistributive impact: income taxation represents two thirds of direct taxation and is very progressive, it has a concentration coefficient of 0.85; urban real state tax represents nearly 15 percent of direct taxation and is almost neutral and it has a concentration coefficient of 0.61; and state tax on private vehicle ownership is approximately 10 percent of direct tax revenue and it is also progressive with a concentration coefficient of 0.74.

From Table 8.4 it is obvious that the regressive impact of indirect taxation on income distribution dominates the progressive impact of direct taxation. This reflects the fact that indirect taxation falls more than proportionally on the income of the middle and low income households (i.e. the relative size of the concentration coefficients with respect to the Gini) and the larger magnitude of indirect taxation with respect to other sources of tax revenue.

Although Indirect Taxation Has a Regressive Impact on Income Distribution of Metropolitan Households of Brazil, Not All Indirect Taxes are Equally Regressive

Table 8.5 shows the decomposition of the distributive effect of indirect taxation by type of goods. Taxation of vehicles has the most progressive effect on income distribution, (concentration coefficient is 0.72). As one could imagine, taxation of tobacco, food items and medications have the most regressive impact, its concentration coefficients are 0.19, 0.31, and 033, respectively. Taxation of leisure activities has a neutral impact on income distribution (concentration coefficient 0.54). The remaining items displayed on Table 8.5 have regressive impact on income distribution: transportation (concentration coefficient 0.44), clothing (concentration coefficient 0.42), housing (concentration coefficient 0.40) and personal expenses (concentration coefficient 0.37).

---

140. Decompositions are based on pre-tax income household ordering. Moreover, they are not exact and are path dependent. However, redistributed bias due to income was found to be negligible, according to our calculations with the post-tax income distribution. See detailed explanation of the decomposition formulas in the appendix.

Table 8.4: Redistributive Impact of Direct and Indirect Taxation by Components Brazil, Metropolitan Areas, 1999

	Magnitude (R$bill)	Share	Concentration Coefficient	Targeting Share of Top 20%	Poorest 40%	Redistributive Effect Delta Gini % points	Relative Redistriutive Efficiency (*)
Indirect taxation	22.0	70%	0.417	50%	15.5%	1.6%	3.5
ICMS goods and services	14.3	45%	0.424	49%	16.7%	1.0%	3.4
PIS	3.4	11%	0.402	49%	16.3%	0.3%	3.8
IPI	4.4	14%	0.406	50%	15.8%	0.4%	3.8
Total indirect							
Direct taxation	9.5	30%	0.735	96%	0.2%	−1.0%	−4.8
Income tax	6.8	22%	0.853	67%	7.0%	−0.9%	−6.0
Urban real state tax	1.6	5%	0.608	80%	2.1%	0.0%	−0.7
State private vehicle tax	1.1	3%	0.735	89%	1.6%	−0.1%	−3.4
Total	**31.6**	**100%**	**0.798**	**62%**	**12%**	**0.7%**	**1**

Note: (*) Relative Redistributive Efficiency is equal to the ratio of the redistributive effect of each tax relative to its share on aggregate tax revenue. Positive is regressive and negative is progressive.

Source: Araújo (2001) and Varsano et al. (1998) Income Expenditure Service 1996, Authors' Calculations.

TABLE 8.5: DECOMPOSING THE DISTRIBUTIVE EFFECT OF INDIRECT TAXATION BY TYPE OF GOODS. BRAZIL METROPOLITAN AREAS, 1999

	Magnitude (R$bill)	Share	Concentration Coefficient	Targeting Share of Top 20%	Poorest 40%	Redistributive Effect Delta Gini % points	Relative Redistriutive Efficiency (*)
Goods and Services							
Vehicles	3.5	16%	0.719	87%	2%	-0.23%	-0.9
Leisure	1.8	8%	0.544	60%	8%	0.03%	0.2
Transportation	2.7	12%	0.440	51%	14%	0.17%	0.9
Clothing	2.7	12%	0.418	49%	15%	0.20%	1.0
Housing	1.2	5%	0.400	27%	29%	0.10%	1.1
Personal expenses	0.9	4%	0.367	44%	17%	0.09%	1.3
Medication	1.2	5%	0.331	41%	19%	0.13%	1.6
Food	6.3	28%	0.311	40%	21%	0.78%	1.7
Tobacco	1.8	8%	0.186	29%	26%	0.34%	2.5
Total	**22.0**	**100%**	**0.417**	**15%**	**51%**	**1.61%**	**1**

Note: (*) Relative Redistributive Efficiency is equal to the ratio of the redistributive effect of each tax relative to its share on aggregate tax revenue. Positive is regressive and negative is progressive.

Source: Araújo (2001) and Varsano et al. (1998) Income Expenditure Service 1996, Authors' Calculations.

Dalton Improving Tax Reforms: Analytical Framework

Dalton welfare improvements are weaker than Pareto improvements. While a Pareto improvement requires that welfare weakly improves for *all* individuals, Dalton Improvement allows for income of one individual to fall provided some poorer individual's income increases equally (that is, "the rich are less deserving than the poor"). In this section we present the analytical framework to identify Dalton Improving Tax Reforms (DITAR hereafter) following Yitzhaki and Slemrod (1991), Mayshar and Yitzhaki (1995), Yitzhaki and Lewis (1996) and Yitzhaki (2001).

Therefore, Dalton's welfare evaluation suppose a decreasing social marginal utility of income.[141] That is, if welfare function $W(.)$ is defined as function of individuals' welfare $Vh, h = 1, \ldots, H; W = W\{V1(q), \ldots, VH(q)\}$; and changes in welfare are given by

$$dW = \sum (h)\; \hat{a}h.\; MBh$$

where $\hat{a}h$ is the social marginal utility of income for individual h, and MBh is the marginal benefit (in income units) for individual h, then the marginal social benefits of income decreases with income level of each individual, i.e., $\hat{a}1 > \hat{a}2 > \hat{a}3 > \cdots > \hat{a}h > 0$.

Definition: A Revenue Neutral Tax Reform is a set of tax revenue changes for each type of good $\ddot{a}' = (\ddot{a}1, \ddot{a}2, \ldots, \ddot{a}n) - (\ddot{a}i > \text{or} < 0)$ – such that total change in revenue is zero

$$\sum (i)i = 0.$$

The impact of the RNTR on welfare is given by

$$dW(\ddot{a}) = \sum (h)\; \hat{a}h.\; MBh(\ddot{a}),$$

where $MBh(\ddot{a})$ is a function of behavioral parameters of the consumer and the characteristics of the prevailing tax system. Assuming individuals welfare is represented by the indirect utility function $Vh(p + t, y)$, by Roy's identity the marginal change in utility of the h individual, produced by *changing tax rate i by dti is equal to*

$$\partial Vh/\partial\, ti = -\, \partial xih\, .\; \partial Vh/\partial y$$

then for individual h all tax changes imply that the total marginal benefit in income units is

$$MBh = \sum (i = 1, \ldots, N)xih\; dti$$

Besides, it is identically true that the change in tax revenue for each tax is equal to marginal revenue times the tax rate change

$$\ddot{a}i = MRi.\; dti \text{ hence } dti = \ddot{a}i\, /\, MRi$$

then substituting and adding for all goods $(i = 1, \ldots, N)$ on the left hand side, and all individuals $(h = 1, \ldots, H)$ on the right hand side we obtain

$$\sum (h = 1, \ldots, H)MBh = -\sum (i = 1, \ldots, N)(Xi\, /\, MRi)\cdot \ddot{a}i$$

where Xi is equal to the aggregate consumption of good i.

---

141. Which is caused by concavity of the social welfare function and/or concavity of the utility function with respect to income.

Since Xi / MRi is equal to the Marginal Efficiency Cost of Public Funds $MECFi$, the welfare impact of tax reform can be rewritten as

$$\partial(h = 1, \ldots, H)MBh = \sum (i = 1, \ldots, N) \, (MECFi) \cdot \ddot{a}i$$

The intuition behind this expression is the following, in income units, the welfare impact of the tax changes on each good is larger than the direct impact of the tax reduction on Xi, $\ddot{a}i$, because $MECFi$ are larger or equal to unity. This follows from the fact that $Xi \geq MRi$ because $MRi \equiv Xi + ti \, . \, Xi/qi + \acute{O} \, in \, ji \, (tj. \, Xj/qi))$ and the difference between them grows with the efficiency cost of taxation which is directly dependent on the price effects on consumer's demand, Xi/qi and Xj/qi. In summary, the $MECFi = F(\tau', (\sigma', \{\varepsilon ji\})$ is a function of the tax rate vector, τ', the price elasticity vector-own and cross-, $\{\varepsilon ji\}$, and the expenditure shares of all goods, σ'. In particular, the $MECFi$ increases with the tax rate and with its own price elasticity. Obviously, the marginal benefits for each individual h is proportional to its share on consumption of each good (xih/Xi). That is, the marginal benefit for individual h is equal to

$$MBh = -\sum (i = 1, \ldots, N)(xih / Xi)(MECFi) \cdot \ddot{a}i$$

Linking the Dalton Improving Reform to Second Order Stochastic Dominance, Using Concentration Curves

Proposition: Second Order Stochastic Dominance of post-reform disposable income relative to pre-reform disposable income is a sufficient condition for a Dalton Improving Marginal Reform $\ddot{a}' = (\ddot{a}1, \ddot{a}2, \ldots, \ddot{a}n)$ where $\Sigma(i)\ddot{a}i = 0$.

Proof:
The Welfare effect of the reform is given by

$$dW(\ddot{a}) = \sum (k = 1, \ldots, H)\hat{a}h \, MBh(\ddot{a}) \tag{1}$$

Second Order Stochastic Dominance of post-reform disposable income relative to pre-reform disposable income implies that Cumulative Marginal Benefits $-CMB \, (\ddot{a}, h)$— produced by the reform are non-negative for every percentile $h = 1, \ldots, H$. That is,

$$CMB \, (\ddot{a}, h) = \sum (k = 1, \ldots, h) \, MBk \geq 0 \; for \; all \; h = 1, \ldots, H \tag{2}$$

Note that

$$MBk(\ddot{a}) = CMB(\ddot{a}, k) - CMB(\ddot{a}, k - 1)$$

Therefore, by substitution in (1) we obtain

$$dW(\ddot{a}) \, CMB(\ddot{a}, H) + (\hat{a}H - \hat{a}(H-1))^* \, CMB(\ddot{a}, H-1) + \cdots + (\hat{a}2 - \hat{a}1)^* \, CMB(\ddot{a}, 1)$$

and since the Dalton criterion implies

$$(\hat{a}k - \hat{a}(k - 1)) \geq 0$$

and from (2)

$$CMB(\ddot{a}, k) \geq 0 \; for \; all \; k$$

then welfare change is non-negative

$$dW(\ddot{a}) \geq 0$$

Definition: $CC(i, h)$ is the vertical coordinate of the concentration curve of good i at household h, therefore 1. $CC(i, h)$ is equal to the share of expenditure of good i of all household up to the hth. Therefore (2) can be rewritten as

$$CMB(\ddot{a},h) = \sum (i = 1, \ldots, n) \; [(MECF\, i)^*(-i)^* \; CC(i, h)] \geq 0 \; \textit{for all } h = 1, \ldots, H \qquad (3)$$

Algorithm and Characterization of the DATOR Solution

Basically the problem is to determine a vector of revenue neutral of tax changes $\ddot{a}^\circ = (\ddot{a}1, \ddot{a}2, \ldots, \ddot{a}n)$ that satisfy equation (3) for all percentiles of the distribution of income. Following Yitzhaki and Lewis (1996) we chose one commodity as the numeraire give it a value $\ddot{a}i = 1$ or $\ddot{a}i = -1$ percent of total indirect tax revenue. Satisfying equation (3) is equivalent to finding a tax reform vector that makes the following equal to zero

$$\mathop{\mathrm{Min}}_{\ddot{a}} \sum_k \{\mathrm{Max}\, [-CMB^k (\ddot{a}), \, 0]\}, \text{ subject to } \sum (i = 1, \ldots, n) \, \ddot{a}i = 0; \; \ddot{a}1 \neq 0^{142}$$

The numerical algorithm was programmed in Excel for 200 percentiles of the income distribution. And it was executed for all 21 potential pairs of tax reform. According to Yitzhaki and Lewis (1996) the whole set of infinite DATOR can be characterized by those extreme solutions.[143]

Identifying Potential Candidates for Raising and Reducing Taxes

The first step to understand condition (3) is to explore its graphical interpretation. That is, the easiest way to identify the existence of a DITAR for two goods is to plot the two concentration curves times their corresponding MECF. If their difference is positive for every percentile—or Second Order Stochastic Dominance holds—then, a DATOR exists for a reduction of the tax on the good corresponding to the curve *above*, and a tax increase for the good corresponding to the curve *below*.

This implies that the best candidates for tax reduction (increase) are for goods subject to larger price distortions (efficiency cost) and which tend to be consumed more than proportionally by lower income groups (and vice versa).

while luxury goods are indicated by larger Concentration coefficients. In other words, the best candidates for tax increase are those goods with lower coordinates of the concentration curves and lower marginal efficiency cost of funds. That implies, raising taxes for luxury goods or goods for which the rich have a large share of expenditure, and/or goods for which tax rates are lower, and/or their own price elasticities are smaller.

According to this criterion, the best candidates for tax reduction are on one hand, goods which exhibit large price distortions. In other words, goods that when taxed, have higher efficiency costs because of the associated distortions on individuals' behavior. Larger price distortions are indicated by larger Marginal Efficiency Cost of Funds (MECF), which are increasing on tax rates and Mashallian price elasticities of demand. That is larger MECF indicates higher efficiency costs. On the other hand, goods which account for important shares in poor individuals' baskets. In other words, goods that when taxed have higher costs in terms of equity. Concentration coefficients indicates the share poor individuals spend on certain good. Lower Concentration coefficients indicates higher shares and vice versa.

Therefore, from all goods displayed in Table 8.6, the best candidates on efficiency grounds for tax reduction because of the large price distortions associated to taxing its consumption (higher

---

142. As stated in Yitzhaki and Lewis (1996), p. 547.
143. All infinite solutions in the DATOR set are convex combinations of the extreme solutions.

TABLE 8.6: EQUITY AND EFFICIENCY OF INDIRECT TAXATION

| | Equity | | Efficiency | |
	Concentration Coefficient	Gini Income Elasticity	Tax Rates	MECF
Vehicle	0.719	1.25	18%	1.23
Leisure	0.544	0.94	30%	
Transportation	0.440	0.76	17%	1.19
Clothing	0.418	0.72	26%	1.33
Housing	0.400	0.69	4%	1.04
Pers. expenses	0.367	0.63	33%	1.51
Medications	0.331	0.57	22%	1.27
Food	0.311	0.54	18%	1.20
Tobacco	0.186	0.32	88%	1.75

Source: Income Expenditure Service 1996, Authors' calculations.

MECF) are tobacco[144] (MECF equal to 1.51), personal expenses (1.51), clothing (1.33), and medications (1.27). On the other hand, the best candidates on equity grounds for tax reduction because of the large share they represent on poor individuals' expenditure (lower Concentration coefficients) are, non-luxury goods such as food (Concentration coefficient equal to 0.31), medications (0.33), and personal expenses (0.37).

Analogously, from Table 8.6 it is shown that the best candidates on efficiency grounds for tax increase because of the small price distortions associated to taxing its consumption—lower MECF—are housing (MECF equal to 1.04), transportation (1.19), and food items (1.2). While on equity grounds the best candidates for tax increase because of the large share they represent on rich individuals' expenditure, are vehicles (Concentration coefficient equal to 0.72), leisure activities (0.54), transportation (0.44), and clothing (0.42).

By comparing the concentration curves of the burden of each tax we identify potential DATOR pairs. In order to check condition (3) we plot the burden of tax by income deciles (Figure 8.2) for food, personal expenses, medications, and vehicles. Goods with the higher tax burden are the candidates for tax reduction, while goods with the lowest tax burden are the candidates for tax increase. As Figure 8.2 shows expenditure on vehicles is highly concentrated on top income deciles. Conversely, personal expenses, food items and medications, represent an important share of lower income deciles. In other words, we can win on equity basis if we reduce taxes for personal expenses, food items or medications. Figure 8.2 also shows that whereas taxing vehicles generates the lower marginal burden per Real of tax, taxing personal expenses generates the higher tax burden. That is, we can win in efficiency basis if we increase taxes for vehicles. Joining efficiency and equity gains, we can see in Figure 8.2 that one DATOR is the reduction of taxes for personal expenses and the increase of taxes for vehicles. By visual inspection, we can see that reducing taxes for medications instead of reducing it for personal expenses would reduce the gains on efficiency grounds. That is because taxing medicines generates a lower marginal burden than taxing personal expenses, which means that reducing taxes for medicines has lower efficiency gains than reducing it for personal expenses.

---

144. Tobacco is an special case because of the health benefits obtained by reducing consumption of this addictive substance.

FIGURE 8.2: DISTRIBUTION OF MARGINAL BURDEN OF INDIRECT TAXATION ON SELECTED GROUP OF GOODS

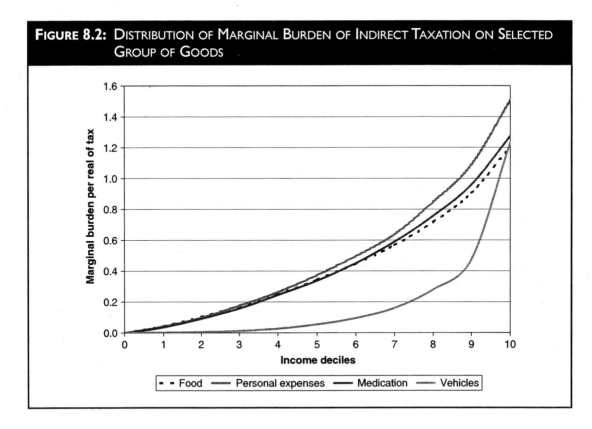

Sen Welfare Index Help for the Identification of Candidates for Tax Reform

Sen's welfare function might be a useful instruments to preidentify candidates for reform, because it provides the necessary conditions for stochastic dominance. Under a Sen (1973) welfare function $W = \mu (1 - G)$, where μ is mean after-tax income, and G is the Gini coefficient of after-tax income; a reform with two tax changes $\ddot{a}1$ and $\ddot{a}2$ will bring the following effects to total welfare.

$$dW(\ddot{a}) = -[\Delta\mu1(1-G\,\eta1)\,\ddot{a}1 + \Delta\mu2(1 - G\,\eta2))\ddot{a}1]$$
$$= MECF1(1 - C1)\,\ddot{a}1 + MECF2(1 - C2)\ddot{a}2$$

Because movements towards optimum taxation would require changes towards equalization of the marginal social burden of each tax, that is towards

$$MECFi(1 - Ci)\,\ddot{a}i = K \text{ for all good } i$$

Therefore, for a tax reform, the goods with higher burden should reduce their tax rates and (vice versa). In the graph below (Figure 8.3) we plot the equity Ci and efficiency cost $MECFi$ for each good. Each curve represents different combinations of tax efficiency and tax progressiveness that produce the same tax burden. Tax burden increases towards the origin. That is, from the three plotted curves in Figure 8.3, the blue curve represents the combinations of tax efficiency and tax progressiveness that produce the lower tax burden, while the red curve represents the combinations that produce the higher tax burden. The green curve plots combinations of efficiency and progressiveness that produce the average marginal tax burden.

Goods below the red line have the associated highest tax burden and thus, are the candidates for tax reduction, for example, food, medications, and personal expenses. Goods above the blue line (housing and vehicles) correspond to the opposite case, they have the lowest tax burden, and

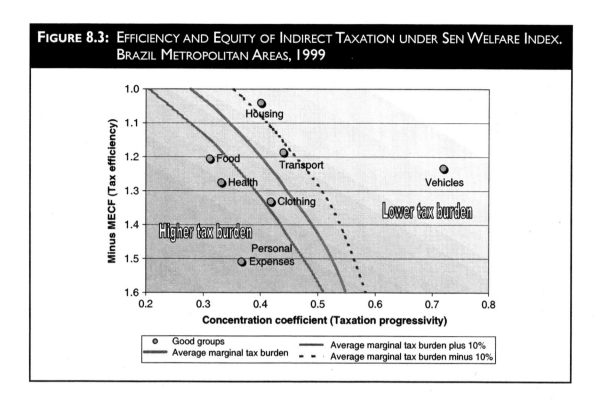

FIGURE 8.3: EFFICIENCY AND EQUITY OF INDIRECT TAXATION UNDER SEN WELFARE INDEX. BRAZIL METROPOLITAN AREAS, 1999

thus they are the candidates for tax increase. From Figure 8.3 we can see that one DATOR alternative is the reduction of taxes for personal expenses and a corresponding tax raise for vehicles. The reason is that personal expenses represent an important share in poor individuals' expenditure and its taxation is not very efficient; and vehicles because its taxation is progressive and it is highly efficient.

The Pairs of Tax Changes that Satisfy the Dalton Improvement Condition

The main questions of this section are the following: is there room for improvement? How large is the DATOR set? How dominant are the simulated reforms when compared to the status quo? Which taxes should be increased or reduced? How do tax reforms rank among themselves? Finally, how robust is the set of DATOR reforms to the variance of the parameter estimates of the demand system?

Our simulations of tax reforms as pairs of tax changes reveal abundant opportunities for improvement. Out of a total of 21 potential pairs of tax reform[145], 13 are Dalton Improvements (Second Order Dominant) relative to the status quo. Table 8.7 displays those reforms as "tax raise-tax reduction" pairs: housing-personal expenses, transport-personal expenses, vehicles-personal expenses, clothing-vehicles, housing-medication, clothing-housing, vehicle-medication, housing-food, clothing-personal expenses, transport-food, clothing-transport, personal expenses-medication and medication-transport.

Moreover, the amplitude of the room for improvement is confirmed by the fact that 6 of those 13 reforms are First Order Dominant relative to the *status quo*. That is, 100 percent of the households affected by those reforms are winners. The reforms are: housing-personal expenses, transport-personal expenses, housing-medication, clothing-housing, clothing-transport, and personal expenses-transport.

---

145. 21 is the total number of pair combinations of 7 taxes: Personal Expenses, housing, transport, vehicles, medication, food, and clothing.

TABLE 8.7: TAX RATES CHANGE AND WELFARE EFFECTS FOR ALTERNATIVE PAIRS OF DALTON IMPROVING INDIRECT TAX REFORMS, BRAZIL

Tax Reform Pair	Tax Rate Changes by Goods and Services							Efficiency Gain*		
	Food	Personal Expenses	Medication	Housing	Clothing	Transport	Vehicles	All	Bottom 50%	Winners*
Housing vs Personal expenses		−6.4%		0.6%				46%	14%	100%
Transport vs Personal expenses		−6.4%				1.2%		32%	13%	100%
Vehicles vs Personal expenses		−6.4%					1.1%	29%	32%	91%
Vehicles vs Clothing					−1.8%		1.1%	12%	24%	91%
Housing vs Medication			−3.5%	0.6%				23%	10%	100%
Housing vs Clothing				0.6%	−1.8%			29%	5%	100%
Vehicle vs Medication			−3.5%				1.1%	35%	34%	91%
Housing vs Food	−0.5%			0.6%				17%	11%	91%
Clothing vs Personal expenses		−6.4%			1.8%			18%	8%	91%
Transport vs Food	−0.5%					1.2%		2%	10%	81%
Transport vs Clothing					−1.8%	1.2%		14%	4%	100%
Medication vs Personal expenses		−6.4%	3.5%					23%	3%	100%
Transport vs Medication			−3.3%			1.1%		9%	9%	81%
Direction of tax change	D	D	D/U	U	U/D	U/D	U			
Initial conditions										
Tax rate	18%	33%	22%	4%	26%	17%	20%			
Tax revenue R$ (Billion)	6.3	0.9	1.2	1.2	2.7	2.7	3.5			

Note. D: Decrease in Tax rete from the initial level. U: Increase in tax rate from the initial level. U/D: Increase or decrease in the tax rate. Max change in revenue of any indirect tax was limited to 1% of total tax revenue. (*) 100% means the first order stochastic dominance relative to status quo.

*As percentage of the revenue swift (1% of total indirect tax revenue).

TABLE 8.8: WELFARE RANKING BETWEEN THE DALTON IMPROVING TAX REFORMS

	First Order Stochastic Dominance	Second Order Stochastic Dominance	Third Order Stochastic Dominance
Housing vs Personal expenses	5	1	2
Transport vs Personal expenses	3	3	3
Vehicles vs Personal expenses	1	4	0
Clothing vs Vehicles	0	1	1
Housing vs Medication	0	3	4
Clothing vs Housing	0	1	4
Vehicle vs Medication	0	1	0
Housing vs Food	0	2	2
Clothing vs Personal expenses	0	2	3
Transport vs Food	0	0	0
Clothing vs Transport	0	1	1
Personal expenses vs Medication	0	0	1
Medication vs Transport	0	0	0

Source: See Table 8A.2 in the appendix.

According to our simulations taxes should be *increased* for housing, vehicles and transport and reduced for personal expenses and food. The magnitude of those changes varies across goods: increased by 0.6 percent for housing, 1.1 percent for vehicles and 1.2 percent for transport, while it should be reduced by 6.4 percent for personal expenses and by 0.5 percent for food. The bigger increase is for transport (1.2 percent) while the bigger reduction is for personal expenses (6.4 percent). Tax changes for medication and clothing do not seem relevant because they increase for some reforms and decrease for others (Yitzhaki and Lewis 1996).

Table 8.8 presents the welfare ranking between the Dalton improving tax reforms. Best reforms are those that dominate—in welfare terms—a larger number of tax reform alternatives. Ranking tax reforms among themselves according to its first order dominance shows that the "best" is housing-personal expenses followed by transport-personal expenses, and vehicles-personal expenses. However, according to its second order dominance, of the thirteen reforms listed in Table 8.8, the most dominant is vehicles-personal expenses, followed closely by transport-personal expenses and housing medications, then by housing-food, clothing-personal expenses, and finally by housing-personal expenses, clothing-vehicles, clothing-housing, vehicles-medication, and clothing-transport. Under the third order dominance criterion, housing-medication and clothing-housing are the dominant, followed in first place by transport-personal expenses, and transport-food, in second place by housing-personal expenses, and housing-food, and in final place by clothing-vehicles, clothing-transport, and personal expenses-medication. As Table 8 shows, neither the transport-food reform nor the medication-transport reform presents any improvement on welfare under these criteria.

DATOR reforms can bring significant efficiency gains relative to the *status quo.* However, their rankings varies with the distribution of those gains. According to the gains for the *average* Brazilian household, the largest gains are for the tax reform involving housing and personal expenses (46 percent), followed closely by a second group of four reforms that includes vehicles-medication (35 percent), transport-personal expenses (32 percent), vehicles-personal expenses

(29 percent) and housing-clothing (29 percent).[146] The second group includes two reforms which gains are 23 percent: housing-medication and personal expenses-medication. The third group includes the following reforms: clothing-personal expenses (18 percent), housing-food (17 percent), clothing-transport (14 percent), and clothing-vehicles (12 percent). The group of reforms that presents the smaller gains for the *average* Brazilian household includes medication-transport (9 percent) and transport-food (2 percent).

However, according to efficiency gains for the poorest 50 percent priorities are different. Preferred tax reforms involves taxing vehicles in exchange for tax reductions of personal expenses, medication and clothing. The maximum benefits for the top 50 percent of the income distribution would be 32 percent of the revenue shift is produced by reducing taxes for Personal Expensed and raising them for housing. In summary, different a distributional perspective make a difference about the preferred good to tax more but not about the preferred good to tax *less*.

Robustness and Sensitivity Analysis

How robust are the reform simulations relative to errors in estimates of the MECF? In order to answer this question we rerun all simulations for DATOR condition after modifying the MECF in order to reduce the chances of satisfying the conditions given by equation (3). MECF were increased and reduced by 10 percent corresponding to expected increased or reduction in taxes in the previous simulations of the DATOR set.

The set of DATOR reforms shows clear robustness under those demanding conditions. The number of feasible DATOR was reduced to nearly half the size (7 instead of 13) and the persistent candidate for tax reduction is still the personal expenses group (see Table 8A.2 in the appendix). Moreover, the set of FOD tax reforms is still not empty (three instead of six options).

Conclusions

The considerable magnitude of the burden of Brazilian indirect taxation (three times that of direct taxation), its dominant regressive effect on regressive direct taxation and the heterogeneity of tax rates across goods and services, clearly justify considering the possibility of indirect tax reform in order to improve Brazilian's welfare.

This paper has identified the set of pair-wise indirect tax reforms that could improve their welfare, according to he Dalton improving criterion. The best indirect tax reform should combine *a reduction of taxes* on personal expenses while *raising* them for private vehicles and housing.

The potential gains from such tax reform are significant when compared to the total tax burden. Efficiency gains can reach as high as 46 percent *of the tax shift* for the average Brazilian and over 30 percent of the tax shift for othe poorest 50 percent. And those estimates are relatively robust. Sensitivity analysis relative to the estimates of the marginal efficiency cost of funds shows that results are persistent and the main conclusion hold.

Appendix
Measuring Incidence of Indirect Taxation[147]

A good example of the heterogeneity of the state VAT taxation across states is the case of food products, which differ on both the number of food items covered, as well as on tax rates. Some states have special tax treatment to groups of commodities defined as essentials so-called "basic food baskets." The "basic food basket" is defined at the state level. Table 8A.1 presents the data of all states related to their VAT taxation of these goods. The bigger basic food basket, in terms of number of items included, is the one defined in the state of Santa Catarina, which includes 44 food items, while the smallest (17 items) is defined in the state of Acre. The "mean" basket

---

146. The efficiency gain as a percentage of the revenue shift, 1 percent.
147. There have not been great difficulties estimating of direct taxation incidence, because in this study we are working just with the payments related by families in Income-Expenditure Survey.

comprises 26 items, and it is defined in the states of Ceará, Espírito Santo, Minas Gerais, and Mato Grosso do Sul. Table 8A.1 illustrates how, while nominal tax rates varies between 17 and 18 percent, with the exception of Espírito Santo (12 percent), effective tax rates varies between 7 and 20.5 percent. Sao Paulo and Rio Grande do Sul have the minimum tax rate, 7 percent, while states such as Acre, Paraíba, Rio Grande do Norte, Sergipe, and Goiás have the maximum tax rate, 20.5 percent.

Calculating the Effect of Taxation on Income Inequality (Gini Coefficient) by Kakwani's Method

$\Delta\, Gini = Gini\,(\{Y_i - T_i, i = 1, \ldots, n\}) - Gini\,(\{Y_i, i = 1, \ldots, n\})$

where

$\{Y_i, i = 1, \ldots, n\}$: income distribution

$\{Y_i - T_i, i = 1, \ldots, n\}$: after tax income distribution

and $T_i = \Sigma\,(j = 1, \ldots, k)\, T_{ij}$, where T_{ij} denotes the taxes paid by individual i on goods j.

$\Delta Gini = CC\,(\{Y_i - T_i, i = 1, \ldots, n\}) - Gini\,(\{Y_i, i = 1, \ldots, n\}) + Gini\,(\{Y_i - T_i, i = 1, \ldots, n\})$
$\quad - CC\,(\{Y_i - T_i, i = 1, \ldots, n\})$

$$\Delta Gini = CC\,(\{Y_i - T_i, i = 1, \ldots, n\}) - Gini\,(\{Y_i, i = 1, \ldots, n\}) + H \qquad (1)$$

where H is the change in inequality due to the re-ranking effect caused by taxation (which should be non-negative)

$$H = Gini\,(\{Y_i - T_i, i = 1, \ldots, n\}) - CC\,(\{Y_i - T_i, i = 1, \ldots, n\})$$

Kakwani showed that (1) can be re-written as an additive decomposition by different type of taxes $(j = 1, \ldots, k)$ as follows:

$$\Delta Gini = \sum\,(j = 1, \ldots, k)\, \Delta Gini(j) + H$$

where the impact of each tax is equal to

$$\Delta Gini\,(j) = -\,[\,CC(T_j) - Gini(Y)\,]\,\phi_j \cdot \theta/(1 - \theta) \qquad (2)$$

and ϕ_j is the share of tax j in total tax revenue and θ is the ratio of tax revenue to total household income –13 percent–. Equation (2) implies that any tax with a Concentration Coefficient smaller that the Gini of income (0.578) will produce a regressive effect, and viceversa. This condition is equivalent to the Gini income elasticity for tax j $GIE_j = CC(T_j)/ Gini(Y)$ being below (or above) unity. Which in terms of the Lorenz curve and the Concentration Curves means that taxes with concentration curves inside the Lorenz curve for income increase inequality and viceversa.

Applying equation (2) to the Brazilian data—tax revenue by tax type and incidence by tax type from the income expenditure survey—we obtain Table 8.4 and Table 8.5.

Table 8A.1: State Level VAT Incidence (Nominal and Effective) on Food Products of State Basic Food Baskets for All Brazilian States

Region/State	Nominal Tax Rate (%)	Food Products in the Basket	Tax Benefit or Credit	Modal Average Tax Burden (%)
NORTH				
Acre	17	17	no	20,5
Amazonas	Not available	Not available	Not available	Not available
Pará	17	30	yes	15,3
Rondônia	17	22	yes	13,6
Roraima	Not available	Not available	Not available	Not available
Tocantins	17	21	yes	10,4
NORTHEAST				
Alagoas	17	24	yes	15,3
Bahia	17	21	yes	7,5
Ceará	17	26	yes	15,3
Maranhão	17	27	yes	12,0
Paraíba	17	21	no	20,5
Pernambuco	17	29	yes	7,9
Piauí	Not available	Not available	Not available	Not available
Rio Grande do Norte	17	22 ·	no	20,5
Sergipe	17	24	no	20,5
SOUTHEAST				
Espírito Santo	12	26	yes	11,2
São Paulo	18	32	yes	7,0
Rio de Janeiro	18	25	yes	16,2
Minas Gerais	18	26	yes	11,2
SOUTH				
Paraná	17	42	yes	11,2
Rio Grande do Sul	17	32	yes	7,0
Santa Catarina	17	44	yes	11,2
CENTER-WEST				
Goiás	17	21	no	20,5
Mato Grosso	17	30	yes	15,3
Mato Grosso do Sul	17	26	yes	10,4
Distrito federal	17	34	yes	15,3

Source: Werneck Vianna *et al.* (2000).

TABLE 8A.2A: WELFARE RANKING OF ALTERNATIVE DALTON IMPROVING INDIRECT TAX REFORMS (PAIR OF TAXES)

	Housing vs Personal Expenses	Transport vs Personal Expenses	Vehicles vs Personal Expenses	Clothing vs Vehicles	Housing vs Medication	Clothing vs Housing
Housing vs Personal expenses			No		No	No
Transport vs Personal expenses			No	No	No	No
Vehicles vs Personal expenses	TOD	TOD		No	TOD	TOD
Clothing vs Vehicles		TOD	SOD		TOD	TOD
Housing vs Medication	FOD	FOD	No	No		TOD
Clothing vs Housing	SOD	SOD	No	No	No	
Vehicle vs Medication	TOD	TOD	FOD	TOD	TOD	
Housing vs Food						
Clothing vs Personal expenses	FOD	FOD	No	No	SOD	
Transport vs Food			SOD	SOD		TOD
Clothing vs Transport	FOD	SOD	SOD		SOD	No
Personal Expenses vs Medication	FOD	SOD	No		SOD	SOD
Medication and transport	FOD	FOD	SOD		SOD	

Policy reforms listed in columns dominate reforms of corresponding row.

Blank in upper diagonal means the pair of reform does not dominate a reform listed in a corresponding row.

Blank in lower diagonal means the pair of reform are not dominted by a reform listed in a corresponding column.

FOD : First Order Stochastic Dominance.

SOD : Second Order Stochastic Dominance.

TOD : Third Order Stochastic Dominance. (Small inequality aversion is sufficient condition for this result).

nd : Ranking was not determined.

TABLE 8A.2B: WELFARE RANKING OF ALTERNATIVE DALTON IMPROVING INDIRECT TAX REFORMS (PAIR OF TAXES)

	Vehicle vs Medication	Housing vs Food	Clothing vs Personal Expenses	Transport vs Food	Clothing vs Transport	Personal Expenses vs Medication	Medication vs Transport
Housing vs Personal expenses	No		No		No	No	No
Transport vs Personal expenses	No		No		No	No	No
Vehicles vs Personal expenses	No	TOD	TOD	No	No	TOD	No
Clothing vs Vehicles	No		TOD	No	No	No	No
Housing vs Medication	No		No		No	No	
Clothing vs Housing				No	TOD	No	
Vehicle vs Medication	No	TOD	TOD	No	No		No
Housing vs Food	No				No		No
Clothing vs Personal expenses					No		
Transport vs Food	SOD	SOD	SOD				
Clothing vs Transport	No						No
Personal Expenses vs Medication							
Medication and Transport	No	SOD	SOD		SOD		No

Policy reforms listed in columns dominate reforms of corresponding row.
Blank in upper diagonal means the pair of reform does not dominate a reform listed in a corresponding row.
Blank in lower diagonal means the pair of reform are not dominted by a reform listed in a corresponding column.
FOD : First Order Stochastic Dominance.
SOD : Second Order Stochastic Dominance.
TOD :Third Order Stochastic Dominance. (Small inequality aversion is sufficient condition for this result).
nd : Ranking was not determined.

References

Ahmad, E. and N. Stern. 1984. "The Theory of Reform and Indian Indirect Taxes." *Journal of Public Economics* 25(3):259–98.

Castro, P. F., and L. C. Magalhães. 1998. "Recebimento e dispêndio das famílias brasileiras: evidências recentes da pesquisa de orçamentos familiares (POF) – 1995/1996." IPEA, Texto para Discussão Interna, n° 614, Brasília.

Creedy, J. 1997. *Are Consumption Taxes Regressives?* WP 20/97, Melbourne Institute Working Paper Series, University of Melbourne, Melbourne.

Dalton, Hugh. 1949. "The Measurement of the Inequality of Income." In *The Inequality of Income.* 1920. Reprint. London: Routledge & Kegan Paul, Ltd.

Decoster, A., Schokkaert, E., and G. Van Camp. 1997. "Is redistribution through indirect taxes equitable?" *European Economic Review* 41.

Feenberg, D., A.W. Mitrusi, and J.M. Poterba. 1997. *Distributional effects of adopting a national retail sales tax.* NBER working paper No. W5885.

Feldstein, Martin. 1972. "Distributional Equity and the Optimal Structure of Public Spending." *American Economic Review* 62(1):32–36.

Hoffmann, R. 1998. *Distribuição de Renda: medidas de desigualdade e pobreza.* São Paulo, Editora da Universidade de São Paulo.

IBGE. 1998. *Pesquisa de Orçamentos Familiares 1995/96.* Rio de Janeiro, IBGE. Mídia digital.

IBGE. 1999. *Pesquisa de Orçamentos Familiares 1995/96.* Rio de Janeiro: IBGE/Departamento de Índices de Preços, v.1. Despesas, recebimentos e características das famílias, domicílios, pessoas e locais de compra.

Kakwani, Nanak C. 1975. "Applications of Lorenz curves in economic analysis". Washington, D.C.: International Bank for Reconstruction and Development.

———. 1977. "Applications of Lorenz Curve in Economic Analysis." *Econometrica* 45(3):719–27.

———. 1983. "Redistribution effects of income tax and cash benefits in Australia." Centre for Applied Economic Research. Kensington, NSW: University of New South Wales. Processed.

———. 1986. *Analyzing redistribution policies: a study using Australian data.* New York: Cambridge University Press.

Lambert, Peter, and Shlomo Yitzhaki. 1995. "Equity, Equality and Welfare." *European Economic Review* 39:674–82.

Lerman, Robert, and Shlomo Yitzhaki. 1994. "The Effect of Marginal Changes in Income Sources on U.S. Income Inequality." *Public Finance Quarterly* 22(4):403–17.

Newbery, D. and N. Stern, eds. 1987. *The theory of taxation for developing countries.* Oxford: Oxford University Press.

Mayshar, Joram, and Shlomo Yitzhaki. 1995. "Dalton-Improving Indirect Tax Reforms." *American Economic Review* 84(4):793–808.

———. 1996. "Dalton-Improving Tax Reforms When Households Differ in Ability and Needs." *Journal of Public Economics.*

Petti, R. H. V. 1993. *ICMS e agricultura: da reforma tributária de 1965/67 à sistemática atual,* Itaguaí, Rio de Janeiro, Dissertação (Mestrado em Planejamento e Políticas de Desenvolvimento Agrícola e Rural na América Latina e Caribe)—Instituto de Ciência Humanas e Sociais—Universidade Federal Rural do Rio de Janeiro.

Rezende, F. 1991. O peso dos impostos no custo da alimentação: análise do problema e propostas de redução, Rio de Janeiro. Processed.

Rodrigues, J. J. 1998. *Carga tributária sobre os salários.* Texto para Discussão n° 1. Brasília—Secretaria da Receita Federal: Coordenação Geral de Estudos Econômico e Tributário.

Siqueira, R.B., J.R. Nogueira, and E.S. Souza. 1998. *Uma análise da incidência final dos impostos indiretos no Brasil.* Departamento de Economia, Universidade de Pernambuco, Recife. Processed.

———. 1999. *Imposto sobre consumo no Brasil: a questão da regressividade reconsiderada,* Departamento de Economia, Universidade de Pernambuco, Recife.

Stern, N. 1987. "Aspect of the Grneral Theory of Tax Reform." In D. Newbery and N. Stern, eds., *The theory of taxation for developing countries.* Oxford: Oxford University Press and World Bank.

Yitzhaki, Shlomo, and Joel Slemrod. 1991. "Welfare Dominance: An Application to Commodity Taxation." *American Economic Review* 81(3):480–9.

Souza, M. C. S. 1996. "Tributação indireta no Brasil: eficiência versus eqüidade." *Revista Brasileira de Economia,* vol.50(1):3–20.

Vianna, S. T. W. 2000. *Tributação sobre renda e consumo das famílias no Brasil: avaliação de sua incidência nas grandes regiões urbanas—1996.* Rio de Janeiro, Dissertação (Mestrado em Economia). Instituto de Economia, Universidade Federal do Rio de Janeiro.

CHAPTER 9

SCHOOLING EXPANSION IN DEMOGRAPHIC TRANSITION: A TRANSIENT OPPORTUNITY FOR INEQUALITY REDUCTION IN BRAZIL

By Carlos Eduardo Velez, Marcelo Medeiros, and Sergei Soares[*]

Abstract

This paper explores the connection between Brazil's schooling inequity and deficiency and demographic transition. The most general versions of the Kuznets curve hipothesis highlight the role of supply side factors (demographic transition and the expansion of education) in redistributing assets and modifying the relative prices of skills, with clear effects on income inequality and growth. The dynamics of this process might be perverse, and unless education opportunities are vigorously equalized, developing economies might converge high inequality equilibria (Kremmer et al. 2002 and Lam 1999). This paper tries to understand how demographic transition in Brazil modifies the time lag required to extend to the whole labor force the educational improvements enjoyed by younger cohorts (the stock-to-cohort time lag). More formally, we want to answer how time correlation between educational efforts and demographic transition affects long term inequality. This paper simulates what would have happened if the educational expansion of the 1990s had occurred one decade earlier—before the demographic transition started. Results show that in the long run taking advantage of this window of opportunity to expand education reduced the stock-to-cohort time lag from 25 to 20 years, and long term inequalities of schooling and labor income. However, in the short run schooling inequality overshoots temporarily, induced by rising between inequality. Another lesson is that, even very strong improvements above the current trend of schooling attainment, take more than two decades to show-up as higher educational endowments for the whole working age population. That is, by taking demographic inertia into account, policy makers conviction about education should be reinforced with patience and the will to monitor educational policy outcomes with a clear long term perspective.

JEL classification: D3, I0, I2, O2.
Keywords: Education: Inequality, Policy evaluation, Kuznets Curve.

Introduction

How long will improvements in schooling of younger cohorts take to change the distribution of educational endowments of the total labor force and, in turn, change the distribution of labor income in Brazil? When rates of return to schooling are significant, as they are in Brazil, the size and distribution of educational endowments determines to a large extent the distribution of labor income. However, improvements in the educational attainment of younger cohorts do not translate immediately into proportional improvements for all cohorts of the economy. Demographics might play an important role in that process.

This paper attempts to develop a demographic model linking the educational profiles of successive cohorts of individuals entering the labor force with the level and inequality of educational endowments of the whole labor force. We ask how the demographic transition might affect the impact of cohort educational profiles on the level and inequality of educational endowments of the entire labor force. For example, an aggressive education policy to improve high school completion should result in large differences between the educational profiles of younger versus older population cohorts in the labor force, with obvious effects on the distribution of the educational stock. However, the size and speed of that effect will depend on the pace of demographic transition in Brazil. Presumably, if demographic transition has not been completed and the fertility rates remain high, the effect will be larger and faster.

The profile of population growth for Brazil will show how large those effects will be, and how long it will take to observe them. Moreover, it will show whether Brazil's position in the demographic transition provides an opportunity (or makes it more difficult) to reduce the inequality, or improve the level, of the educational stock of the labor force. Hopefully this model could be a device to show how much time is required to recover the full social benefits of sustained investments in education. That is, to understand the links and the lags between current policy actions and future outcomes. In other words, it would enhance the value of current policies in terms of the equity improvements for present and future generations.

Considered within the Latin American context, Brazilian educational outcomes are lacking and the allocation of resources towards education is low. From the outcome side, educational attainment is too low and the differentials in access to education are significant both across regions, and income groups. From the allocation of resources side, public expenditure in Brazil is too biased towards public pension subsidies, while the share of education is small. These characteristics of the educational system of Brazil become particularly worrying given the fact that Brazil has one of the highest levels of income inequality in the world and it is clearly linked to inequality of education. Bourguignon, Ferreira, and Leite (2002) show that nearly 30% of excessive inequality relative to the US is explained by educational inequities.

The original version of Kuznets Curve hypothesis emphasized the role of demand-side forces to shape the relation between income inequality and economic development. Basically, the dynamics interaction of technological change and the induced demand for capital skills where supposed to explain why inequality first rise and the fell with development. A more general version adds the role of supply side determinants, namely arguing the impact of demographic transition forces could flood the market with young unskilled workers reducing the rise of inequality. Hence the age-earning curve would be flatten once those fat cohorts reach the pick earning age.[148]

---

148. The analysis of adverse supply effect on the relative wages of the baby-boom cohort in the United States is presented in Easterlin 1980; Freeman 1979; Welch, 1979; Lam, 1997; Murphy and Welch, 1992; and Murphy and Katz, 1992.

Demographics is particularly relevant for developing countries because as Higgins and Williams (1999) show, the demographic transition in these countries "has generated much more dramatic changes in relative cohort size than did the baby-boom in OECD countries." Evidence from Higgins and Williams provides support for a link between cohort size aggregate inequality. The estimated quantitative impact is considerable: a one standard deviation increase in the fraction of population in peak earnings would increase in the fraction of population in peak earnings would lower a country's Gini coefficient by 6.5.[149]

However, decomposition exercises show that the demographic transition has two opposite effects on inequality. The first effect which increases inequality, is the change in the composition of the labor force and while the second one, the change in the age-earning profile, reduces inequality.

A more sophisticated perspective by Kremmer and Chen (2002) shows that on its own course, the dynamics of education inequality could lead to a perverse cycle of increasing inequality in a country such as Brazil. Nevertheless, according to their model the timely enhancement of educational opportunities for the poor is critical to avoid this outcome, and position the economy on path leading to a steady state with a more balanced distribution of skilled and un-skilled workers. Empirical evidence, by Kremer and Chen (2002), suggests that the fertility differentials between educated and uneducated parents is stronger in more unequal countries (like Brazil).[150] If children of uneducated parents are less likely to become educated, the fertility differential will induce an increasing proportion of unskilled workers in the next generation. Which in turn tend to depress their wages and increase their chances of having more children and so on.[151] Based on a dynamic markovian framework of fertility and education inequality across generations, Kremer and Chen (2002) show depending on the initial conditions the economy might converge to high or low inequality scenarios. "If the initial proportion of skilled workers is too low, inequality will be self reinforcing and the economy may approach a steady state with a low proportion of skilled workers and greater inequality between the skilled and unskilled."

These findings have the most important implications for the timing and efficiency of educational policy. According to their estimates, in middle income economies like Brazil a temporary increase in schooling opportunities for the children of the poor that raise the share of skilled workers above a certain critical value, would induce a virtuous dynamics of education equalization across generations. The key question then is, could the window of opportunity for this policy intervention been expiring? As time passes, have Brazil reached the point in which for producing the desired outcome the required effort is too large? Moreover, given the fact that lower fertility rates reduces the demographic weigh of younger cohorts, is the leverage of current educational policies to modify the distribution of the whole labor force still available?

Kremer et al. (2002) show that any effort to reduce the unit cost of taking the children of the poor to reach high educational attainment has the same consequences. Hence a whole range of policy instruments can produce the desired effect: from improvements in nutrition and childcare to the incentives to reduce unit cost and improve quality in the allocation of public educational funds. Moreover, they also show that if fertility is endogenous to skill wage differentials temporary policy interventions can have even larger multiplier effects.

This paper is organized as follows, the next section describes the demographic background of Brazil, the second section presents the methodology and data used in this paper, the third section depicts the evolution of education between cohorts, the fourth section defines the stock-to-cohort lag of educational attainment, the fifth section shows the results of the simulations, and finally, the sixth section presents the conclusions.

---

149. Over time the relation is becoming weaker: stronger in the 1970s and 1980s but non existent in the 1990s.

150. Most Latin American countries show very high fertility differentials. Well above the predicted level conditional on ine-quality. Those error terms are the highest in the case of Colombia in the 1990s.

151. Assuming the substitution effect dominates the income effect.

Demographic Background

According to the 2000 Census, the Brazilian population amounts to 170 million people, most of which live in the coastal urban area. Spatial differences are strong. Brazil is divided by geographers into five regions: South, Southeast, Center-West, North, and Northeast. The first two are the most developed and rich, the last one is the poorest. Population density can be considered high in the metropolitan areas of all regions, medium in non-metropolitan areas of the Southern and Southeastern regions and low in rural areas of the Northern and Center-western regions.

As in other countries, the Brazilian demographic history of the last hundred years can be divided into three periods. The first ranges from the early 1900s to the late 1930s, when birth and death rates were high. However, as mortality balances birthrate, a good part of population growth was due to international immigration. The second period begins after the 1930, when international migration is reduced and the falling mortality together with high fertility became the main reason for rapid population growth. Rates were at their peak, around 2.9 percent per year, during the decades of 1950 and 1960. The third period begins at the late 1960s, with a rapid fall in fertility rates and, therefore, of the population growth. Mortality keeps falling during the period but its level is not enough to undo the effects of the reduction in fertility. Population growth rates are estimated at 1.3 percent in the late 1990s.

The story above happened in all Brazilian regions, but not at exactly the same time. Except for migration, the demographic patterns of all regions followed, with some delay, what happened in the Southeast. Furthermore, in the last decades the demographic patterns of all regions became much more homogeneous than before, although we can still identify clear differences among them.

During the 1990s infant mortality has fallen significantly, but not enough to compensate reduced fertility. As a result, during this decade younger cohorts are smaller than their predecessors. Although the pressures for the supply of schooling caused by total population growth are reduced, other factors of pressure such as short distance migration and the increase of school enrollment are still in effect.

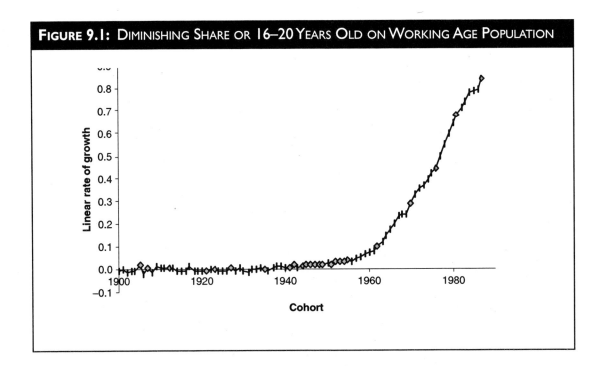

FIGURE 9.1: DIMINISHING SHARE OR 16–20 YEARS OLD ON WORKING AGE POPULATION

The net effect of the *demographic transition of Brazil* on the age composition of the labor force is shown on Figure 9.1 above. This Figure shows the composition of the whole working-age population every 10 years from 1950 to 2000, and provides some forecast for the period 2010 to 2040, namely all those between 16 and 70 years of age in any given calendar year, in terms of cohorts. It is clear, that the decreasing demographic weight of the youngest cohort of the labor force (16–20 year olds) that started in the 1980s. It is notable that for the labor force of 1970 the demographic share of the youngest cohorts peaks for the labor force borne in 1954 (4.2 percent) and then falls significantly for the labor force in 1990 and 2000. That is, for the cohorts born in 1974 and 1984 the demographic share fell to 3.5 and 3.2 percent respectively. Up to the year 2000 population, younger cohorts are always more numerous than older ones. From year 2010 onwards, the functions are no longer monotonously increasing and there is a point from which newer cohorts become less numerous.

Our thesis is that the strongest educational expansion should coincide with the peak of demographic "replacement"—when young workers have the largest population share. This window of opportunity for education should not be missed if there is a concern for closing the educational gap and reach more equitable access to education.

Methodology and Data

The methodology to be used in this paper will be the simplest possible capable of providing an answer to the questions on the interplay between the educational level and inequality of each cohort and the educational level and inequality of the population as a whole in a given calendar year. Let:

T   index calendar years (year of observation)
t   index cohorts
S_t be the final average educational level of cohort t.
I_t be a decomposible measure of final educational inequality of cohort t.
$è(T,t)$ be the weight of cohort t in the population aged 16 to 70 in year T.

Then:

$ST = Ótè (T,t)St$ the final educational level of the 16–70 population in year T is a weighted average of the final educational level of each cohort
$è(T,t)$ Weights vary over time due to demographic transition.
$IT = Ót f(T,t) It + Ót g (T,t)St$ the *final* educational inequality of the 16–70 population. We adopt decomposable entropy inequality measure E2.

The methodology consists of: (i) eEstimating the *final* educational attainment—mean and inequality—of each cohort (including those younger cohorts which have not converged yet), (ii) measuring the stock-vs-cohort time lag for the calendar years 1970–1998, and (iii) measuring the impact of the *timing* of educational attainment (simulating temporary deviations from the path of cohort education expansion in periods of higher demographic growth and establish its impact on the stock-vs-cohort time lag and on aggregate inequality).

The decomposable inequality measure we decided to use is one of most common: one-half of the squared coefficient of variation. According to Shorrocks (1980), this measure corresponds to the member of the generalized entropy class with an inequality aversion parameter of 2. This inequality measure can be decomposed into within and between components by using the following decomposition weights:

$$W(T,t) = è(T,t) \cdot (S_t/S_T)^2$$

Hence forth, we will always refer to this inequality measure as I_2.

Keep in mind that the inequality of education is linked to the inequality of labor income var ($\log y$):

$$\text{var}(\log y) = \beta^2 \, \text{var}(E) + \text{var}(\mu)$$

where β is the return to education in a linear Mincerian equation and μ the error term,[152] and

$$\text{var}(E) = I_2 \cdot \text{mean}(E)^2$$

The data we use are all from the *Pesquisa Nacional por Amostragem de Domicílio* (PNADs) from 1977 to 1999. These are surveys covering the whole nation, except for the rural area of the Northern region, where the vast distances make a yearly survey too costly. The sampling scheme has been the same—stratified and clustered—but the strata change every time the Census Bureau Grid changes, which happens every 10 years with the national Census. The questionnaire has changed considerably over time, but schooling and age, the only variables important in this study, have been largely spared.

The PNAD imposes two shortcomings upon our analysis. The first is that the same people are not followed over time. This means that we do not have real cohorts but pseudo-cohorts. In principle, this should not be a problem, if we believe in the PNAD sampling scheme. The second problem is that the PNADs exist only from 1977 to 1999. This means that any one cohort was followed only during a part of its evolution.

The Evolution of Education Between Cohorts: Monotonically Increasing Mean, Decreasing Inequality and Inverted U-Shaped Mean-Variance Schedule

Figure 9.2 shows educational progress in Brazil. On the horizontal axis is the year of birth of each successive cohort from 1900 to 1983, on the vertical axis is the estimated final average educational level of the cohort. We will explain exactly how this estimate is made later on, but for now what is important is that average education is a monotonically increasing function of cohort date of birth but the rate of increase is not fixed. Figure 9.2 shows that the education of each cohort increased at a more or less steady rate until about the 1940 cohort, accelerated for those born between 1940 and 1960, slowed its rate of growth for the 1960's cohorts and then accelerated again for the cohorts born after 1970.

Figure 9.3 shows the same for the I_2 measure of education of the cohort. Once again, the most important fact is a monotonic relation—each successive cohort has less internal inequality the previous one. It is important to note that the I_2 measure does not bear a linear relation to the amount of income inequality explained by education, and this is due to the highly nonlinear returns to education in Brazil.

As a result of this evolution the educational attainment by Cohorts has taken an interesting shape: an inverted U of the mean-variance schedule , with decreasing variance since the early 1960's. Figure 9.4 shows a wide range for both mean education and variance and wide oscillations in the variance. The latter would be approximately 65 percent of the level achieved in 1959. This trend over the last four decades is due to the reduction in education inequality much faster than the increase of average education (square).

Demographic simulations suggest that it takes more than two decades to see the benefits of increasing educational attainment for the younger cohorts reflected on the whole labor force. One way of looking at how contemporary educational policy affects the distribution of educational endowments of the whole labor force is to measure how many years it takes for the whole labor

---

152. For a general version see Lam (1999).

FIGURE 9.2: AVERAGE YEARS OF EDUCATION BY COHORT

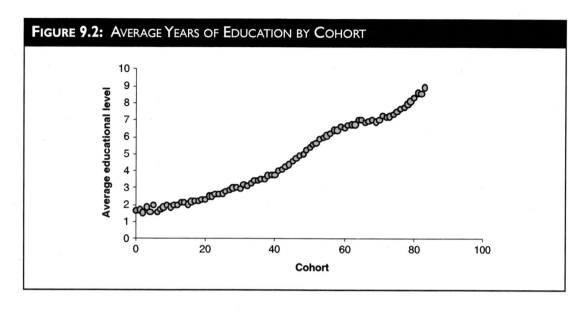

FIGURE 9.3: INEQUALITY IN EDUCATIONAL ATTAINMENT BY COHORT

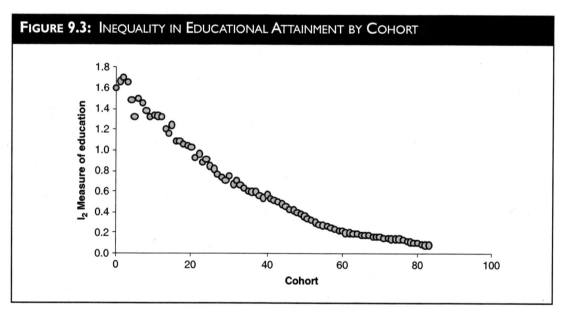

force to reach the level of educational attainment of one cohort. Our observations show that the labor force of 1970s had the same number of years of education of the cohort born in 1940, which on average was finishing school in 1951 (entering school at 7 years of age and attaining nearly 4 years of schooling). Resulting in a gap of 19 years between 1951 and 1970. That gap grew over time to a maximum of 25 years at the end of the century. That is, the labor force of 1998 had 6.5 years of schooling, which was the same educational attainment obtained by the cohort born in 1960, that on average was leaving school in 1973–74. The fact that the gap between the cohort and the whole labor force grew more that the marginal increase in schooling (6 more years for the gap versus 2.5 years of mean school attainment) is associated with the demographic transition. That is, the decreasing demographic weight of the youngest cohort of the labor force of 1990 and 2000 vis a vis the labor force of 1970 and 1980.

Before going into the interactions between the aggregate educational level of the whole labor force and educational inequality of each cohort, its weight in the population and the education

FIGURE 9.4: EDUCATIONAL ATTAINMENT BY COHORT: MEAN-VARIANCE SCHEDULE. OBSERVED AND SIMULATED. BRAZIL 1920–2009

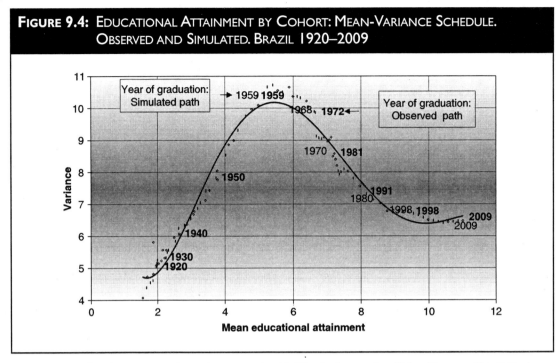

Note: Year of graduation is equal to cohort year plus 12. That is, the year in which a 12 years old individual graduates from 5th grade if entered school when 7 years old.

levels and inequalities of the whole population by year, it is important to note how education levels and inequality converge within each cohort over time. In principle, all cohorts are born with zero average education, and over time this number increases up to the point at which there is no one in the cohort that still in school and then stabilizes. Basically, early observations of younger cohorts *underestimate* mean educational attainment and *overestimate* inequality of education. Cohorts below 30 years of age are still changing, hence we *model their final convergence levels* for mean and coefficient of variation. In order to associate a unique pair of distributional parameters to each cohort.[153]

The Increasing Stock–to–Cohort Time Lag of Educational Attainment

Figures 9.5 and 9.6 show how educational levels and inequality have evolved from one calendar year to the next from 1969 to 1999, in addition to a projection to 2013.[154] What is shown does not correspond exactly to what is observed in more recent years because those cohorts still increasing their education are imputed their final educational levels and inequality as explained above. These figures illustrates the increasing stock-to-cohort lag of educational attainment. That is, the time lag required to extend to the whole *labor force* the educational improvements enjoyed by younger cohorts. For comparison, the education of each cohort is also shown on the same graph. These Figures can be thought of as depicting the "permanent education levels and inequality" of people aged 16 to 70 in each year, even if they have not yet achieved these levels. Some interesting things are apparent from these graphs. The first is that educational levels appear to be increasing in very monotonous, slow, and linear fashion. This is not really surprising, given the monotonous and slow increase in educational levels of each cohort.

153. See Appendix 1 explains the convergence of educational attainment within cohorts.
154. The projection is very simple: the education of cohorts born after 1984 is linearly projected based on those born from 1961 to 1983.

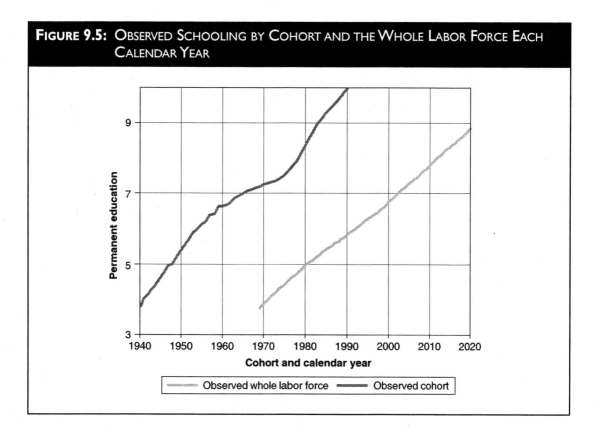

FIGURE 9.5: OBSERVED SCHOOLING BY COHORT AND THE WHOLE LABOR FORCE EACH CALENDAR YEAR

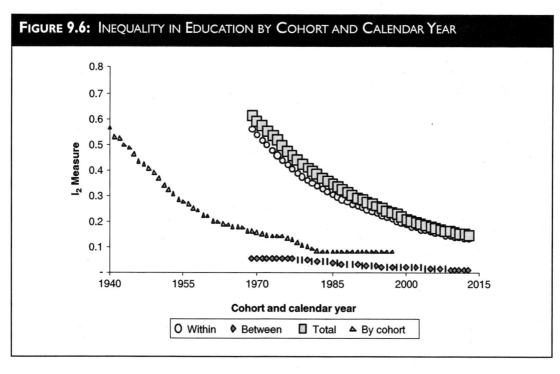

FIGURE 9.6: INEQUALITY IN EDUCATION BY COHORT AND CALENDAR YEAR

FIGURE 9.7: EVOLUTION OF EDUCATIONAL ATTAINMENT OF THE LABOR FORCE—MEAN AND VARIANCE. OBSERVED. BRAZIL, 1962–2013

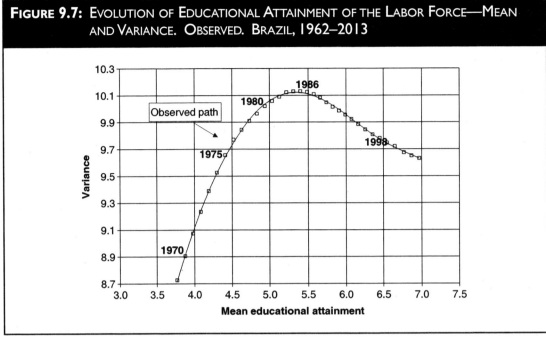

Note: Labor force includes individuals 14–65 years old.

The second interesting fact is that inequality, a measured by the I_2 measure, is falling continuously. This fall is mostly due to within cohort inequality, as between cohort inequality is much smaller.[155] This is surprising, as it is not evident that within cohort inequality dominates total inequality. It is important to note that this fall does not necessarily mean that income inequalities due to education are falling—given Brazil's highly convex returns to education, the two may well go in different directions.

Interestingly, the shape of the Educational attainment (mean and variance schedule) for the *whole* labor force (Figure 9.7) has the *same* inverted U shape of the corresponding schedule for cohorts (Figure 9.4). However important differences are evident, the stock-to-cohort time lag (approximately 25 years) and has been increasing during the last decade. Moreover, the range of variation of variance and the mean is much smaller. While the variance for cohorts goes from 7 to 10 in a period of 15 years ending in 1959, the variance of the stock increases from 9 to 10.1 in a similar period culminating in 1986.

Simulations: Permanent and Temporary Acceleration of Educational Attainment

Permanent Acceleration of Educational Expansion

Figures 9.8 and 9.9 are identical to Figures 9.5 and 9.6, except that they show a simulation as well. In this simulation, we increase the education of all cohorts born after 1959 by (t −1959)/10 years, where t is the cohort's year of birth. The final impact on average education of this very large increase in education of each is an increase of 1.74 years in 2013. On the other hand, the increase in inequality is very small—in 2013, the I_2 measure would be 0.162, and not 0.148, due to the smaller rate of reduction in between cohort inequality.

---

155. We have assumed constant within cohort inequality for cohorts born after 1987.

FIGURE 9.8: OBSERVED AND SIMULATED SCHOOLING BY COHORT AND CALENDAR YEAR

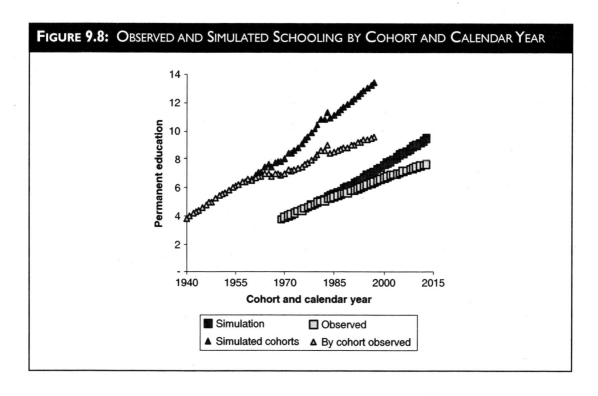

FIGURE 9.9: OBSERVED AND SIMULATED INEQUALITY IN EDUCATION BY COHORT AND CALENDAR YEAR

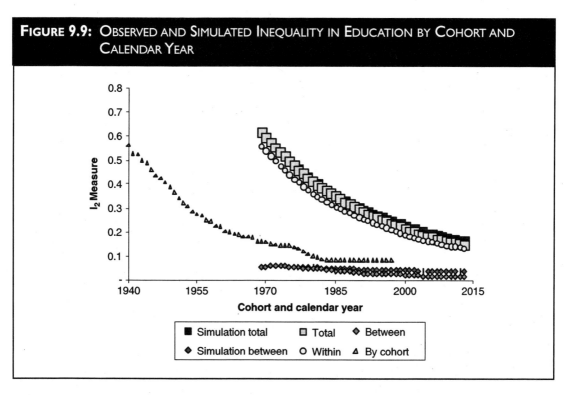

The fact that even a very large intervention, operated on more recent cohorts, does not significantly affect educational inequality is due to the dominant effect of within cohort inequality. Within inequality, as measured by I_2, is not independent from between cohort inequality because average cohort education composes the weights, but this effect is almost insignificant. On the other hand, average income increases, but relatively slowly, given the dramatic nature of the simulation at the cohort level. Both of these effects suggest the existence of strong demographic inertia.

Temporary Acceleration of Educational Expansion Before Demographic Transition

The simulation above supposes very strong and incremental improvements in the educational system, which ignore reasonable fiscal constraints. A second, more interesting, simulation is temporary acceleration of educational expansion before demographic transition, which basically maintains the accelerated expansion during the 1970s and 1980s. This is equivalent to accelerating through the Mean-Variance path of educational attainment for cohorts (Figure 9.4) when demographic growth of schooling cohorts is at its maximum. In particular, keeping the acceleration observed for cohorts born in the 1940–60 period for the cohorts 1961–72 period (policy period 1973–84). This policy is equivalent to anticipating by nearly one decade the improvements of the educational system enjoyed by younger cohorts during the 1990s—the light blue line versus the yellow line. We should remark that the deviation of the expansion path is *temporary* and after 1998 graduation year (cohort years) simulated and observed paths coincide again.

The Expected Impact on the Educational Attainment of the Labor Force

Because of the fact that the demographic transition has not yet been completed in Brazil, providing a rationale for an "educational push" in the first decade of the XXI century, one would expected that the simulation shows firstly that heavier cohorts have higher mean educational attainment. Secondly, lower *within inequality*. The reason of why *within inequality* falls much faster than *between inequality* is because the largest cohorts receive the lowest levels of inequality. Thirdly, an overshooting of *between inequality*, with a reduction under the historical trend after two or three decades. This behavior is explained because the large cohorts where already more educated, therefore closer to the mean. In the *short run*, the expected effect of the simulations on the *overall inequality* would depend on which component dominates the other. While in the *long run*, one would expect a *lower overall inequality*. The expected effect on variance depends on whether inequality falls enough to compensate the growth of mean educational attainment. Finally, as labor inequality changes are proportional to changes in the variance of education (approximation under linear Mincerean equation). Hence, long term inequality is expected to fall (General equilibrium could reduce B the wage skill gap and reduce inequality even further).

Simulations Results

The results from the simulation confirmed our expectations about faster achievement of mean educational attainment goals, overshooting of the inequality and the variance of education with lower long term levels for both and consequently.

The magnitude of shift in the mean educational attainment is considerable, seven years to the left and 0.6 years upwards for the year 2002, which means that the time-gap falls from 25 to 18 years. The results also confirmed the anticipated temporary overshooting of the inequality and variance of education from mean 5.3 to 7.4 years of schooling, maximum 4 percent at mean 6.5. The long term levels reached by these variables by 2013 are 15 percent in inequality and 6 percent in variance of education.

Figure 9.10 shows the temporary deviations in the cohort-path as the simulation of policy changes that anticipate by nearly one decade the improvements of the educational system enjoyed by younger cohorts during the 1990s—the light blue line versus the yellow line. That is, maintaining the rate of growth of educational attainment enjoyed by the cohorts borne in the 1940s and 1950s for the generations borne in the 1960s and early 1970s. For example, the simulated average education of the individual borne in 1970 (which was leaving school in 1984)

FIGURE 9.10: OBSERVED AND SIMULATED SCHOOLING BY COHORT AND CALENDAR YEAR

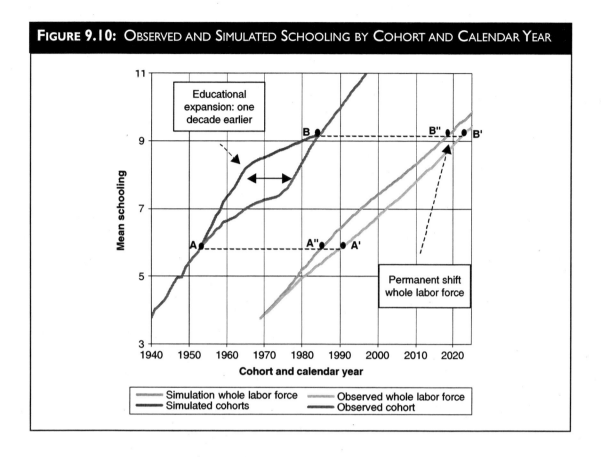

was nearly seven years of schooling, the same as the value observed for the person borne in 1980 (which was leaving school by the year 1994). The consequences for the school attainment of whole labor force is a permanent North-West shift—the blue line versus the orange line. The magnitude of the shift is considerable, seven years to the left and 0.6 years upwards for the year 2002, which means that the time-gap falls from 25 to 20 years.

Because the transformations are much less dramatic than those in the first simulation, the impact on average education is also much less dramatic. The educational level of the 16 to 70 population in the final calendar year we look at, 2013, rises from 7.7 years to 8.1. The effects on inequality are also not very impressive: there is a small increase as the cohorts whose education was increased come into adult age, but it wears out by the year 2000.

Figure 9.11 illustrates the temporary overshooting of the inequality of education along with its long term reduction. The black line illustrates the observed the mean educational attainment and the inequality of education, while the gray line depicts the relation for the simulation case. relation between the observed path.

Because the demographic transition will be almost completed in the first two decades of the XXI century there is an opportunity to reduce the lag between current educational policy and its impact on the whole labor force. Therefore, delaying a vigorous "educational push" beyond demographic opportunities would have a significant permanent cost in terms of extending the benefits of current educational policy to the whole populations and catchup with the rest of the world.

Conclusions

The main conclusion is that demographic inertia is strong in Brazil and improvements in the school system today will take long to translate into more education for the population as a whole. Between cohort inequality will always increase because increasing the educational level of younger

FIGURE 9.11: COVARIANCE COEFFICIENT VS. MEAN EDUCATIONAL ATTAINMENT

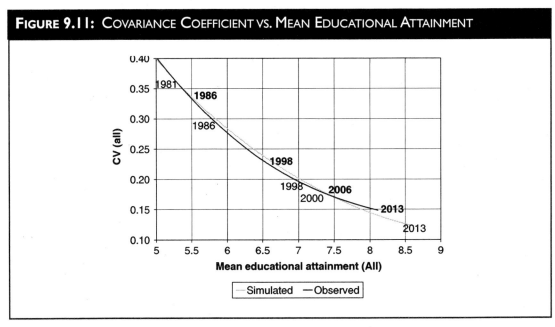

Note: Labels correspond to stock year.

FIGURE 9.12: EVOLUTION OF EDUCATIONAL ATTAINMENT OF THE LABOR FORCE: MEAN AND VARIANCE. OBSERVED AND SIMULATED. BRAZIL 1969–2013

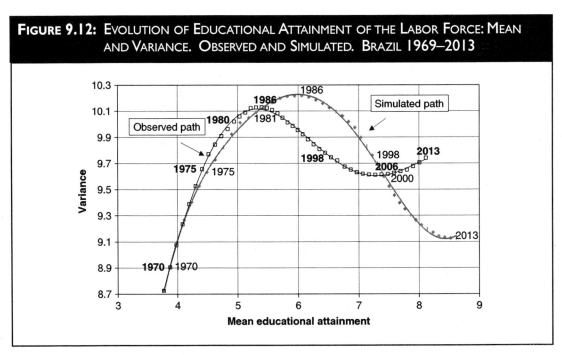

Note: Labor force includes individuals 14–65 years old.

cohorts is equivalent to giving more education to those cohorts that already have the most. On the other hand, total inequality would relatively unaffected because within cohort inequality of older cohorts dominates total educational inequality within the population.

The paper gives a response to the implicit question raised in the title: there is a transient window of opportunity for long term inequality reduction via schooling expansion in the short and medium term. Part of that temporary window has already been lost. However, given the slow nature of demographic transition, this window is really wide and there is still time to take advantage of it by expanding education vigorously. The main conclusions of this report are:

- Previous educational policy, especially in the 1980s, did not take full advantage of *demographic opportunities*. The stock-to-cohort time lag could have been reduced substantially (25 percent) if a country like Brazil had maintained the historical rate of growth of schooling during the 1980s.
- Educational Policy makers should maintain a patient long term perspective, because the stock-to-cohort time lag is considerable (from two to three decades). Therefore, policy makers should put in place monitoring mechanisms to follow both the performance of younger cohort and the demographic transition.
- The appropriate time correlation between educational efforts and pre-demographic transition would reduce long term inequality. However there might be a labor income inequality overshoot in the short run, the period in with inequality between cohorts might run dominant. Additional reductions labor income inequality would follow if the wage skill gap responds to the supply changes, and even further if income-fertility differentials persist (Kremmer et al. 2002). *Demographic* opportunities *are still available*, but they are smaller and transient. Because the demographic transition will be almost completed in the first two decades of the XXI century, there is still an opportunity to reduce the stock-vs-cohort time *lag* via educational expansion.
- *Delaying "educational push" would have a permanent long term equity cost for Brazil.* Therefore, delaying a vigorous "educational push" beyond demographic opportunities would have a significant permanent cost in *terms* of extending the benefits of educational policy to the whole populations and catch-up with the rest of the world.

Perhaps there is a corollary in terms of the specific role of foreign credit (vis a vis domestic credit) to finance education expansion before demographic transition takes place. Fiscal constraints might be too binding precisely when countries like Brazil face optimal demographic opportunities. Own country resources are the most limited at this point in time because dependency ratios are the highest and productivity per worker is very low. Hence this constraint might be efficiently relaxed via foreign credit from multilateral institution. In summary, the level of schooling of the labor force in Brazil is clearly insufficient and efforts to make educational attainment higher and more equitable should be emphasized. Nevertheless policy makers and policy observers should be aware that any expected impact of education on inequality of income will not be immediate. Hence they should be willing to establish monitoring systems can follow to young cohorts of students trough the different stages of the educational ladder and evaluate educational outcomes with an explicit long term perspective.

Appendix: Converge Estimation for Educational Attainment (Mean and Inequality) Within Cohorts

In principle, all cohorts are born with zero average education, and over time this number increases up to the point at which there is no one in the cohort that still in school and then stabilizes. In Brazil, after 30 years of age, very few people are still in school. In 1999, only 2.9 percent of the population 30 or over were still in any kind of regular learning. The year of 1999 may be used as an upper bound, given that each successive cohort is completing more education than its predecessors.[156]

Because we observed cohorts from 1977 to 1999, this means that any cohort born previous to 1947 should no longer show any increases in education over the period of observation and even

---

156. For example, in 1995 only 1.6 percent of people 30 or older were involved in education.

those born previous to 1952 (those 25 and older in 1977) should show very little. This is indeed what we observe, Figure 9A.1 shows the slope linear trend line showing the increase in education of each cohort over the 1977–1999 period. It is flat for cohorts born from 1900 to the mid-1940s and then increases strongly and monotonously up the last cohort observed—the one born in 1987.

A related pattern can be seen in the evolution of inequality. Figure 9A.2 shows that the I_2 measure does not change significantly until the 1965 cohort and then there is a strong downward trend for all successive cohorts. In other words, cohorts aged 12 have already achieved their final inequality, as measured by one half of the coefficient of variation squared. This is not as intuitive as the effect on average education.

The I_2 measure is one-half of the variance divided by the square of the mean. When each cohort comes into the world none of its members has any education, the mean is zero, and I_2 is not even defined. Once at least one child finished one year of schooling, I_2 becomes defined and then increases very quickly as a part of the cohort acquires some education, yielding a positive denominator, but the numerator, average years of education, remains very low. I_2 then falls mostly because this denominator is increasing. Since we only observe each cohort after it is 10 years old, we do not observe the increasing part of the curve, only the downward part. We will also see later on that it becomes stable within each cohort before average educational level does. This is why we observe changes in the I_2 measure over the 1977–1999 period only with the 1965 cohort while the average changes over the same period for all cohorts after the one born in 1945.

Another way to observe the evolution within cohorts and over time is to look at the average education of each cohort from 1977 to 1999. Figures 9A.3 through 9A.5 show this for ten cohorts born from 1920 to 1975. Figure 9A.3 shows that the cohorts born in 1920, 1930, and 1940 show no increase at all in average education over the period; Figure 9A.4 shows very slight increases for cohorts born in 1945, 1950, and 1955; and finally Figure 9A.5 shows the large increases in the education of cohorts born from 1960 onwards, whose members were still overwhelmingly in school during the observation period. Finally, each successive cohort attains a final educational level superior to that of its predecessors

Figures 9A.6 through 9A.8 show the I_2 measure for the same cohorts as Figures 9A.3 through 9A5. The message is again clear: the inequality of education is stable from 1977 to 1999 for cohorts born until 1965 but falls over the observation period for those born after 1965. Of course, the final value of I_2 for each cohort is lower than for its predecessor.

Finally, if we shift the curves on Figures 9A.5 and 9A.8, we can see how the level and inequality in education vary as different cohorts age. This is what is shown on Figures 9A.9 and 9A.10, which may be the most important figures thus far. Let us start with Figure 9A.9.

Figure 9A.9 appears to show that successive cohorts, at least those born from 1960 to 1975, have higher education levels at any given age and appear to level off at more or less the same age. This is equivalent to saying that most educational improvement involves advancing further in the educational ladder in the same time rather than staying longer in school. In other words, kids are doing better because they are repeating less. This is coherent with most analysis in the education literature in recent years.

The practical impact of this upon our analysis is on how we will model final educational level of the cohorts born from 75 to 83, whose years of schooling had not yet reached its final value in 1999. What we do is take the 1974 cohort as a baseline and see how much more education a given younger cohort has at each observed age and then attribute to these newer cohorts the 1974 cohort final value multiplied by the average percentage difference between the two over the years of observation.

Figure 9A.10 is easier to interpret. By age 20, educational inequality, as measured by the I_2 measure, levels off. This means that additional increases in the variance of education are matched by equal increases in the square of average education, leaving this inequality measure unchanged.

FIGURE 9A.1: RATE OF GROWTH OF AVERAGE EDUCATION WITHIN EACH COHORT OVER THE PERIOD OF OBSERVATION

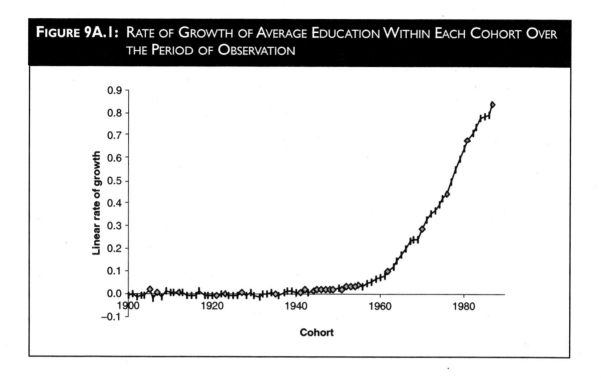

FIGURE 9A.2: RATE OF GROWTH OF INEQUALITY WITHIN EACH COHORT OVER THE PERIOD OF OBSERVATION

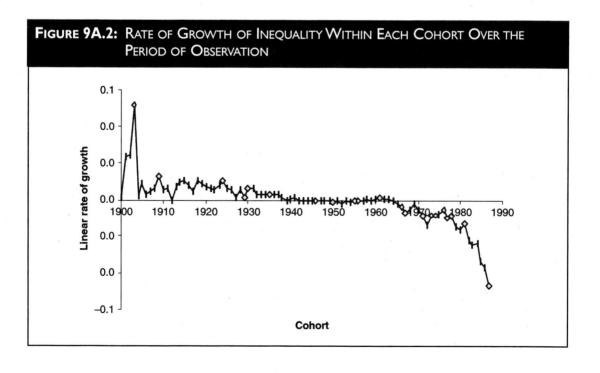

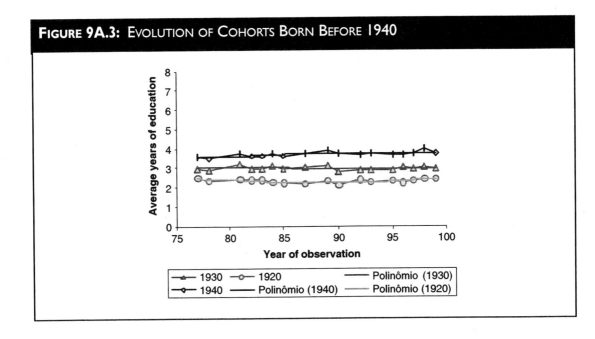

Figure 9A.3: Evolution of Cohorts Born Before 1940

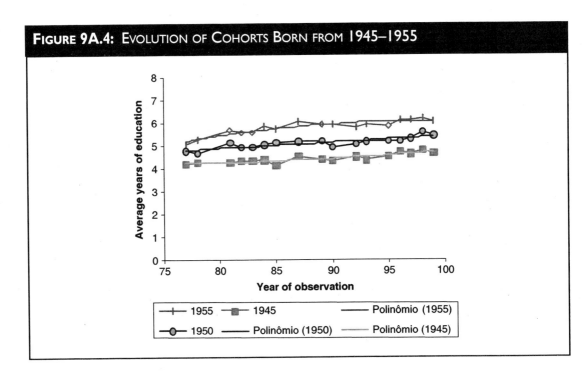

Figure 9A.4: Evolution of Cohorts Born from 1945–1955

FIGURE 9A.5: EVOLUTION OF COHORTS BORN FROM 1960–1975

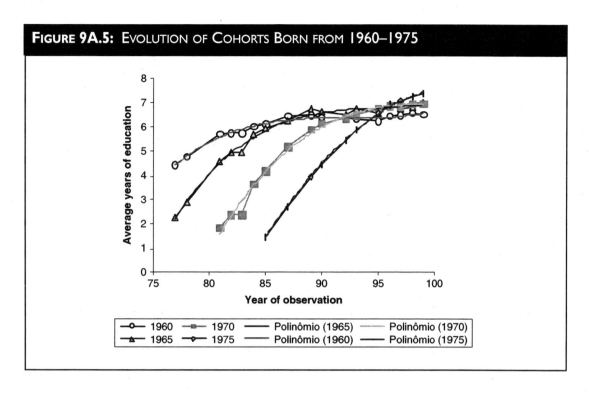

FIGURE 9A.6: EVOLUTION OF COHORTS BORN BEFORE 1940

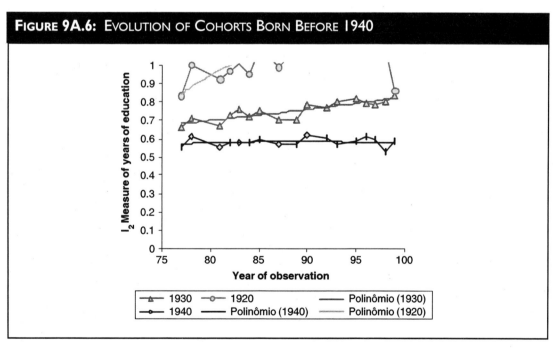

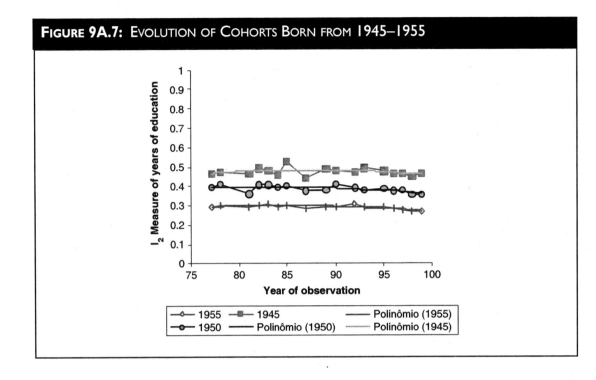

FIGURE 9A.7: EVOLUTION OF COHORTS BORN FROM 1945–1955

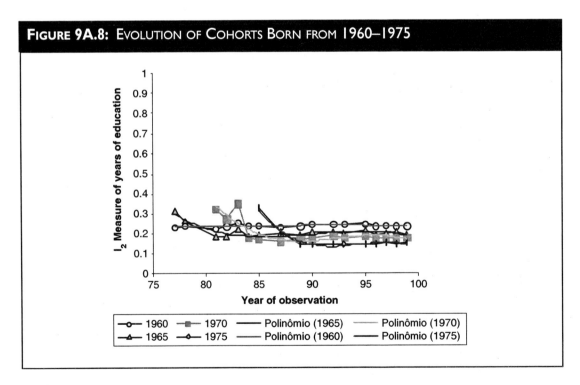

FIGURE 9A.8: EVOLUTION OF COHORTS BORN FROM 1960–1975

FIGURE 9A.9: EVOLUTION OF EDUCATION LEVELS OF COHORTS BORN FROM 1955–1975

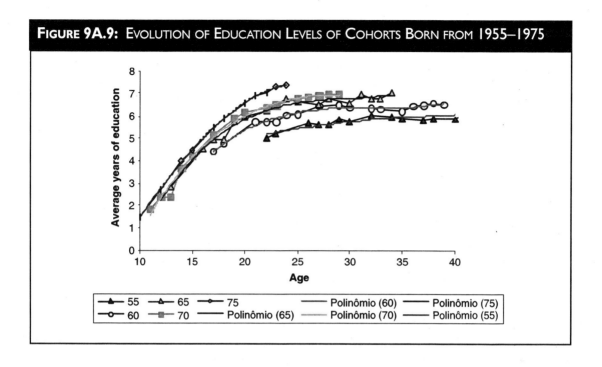

FIGURE 9A.10: EVOLUTION OF INEQUALITY OF COHORTS BORN FROM 1955–1975

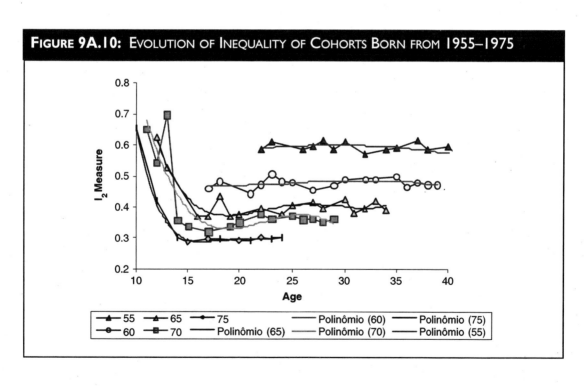

Bibliography

Anand, S. and S. Kanbur. 1993. "Inequality and Development: A Critique," *Journal of Development Economics* 41:19–43.

Ahluwalia, M. 1976. "Inequality, Poverty and Development" *Journal of Development Economics* 3:307–42.

Barros, Ricardo, and David Lam. 1996. "Income and Education Inequality and Children's Schooling Attainment in Brazil." In Nancy Birdsall and Richard Sabot, eds., *Opportunity Foregone: Education in Brazil*. Washington: Inter-American Development Bank.

Birdsall, Nancy, and Richard Sabot, eds. 1996. *Opportunity Foregone: Education in Brazil*. Washington: Inter-American Development Bank.

Bloom and Willimason. 1998. "Demographic Transitions and Economic Miracles in Emerging Asia" *World Bank Economic Review* 12:419–55.

Case, Anne, and Angus Deaton. 1999. "School Inputs and Education Outcomes in South Africa." *Quarterly Journal of Economics*, forthcoming

Deaton, Angus and Paxson, Christina. 1997. "The effects of economic and population growth on national saving and inequality." *Demography* 34(1).

Deninger, Klaus, and Lyn Squire. 1996. "A New Data Set Measuring Income Inequality." *The World Bank Economic Review* 10(3):565–91.

Duryea, Suzanne, and Miguel Székely. 1999. "Decomposing Schooling Differences in Latin America." IDB. Processed.

Higgins, Matthew, and Jeffrey G. Williamson. 1999. "Explaining Inequality the World Round: Cohort Size, Kuznets Curves, and Openness." NBER Working Paper No. 7224.

Katz, L., and K. Murphy. 1992. "Changes in Relative Wages, 1963–1987: Supply and Demand Factors." *Quarterly Journal of Economics* 107:35–78.

Kremer, M., and D. Chen. 2002. "Income Distribution Dynamics with Endogenous Fertility." *Journal of Economic Growth* 7(3):227–58.

Kuznets, S. 1979 "Growth, population and income distribution, selected essays." New York: Norton.

Lam, David. "Generating Extreme Inequality: Schooling, Earnings, and Intergenerational Transmission of Human Capital in South Africa and Brazil." Report No. 99-439 Research Report. Population Studies Center at The Institute For Social Research University Of Michigan

Lam, D. 1986. "The Dynamics of Population Growth, Differential Fertality and Inequality." *Economic Review* 76(5)1103–1116.

Levison, D., and D. Lam. 1991. "Declining Inequality in Schooling in Brazil and Its Effects on Inequality in Earnings." *Journal of Development Economics* 37:1992.

Mookherjee, D. and A. Shorrocks. "A decomposition analysis of the trend in UK income inequality." *The Economic Journal* 92(368).

Ram, R. 1990. "Educational expansion and schooling inequality: international evidence and some implications." *The Review of Economic and Statistics* 72(2).

Shorrocks, A.F. 1980. "The class of additively decomposable inequality measures." *Econometrica* 48(3).

CHAPTER 10

EX ANTE EVALUATION OF CONDITIONAL CASH TRANSFER PROGRAMS: THE CASE OF BOLSA ESCOLA[157]

By François Bourguignon, Francisco H. G. Ferreira, and Phillippe G. Leite[158]

Abstract

Cash transfers targeted to poor people, but conditional on some behavior on their part, such as school attendance or regular visits to health care facilities, are being adopted in a growing number of developing countries. Even where ex post *impact evaluations have been conducted, a number of policy-relevant counterfactual questions have remained unanswered. These are questions about the potential impact of changes in program design, such as benefit levels or the choice of the means-test, on both the current welfare and the behavioral response of household members. This paper proposes a method to simulate the effects of those alternative program designs on welfare and behavior, based on micro-econometrically estimated models of household behavior. In an application to Brazil's recently introduced federal* Bolsa Escola *program, we find a surprisingly strong effect of the conditionality on school attendance, but a muted impact of the transfers on the reduction of current poverty and inequality levels.*

JEL Codes: I38, J13, J22, J24
Key Words: Conditional Transfers; Demand for Schooling, Child Labor

Introduction

During the 1990s, a new brand of redistribution programs was adopted in many developing countries. Although local versions varied, programs such as *Food for Education* in Bangladesh,

---

157. Paper to be presented at the WB/UNICEF/ILO conference on Chile Labor, Oslo May 28–29, 2002.

158. Respectively, Delta and World Bank, Paris, PUC, Rio and PUC, Rio.

Bolsa Escola in Brazil, and *Progresa* in Mexico are all means-tested conditional cash transfer programs. As the name indicates, they share two defining features, which jointly set them apart from most pre-existing programs, whether in developing or developed countries. The first of these is the means-test, defined in terms of a maximum household income level, above which households are not eligible to receive the benefit.[159] The second is the behavioral conditionality, which operates through the requirement that applicant households, in addition to satisfying the income targeting, have members regularly undertake some pre-specified action. The most common such requirement is for children between 6 and 14 years of age to remain enrolled and actually in attendance at school. In Mexico's *Progresa*, additional requirements applied to some households, such as obligatory pre- and post-natal visits for pregnant women or lactating mothers.

The implementation of these programs have generated considerable interest, both in the countries where they took place and in the international academic and policy-making communities. Accordingly, a great deal of effort has been placed in evaluating their impact. There are two types of approach for evaluating the effects of these programs on the various aspects of household welfare that they seek to affect. *Ex post* approaches consist of comparing observed beneficiaries of the program with non-beneficiaries, possibly after controlling for selection into the first or the second group if truly random samples are not available. An important literature has recently developed on these techniques and many applications to social programs have been made in various countries.[160]

Ex ante methods consist of simulating the effect of the program on the basis of some model of the household. These models can vary widely in complexity and coverage. Arithmetic simulation models simply apply official rules to determine whether or not a household qualifies for the program, and the amount of the transfer to be made, on the basis of data commonly available in typical household surveys. More sophisticated models include some behavioral response by households.

Ex ante and *ex post* evaluation methods are complements, rather than substitutes. To begin with, they have different objectives. *Ex post* methods are meant to identify the actual effects of a program on various dimensions of household welfare, by relying on the direct observation of people engaged in the program, and comparing them with those same dimensions in a carefully constructed comparison group, selected so as to provide a suitable proxy for the desired true counterfactual: "how would participants have fared, had they not participated?" In some sense, these are the only "true" evaluations of a program.

Even when comparison groups are perfectly believable proxies for the counterfactual, however, *ex post* evaluations leave some policy-relevant questions unanswered. These questions typically refer to how impact might change if some aspect of the program design changes—such as the level of the means-test; the nature of the behavioral conditions imposed; or the level of the transfer benefits. It is difficult enough to obtain an actual control group to compare with a single program design in reality. It is likely to be impossible to "test" many different designs in experimental conditions. *Ex ante* methods are valuable tools exactly because it is easier to experiment on computers than on people. These methods are essentially prospective since they rely on a set of assumptions about what households are likely to do when faced with the program. They also permit direct counterfactual analysis of alternative programs for which no *ex post* data

---

159. For verification and enforcement reasons, the means-test is often specified in terms of a score based on responses to a questionnaire and/or a home visit by a social worker. In some countries, the score is 'calibrated' to be approximately equivalent to a pre-determined level of household income per capita. See Camargo and Ferreira (2001) for a discussion of the Brazilian case.

160. This literature relies heavily on matching techniques, and draws extensively on the early work by Rubin (1977) and Rubin and Rosenbaum (1985). For a survey of recent applications, see Heckman and Vytlacil (2002). For a study of the effects of the *Food for Education* program in Bangladesh, see Ravallion and Wodon (2000). A number of important studies of *Progresa* were undertaken under the auspices of the International Food Policy Research Institute (IFPRI). See, in particular, Parker and Skoufias (2000) and Schultz (2000).

can be available. Thus, they are indispensable when designing a program or reforming existing ones.

Simulation models of redistribution schemes based on micro data sets are widely used in developed countries, especially to analyze the effect of the numerous and often complex cash transfer instruments found in those countries. Given the progress of direct cash transfers in developing countries, building the same type of models in developing countries may become necessary.[161] However, the specific behavioral conditionality that characterizes these programs requires modifications, and a focus on different aspects of household behavior. The present paper takes a step in that direction by proposing a simple *ex ante* evaluation methodology for conditional means-tested transfer programs. We apply the method to the new federal design of *Bolsa Escola*, in Brazil, and we are concerned with both dimensions cited by the program administrators as their objectives: (i) the reduction of current levels of poverty and inequality; and (ii) the provision of incentives for the reduction of future poverty, through increased school enrollment among poor children today.

The paper is organized as follows. The next section describes the *Bolsa Escola* program, as it was launched at the federal level in Brazil in 2001. The third section presents the simple econometric model used for simulating the effects of the program. Given the conditionality of *Bolsa Escola*, this model essentially deals with the demand for schooling and therefore draws on the recent literature on child labor. The estimation of the model is dealt with in fourth section, whereas the simulation of program effects and a comparison with alternative program designs are discussed in fifth section. The sixth section concludes.

Main Features of the *Bolsa Escola* Program

The Brazilian national *Bolsa Escola* program, created by a law of April 2001 within the broader context of the social development initiative known as Projeto Alvorada, is the generalization at the federal level of earlier programs, which were pioneered in the Federal District and in the city of Campinas (SP) in 1995, and later extended to several other localities.[162] The law of April 2001 made these various programs uniform in terms of coverage, transfer amounts and the associated conditionality. It also provided federal funding. Yet, the monitoring of the program itself is left under the responsibility of municipal governments.

The rules of the program are rather simple. Households with monetary income per capita below 90 Reais (R$)42 per month—which was equivalent to half a minimum wage when the law was introduced—and with children aged 6 to 15 qualify for the *Bolsa Escola* program, provided that children attend school regularly. The minimum rate of school attendance is set at 85 per cent and schools are supposed to report this rate to municipal governments for program beneficiaries. The monthly benefit is R$15 per child attending school, up to a maximum of R$45 per household. Transfers are generally paid to the mother, upon presentation of a magnetic card that greatly facilitates the monitoring of the whole program.

The management of the program is essentially local. Yet, control will be operated at two levels. At the federal level, the number of beneficiaries claimed by municipal governments will be checked for consistency against local aggregate indicators of affluence. In case of discrepancy, local governments will have to adjust the number of beneficiaries on the basis of income per capita rankings. At the local level, the responsibility for checking the veracity of self-reported incomes is left to municipalities.

---

161. See, for instance, Harding (1996). On the need for and difficulties with building the same type of models in developing countries, see Atkinson and Bourguignon (1991).

162. Early studies of these original programs include Abramovay et. al. (1998); Rocha and Sabóia (1998) and Sant'Ana and Moraes (1997). A comprehensive assessment of different experiences with *Bolsa Escola* across Brazil can be found in World Bank (2001). There is much less written on the federal program, for the good reason that its implementation in practice is only just beginning. The description given in this section draws on the official Ministério da Educação website, at http://www.mec.gov.brhome/bolsaesc.

163. Approximately US$ 30, at August 2002 exchange rates.

It is estimated that some ten million children (in six million households) will benefit from this program. This represents approximately 17 percent of the whole population, reached at a cost slightly below 0.2 percent of GDP. The latter proportion is higher in terms of household disposable income: 0.45 percent when using household income reported in the PNAD survey and 0.3 per cent when using National Accounts. Of course, this figure is considerably higher when expressed in terms of targeted households. Even so, it amounts to no more than 5 percent of the income of the bottom two deciles.

A Simple Framework for Modeling and Simulating *Bolsa Escola*

The effects of such a transfer scheme on the Brazilian distribution of income could be simulated by simply applying the aforementioned rules to a representative sample of households, as given for instance by the Pesquisa Nacional por Amostra de Domicílios (PNAD), fielded annually by the Brazilian Central Statistical Office (IBGE). This would have been an example of what was referred to above as "arithmetic" simulation. Yet, for a program which has a change in household behavior as one of its explicit objectives, this would clearly be inappropriate. After all, *Bolsa Escola* aims not only to reduce current poverty by targeting transfers to today's poor, but also to encourage school attendance by poor children who are not currently enrolled, and to discourage evasion by those who are. Any *ex ante* evaluation of such a policy must therefore go beyond simply counting the additional income accruing to households under the assumption of no change in schooling behavior. Simulating *Bolsa Escola* thus requires some structural modeling of the demand for schooling. This section presents and discusses the model being used in this paper.

There is a rather large literature on the demand for schooling in developing countries and the related issue of child labor. The main purpose of that literature is to understand the reasons why parents would prefer to have their kids working within or outside the household rather than going to school. Various motives have been identified and analyzed from a theoretical point of view,[164] whereas numerous empirical attempts have been made at testing the relevance of these motives, measuring their relative strength and evaluating the likely effects of policies.[165] The empirical analysis is difficult for various interrelated reasons. First, the rationale behind the decision on child labor or school enrollment is by itself intricate. In particular, it is an inherently intertemporal decision, and it will differ depending on whether households behave as a unitary model, or whether internal bargaining takes place. Second, it is difficult to claim exogeneity for most plausible explanatory variables, and yet no obvious instrument is available for correcting the resulting biases. Third, fully structural models that would permit a rigorous analysis of policies are complex and therefore hard to estimate while maintaining a reasonable degree of robustness.

In light of these difficulties, our aims are modest and our approach is operational: rather than proposing a new, more complete structural model of the demand for schooling and intra-household labor allocation, we aim simply to obtain reasonable orders of magnitude for the likely effects of transfer programs of this kind. We thus make the choice to limit the structural aspects of the modeling exercise to the minimum necessary to capture the main effects of the program.

In particular, we make four crucial simplifying assumptions. First, we entirely ignore the issue of how the decision about a child's time allocation is made within the household. We thus bypass the discussion of unitary versus collective decisionmaking models of household. Instead, we treat our model of occupational choice as a reduced-form reflection of the outcome of whichever

---

164. See the well-known survey by Basu (1999) as well as the recent contribution by Baland and Robinson (2001).

165. Early contributions to that literature include Rosenzweig and Evenson (1977), as well as Gertler and Glewwe (1990). For more recent contributions and short surveys of the recent literature see Freije and Lopez-Calva (2000), Bhalotra (2000). On policy see Grootaert and Patrinos (1999).

decisionmaking process took place within the household.[166] Second, we consider that the decision to send a child to school is made after all occupational decisions by adults within the household have been made, and does not affect those decisions. Third, we do not discuss here the issue of various siblings in the same household and the simultaneity of the corresponding decision. The model that is discussed thus is supposed to apply to all children at schooling age within a household. Fourth, we take the composition of the household as exogenous.

Under these assumptions, let S_i be a qualitative variable representing the occupational choice made for a child in household i. This variable will take the value 0 if the child does not attend school, the value 1 if she goes to school *and* works outside the household and the value 2 if she goes to school and does not work outside the household. When $S_i = 0$, it will be assumed that the child works full time either at home or on the market, earnings being observed only in the latter case. Similarly, $S_i = 2$ allows for the possibility that the child may be employed in domestic activities at the same time he/she goes to school. The occupational choice variable S_i will be modeled using the standard utility-maximizing interpretation of the multinomial Logit framework, so that:

$$S_i = k \text{ iff } S_k(A_i, X_i, H_i; \Upsilon_{-i} + y_{ik}) + v_{ik} > S_j(A_i, X_i, H_i; \Upsilon_{-i} + y_{ij}) + v_{ij} \text{ for } j \neq k \quad (1)$$

where $S_k(\ )$ is a latent function reflecting the net utility of choosing alternative k ($= 0$, 1 or 2) for deciders in the household. A_i is the age of the child I; X_i is a vector of her characteristics; H_i, is a vector of the characteristics of the household she belongs to (size, age of parents, education of parents, presence of other children at school age, distance from school, etc.); Υ_{-i} is the total income of household members other than the child and y_{ij} is the total contribution of the child towards the income of the household, depending on her occupational choice j. Finally, v_{ij} is a random normal variable that stands for the unobserved heterogeneity of observed schooling/participation behavior. If we collapse all non-income explanatory variables into a single vector Z_i and linearize, (1) can be written as:

$$U_i(j) = S_j(A_i, X_i, H_i; \Upsilon_{-i} + y_{ij}) + v_{ji} = Z_i.\gamma_j + (\Upsilon_{-i} + y_{ij})\alpha_j + v_{ij} \quad (2)$$

This representation of the occupational choice of children is very parsimonious. In particular, by allowing the coefficients γ_j and α_j to differ without any constraints across the various alternatives, we are allowing all possible tradeoffs between the schooling of the child and his/her future income, and the current income of the household. Note also that the preceding model implicitly treats the child's number of hours of work as a discrete choice. Presumably that number is larger in alternative 0 than in alternative 1 because schooling is taking some time away. This may be reflected in the definition of the child income variable y_{ij} as follows. Denote the observed market earnings of the child as w_i. Assuming that these are determined in accordance with the standard Becker-Mincer human capital model, write:

$$\log w_i = X_i.\delta + m^*\text{Ind}(S_j = 1) + u_i \quad (3)$$

where X_i is a set of individual characteristics (including age and schooling achieved) and where u_i is a random term that stands for unobserved earnings determinants. Assumptions on that term will be discussed below. The second term on the right hand side takes into account the preceding remark on the number of hours of work. Children who attend school and are also reported to work on the market presumably have less time available and may thus earn less. Based on (3), the child's contribution to the household income, y_{ij}, in the various alternative j is defined as follows:

$$y_{i0} = Kw_i ; \quad y_{i1} = M y_{i0} = MKw_i ; y_{i2} = D y_{i0} = D Kw_i \quad \text{with } M = \text{Exp}(m) \quad (4)$$

---

166. For a discussion of how intra-household bargaining affects the occupational choice of members, see Chiappori (1992). See also Bourguignon and Chiappori (1994) and Browning et al. (1994).

where it is assumed that y_{ij} covers both market and domestic child labor. Thus domestic income is proportional to actual or potential market earnings, w_i, in a proportion K for people who do not go to school. Going to school while keeping working outside the household means a reduction in the proportion $1-M$ of domestic and market income. Finally, going to school without working on the market means a reduction in the proportion $1-D$ of total child income, which in that case is purely domestic. The proportions K and D are not observed. However, the proportion M is taken to be the same for domestic and market work and may be estimated on the basis of observed earnings.

Replacing (4) in (2) leads to:

$$U_i(j) = S_j(A_i, X_i, H_i; \Upsilon_{-i} + y_{ij}) + v_{ji} = Z_i.\gamma_j + \Upsilon_{-i}\,\alpha_j + \beta_j.w_i + v_{ij}$$
$$\text{with: } \beta_0 = \alpha_0\,K; \quad \beta_1 = \alpha_1 MK; \quad \beta_2 = \alpha_2\,DK \tag{5}$$

We now have a complete simulation model. If all coefficients α, β, γ are known, as well as the actual or potential market earnings, w_i and the residual terms v_{ij}, then the child's occupational type selected by household i is:

$$k^* = \text{Arg max}[\,U_i(j)] \tag{6}$$

Equation (5) represents the utility of household i under occupational choice j $[\,U_i(j)]$ in the benchmark case. If the *Bolsa Escola* program entitled all children[167] going to school to a transfer T, (5) would be replaced by:

$$U_i(j) = Z_i.\gamma_j + (\Upsilon_{-I} + \text{BE}_{ij}).\alpha_j + \beta_j.w_i + v_{ij} \quad \text{with BE}_{i0} = 0 \text{ and BE}_{i1} = \text{BE}_{i2} = T \tag{7}$$

Under the assumptions we have made, equation (7) is our full reduced-form model of the occupational choice of children, and would allow for simulations of the impact of *Bolsa Escola* transfers on those choices. All that remains is to obtain estimates of β, γ, α, w_i and the v_{ij}'s.

Estimation of the Discrete Choice Model

Assuming that the v_{ij} are iid across sample observations with a double exponential distribution leads to the well-known multi-logit model. However, some precautions must be taken in this case. It is well known that the probability that household i will select occupational choice k is given by:

$$p_{ik} = \frac{\text{Exp}(Z_i.\gamma_k + \Upsilon_{-i}.\alpha_k + w_i.\beta_k)}{\sum_j \text{Exp}(Z_i.g_j + \Upsilon_{-i}.a_j + w_i.b_j)} \tag{8}$$

Taking regime $j = 0$ as a reference, the preceding probability may be written as:

$$p_{ij} = \frac{\text{Exp}[Z_i.(\gamma_j - \gamma_0) + \Upsilon_{-i}.(\alpha_j - \alpha_0) + w_i(\beta_j - \beta_0)]}{1 + \sum_{j=1}^{2} \text{Exp}[Z_i.(\gamma_j - \gamma_0) + \Upsilon_{-i}.(\alpha_j - \alpha_0) + w_i(\beta_j - \beta_0)]} \quad \text{for } j = 1, 2 \tag{9}$$

and $p_{i0} = 1 - p_{i1} - p_{i2}$.

The difficulty is that the Multinomial logit estimation permits identifying only the differences $(\alpha_j - \alpha_0)$, $(\beta_j - \beta_0)$, and $(\gamma_j - \gamma_0)$ for $j = 1, 2$. Yet, inspection of (6) and (7) indicates that, because the *Bolsa Escola* transfer is state-contingent, meaning that the income variable is asymmetric across

---

167. It will prove simpler to discuss the estimation problem under this simplifying assumption. We reintroduce the means test, without any loss of generality, at the simulation stage.

alternatives, it is necessary to know *all three* coefficients α_0, α_1 and α_2 in order to find the utility maximizing alternative, k^*.

This is where the only structural assumption made so far becomes useful. Call $\hat{a}_j$ and $\hat{b}_j$ the estimated coefficients of the multilogit model corresponding to the income and the child earning variables for alternatives $j = 1, 2$, the alternative 0 being taken as the default. Then (5) implies the following system of equations:

$$\alpha_1 - \alpha_0 = \hat{a}_1$$

$$\alpha_2 - \alpha_0 = \hat{a}_2$$

$$(\alpha_1 M - \alpha_0).K = \hat{b}_1 \tag{10}$$

$$(\alpha_2 D - \alpha_0)K = \hat{b}_2$$

M is known from equation (3). It follows that arbitrarily setting a value for K or for D allows us to identify α_0, α_1 and α_2 and the remaining parameter in the pair (K, D). The identifying assumption made in what follows is that kids working on the market and not going to school have zero domestic production, i.e. $K = 1$. In other words, it is assumed that the observed labor allocations between market and domestic activities are corner solutions in all alternatives.[168] It then follows that:

$$\alpha_1 = \frac{\hat{a}_1 - \hat{b}_1}{1 - M} \quad \text{and} \quad \alpha_2 = \alpha_1 + \hat{a}_2 - \hat{a}_1 \tag{11}$$

Of course, a test of the relevance of the identifying assumption is that both α_1 and α_2 must be positive. One could also require that the value of D obtained from system (9) with $K = 1$ be in the interval $(0,1)$.

For completeness, it remains to indicate how estimates of the residual terms $v_{ij} - v_{i0}$ may be obtained. In a discrete choice model these values cannot be observed. It is only known that they belong to some interval. The idea is then to draw them for each observation in the relevant interval, that is: in a way consistent with the observed choice. For instance if observation i has made choice 1, it must be the case that :

$$Z_i.\gamma_1 + \Upsilon_{-i}. \hat{a}_1 + \hat{b}_1.w_i + (v_{i1} - v_{i0}) > \text{Sup}[0, Z_i.\gamma_2 + \Upsilon_{-i}. \hat{a}_2 + \hat{b}_2.w_i + (v_{i2} - v_{i0})]$$

The terms $v_{ij} - v_{i0}$ must be drawn so as to satisfy that inequality. All that is missing now is a complete vector of child earnings values, w_i.

Estimation of Potential Earnings

The discrete choice model requires a potential earning for each child, including those who do not work outside the household. To be fully rigorous, one could estimate both the discrete choice model and the earning equation simultaneously by maximum likelihood techniques. This is a rather cumbersome procedure. Practically, a multinomial probit would then be preferable to a multinomial logit in order to handle simultaneously the random terms of the discrete choice model and that of the earning equation. Integrating tri-variate normal distributions would then be required. Also, other issues which are already apparent with a simpler technique would not necessarily be solved.

---

168. In effect, this assumption may be weakened using some limited information on hours of work available in the survey.

We adopt a simpler approach, which has the advantages of transparency and robustness. It consists of estimating (3) by OLS, and then to generate random terms u_i for non-working kids, by drawing in the distribution generated by the residuals of the OLS estimation.

There are several reasons why correcting the estimation of the earning function for a selection bias was problematic. First, instrumenting earnings with a selection bias correction procedure requires finding instruments that would affect earnings but not the schooling/labor choice. No such instrument was readily available. Second, the correction of selection bias with the standard two-stage procedure is awkward in the case of more than two choices. Lee (1983) proposed a generalization of the Heckman procedure, but it has been shown that Lee's procedure was justified only in a rather unlikely particular case (Bourguignon et. al. 2001). For both of these reasons, failing to correct for possible selection bias in (3) did not seem too serious a problem. On the other hand, trying to correct using standard techniques and no convincing instrument led to rather implausible results.

Simulating Programs of the Bolsa Escola Type

As mentioned in footnote 11, the model (6)–(7) does not provide a complete representation of the choice faced by households in the presence of a program such as *Bolsa Escola*. This is because it takes into account the conditionality on the schooling of the children, but not the means-test. Taking into account both the means-test and the conditionality leads to choosing the alternative with maximum utility among the three following conditional cases:

$$U_i(0) = Z_i.\gamma_0 + \alpha_0 \Upsilon_{-I} + \beta_0 w_i + v_{i0}$$

$$U_i(1) = Z_i.\gamma_1 + \alpha_1(\Upsilon_{-I} + T) + \beta_1 w_i + v_{i1} \quad \text{if } \Upsilon_{-I} + M w_i \leq \Upsilon^\circ$$

$$U_i(1) = Z_i.\gamma_1 + \alpha_1 \Upsilon_{-I} + \beta_1 w_i + v_{i1} \quad \text{if } \Upsilon_{-I} + M w_i > \Upsilon^\circ \qquad (12)$$

$$U_i(2) = Z_i.\gamma_2 + \alpha_2(\Upsilon_{-I} + T) + \beta_2 w_i + v_{i2} \quad \text{if } \Upsilon_{-I} \leq \Upsilon^\circ$$

$$U_i(2) = Z_i.\gamma_2 + \alpha_2 \Upsilon_{-I} + \beta_2 w_i + v_{i2} \quad \text{if } \Upsilon_{-I} > \Upsilon^\circ$$

where Υ° stands for the means test. Of course, as mentioned above, only the differences between the utility corresponding to the three cases matter, so that one only need to know the differences $(\beta_j - \beta_0)$, $(\gamma_j - \gamma_0)$ and $(v_{ij} - v_{i0})$—but the three coefficients α_j. In this system, one can see how the introduction of *Bolsa Escola* might lead households from choice (0)—no schooling—to choices (1) or (2), but also from choice (1) to choice (2). In the latter case, a household might not qualify for the transfer T when the child both works and attends school, but qualifies if she stops working.

A wide variety of programs may be easily simulated using this framework. Both the means-test and the transfer T could be made dependent on characteristics of either the household or the child (X and H). In particular, T could depend on age or gender. Some examples of such alternative designs are simulated and discussed in the fifth section.

Before presenting the model estimations results, we should draw attention to two important limitations of the framework just described. Both arise from the set of assumptions discussed in the beginning of this section. The first limitation is that we can not take into account the household transfer ceiling of R\$45 per household. The reason is that by ignoring multi-children interactions in the model, it is as though we had effectively assumed that all households were single-child, from a behavioral point of view. In the non-behavioral part of the welfare simulations which are reported in the next section, however, each child was treated separately, and the R\$45 limit was applied.

The second limitation has to do with the exogeneity of non-child income Υ_{-I}. This exogeneity would clearly be a problem when there are more than one child at schooling age. Yet, it is also unrealistic even when only adult income is taken into account. It is clearly possible that the presence of the means-test might affect the labor supply behavior of adults, because there are

TABLE 10.1: SCHOOL ENROLLMENT AND OCCUPATION OF CHILDREN BY AGE (10–15 YEARS OLD)							
	10	11	12	13	14	15	Total
Not Studying	2.5%	2.3%	3.3%	5.6%	8.0%	13.0%	5.8%
Working and Studying	8.1%	10.9%	14.0%	18.3%	22.6%	27.3%	16.9%
Studying	89.4%	86.8%	82.7%	76.1%	69.4%	59.6%	77.3%
Total	100.0%	100.0%	100.0%	100.0%	100.0%	100.0%	100.0%

Source: PNAD/IBGE 1999 and author's calculation.

circumstances in which it might be in the interest of the family to work slightly less in order to qualify for *Bolsa Escola*. Note, however, that this might not be so sharply the case if the means-test is based, not on current income, but on some score-based proxy for permanent income, as appears to be the case in practice.

Descriptive Statistics and Estimation Results

The model consisting of equations (3) and (12) was estimated on data from the 1999 PNAD household survey. This survey is based on a sample of approximately 60,000 households, which is representative of the national population[169]. Although all children aged 6–15 qualify for participation in the program, the model was only estimated for 10–15 year-olds, since school enrollment below age 10 is nearly universal.[170] At the simulation stage, however, transfers are of course simulated for the whole universe of qualifying 6–15 year-olds.

Table 10.1 contains the basic description of the occupational structure of children aged 10–15 in Brazil, in 1999. In this age range, 77 percent of children report that they dedicate themselves exclusively to studying. Some 17 percent both work and study, and 6 percent do not attend school at all. This average pattern hides considerable variation across ages: school attendance declines—and work increases—monotonically with age. Whereas only 2.5 percent of ten year-olds are out of school, the figure for fifteen year-olds is 13 percent. Whereas 90 percent of ten year-olds dedicate themselves exclusively to studying, fewer than 60 percent of fifteen year-olds do so. From a behavioral point of view, it is thus clear that most of the action is to be found among the eldest children.

Table 10.2 presents the mean individual and household characteristics of those children, by occupational category. Children not going to school are both older and less educated than those still enrolled. As expected, households with school drop-outs are on average poorer, less educated and larger than households where kids are still going to school. Dropping out of school and engaging in child labor are relatively more frequent among non-whites and in the North East. Both forms of behavior are least common in metropolitan areas, but proportionately more common in non-metropolitan urban areas than in rural areas. Interestingly, households where children both work and go to school are in an intermediate position, along all dimensions, between those whose children specialize, but are generally closer to the group of drop-outs.

A remarkable feature of Table 10.2 is the observed amount of children's earnings, when they work and do not study. Ranging from around R$80 to R$120 per month, children's earnings represent approximately half the minimum wage, an order of magnitude that seems rather reasonable.

---

169. Except for the rural areas of the states of Acre, Amazonas, Pará, Rondônia and Roraima.

170. We know that school enrollment is nearly universal from answers to schooling questions in the PNAD. An additional reason to limit the estimation of the behavioral model to children aged ten or older is that the incidence of child labor at lower ages is probably measured with much greater error, since PNAD interviewers are instructed to pose labor and income questions only to individuals aged ten or older.

TABLE 10.2: SAMPLE MEANS. CHARACTERISTICS OF CHILDREN AND THE HOUSEHOLD THEY BELONG TO (10–15 YEARS OLD ONLY)

	Not studying	Working and Studying	Studying	Total
Age	13.5	13.2	12.3	12.51
Years of schooling	2.9	3.9	4.1	3.97
Household per capita income	80.9	104.5	202.0	178.25
Earning's children (observed)				
10	118.4	34.2	—	38.0
11	98.3	44.6	—	50.4
12	100.7	50.8	—	57.0
13	76.8	66.9	—	68.5
14	100.5	83.8	—	87.8
15	127.6	109.3	—	113.9
Years of schooling of the most educated parent	3.2	4.0	6.4	5.79
Age of the oldest parent	46.4	46.1	44.5	44.89
Number of household members	5.8	5.9	5.2	5.39
Race (White)	36.9%	40.9%	51.6%	48.9%
Gender (Male)	53.0%	65.2%	46.9%	50.3%
North	6.1%	5.6%	6.0%	5.9%
Northeast	40.4%	45.6%	29.9%	33.2%
Southeast	32.8%	26.1%	43.5%	39.9%
South	14.1%	15.9%	13.7%	14.1%
Center-West	6.6%	6.7%	6.9%	6.9%
Metropolitan area	18.2%	12.8%	30.9%	27.1%
Urban non metroplitan	34.0%	49.2%	16.0%	22.7%
Rural areas	47.8%	38.0%	53.0%	50.2%
Proportion of universe	6.1%	16.8%	77.1%	100.0%
Population	**1,208,313**	**3,345,075**	**15,329,237**	**19,882,625**

Source: PNAD/IBGE 1999 and author's calculation.

These amounts compares with the R$15 transfer that is granted by the *Bolsa Escola* program for children enrolled in school. Note, however, that the R$90 figure is not a good measure for the opportunity cost of schooling, since school attendance is evidently consistent with some amount of market work.

Tables 10.3 and 10.4 contain the estimation results. Because of the great behavioral variation across ages even within the 10–15 range—as revealed, for instance, in Table 10.1—we estimated the (identically specified) model separately for each age, as well as for the pooled sample of all 10–15 year-olds. The simulations reported in the next section rely on the age-specific models, but in this section we focus on the joint estimation, both for ease of discussion and because the larger sample size allowed for more precise estimation in this case.

TABLE 10.3: LOG EARNIGNS REGRESSION (10–15 YEARS OLD CHILDREN REPORTING EARNINGS)

		10 to 15 years old			15 years old		
		Coefficient	Std	P > |z|	Coefficient	Std	P > |z|
	n obs	2444			1010		
	R^2	0.43			0.54		
Dummy WS		−0.4118	0.0324	0.0000	−0.2285	0.0385	0.0000
Years of schooling		−0.0136	0.0198	0.4920	−0.0409	0.0244	0.0930
Years of schooling^2		0.0110	0.0021	0.0000	0.0077	0.0025	0.0020
Male		0.1746	0.0283	0.0000	0.1349	0.0355	0.0000
White		0.0658	0.0295	0.260	0.0600	0.355	0.0910
North		−0.2329	0.0447	0.0000	−0.1515	0.0748	0.0430
Northeast		−0.2054	0.0379	0.0000	−0.1529	0.0472	0.0010
South		−0.0461	0.0422	0.2750	−0.0165	0.0475	0.7290
Center-West		−0.1082	0.0426	0.0110	−0.0801	0.0490	0.1020
Urban non metropolitan		−0.0284	0.0408	0.4870	0.0472	0.0538	0.3810
Rural		0.0042	0.0327	0.8980	0.0507	0.0393	0.1970
Log of means earnings by cluster		0.3788	0.0148	0.0000	0.4756	0.0199	0.0000
Intercept		3.5266	0.0751	0.0000	2.7600	0.1176	0.0000

Source: PNAD/IBGE 1999 and author's calculation.

Table 10.3 shows the results of the OLS estimation of the earnings function (3), both for the pooled sample and for the 15 year-old group.[171] Geographical variables,[172] race and gender have the expected sign, and the same qualitative effect as for adults. So does (the logarithm of) the average earnings of children in the census cluster, which is included as a proxy for the spatial variation in the demand for child labor. The effect of previous schooling is best described as insignificant. Even though the coefficient of the squared term is positive and significant, the influence of the (negative and insignificant) linear term implies that earnings decline with schooling in the range relevant for 10–15 year-olds. It should be noted that our separate specifications mask the main determinant of earnings for children, namely age. In an alternative (unreported) specification for the pooled sample, when age was included as an explanatory variable, an additional year of age increased earnings by approximately 40 per cent. However, there was a clear non-linearity in the way age affected earnings, which is reflected in changes in the coefficient estimates when the model is separately estimated. These non-linearities and interactions between age and other determinants are the reason why the separate specification was preferred.

The estimate for m (the coefficient for "dummy WS" in Table 10.3) reveals that, as expected, the fact that a child goes to school at the same time as she works outside the household reduces total earnings in comparison with a comparable child who dedicates herself exclusively to market

171. Analogous results for the 10, 11, 12, 13 and 14 year-old samples are available from the authors on request.
172. With the South being insignificantly different from the reference Southeast region, as expected.

TABLE 10.4: MULTINOMIAL LOGIT COEFFICIENTS

	Pseudo-R^2	#obs	Working and Studying			Studying		
			Coefficient	Std	P > |z|	Coefficient	Std	P > |z|
10 to 15 years old	0.1586	42153						
Total household income			0.0004	0.0001	4.6300	0.0006	0.0001	7.8200
Earning's children (What)			−0.0075	0.0018	−4.2100	−0.0074	0.0015	−4.9300
Total people by household			−0.0343	0.0169	−2.0300	−0.1751	0.0157	−11.1400
Years of schooling			0.6635	0.0407	16.3100	0.8338	0.0378	22.0500
Years of schooling^2			−0.0383	0.0051	−7.5300	−0.0837	0.0048	−17.6000
White			0.0138	0.0628	0.2200	0.1613	0.0566	2.8500
Male			0.7447	0.0567	13.1400	−0.1841	0.0503	−3.6600
Max parent's education			0.0371	0.0104	3.5700	0.1300	0.0093	13.9100
Max parent's age			−0.0035	0.0027	−1.2900	0.0023	0.0024	0.9600
Number of children below 7			−0.0108	0.0362	−0.3000	0.0875	0.0332	2.6400
Rank of child			0.6433	0.0538	11.9500	0.9099	0.0504	18.0500
North			0.5673	0.1113	5.1000	0.0980	0.0998	0.9800
Northeast			0.7086	0.0789	8.9800	0.2854	0.0717	3.9800
South			0.1901	0.0867	2.1900	−0.3569	0.0778	−4.5800
Center-West			0.2757	0.0977	2.8200	−0.1013	0.0869	−1.1700
Urban non metropolitan			1.1803	0.0807	14.6200	−0.4999	0.0728	−6.8700
Rural			0.2030	0.0735	2.7600	−0.1835	0.0628	−2.9200
Means of earnings by cluster			0.0118	0.0073	1.6200	0.0022	0.0057	0.4000
Intercept			−2.3104	0.2071	−11.1600	0.4412	0.1846	2.3900

Source: PNAD/IBGE 1999 and author's calculation.

work. If one interprets this coefficient as reflecting fewer hours of work, then a child going to school works on average 40 per cent less than a dropout (for the pooled sample), or just under a quarter less for fifteen year-olds. These seem like reasonable orders of magnitude.

The results from the estimation of the multinomial logit for occupational choice also appear eminently plausible. They are reported in Table 10.4 (for the pooled sample) and Tables 10.4a and 10.4b for 10–12 and 13–15 year-olds, respectively. The reference category was "not studying" ($j = 0$), throughout. As expected, household income (net of the child's) has a positive effect on schooling, whereas the child's own (predicted) earnings have a negative effect. Household size reduces the probability of studying, compared to the alternatives.[173] Previous schooling at a given age has a positive (but concave) effect. Race has an insignificant effect on occupational choice,

---

173. To the extent that household size reflects a larger number of children, this is consistent with Becker's quantity-quality trade-off.

TABLE 10.4a: MULTINOMIAL LOGIT COEFFICIENTS

	Pseudo-R^2	#obs	Working and Studying			Studying		
			Coefficient	Std	P > |z|	Coefficient	Std	P > |z|
10 years old	0.2393	6853						
Total household income			0.0001	0.0004	0.8570	0.0006	0.0003	0.0760
Earning's children (What)			−0.0711	0.0273	0.0090	−0.0460	0.0251	0.0670
Total people by household			−0.0072	0.0769	0.9250	−0.0766	0.0679	0.2590
Years of schooling			2.5342	0.2466	0.0000	2.8347	0.2138	0.0000
Years of schooling^2			−0.4023	0.0599	0.0000	−0.4993	0.0513	0.0000
White			−0.2006	0.2611	0.4420	−0.1311	0.2375	0.5810
Male			0.6865	0.2057	0.0010	−0.2596	0.1803	0.1500
Max parent's education			0.0235	0.0396	0.5530	0.0621	0.0343	0.0710
Max parent's age			−0.0030	0.0094	0.7460	−0.0037	0.0079	0.6430
Number of children below 7			0.1721	0.1294	0.1840	0.0682	0.1145	0.5510
Rank of child			0.1935	0.1354	0.1530	0.0982	0.1179	0.4050
North			1.8948	0.4854	0.0000	0.7064	0.4214	0.0940
Northeast			1.7310	0.3279	0.0000	0.8418	0.2865	0.0030
South			0.5136	0.3755	0.1710	−0.2513	0.3263	0.4410
Center-West			1.5302	0.4621	0.0010	0.8179	0.4202	0.0520
Urban non metropolitan			3.1158	0.3732	0.0000	0.5128	0.3077	0.0960
Rural			1.0942	0.3324	0.0010	0.1258	0.2610	0.6300
Means of earnings by cluster			0.3847	0.1175	0.0010	0.1872	0.1090	0.0860
Intercept			−3.4075	0.7173	0.0000	1.4643	0.5863	0.0140
11 years old	0.2610	7022						
Total household income			−0.0001	0.0002	0.7180	0.0002	0.0002	0.3690
Earning's children (What)			−0.0247	0.0313	0.4310	0.0481	0.0296	0.1050
Total people by household			0.1202	0.0750	0.1090	0.1143	0.0698	0.1020
Years of schooling			1.8700	0.2440	0.0000	1.9526	0.2194	0.0000
Years of schooling^2			−0.2545	0.0500	0.0000	−0.2714	0.0451	0.0000
White			0.0327	0.2585	0.8990	0.0935	0.2424	0.7000
Male			0.3583	0.2115	0.0900	−0.4660	0.1970	0.0180
Max parent's education			0.0057	0.0416	0.8910	0.0850	0.0381	0.0260
Max parent's age			−0.0061	0.0094	0.5180	0.0020	0.0085	0.8180
Number of children below 7			−0.1829	0.1392	0.1890	−0.2591	0.1310	0.0480
Rank of child			−0.0341	0.1468	0.8160	−0.2566	0.1372	0.0610

(continued)

TABLE 10.4a: MULTINOMIAL LOGIT COEFFICIENTS (CONTINUED)

	Pseudo-R²	#obs	Working and Studying			Studying		
			Coefficient	Std	P > |z|	Coefficient	Std	P > |z|
North			1.2805	0.4554	0.0050	0.5387	0.4270	0.2070
Northeast			0.8725	0.3029	0.0040	−0.1828	0.2794	0.5130
South			1.4466	0.4633	0.0020	0.3018	0.4463	0.4990
Center-West			0.4704	0.3925	0.2310	−0.5806	0.3546	0.1020
Urban non metropolitan			1.6909	0.3100	0.0000	−0.0622	0.2874	0.8290
Rural			−0.0171	0.2962	0.9540	−0.1303	0.2621	0.6190
Means of earnings by cluster			0.0277	0.0313	0.3750	−0.0778	0.0313	0.0130
Intercept			−2.4141	0.6731	0.0000	1.6659	0.6096	0.0060
12 years old	0.2258	7196						
Total household income			0.0000	0.0002	0.8790	0.0003	0.0002	0.1610
Earning's children (What)			−0.0093	0.0084	0.2680	−0.0150	0.0084	0.0730
Total people by household			−0.0005	0.0581	0.9940	−0.0769	0.0554	0.1650
Years of schooling			1.3963	0.1728	0.0000	1.5883	0.1572	0.0000
Years of schooling²			−0.1405	0.0305	0.0000	−0.1787	0.0278	0.0000
White			0.1590	0.2030	0.4330	0.2339	0.1907	0.2200
Male			0.9392	0.1726	0.0000	0.0547	0.1580	0.7290
Max parent's education			0.0072	0.0319	0.8220	0.0795	0.0289	0.0060
Max parent's age			−0.0023	0.0089	0.8010	0.0001	0.0082	0.9920
Number of children below 7			−0.0121	0.1164	0.9170	0.0150	0.1082	0.8900
Rank of child			0.6002	0.1712	0.0000	0.4909	0.1601	0.0020
North			1.2716	0.3599	0.0000	0.6064	0.3377	0.0720
Northeast			0.8998	0.2481	0.0000	0.3845	0.2312	0.0960
South			0.0463	0.2760	0.8670	−0.5530	0.2496	0.0270
Center-West			−0.0045	0.3113	0.9890	−0.2569	0.2818	0.3620
Urban non metropolitan			2.5243	0.2654	0.0000	0.1413	0.2319	0.5420
Rural			1.0872	0.2437	0.0000	0.2634	0.2035	0.1960
Means of earnings by cluster			0.0214	0.0184	0.2440	−0.0046	0.0188	0.8080
Intercept			−4.0732	0.6442	0.0000	−0.1458	0.5756	0.8000

Source: PNAD/IBGE 1999 and author's calculation.

TABLE 10.4b: MULTINOMIAL LOGIT COEFFICIENTS

	Pseudo-R^2	#obs	Working and Studying			Studying		
			Coefficient	Std	P > |z|	Coefficient	Std	P > |z|
13 years old	0.1813	7077						
Total household income			0.0003	0.0002	0.1390	0.0004	0.0002	0.0280
Earning's children (What)			−0.0211	0.0078	0.0070	−0.0143	0.0078	0.0660
Total people by household			0.0422	0.0434	0.3310	−0.0561	0.0402	0.1630
Years of schooling			0.7544	0.1192	0.0000	0.9879	0.1135	0.0000
Years of schooling^2			−0.0431	0.0184	0.0190	−0.0737	0.0176	0.0000
White			0.0422	0.1606	0.7930	0.1379	0.1492	0.3560
Male			0.8550	0.1365	0.0000	−0.0430	0.1270	0.7350
Max parent's education			0.0097	0.0250	0.6990	0.0798	0.0232	0.0010
Max parent's age			−0.0022	0.0064	0.7260	−0.0020	0.0059	0.7300
Number of children below 7			−0.1093	0.0921	0.2350	−0.0676	0.0856	0.4300
Rank of child			0.1376	0.1495	0.3570	0.0841	0.1422	0.5540
North			0.7935	0.2676	0.0030	0.4388	0.2477	0.0760
Northeast			1.0844	0.1923	0.0000	0.7627	0.1812	0.0000
South			0.4987	0.2313	0.0310	−0.2157	0.2142	0.3140
Center-West			0.4728	0.2452	0.0540	0.1034	0.2218	0.6410
Urban non metropolitan			1.1527	0.2210	0.0000	−0.5803	0.2061	0.0050
Rural			0.2636	0.2008	0.1890	−0.1524	0.1824	0.4030
Means of earnings by cluster			0.0342	0.0131	0.0090	−0.0090	0.0138	0.5140
Intercept			−2.4040	0.5116	0.0000	0.3448	0.4679	0.4610
14 years old	0.1795	7052						
Total household income			0.0002	0.0002	0.2150	0.0004	0.0001	0.0060
Earning's children (What)			−0.0029	0.0039	0.4590	0.0077	0.0049	0.1190
Total people by household			0.0431	0.0362	0.2350	−0.0256	0.0349	0.4630
Years of schooling			0.4374	0.0924	0.0000	0.7161	0.0946	0.0000
Years of schooling^2			−0.0041	0.0132	0.7530	−0.0385	0.0132	0.0040
White			−0.0286	0.1310	0.8270	0.1265	0.1233	0.3050
Male			0.6975	0.1151	0.0000	−0.2034	0.1092	0.0630
Max parent's education			0.0369	0.0233	0.1130	0.1091	0.0218	0.0000
Max parent's age			−0.0137	0.0060	0.0220	−0.0024	0.0056	0.6750
Number of children below 7			−0.1234	0.0769	0.1090	−0.1285	0.0750	0.0870
Rank of child			−0.1313	0.1638	0.4230	−0.2028	0.1582	0.2000

(continued)

TABLE 10.4b: MULTINOMIAL LOGIT COEFFICIENTS (CONTINUED)

	Pseudo-R^2	#obs	Working and Studying			Studying		
			Coefficient	Std	P > |z|	Coefficient	Std	P > |z|
North			0.6328	0.2363	0.0070	0.4337	0.2236	0.0520
Northeast			0.9830	0.1634	0.0000	0.8621	0.1573	0.0000
South			0.0849	0.1802	0.6380	−0.5569	0.1678	0.0010
Center-West			0.5093	0.2100	0.0150	0.2439	0.1995	0.2220
Urban non metropolitan			0.9129	0.1687	0.0000	−0.7278	0.1599	0.0000
Rural			0.2720	0.1529	0.0750	−0.1551	0.1388	0.2640
Means of earnings by cluster			0.0016	0.0051	0.7620	−0.0397	0.0078	0.0000
Intercept			−1.4708	0.4538	0.0010	−0.0760	0.4350	0.8610
15 years old	0.1549	6953						
Total household income			0.0002	0.0001	0.1800	0.0004	0.0001	0.0000
Earning's children (What)			−0.0029	0.0028	0.2860	−0.0049	0.0032	0.1290
Total people by household			0.0752	0.0294	0.0110	0.0195	0.0291	0.5040
Years of schooling			0.2210	0.0719	0.0020	0.3994	0.0735	0.0000
Years of schooling^2			0.0109	0.0087	0.2130	−0.0052	0.0088	0.5510
White			−0.1459	0.1070	0.1730	0.1201	0.1015	0.2370
Male			0.6201	0.0949	0.0000	−0.1786	0.0903	0.0480
Max parent's education			0.0503	0.0173	0.0040	0.1109	0.0162	0.0000
Max parent's age			0.0103	0.0050	0.0400	0.0214	0.0049	0.0000
Number of children below 7			−0.2800	0.0669	0.0000	−0.2619	0.0638	0.0000
Rank of child			—	—	—	—	—	—
North			0.3019	0.1848	0.1020	0.3707	0.1741	0.0330
Northeast			0.6628	0.1291	0.0000	0.6156	0.1260	0.0000
South			−0.0736	0.1440	0.6090	−0.5285	0.1384	0.0000
Center-West			0.1186	0.1635	0.4680	−0.0937	0.1538	0.5420
Urban non metropolitan			0.4465	0.1439	0.0020	−0.7331	0.1403	0.0000
Rural			−0.1145	0.1298	0.3780	−0.3243	0.1216	0.0080
Means of earnings by cluster			0.0048	0.0038	0.2030	−0.0100	0.0050	0.0440
Intercept			−2.2590	0.3516	0.0000	−1.4724	0.3444	0.0000

Source: PNAD/IBGE 1999 and author's calculation.

unlike gender which reflects the usual asymmetry between market work for males and domestic work for females. Parents' education has the expected positive effect—on top of the income effect—on children's schooling.

In view of this general consistency of both the earnings and the discrete occupational choice models, the question now arises of whether the structural restrictions necessary for the consistency of the proposed simulation work (positive α_1 and α_2, and $0 < D < 1$) hold or not. For the pooled sample and using (11), we find that:

$$\alpha_1 = \frac{\hat{a}_1 - \hat{b}_1}{1 - M} = \frac{0.0004 + 0.0075}{1 - \text{Exp}(-0.4118)} = 0.023 \quad \text{and} \quad \alpha_2 = \alpha_1 + \hat{a}_2 - \hat{a}_1 = .024$$

The coefficients of income in the utility of alternatives $j = 1$ and 2 is thus positive, which is in agreement with the original model. This is also true of the utility of alternative $j = 0$ since it may be computed that $\alpha_0 = 0.023$. The value of the parameter D may also be derived. Under the identifying assumption that $K = 1$, it is given by:

$$D = \frac{\hat{b}_2 + \alpha_0}{\alpha_2} = \frac{-0.0074 + 0.023}{0.024} = 0.6609$$

This figure means that children who are going to school but do not work on the market are estimated to provide domestic production for approximately two-thirds of their potential market earnings. Note that this is almost identical to the estimated value for M [$=\text{Exp}(-0.4118) = 0.6625$]. Because M denotes the average contribution to household income from children both studying and working, as a share of their potential contribution if not studying, this implies that the estimated value of non-market work by children studying (and not working in the market) is approximately equal to the market value of work by those studying (and working in the market). If there was little selection on unobservables into market work, this is exactly what one would expect.

Overall, the estimates obtained from the multinomial discrete occupational choice model and the earning equation seem therefore remarkably consistent with rational, utility-maximizing behavior. We may thus expect simulations run on the basis of these models and the identifying structural assumptions about the parameter K to yield sensible results. We can now turn to our main objective: gauging the order of magnitude of the effects of programs such as *Bolsa Escola*.

An *ex ante* Evaluation of *Bolsa Escola* and Alternative Program Designs

Bolsa Escola—and many conditional cash transfer schemes like it—are said to have two distinct objectives: (i) to reduce current poverty (and sometimes inequality) through the targeted transfers, and (ii) to reduce future poverty, by increasing the incentives for today's poor to invest in their human capital. Later on in this section, we will turn to the first objective. We begin by noting, however, that, as stated, the second objective is impossible to evaluate, even in an *ex ante* manner. Whether increased school enrollment translates into greater human capital depends on the trends in the quality of the educational services provided, and there is no information on that in this data set.[174] Finally, whether more "human capital", however measured., will help reduce poverty in the future or not, depends on what happens to the rates of return to it between now and then. This is a complex, general equilibrium question, which goes well beyond the scope of this exercise.

What we might be able to say something about is the intermediate target of increasing school enrollment. While the preceding remarks suggest that this is not sufficient to establish whether the

---

174. There is limited information in other data sets, such as the Education Ministry's Sistema de Acompanhamento do Ensino Básico (SAEB), but not for sufficiently long periods of time. See Albernaz et al. (2002).

TABLE 10.5: SIMULATED EFFECT OF *BOLSA ESCOLA* ON SCHOOLING AND WORKING STATUS (ALL CHILDREN 10–15 YEARS OLD)

	All Households			
	Not Studying	**Working and Studying**	**Studying**	**Total**
Not Studying	66.6%	9.0%	24.4%	5.8%
Working and Studying	—	98.1%	1.9%	16.9%
Studying	—	—	100.0%	77.3%
Total	**3.9%**	**17.1%**	**79.1%**	**100.0%**

	Poor Households			
	Not Studying	**Working and Studying**	**Studying**	**Total**
Not Studying	52.0%	13.4%	34.6%	9.1%
Working and Studying	—	99.0%	1.0%	23.7%
Studying	—	—	100.0%	67.2%
Total	**4.7%**	**24.7%**	**70.6%**	**100.0%**

Source: PNAD/IBGE 1999 and author's calculation.

program will have an impact on future poverty, it is at least necessary.[175] An *ex ante* evaluation of impact on this dimension of the program thus requires simulating the number of children that may change schooling and working status because of it.

This is done by applying the decision system (12)—with behavioral parameter values (α, β, γ, M and D) estimated from (9)–(11), and policy parameter values (T and Υ^0) taken from the actual specification of *Bolsa Escola*—to the original data. Equation (12) is then used to simulate a counterfactual distribution of occupations, on the basis of the observed characteristics and the restrictions on residual terms for each individual child. Comparing the vector of occupational choices thus generated with the original, observed vector, we see that the program leads to some children moving from choice $S_i = 0$ to choices $S_i = 1$ or 2, and from $S_i = 1$ to choices $S_i = 2$. The corresponding transition matrix is shown in Table 10.5 for all children between 10 and 15, as well as for all children in the same age group living in poor households.[176]

Despite the small value of the proposed transfer, Table 10.5 suggests that one in every three children (aged 10–15) who are presently not enrolled in school would get enough incentive from *Bolsa Escola* to change occupational status and go to school. Among them, just over a quarter would enroll, but remain employed on the labor market. The other three quarters would actually cease work outside their household. This would reduce the proportion of children outside school from 5.8 to 3.9 percent.

The impact on those currently both studying and working would be much smaller. Barely 2 percent of them would abandon work to dedicate themselves exclusively to their studies. As a

175. One could argue that it is not even necessary, since the transfers might, by themselves, alleviate credit constraints and have long-term positive impacts, e.g. through improved nutrition. We focus on whether the conditional nature of these transfers actually have any impact of the children's occupational choices (or time allocation decisions).

176. A household was considered poor if its (regionally price-deflated and imputed rent-adjusted) per capita income was less than R$74.48 in the reference month of the 1999 PNAD survey. For the derivation of the poverty line, see Ferreira et al. (forthcoming).

result of this small outflow, combined with an inflow from occupational category 1, the group of children both studying and working would actually grow in the simulated scenario, albeit marginally.

The impacts are even more pronounced, as one would expect, among the poor who are the target population for the program. According to the poverty line being used, the incidence of poverty in Brazil is 30.5 percent. However, because there are more children in poor households (this being one of the reasons why they are poor), the proportion of 10–15 children in poor households is much higher: 42 percent. The second panel in Table 10.5 shows that dropouts are much more frequent among them (9.1 instead of 5.8 per cent for the whole population). It also shows that *Bolsa Escola* is more effective in increasing school enrollment. The fall in the proportion of dropouts is one-half, rather than one-third. As a result, the simulation suggests that *Bolsa Escola* could increase the school enrollment rate among the poor by approximately 4.4 percentage points. Once again, this increase comes at the expense of the "not studying" category, whose numbers are halved, rather than of the "working and studying" category, which actually becomes marginally more numerous.

A 50 percent reduction in the proportion of poor children outside school is by no means an insubstantial achievement, particularly in light of the fact that it seems to be manageable with fairly small transfers (R$15 per child per month). This is partly due to the fact that the value of the current contributions of children who are enrolled in school is a sizable proportion of their potential earnings when completely outside school. Those proportions are exactly the interpretation of the parameters M (for those who work on the market as well as study) and D (for those who work at home as well as study), which we estimated to be of the order of 0.66. Applying that factor to R$100, as a rough average of the earnings of children in category $j = 0$ (see Table 10.2), we are left with some R$33 as the true opportunity cost of enrolling in school. Consequently, those children who change occupation from that category in response to the R$15 transfer must have average personal present valuations of the expected stream of benefits from enrolling greater than R$18. Those who don't, must on average value education at less than that.

Because our simulations suggest that *Bolsa Escola*, as currently formulated, would still leave some 4 percent of all 10–15 year-olds (4.7 percent among the poor ones) outside school, it is interesting to investigate the potential effects of changing some of the program parameters. This was, after all, one of the initial motivations for undertaking this kind of *ex ante* counterfactual analysis. Table 10.6 shows the results of such a comparative exercise in terms of occupational choice, using transition matrices analogous to those in Table 10.5, once again both for all children and then separately for poor households only. Table 10.7 compares the impact of each scenario with that of the benchmark program specification, in terms of poverty and inequality measures. Four standard inequality measures were selected, namely the Gini coefficient and three members of the Generalized Entropy Class: the mean log deviation, the Theil-T index and (one half of) the square of the coefficient of variation. For poverty, we present the three standard FGT (0, 1, 2) measures, with respect to the aforementioned Ferreira et. al. (forthcoming) poverty line. This later table allows us to gauge impact in terms of the first objective of the program, namely the reduction of current poverty (and possibly inequality).

In both tables, the simulation results for six alternative scenarios are presented. In scenario 1, the eligibility criteria (including the means test) are unchanged, but transfer amounts (and the total household ceiling) are both doubled. In scenario 2, the uniform R$15 per child transfer is replaced by an age-contingent transfer, whereby 10 year-olds would receive R$15, 11 year-olds would receive R$20, 12 year-olds would receive R$25, 13 year-olds would receive R$35, 14 year-olds would receive R$40, and 15 year-olds received R$45.[177] In scenario 3, transfer amounts were unchanged, but the means-test was raised from R$90 to R$120. Scenario 4 combines scenarios 1 and 3: the transfer was doubled, and the means-test raised to R$120. Scenario 5 combines

---

177. The household ceiling was also doubled to R$90 in this case.

TABLE 10.6: SIMULATED EFFECT ON SCHOOLING AND WORKING STATUS OF ALTERNATIVE SPECIFICATIONS OF CONDITIONAL CASH TRANSFER PROGRAM (ALL CHILDREN 10–15 YEARS OLD)

	Original	Bolsa Escola's Program	Scenario 1	Scenario 2	Scenario 3	Scenario 4	Scenario 5	Scenario 6
All Households								
Not going to school	5.8%	3.9%	2.8%	2.8%	3.6%	2.4%	2.3%	5.8%
Going to school and working	16.9%	17.1%	17.1%	17.1%	17.2%	17.2%	17.2%	16.8%
Going to school and not working	77.3%	79.1%	80.1%	80.1%	79.3%	80.4%	80.4%	77.4%
Total	**100.0%**	**100.0%**	**100.0%**	**100.0%**	**100.0%**	**100.0%**	**100.0%**	**100.0%**
Poor Households								
Not going to school	9.1%	4.7%	2.5%	2.5%	4.7%	2.5%	2.5%	9.0%
Going to school and working	23.7%	24.7%	25.1%	25.1%	24.8%	25.3%	5.3%	23.6%
Going to school and not working	67.2%	70.6%	72.4%	72.3%	70.5%	72.2%	72.2%	67.3%
Total	**100.0%**	**100.0%**	**100.0%**	**100.0%**	**100.0%**	**100.0%**	**100.0%**	**100.0%**

Source: PNAD/IBGE 1999 and author's calculation.

TABLE 10.7: SIMULATED DISTRIBUTIONAL EFFECTS OF ALTERNATIVE SPECIFICATIONS OF THE CONDITIONAL CASH TRANSFER PROGRAM

	Original	Bolsa Escola's Program	Scenario 1	Scenario 2	Scenario 3	Scenario 4	Scenario 5	Scenario 6
Mean Income per capita	253.9	255.0	256.1	255.8	255.2	256.5	256.3	255.1
Inequality measures								
Gini coefficient	0.594	0.589	0.584	0.585	0.588	0.583	0.584	0.589
Mean logarithmic deviation	0.704	0.670	0.647	0.652	0.669	0.644	0.649	0.668
Theil index	0.710	0.700	0.690	0.692	0.699	0.687	0.689	0.699
Generalized Entropy (2)	1.605	1.589	1.572	1.575	1.585	1.565	1.569	1.587
Poverty measures								
Poverty headcount	30.5%	29.5%	28.2%	28.5%	29.5%	28.2%	28.5%	29.4%
Poverty gap	13.5%	12.4%	11.2%	11.5%	12.4%	11.2%	11.5%	12.3%
Total square deviation from poverty line	8.1%	7.1%	6.2%	6.4%	7.1%	6.2%	6.4%	7.0%
Annual cost of the program (million Reais)		1,668	3,228	3,000	1,944	3,984	3,720	1,668

Source: PNAD/IBGE 1999 and author's calculation.

scenarios 2 and 3 in the same way: an age-progressive transfer with a R$120 means-test. Scenario 6 simulated a targeted transfer exactly as in *Bolsa Escola*, but with no conditionality: every child in households below the means-test received the benefit, with no requirement relating to school attendance.

Table 10.6 gives rise to three main results. First of all, a comparison of Scenario 6 and the actual *Bolsa Escola* program suggests that conditionality plays a crucial role in inducing the change in children's time-allocation decisions. The proportions of children in each occupational category under Scenario 6 are almost identical to the original data (that is, no program). This suggests that it is the conditional requirement to enroll in order to receive the benefit—rather than the pure income effect from the transfer—which is the primary cause of the extra demand for schooling evident in the *Bolsa Escola* column.

Second, scenario 1 reveals that the occupational impact of the program is reasonably elastic with respect to the transfer amount. The proportion of un-enrolled children drops another percentage point (to some 25 percent) in response to a doubling of the transfers. The proportion of children in the "studying only" category rises by the same percentage point. Scenario 2 suggests that it doesn't matter much, in aggregate terms, whether this increase in transfers is uniform across ages, or made to become increasing in the age of the child. Finally, scenario 3 (and the combinations in scenarios 4 and 5) suggest that occupational effects are less sensitive to the means-test than to the transfer amount.

Results are considerably less impressive in terms of the program's first stated objective, namely the reduction in current poverty (and inequality) levels. Table 10.7 suggests that the program, as currently envisaged, would only imply a one percentage point decline in the short-run incidence of poverty in Brazil, as measured by $P(0)$. However, there is some evidence that the transfers would be rather well targeted, since the inequality-averse poverty indicator $P(2)$ would fall by proportionately more than $P(0)$, from 8 to 7 percent. This is consistent with the inequality results: whereas the Gini would fall by only half a point as a result of the scheme, measures which are more sensitive to the bottom, such as the mean log deviation, fall by a little more. Overall, however, the evidence in column 2 of Table 10.7 falls considerably short of a ringing endorsement of *Bolsa Escola* as a program for the alleviation of current poverty or inequality.

The situation could be somewhat improved by increases in the transfer amounts (scenarios 1 and 2). Nevertheless, even a doubling of the transfer amount to R$30 per month would only shave another 1.3 percentage points off the headcount.[178] An increase in the means-test would not help much, as indicated by Scenario 3. This is consistent with our earlier suggestion that the program already appears to be well-targeted to the poor. If it fails to lift many of them above the poverty line, this is a consequence of the small size of the transfers, rather than of the targeting.

These results contrast with the arithmetic simulations reported by Camargo and Ferreira (2001), in which a somewhat broader, but essentially similar program would reduce the incidence of poverty (with respect to the same poverty line and in the same sample) by two-thirds, from 30.5 to 9.9 percent. This was despite the fact that the absence of a behavioral component to the simulation weakened its power, by excluding from the set of recipients those households whose children might have enrolled in response to the program. The reason is simple: Camargo and Ferreira simulate much higher transfer levels, ranging from R$150 to R$220 per household (rather than child).

Conclusions

In this paper, we proposed a micro-simulation method for evaluating and experimenting with conditional cash-transfer program designs, *ex ante*. We were concerned with the impacts of the Brazilian *Bolsa Escola* program, which aims to reduce both current and future poverty by providing small targeted cash transfers to poor households, provided their children are enrolled in and in actual attendance at school. We were interested in assessing two dimensions of the

---

178. The simulated one-percentage-point fall in $P(2)$ is, once again, more respectable.

program: its impact on the occupational choice (or time-allocation) decisions of children, and the effects on current poverty and inequality.

For this purpose, we estimated a discrete occupational choice model (a multinomial logit) on a nationally representative household-level sample, and used its estimated parameters to make predictions about the counterfactual occupational decisions of children, under different assumptions about the availability and design of cash transfer programs. These assumptions were basically expressed in terms of different values for two key policy parameters: the means-test level of household income; and the transfer amount.

Because predicted earnings values were needed for all children in the simulation, this procedure also required estimating a Mincerian earnings equation for children in the sample, and using it to predict earnings in some cases. Also, because the income values accruing to each household were not symmetric across different occupational choices, standard estimation procedures for the multinomial logit were not valid. An identification assumption was needed, and we chose it to be that children not enrolled in school work only in the market, and have a zero contribution to domestic work. Under this assumption, the estimation of the model generated remarkably consistent results: marginal utilities of income were always positive, and very similar across occupational categories. Time spent working by those enrolled in school, as a fraction of time spent working by those not enrolled, was always in the $(0, 1)$ interval and was basically identical—and equal to two-thirds—whether work was domestic or in the market.

When this estimated occupational choice model was used to simulate the official (April 2001) design of the federal Brazilian *Bolsa Escola* program, we found that there was considerable behavioral response from children to the program. About one third of all 10–15 year-olds not currently enrolled in school, according to the model, would enroll in response to the program. Among poor households, this proportion was even higher: one half would enter school. The proportion of children in the middle occupational category ("studying and working in the market") would not fall. In fact, it would rise, marginally.

Results in terms of the reduction of current poverty, however, were less heartening. As currently designed, the federal *Bolsa Escola* program would reduce poverty incidence by one percentage point only, and the Gini coefficient by half a point. Results were better for measures more sensitive to the bottom of the distribution, but the effect was never remarkable.

Both the proportion of children enrolling in school in response to program availability and the degree of reduction in current poverty turn out to be rather sensitive to transfer amounts, and rather insensitive to the level of the means-test. This suggests that the targeting of the Brazilian *Bolsa Escola* program is adequate, but that poverty reduction through this instrument, although effective, is not magical. Governments may be transferring cash in an intelligent and efficient way, but they still need to transfer more substantial amounts, if they hope to make a dent in the country's high levels of deprivation.

References

Abramovay, M., C. Andrade, and J.J. Waiselfisz. 1998. *Melhoria Educacional e Redução da Pobreza*. Brasília: Edições UNESCO.

Albernaz, Ângela, Francisco H.G. Ferreira, and Creso Franco. 2002. "Qualidade e Eqüidade na Educação Fundamental Brasileira." Discussion Paper #455, Departamento de Economia, Pontifícia Universidade Católica, Rio de Janeiro.

Atkinson, Anthony, and François Bourguignon. 1991. "Tax-Benefit Models for Developing Countries: Lessons from Developed Countries." In J. Khalilzadeh-Shirazi and A. Shah, eds., *Tax Policy in Developing Countries*. Washington, D.C.: World Bank.

Baland, Jean-Marie, and James A. Robinson. 2000. "Is Child Labor Inefficient?" *Journal of Political Economy* 108:663–679.

Basu, Kaushik. 1999. "Child Labor: Cause, Consequence and Cure, with Remarks on International Labor Standards." *Journal of Economic Literature* XXXVII:1083–1119.

Bhalotra, Sonia. 2000. "Is Child Work Necessary?" Cambridge University. Processed.

Bourguignon, François, M. Fournier, and M. Gurgand. 2001. "Selection Bias Correction Based on the Multinomial Logit Model." Working Paper #20023-04, CREST/INSEE, Paris.

Bourguignon, François, and Pierre-Andre Chiappori. 1994. "The Collective Approach to Household Behavior." In Blundell, Preston, and Walker, eds., *The Measurement of Household Welfare*. Cambridge: Cambridge University Press.

Browning, Martin, François Bourguignon, Pierre-Andre Chiappori, and Valerie Lechene. 1994. "Income and Outcomes: A Structural Model of Intra-Household Allocation." *Journal of Political Economy* 102(6):1067–1096.

Camargo, José Márcio, and Francisco H.G. Ferreira. 2001. "O Benefício Social Único: uma proposta de reforma da política social no Brasil." Discussion Paper #443, Departamento de Economia, Pontifícia Universidade Católica, Rio de Janeiro.

Chiappori, Pierre-Andre. 1992. "Collective Labor Supply and Welfare." *Journal of Political Economy* 100:437–467.

Ferreira, Francisco H.G., Peter Lanjouw, and Marcelo Neri. Forthcoming. "A Robust Poverty Profile for Brazil Using Multiple Data Sources." *Revista Brasileira de Economia*.

Freije, Samuel, and Luiz F. Lopez-Calva. 2000. "Child Labor and Poverty in Venezuela and Mexico." El Colégio de Mexico, Mexico City. Processed.

Gertler, Paul, and Paul Glewwe. 1990. "The Willingness to Pay for Education in Developing Countries: Evidence from Rural Peru." *Journal of Public Economics* 42:251–275.

Grootaert, Christiaan, and Harry Patrinos, eds. 1999. *The Policy Analysis of Child Labor: A Comparative Study*. New York: St Martin's Press.

Harding, Ann, ed. 1996. *Microsimulation and Public Policy*. Amsterdam: Elsevier.

Heckman, James, and E. Vytlacil. 2002. "Econometric evaluation of social programs." In J. Heckman and E. Leamer, eds., *Handbook of Econometrics*. Vol. 5, Amsterdam: North-Holland.

Parker, Susan, and Emmanuel Skoufias. 2000. "The Impact of Progresa on Work, Leisure and Time Allocation." IFPRI Final Report on Progresa, IFPRI, Washington, D.C.

Ravallion, Martin, and Quentin Wodon. 2000. "Does Child Labor Displace Schooling? Evidence on Behavioral Responses to an Enrollment Subsidy." *Economic Journal* 110:C158–C175.

Rocha, Sônia, and João Sabóia. 1998. "Programas de Renda Mínima: Linhas Gerais de uma Metodologia de Avaliação." Discussion Paper #582, IPEA/UNDP, Rio de Janeiro.

Rosenzweig, Mark, and Robert Evenson. 1977. "Fertility, Schooling and the Economic Contribution of Children in Rural India: An Econometric Analysis." *Econometrica* 45(5):1065–1079.

Rubin, Donald. 1977. "Assignment to a Treatment Group on the Basis of a Covariate." *Journal of Educational Statistics* 2:1–26.

Rubin, Donald, and Paul Rosenbaum. 1985. "The Bias Due to Incomplete Matching." *Biometrica* 41(1):103–116.

Sant'Ana, S.R., and A. Moraes. 1997. *Avaliação do Programa Bolsa Escola do GDF*. Brasília: Fundação Grupo Esquel Brasil.

Schultz, T. Paul. 2000. "The Impact of Progresa on School Enrollment." IFPRI Final Report on Progresa, IFPRI, Washington, D.C.

World Bank. 2001. "Brazil: An Assessment of the Bolsa Escola Programs." Report 20208-BR, Washington, D.C.

CHAPTER 11

THE DYNAMICS OF THE SKILL-PREMIUM IN BRAZIL: GROWING DEMAND AND INSUFFICIENT SUPPLY?

By Andreas Blom and Carlos Eduardo Vélez[179]

Abstract

Labor market income in Brazil is extremely unequal. Previous literature, such as Ferreira and Paes de Barros (1999) has found that the persistent rise in skill-premium explains a large part of the increasing wage-inequality. During the last decades, the marginal returns to higher education have increased dramatically and have generated an increasing "convexification" of the earnings function deteriorating income inequality in two ways: first by increasing the income differences between the skilled and unskilled and by severely weakening the potential income equalization that could be obtained from the higher and more equally distributed educational endowments among new cohorts of workers, Vélez, et al. (2001). This paper uses the framework of Katz and Murphy (1992) and Murphy, Riddell, and Romer (1998), to explain the evolution of returns to labor skills in terms of specific supply and demand changes during the last two decades. Our findings suggest the substantial but asymmetric expansion of the education system in Brazil—with weaker growth of tertiary education—combined with a steady skill-biased change in labor demand explains the increasing skill premium. Our simulations suggest that an aggressive long term expansion in the supply, ceteris paribus, reducing the skill-premium to levels observed in developed countries would lead to a 4.5 gini points reduction in the gini coefficient of individual labor market income. Therefore, expanding tertiary education aggressively would not only increase economic growth by investing in high return assets, but it would also mitigate wage-inequality in the long run. The policy challenge is finding ways to expand tertiary education at reasonable marginal costs—well below the current level observed in average Brazilian universities—and with minimum burden on the public budget.

179. The authors are grateful for comments and suggestions from Mauricio Santamaria, Serguei Soares and from participants at the World Bank presentation.

Introduction

Brazil has one of the most skewed income distributions in the world. The huge disparity between those that have and those that have not, receives growing attention among policymakers and in the public. Multiple factors lie behind the notorious income-inequality. The increasing wage disparity between those who have tertiary education and those that do not appears to be one key piece in the inequality-puzzle. This paper models the evolution of returns to labor skills in Brazil in terms of specific supply and demand changes during the last two decades.

The role of education for wage-inequality dates back to the human capital revolution in economics, Becker (1965) and Mincer (1974). In particular Tinbergen emphasizes that differences in salary between workers to a large extent can be attributed to differences in attained schooling and that a thorough inequality analysis has to encompass both supply and demand:

> Quite often the opinion is held that income differences in a rigid way reflect differences in the pro-
> ductive qualities of people. As a consequence, the inequality between human beings is seen as a
> reason for income inequality to persist, not to say to be preordained. Even if we assume for a while
> that differences in ability cannot be changed [. . .] what matters (for inequality) is the difference
> between qualities *available* and qualities *required* by the demand side.
> —Jan Tinbergen (1975)

In the case of Brazil, abundant evidence shows that the distribution and reward of education matters for wage-inequality, for example Birdsall and Salbot (1996). They find that the Brazilian workforce both in the past and in the present has accumulated less education compared to other countries with the same per capita income. Furthermore, they present findings similar to Patrinos (2001) and Psacharopoulos (1993) emphasizing that returns to schooling in Brazil in the 1970s and 1980s exceeded returns to schooling in most other nations in the world.[180]

The returns to schooling by education level display large variation between education levels and over time. Ferreira and Barros (1999); Blom, Holm-Nielsen and Verner (2001); as well as Arbache, Green and Dickerson (2001) show that the reward of lower and middle levels of education in the early 1980s substantially exceeded those currently prevailing. While the wage of tertiary graduates relentlessly increased during the same period. Blom, Holm-Nielsen, and Verner (2001) finds that for the period 1982 to 1998, returns to 4, 8, and 11 years of completed schooling dropped 26 percent, 35 percent and 8 percent, respectively, while returns to tertiary schooling surged 24 percent. Hence, the reward of education became increasingly convex implying that the marginal reward of education increased with the years of education.

In Brazil, increased return to skills exacerbates existing income-inequality. This is a result of two opposite directed impacts. On the one hand, the decline in returns to schooling for workers with middle levels of education, 5–11 years of schooling, entails that the wage difference between workers with middle levels of education and workers with less schooling decreases. Due to the comparatively small stock of education in Brazil, workers with middle levels of education generally earn above the average wage. Consequently, a decline in returns to middle levels of education diminishes wage-inequality. On the other hand, the surging returns to tertiary schooling raises the wage of workers predominantly positioned in the highest deciles of the income distribution. Therefore, increased convexity also worsens wage-inequality. Ferreira and Paes de Barros (1999)

---

180. The finding of below-average accumulation of education relative to per capita income and above average returns to schooling, supports the analysis of Tinbergen (1975). The essence of Tinbergen's idea is a race between technology and accumulated education, where returns to education is interpreted as a price of education. Specifically, the returns to schooling is an outcome of supply determined by outcome of the education system and demand for schooling determined by the marginal productivity of different types of labor, which Tinbergen strongly associates with the level of technology. In the case of Brazil, the relative low stock of accumulated education relative to the GDP-level suggests that technology "leads the race" and returns to schooling therefore exceed that found internationally.

find that for the 1976–1996 period, the former effect dominated the latter. That is, the change in returns to schooling decreased wage-inequality. These findings indicate that (a) education policy is a powerful tool to reduce wage-inequality and (b) the rise in the returns to tertiary education exacerbates wage-inequality.

In addition to the previous direct effect, there is another unequalizing indirect effect of earnings convexification on income inequality. Vélez et al. (2001) show that beyond a certain level of convexity of the earning function, an increase in mean education produces an (unexpected) un-equalizing effect on income inequality. That is, if rates of return rise with the level of schooling, accumulation of schooling worsens income inequality unless the accumulation of schooling is sufficiently egalitarian.[181] Thus, increasing returns to education also weaken the potential income equalization that could be obtained from the higher and more equally distributed educational endowments of new cohorts of workers entering the labor market in Brazil.

The increased convexity in the human capital earnings function has attracted a fair amount of attention due to the proliferation of the phenomenon. Several major economies in Latin America experienced increased convexity during the 1980s and 1990s; see Beyer et al. (1999), Santamaria (2000) and Veléz et al. (2001), Lächler (1998), Galiani and Sanguinetti (2000) for evidence on Chile, Colombia, Mexico and Argentina, respectively. Some low and middle-income countries in other regions underwent the same change, see Foley (1997) as well as Muraimy and Lam (1999) for studies on South Africa and India. Furthermore, the trend is not confined to developing countries. Katz and Murphy (1992); Romer, Riddle and Murphy (1998); and Card and Lemieux (2000) reveal that the United States, United Kingdom, and Canada to different degrees all experienced a rise in the income disparity between workers with tertiary education and workers with secondary education.

The suggested explanations for increased reward of advanced human capital generally evolve around (a) the relative supply of tertiary graduates or (b) increased demand for skill due to trade-liberalization and the revolution in information and communication technology (ICT). In a seminal paper Katz and Murphy (1992) demonstrate how the relative supply of college graduates to high school graduates combined with a time-linear increase in labor demand for college graduates drive the relative wage of the two education groups. Later studies corroborate and refine this finding for the United States, Card and Lemieux (2000) and Romer, Riddle, and Murphy (1998). Other studies have examined reasons for increased skill-premium to highly educated workers in middle-income countries, but they mostly concentrate on the role of trade-liberalization. Few studies focus on the role played by relative supply with the exception of Santamaria (2000) for Colombia. The supply focus is crucial for policy analysis, because it yields estimates of how policymakers through education policy can impact on long-term wage-inequality.

The paper provides policymakers with information on the scope for long term reduction of wage inequality by turning the handles of the education system, and in particular the number of graduates from tertiary education. We estimate the Katz and Murphy-model in order to understand how long-run education policy influences the wage premium and identify policy initiatives that could reduce inequality. The Katz and Murphy model has to our knowledge not been fully applied to the case of Brazil. Arbache, Green, and Dickerson (2001) use the framework to investigate how labor demand for advanced skills developed over time.

In addition to applying the Katz and Murphy model that links the supply of skilled labor with relative wage, we examine the role of wages of tertiary graduates for wage inequality. We utilize the by now fairly standard technique of wage simulation. First, we express the relative wage of tertiary graduates as returns to tertiary schooling. By using the technique of wage-simulation we evaluate how returns to schooling impacts on wage-inequality. Hence, the paper directly links supply of skilled labor that policymakers strongly influence in the medium to the long run, and wage-inequality.

---

181. Ibid., p. 31.

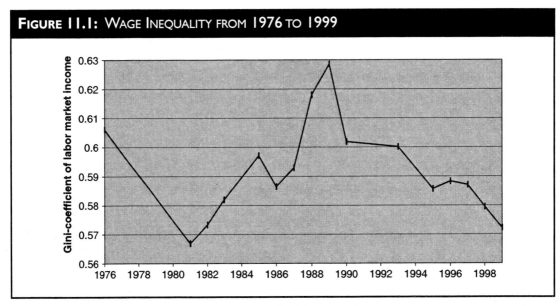

FIGURE 11.1: WAGE INEQUALITY FROM 1976 TO 1999

Note: Hourly wage from principal and secondary job for full time workers.
Source: Authors' own calculation based on PNAD.

The paper is organized as follows. The subsequent section presents the level and evolution of wage-inequality as well as the distribution, evolution and remuneration of education from 1976 to 1999. In section three we estimate the Katz and Murphy model. The analysis enables us subsequently in section four to perform counterfactual policy analysis to illustrate the impact of education policy on wage-inequality. More specifically, we ask how wage-inequality would have developed if the education policy in the 1980s and 1990s had differed from the observed policy. The final section provides an assessment of the scope for reducing wage-inequality by expanding tertiary education.

Wage-inequality and Education

Inequality manifests itself in numerous ways in a society. In this paper, we focus on income inequality and more specifically on pre-tax wage-inequality. Wage-inequality is measured for individual wage earners. This provides a well-defined and quantitatively solid starting point. However, this paper does not cover a number of important aspects of inequality, such as government transfers, taxation, distribution of assets and unemployment. The analysis adopts the gini-coefficient as the general measure of inequality.

The Brazilian national household survey, PNAD, provides the household information. We consider income from both primary and secondary employment and deflated by the national consumer price index, INPC, to obtain real wages.[182] All wages are expressed as hourly wage in fixed September 1997 prices. We use all existing household surveys from 1976 to 1999 with the exception of 1984 and 1992. Figure 11.1 presents the evolution of wage-inequality in Brazil in the examined period.

182. In 1976, the Brazilian statistical office, IBGE, did not assemble the INPC. Alternatively, we deflate the wage by the IPC price index also collected by the IBGE. The two price indexes follow similar paths during the 1980s. Hence, they seemingly measure price changes in a similar way. The necessary change in deflators should therefore not significantly reduce the comparability of the wage series from 1976 to 1981. The appendix provides detailed information about the computation of each data series presented in this paper.

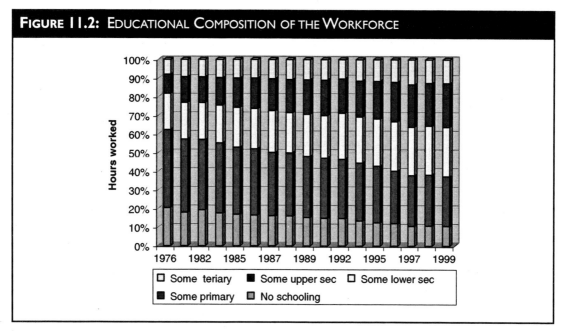

FIGURE 11.2: EDUCATIONAL COMPOSITION OF THE WORKFORCE

Note: Hours worked by full time workers.

Source: Authors' own calculation based on PNAD.

From 1976 to 1981, wage-inequality decreased from an internationally remarkably high level of 0.61. The so-called "lost decade" of the 1980s plagued by negative growth and heavy economic distress severely exacerbated wage-inequality that peaked in 1989 at 0.63. Hereafter, the distribution of wages became less unequal. From 1989 to 1999, the gini-coefficient fell 6 gini-points from 0.63 to 0.57. Notably with two substantial drops in 1990 and in 1994. The latter drop is consistently linked to the economic stabilization following the *Real* plan. The evolution depicted by Figure 11.1 corresponds to similar findings by IPEA (2001), Neri and Camargo (1999) as well as Ferreira and Barros (1999). Despite the reduction in wage-inequality in the 1990s, the distribution of wage still remains notoriously inequal in international comparison, Ferreira and Bourguignon (2000).

Educational Composition of the Labor Force from 1976 to 1999

During the 1970s, 1980s and 1990s, policymakers strived to provide universal primary education and as well as to turn the secondary education system into a mass-system.[183] As a consequence, the schooling system expanded in these decades. Nevertheless, the speed of expansion in 1970s and 1980s was moderate on an international scale, Birdsall and Sabot (1996). The fruits of these efforts are clearly visible today. The educational attainment of the workforce steadily improved. The average number of attained years of schooling increased from 4.8 in 1976 to 6.9 in 1999. Figure 11.2 shows how the improvement in the education system gradually translated into increased education attainment of the workforce.

In 1976, over 60 percent of the workforce had at most a diploma from primary school (four years of schooling). As older primarily less educated workers were replaced by younger peers with considerably more schooling, the share of workers with 4 years of schooling or less declined

---

183. The Brazilian education system consists of four levels with national graduation exams; primary education from 1–4 years of schooling, lower secondary education (sometimes called upper primary) from 5–8 years of schooling, upper secondary education from 9–11 years of schooling and, lastly, tertiary education from 12–15/17 years of schooling.

to 38 percent. In 1999, more than half of the workers had graduated from lower secondary school (eight years of schooling).

The distribution of schooling became considerably more equitable over the examined period. Inequality of schooling, measured by the gini-coefficient of the years of schooling, decreased every single year from 1976 to 1999. In 1976, the gini-coefficient for years of schooling was 0.49. By 1999, inequality in schooling had dropped to 0.37.

Education and Wages

Education continues to be the main determinant of an individual's labor market income. Generally, wage increases monotonically with the level of education. We compute the evolution of wage by education group using a so-called fixed-weight wage method developed by Freeman (1980) and applied by Katz and Murphy among others. The method calculates the wage for a fixed demographic composition of the work force in order for alteration over time in demographic characteristics (age and gender) not to affect the wage-series. Specifically, we divide the labor force into demographic cells by age and gender.[184] Weights are assigned to each cell on the basis of the average number of workers in each cell during the entire period. The wage of an education group is given by a weighted average of the average wage of each demographic cell with that level of education. Figure 11.3 presents the results.

Notably, the wages display high sensitivity to economic cycles. The spikes in wages 1986, 1989 and 1994/5 correspond to economic expansions. The average wage of all levels of education decreased during the two decades considered.[185] However, the wages across education groups declined by different magnitudes. In particular, the workers with tertiary education endured a small decline in wages.

As the wage of secondary graduates and tertiary graduates drifted apart, the relative wage of tertiary graduates increased. In 1976, a typical worker with tertiary education earned in 320 percent and 210 percent more than a colleague with lower secondary education and upper secondary education, respectively. By 1999, the same wage gap had expanded to 450 percent and 240 percent, respectively. Oppositely, the wage of lower secondary graduates and upper secondary graduates declined substantially relative to workers with less education.

Returns to Schooling

In order to purge the relationship between wage and education further, we estimate returns to schooling. By estimating returns to schooling from Mincerian regressions, we control for additional factors than in the above Katz and Murphy (1992) method. We estimate the following Mincerian regression for every year in our sample.

$$\ln y_i = \beta_{sch}^* S_i + X_i' \gamma + \varepsilon_i \qquad (1)$$

Where y_i and S_i indicate wage and number of years of schooling for individual i. X stands for a matrix of control variables. γ is the vector of estimated coefficients for control variables. We control for age (quadratic formulation), gender, labor market status (formal employee, informal employee,[186] self-employed, or employer), region of living (5 major regions) and rural residence.

---

184. We divide the workforce into 9 age-cohorts, 2 genders and 7 education groups (no schooling, incomplete primary, complete primary, lower secondary, upper secondary, incomplete tertiary and complete tertiary), which yields 126 demographic cells.

185. This does not imply that income per worker decreased over the period, since the size of education groups with secondary and tertiary education increased over time. Actually, the per capita income fell during the 1980s, but recovered more than fully in 1990s.

186. The partition of employees into a formal and an informal group is done on the basis of "*carteira assinada,*" signed workcard. Holding a signed workcard entitles an employee to a series of rights and benefits, he or she can therefore meaningfully be classified as working in the formal (regulated) sector of the economy.

FIGURE 11.3: HOURLY WAGE BY EDUCATION LEVEL (FIXED DEMOGRAPHIC COMPOSITION)

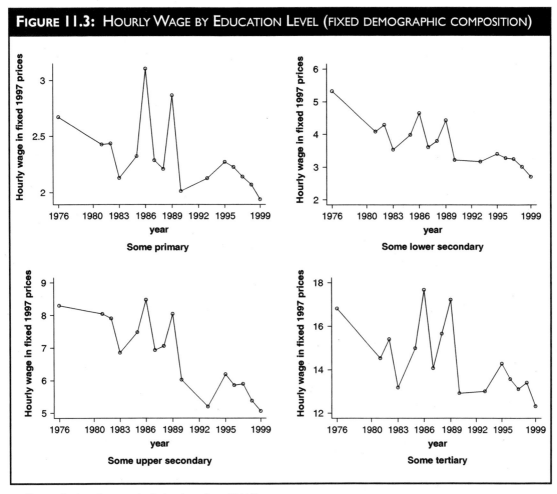

Source: Authors' own calculation based on PNAD.

Furthermore, we estimate the returns to each level of schooling separately by adopting a spline specification. The full form of (1) is then (1b).

$$\ln y_i = \beta_{pri} * S_{i,pri} + \beta_{lsec} * S_{i,lsec} + \beta_{usec} * S_{i,usec} + \beta_{ter} * S_{i,ter} + X_i' \gamma + \varepsilon_i \qquad (1b)$$

Where, S_i indicates the number of years of schooling attended at each level of education (primary, lower secondary, upper secondary and tertiary). The βs are estimated returns to school to one additional year in primary, lower secondary, upper secondary and tertiary schooling, respectively.[187] Figure 11.4 displays the returns to schooling to each education level.

Controlling for additional factors, we confirm the findings from the average wage data. The returns to primary, lower secondary, and upper secondary schooling declined over the period, while returns to tertiary schooling persistently increased through out the two decades. These findings correspond to previous findings by Blom, Holm-Nielsen and Verner (2001) based on metropolitan labor market data.

---

187. We tested an alternative formulation with dummies for completion of each education level. The spline specification proved the most explanatory indicating that years of schooling in between graduation years matter in the wage determination process. Although, clear signs of so-called sheep-skin effects exist.

FIGURE 11.4: RETURNS TO SCHOOLING BY EDUCATION LEVEL

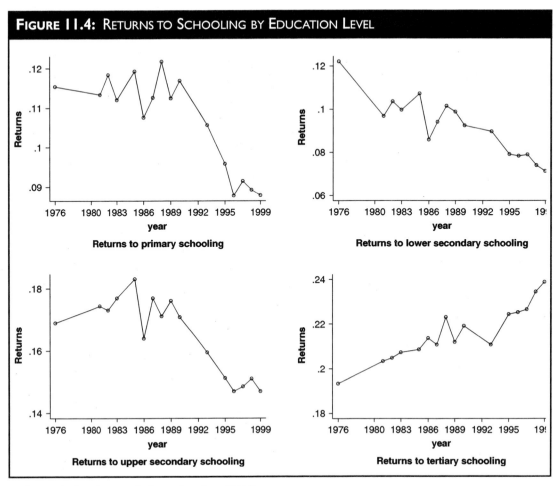

Source: Authors' own calculation based on PNAD.

Remuneration of Education and Wage-inequality

How did the shifts in returns to schooling affect wage-inequality? To answer this question, we apply the technique of wage-simulations. Specifically, the technique consists in estimating a mincerian regression for the year under investigation as done above in (1b). From (1b) we obtain a predicted log wage for each worker, $\ln \hat{y}_i$. We subtract the estimated effect of education as given by the estimated vector of returns to schooling $\hat{\beta}_{sch}$. We then add the effect of education given a simulated (hypothetical) vector of returns to schooling, $\hat{\beta}_{sim}$. Hence, the simulated wage for individual i, $y_{sim,i}$ is computed as:

$$\ln y_{sim,i} = \ln \hat{y}_i - S_i' \hat{\beta}_{sch} + S_i' \beta_{sim} + e \qquad (2)$$

The unexplained residual from (1), e, is added to the simulated wage, so that unexplained wage-variation remains constant.[188] By analyzing the wage-distribution of the simulated wage, y_{sim}, we assess the impact of returns to schooling on wage-inequality.

---

188. In order for the simulations not to be biased, we need to assume that the error term is independent of attained schooling, see Velez et al. (2001).

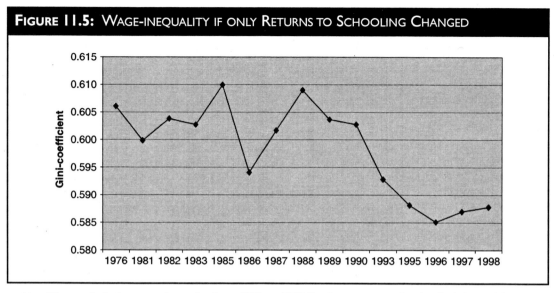

FIGURE 11.5: WAGE-INEQUALITY IF ONLY RETURNS TO SCHOOLING CHANGED

Note: The graph depicts wage-inequality from 1976 to 1999 if only returns to schooling had changed from 1976 to 1999. All other factors are kept constant at the 1976 level.

Source: Authors' own calculation based on PNAD.

Figure 11.5 depicts how wage inequality would have developed from 1976 to 1999 if only returns to schooling changed. Hence, all other factors including control variables, attained schooling and residual wage remain identical to the 1976 level.

The decline in returns to lower and medium levels of schooling that took place from 1988 to 1996 accounts for a drop in the gini-coefficient of more than 2 gini-points. Changing the base year of the simulation, the endowments, from 1976 to 1989 or 1999 marginally reduces the bearing that returns to schooling exert on wage-inequality. For all three base years, the drop in wage-inequality exceeds 2 gini-points. Consequently, we conclude that the decline in returns to schooling, ceteris paribus, explains at least a third of the reduction in wage-inequality from 1989 to 1996.

The Skill-premium and Wage Inequality

Workers with tertiary education experienced as the only education group rising returns to schooling. Since the salary of this education group lies above the national average, the rise in returns to schooling lead to a deterioration of wage inequality. We assess the role of returns to tertiary schooling for wage inequality by observing the change in wage-inequality as the returns to tertiary schooling change. This is done by the same simulation technique as above where we only change the fourth element of the vector of returns to schooling. That is, we vary the returns to tertiary schooling while keeping returns to the other three education levels constant. Figure 11.6 presents the findings for the level of wage-inequality in 1999 as a function of returns to tertiary schooling.

A hypothetical reduction in demand for workers with tertiary education that causes returns to tertiary schooling to decline from the 1999-level of 23.9 percent to 13 percent—the level of returns in the United States—would reduce wage-inequality from 0.575 to 0.530. This simulation shows that a reduction in the skill-premium leads to a substantially more equitable income distribution. The returns to schooling for the other three education levels influence less on wage-inequality (Figures 11A.1–4). Nevertheless, the return to upper secondary education still impacts considerably on wage-inequality, whereas returns to lower secondary and primary education

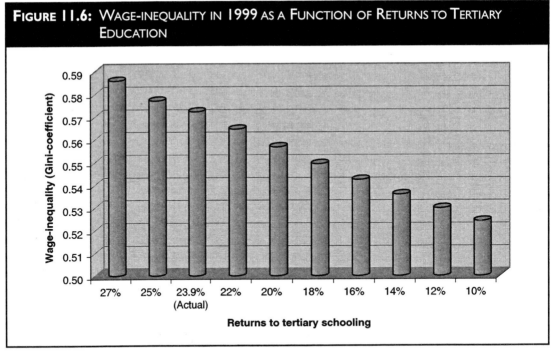

FIGURE 11.6: WAGE-INEQUALITY IN 1999 AS A FUNCTION OF RETURNS TO TERTIARY EDUCATION

Note: The graph depicts wage-inequality in 1999 if only returns to tertiary schooling changed to the hypothetical level given by the horizontal axis. All other factors are kept constant.

Source: Authors' own calculation based on PNAD.

matters less for wage-inequality. This finding motivates the rest of the paper, which investigates how policymakers can influence the skill-premium and thereby reduce wage-inequality.

Relative Supply, Relative Demand, and the Skill-premium

The skill-premium is a price on advanced human capital. As all other prices, the interaction of demand and supply determines the skill-premium. In a seminal work, Katz and Murphy (1992) investigate how demand and supply for tertiary graduates determine the skill-premium in the United States. This section applies the Katz and Murphy model to the case of Brazil. The analysis will help us understand why the skill-premium rose during the last two decades. Furthermore, because output of the education system in the long run dictates the educational composition of labor supply, the analysis yields valuable insight into how education policy, through the impact on supply, affects the skill-premium and wage-inequality.

A Stylized Relationship between Demand, Supply, and Wages

This subsection provides the theoretical foundation for the estimated models. Katz and Murphy (1992) develop an empirical model based on a simple CES production function:[189]

$$\Upsilon = \left[L_{ter}^{\frac{\sigma-1}{\sigma}} + L_{usec}^{\frac{\sigma-1}{\sigma}} \right]^{\sigma/\sigma-1} \tag{3}$$

189. The usual notations denote two education groups; unskilled and skilled workers. The actual educational attainment of the two reference groups often differs from one study to another. Because we do not perceive graduates from upper secondary schooling to be unskilled, we prefer to denote the two groups by their education level, upper secondary and tertiary.

Where Y, L, σ refers to output, labor of the type indicated by the subscripts and the elasticity of substitution between the two types of labor, respectively. The subscripts *ter* and *usec* stand for tertiary and upper secondary. Many similar models exist, Murphy, Riddle and Romer (1998), Card and Lemieux (2000), Haskel (2000) and Santamaria (2000). Assuming labor supply to be predetermined in the short run, hence a vertical supply curve, the relative labor demand curve arising from (3) determines the relative wage. These assumptions can be shown to imply the following simple relationship between wage, demand and supply:

$$\log\left(\frac{w_{ter,t}}{w_{usec,t}}\right) = \frac{1}{\sigma}\left[\log\left(\frac{D_{ter,t}}{D_{usec,t}}\right) - \log\left(\frac{S_{ter,t}}{S_{usec,t}}\right)\right] \qquad (4)$$

Where w, D and S indicate wage, demand and supply, respectively. The key parameter for the analysis is the economy wide elasticity of substitution, σ. A high elasticity of substitution implies that secondary graduates easily substitute tertiary graduates. The higher the elasticity, the smaller the impact of relative supply on output and the smaller the impact of relative supply and demand on relative wage (and wage-inequality). The economy wide elasticity of substitution is determined by (a) sector specific elasticity of substitution embodied in each sector's choice of production technology and (b) the ease with which labor flows between sectors with different intensity of skilled labor.

The model is an aggregate labor market model that assumes clearing of the labor market across sectors within each year. While the assumption plausibly holds in the long run, there exist short run barriers to flow of labor across sectors in the economy. That is, in the short run firms face a sector specific upward sloping supply curve due to sector specific experience and different geographical locations of sectors. Sector specific shocks translating into sector specific changes in relative labor demand might therefore create short run deviations from the long run equilibrium. The estimated model is therefore expected to hold only in the long run.[190]

The estimated regression version of (4) is (5):

$$\log\left(\frac{w_{ter,t}}{w_{usec,t}}\right) = \alpha + \beta\left[\log\left(\frac{D_{ter,t}}{D_{usec,t}}\right) - \log\left(\frac{S_{ter,t}}{S_{usec,t}}\right)\right] + \varepsilon_t \qquad (5)$$

Where the error term, ε_t, picks up misspecifications, unobserved factors and measurement errors. From the coefficient estimate of β, we compute the elasticity of substitution between the two types of labor as

$$\sigma = \frac{1}{\beta} \qquad (6)$$

In order to force the elasticity of substitution to be similar for demand and for supply, we compute the change in net-supply, NS.

$$\log\left(\frac{w_{S,t}}{w_{U,t}}\right) = \alpha + \beta_1 \log\left(\frac{NS_{S,t}}{NS_{U,t}}\right) + \varepsilon_t \qquad \text{model (1)}$$

---

190. Card and Lemieux (2000) find that in the case of the United States, Canada, and United Kingdom the rise in the relative wage almost exclusively benefited the younger cohorts between 26 and 40 years old. They refine the Katz and Murphy model to take account for imperfect substitution between age-cohorts. Additionally, Santamaria (2000) shows that the relative wage differs between genders, which strongly suggests imperfect substitution between these two segments of the labor market. These shortcomings of (4) underscore the aggregate nature of the model.

Model (1) is the first model that we estimate. The model estimated by Katz and Model includes a time trend to capture a skill-biased change in labor demand. The change in demand is caused by an increase in the productivity of workers with tertiary education relative those with secondary education.[191] Murphy, Riddle and Romer (1998) provide a theoretical foundation based on skill-biased technological progress for the inclusion of the time trend. We equally estimate this model, henceforth called model (2):

$$\log\left(\frac{w_{S,t}}{w_{U,t}}\right) = \alpha + \beta_1 \log\left(\frac{NS_{S,t}}{NS_{U,t}}\right) + \beta_2 t + \varepsilon_t \qquad \text{model (2)}$$

Furthermore, we consider an alternative model where we estimate the impact of demand and the impact of supply separately. The motivation is twofold: (a) For reasons discussed in the following section, the applied demand indicator underestimates the increase in the demand for highly skilled labor; (b) The shock to supply might impact wages differently than shocks to demand. Why? Innovations in supply almost exclusively occur when young cohorts of school-leavers enter the labor market. Since school-leavers possess little sector experience, they are relatively more flexible in terms of sector of employment (and region of employment). Hence, innovations in supply tend to have high elasticity of substitution due to high sector and geographical mobility. Oppositely, sector specific demand shocks affect workers that already hold sector specific experience. The latter reduces mobility across sectors, because workers loose the reward of sector specific experience by switching sector. Therefore, innovations in demand impact relative wage to a larger extent than supply.[192] In this scenario, a negative sector specific shock to a skill-intensive sector that decreases the demand for tertiary graduates by 1 percent would reduce the relative wage of tertiary graduates more than the impact of a 1 percent increase in the supply of tertiary graduates. Hence, we propose the following model, henceforth model (3):

$$\log\left(\frac{W_{ter,t}}{W_{sec,t}}\right) = \alpha + \frac{1}{\sigma_S} * \log\left(\frac{S_{ter,t}}{S_{sec,t}}\right) + \frac{1}{\sigma_D} * \log\left(\frac{D_{ter,t}}{D_{sec,t}}\right) + \beta^* t + \varepsilon_t \qquad \text{model (3)}$$

Where σ_S and σ_D refer to the elasticity of substitution estimated for supply and demand, respectively.

Applying the Model to a Middle-income Country

Like Katz and Murphy (1992), this paper focuses on the wage of workers with tertiary education relative to those with secondary education. However, the educational composition of the United States and that of a middle-income country like Brazil differ dramatically. In the United States, the two reference education groups encompass more than 90 percent of the workforce, while only a little bit more than a third have attended upper secondary education in Brazil.[193] Robbins and Gindling (1999) argue that the cutoff point on the education scale between low skilled and high

---

191. The assumption of a constant rise in the relative productivity of highly skilled labor differs from the assumption of a constant increases in either Total Factor Productivity (TFP) or output per labor, since the two latter concepts consider the productivity of the labor force as a whole without distinguishing between different types of labor. An increase in TFP could both favor and disfavor highly skilled labor depending upon the sector or education group in which the productivity gains take place.

192. Birdsall and Salbot (1996), Menezes et al. (2000) and Blom, Pavcnik and Schady (forthcoming) document that wages indeed vary across sectors and industries of employment, even controlling for observable personal characteristics. Such high wage-differences between sectors testify to the importance of sector specific experience.

193. Measured in hours of work, figure 11.2.

skilled should be placed lower when analyzing the skill-premium in a middle-income country than in a developed country. As a consequence they examine the wage-difference between graduates from primary education and graduates from tertiary education in the case of Costa Rica. Nevertheless, we uphold the original cutoff point because we explicitly focus on explaining the rising skill-premium to tertiary education. Hence, the only sensible cutoff point on the education scale is between upper secondary education and tertiary education. Furthermore, the sharp divergence in wages between the two reference groups undoubtedly demonstrate that the labor market distinguish between the two education groups. In the case of Brazil, the relative small coverage of the two groups might reduce the overall relevance of the analysis, but the fact that returns to tertiary education substantially matter for wage-inequality, warrants, in your eyes, the choice of focusing on the wage premium to tertiary education only.

Computation of Relative Wage, Relative Supply and Relative Demand
Relative Wage
We follow Katz and Murphy (1992) and compute relative wage with fixed demographic weights as outlined previously. The computation excludes other education groups than complete upper secondary graduates and complete tertiary graduates. The opposite would affect relative wage to the extent that the relative share or the wage of dropouts changes during the period.[194]

Supply
We measure supply as the share of working hours supplied by each education group out of the total number of working hours. Arguably, this choice of method misses some aspects of supply that might impact wages.[195] We include both genders in the supply series. Hence, we assume full substitutability between male and female colleagues. Although the assumption is not fully correct, it is preferred to the alternative assumption of no substitutability.

The analysis focuses on explaining the relative wage of upper secondary graduates to tertiary graduates. However, the evolution in the supply of other education groups likely influences this wage-ratio. For example, an abundant supply of lower secondary graduates potentially adds to the supply of upper secondary due to the higher degree of substitutability with upper secondary graduates than with tertiary graduates. Therefore, the supply of upper secondary graduates and tertiary graduates should be adjusted. Ideally, the adjustment should be substituted for a multi-equilibrium framework estimating elasticities of substitution between all education groups. A such model has so far not been developed, we therefore follow the literature and add a weighted supply of the excluded education groups to the two reference groups. Several suggestions exist for how to determine the weights. We adopt the "wage-level approach" suggested by Card and Lemieux (2000). They base the weights on the relative wage of the excluded education group to

---

194. Murphy, Riddle and Romer (1998) propose an alternative to the fixed demographic weights method. They estimate a mincerian regression for each year with dummies for completed college and completed high school controlling for age and gender. The difference between the two coefficient estimates is used as a measure for relative wage.

195. For example, the computed supply series do not reflect the incidence of open unemployment. A difference in unemployment level between the two education groups could affect the relative wage. However, if insiders determine the wages, unemployment exert no influence on wages. Accounting for unemployment could therefore introduce noise into the supply series and thereby blur the association between supply and wages. A similar argument pertains to the failure of the supply series to account for the educational attainment of the people not participating in the labor market or part-time employees. Additionally, Katz and Murphy (1992) measure supply series in terms of so-called efficiency units. The idea is that more experienced workers supply more efficient labor. Therefore, the supply series should take account of this difference in efficiency. Katz and Murphy (1992) weigh the supply of each age-cohort by the wage in order for the supply series to reflect possible differences in effective supply. Santamaria (2000) applies both methods in the case of Colombia and finds only a marginal difference.

the wage level of the two reference groups. For example, the hours worked by dropouts from tertiary education are added to the supply of upper secondary graduates with the weight ö computed as:[196].

$$\varphi_{\text{completeusec}} = (w_{\text{completeter}} - w_{\text{incompleteter}}) / (w_{\text{completeter}} - w_{\text{completeusec}}) \quad (7)$$

Applying (7), the hours of work by tertiary dropouts are split 66 percent to the supply of completed upper secondary and 33 percent to completed tertiary. The weights are more important in the case of Brazil than in the case of developed countries, since the excluded education groups contain the bulk of the working force. As a robustness check, we estimate the model (1)—model (3) without adjusting for the supply of lower secondary and primary education.

Relative Demand
Contrary to supply, we do not observe demand for labor. Changes in relative demand for education arise from two sources;

(a) *Within-sector demand shifts.* That is, the same products are produced, but firms have changed production technology. The change in production technology implies a change in relative demand for labor. For example, if shoe manufactures replace cutters or/and sewers with machines, then the demand for unskilled labor decreases while demand for skilled technicians increases. Within-sector demand shifts closely relate to the installation of skill-biased technology.[197]

(b) *Between-sector demand shifts.* Sectors differ in their demand for skilled workers. When some sectors expand and others retract, the economy's relative demand for skilled labor shifts. For example, if the relative size of the agriculture sector decreases, the demand for unskilled workers declines, since agriculture intensively employs unskilled labor.

We measure "*between-sector demand shift*" by the fixed coefficient "manpower requirements" index developed by Freeman(1975) and ditto (1980):

$$\Delta D_{e,t} = \frac{1}{N_e} \sum_j \mu_{e,j} \Delta N_{j,t}, \ \mu_{e,j} = N_{e,j} / N_j \quad (8)$$

Where $\Delta D_{e,t}$ stands for the demand shift for education group e in time period t. $\mu_{e,j}$ indicates the employment share of education group e in sector j. The weight equals the share of employment at the beginning of the period and is constant. N indicates the absolute number of employees.

Intuitively, the demand shift measures the aggregate change in labor demand due to a change in the sectoral composition of the economy. That is, if a sector intensive in skilled labor (μ_{ter} high)

---

196. Alternatively, Katz and Murphy (1992) proposes weighting according to wage level and wage-evolution as determined in the following regression (with no constant):

$$w_{\text{incom ter}} = \varphi_{\text{com ter}} * w_{\text{com ter}} + \varphi_{\text{com upper sec}} * w_{\text{com upper sec}}$$

Additionally, Robbins and Gindling (1999) propose some a-priori reasonable weights. Appendix table 3 presents the weights arising from the proposed methods. The alternative approaches give weights similar to those of the adopted Card and Lemieux method. Consequently, the chosen method does not affect the findings.

197. Changes in technology lead firms to demand more skilled labor if the installed technology is skill-biased. These within-sector shifts can be observed by keeping the production volume of each sector constant and compute the change in labor intensity across sectors. Hence, the opposite of the between-sector shifts. Katz and Murphy (1992) estimate the within-sector shifts by observing the change in labor input intensity for 3 occupation groups. However, the PNAD survey do not have well-structured occupation data, we therefore choose not to compute this indicator.

expands ($\Delta N_j > 0$), then demand for skilled labor increases ($\Delta D_{ter} > 0$). The estimated demand shift is biased, because the shift only reflects changes in employment and not in wages (quantity). The bias will be the opposite of the movement in wage. For instance, if demand for tertiary graduates increased causing the wage to rise, firms will respond by hiring a smaller number of graduates. Hence, in this case, the demand indicator underestimates the "true" demand shift. The degree of bias varies from one education group to the other depending on the evolution of wages; Johnson (1992), Katz and Murphy (1992) as well as Santamaria (2000). Tables 11A.5 and 11A.6 display the factor intensity and the employment share, respectively, which are the two components needed to construct the demand shifts. Table 11A.7 presents labor demand shifts in sub-periods of 1976–1999, while Figure 11A.1 graphs the yearly between-sector demand shifts.

The between-sector shifts show that sectors intensive in low human capital labor (predominantly agriculture and mining) decreased consistently from 1976 to 1999. All other education groups experienced rising demand in the period taken as a whole, although demand decreased for certain groups in sub-periods. A part from the sub-period 1990–1995, sectors relatively intensive in skilled labor expanded.[198] The largest rise in demand occurred for upper secondary graduates. The demand for this group surged 20.8 percent from 1976 to 1999 due to changes in the sectoral composition. The period from 1976 to 1981 stands out as a period with large flows towards skill intensive sectors.

Figure 11.7 presents the net supply and wage series. In Brazil, the log relative wage in 1976 was 0.88, which widened to 1.09 in 1999. The relative wage in Brazil substantially exceeds the relative wage prevailing in developed countries. In the Unites States, log relative wage bottomed out at an all time low at around 0.39 in the late 1970s. Thereafter, the log relative wage grew to 0.52 in 1987, where the Murphy, Riddle and Romer (1998) series end. In Canada, the log relative wage oscillated around 0.48 from 1981 to 1994 with no observable trend line.

The figure displays the expected negative association between relative net supply and relative wage. Furthermore, as expected from the discussion of the model's characteristics, the supply curve displays less volatility than the wage curve.

Estimation

The theoretical considerations suggested three ways to estimate the relationship between relative wage, relative supply and relative demand. Table 11.1 presents the estimation results.

In model (1), relative net-supply statistically significantly affects relative wage with a coefficient close to minus one. The inferred elasticity of substitution becomes 1. Given the simplicity of the model, the explanatory power is unexpectedly high. The R^2 reaches 0.89, which in part can be explained by the few number of observations. The constant is statistically insignificant.

In model (2), we introduces time trend to capture a constant skill-biased change in labor demand. The addition of a time trend slightly augments the explanatory power from 0.89 to 0.92. The constant equally increases marginally and turns statistically significant. The estimated elasticity of substitution alters completely. The coefficient (numerically) drops from –0.98 to –0.21 and becomes statistically insignificant. Oppositely, the introduced time trend is statistically significant, but only on a 5 percent level. Hence, the standard errors appear substantially inflated considering the model's high explanatory power. The size of the coefficient of the time trend suggests that, all

---

198. The period of exception, 1990–1995, coincides with the trade-liberalization period. The simultaneity suggests that trade-liberalization lead to a specialization in sectors intensive in unskilled labor. The observed specialization corresponds to the prediction of the Hekscher-Ohlin model; Countries that are relatively abundant in low-skilled workers specialize in sectors with low skill intensity. The drop in demand for skilled labor could hence be a consequence of falling profits and reductions in outputs taking place in the skill-heavy sectors as the price of their product fell due to increased foreign competition following reductions in tariffs.

FIGURE 11.7: RELATIVE WAGE AND RELATIVE NET SUPPLY OF TERTIARY TO UPPER SECONDARY GRADUATES

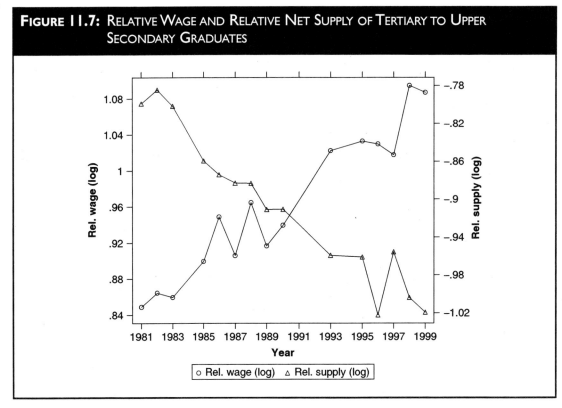

Source: Authors' own calculation based on PNAD.

other things equal, the skill-premium to tertiary education increases by 1.5 percent annually due to skill-biased change in labor demand.

The difference between the two models is striking. Following model (1), the asymmetric development in the educational composition of labor supply almost fully explains the rising skill-premium to tertiary education. The expansion of lower and upper secondary education during the 1980s and 1990s reduced the marginal productivity of these types of labor and therefore decreased the wage relative to that of tertiary graduates.[199] According to model (2), a constant skill-biased change in labor demand causes the relative wage to rise. In this setting the relative supply played a statistically insignificant role for the rise in the skill-premium.[200]

199. The decrease in marginal productivity does not imply that investment in education at this level is unprofitable. On the contrary, an individual still significantly increases his/her revenue by attending secondary school. However, the marginal increase in wage derived from the completion of secondary education decreased over time.

200. The lack of relationship between relative supply and wage could be explained by the *Rybczynski effect* (as derived in a Heckscher-Ohlin model): In a multi sector economy with a higher number of products than factors, the zero-profit conditions determine relative factor prices. Although each sector faces a downward sloping demand curve, the aggregated economy wide demand curve is horizontal. An increase in relative supply of skilled workers causes skill-intensive sectors to expand production and employment whereas skill-extensive sectors retract. Hence, in this setting relative supply does not change relative wage. However, the models predictions do not hold if (a) the number of factors exceed number of products manufactured, (b) the production composition (type of products) alters, and (c) barriers to labor flow exist across sectors, for example sector specific experience; see Haskel (1999).

TABLE 11.1: ESTIMATION RESULTS

Model	(1)	(2)	(3)
Time Sample	1981–1999	1981–1999	1981–1999
Constant	0.076	0.063[**]	0.056[***]
	(0.087)	(0.24)	(0.16)
Net Supply $(-1/\sigma)$	−0.98[***]	−0.21	−0.62[***]
	(0.095)	(0.33)	(0.18)
Time trend	—	0.015[**]	0.011[***]
		(0.0056)	(0.002)
Demand	—	—	3.55[***]
			(0.69)
R2	0.89	0.92	0.98
Observations	15	15	15
Tests for misspecification			
Durbin-Watson test	2.27	2.30	2.00
RESET test	0.39	0.87	0.93
Implied elasticity (σ)	1.0	4.7	1.61

Note: *, ** and *** denote statistical significance at the 10%, 5% and 1% level, respectively. The value for RESET test is the probability of correct specification.

The disappearance of the impact of supply arises due to multicollinearity between the supply series and the time trend. That is, the evolution of relative supply is almost identical to a line. The correlation between the relative supply and the time trend is 0.94. The Variance Inflation Factor (VIF) for model (2) is 16.5, which clearly exceeds the rule of thump value of 10 indicating high incidence of multicollinarity. This implies that the separation of the impact of supply from the impact of the time trend hinges on short term (yearly) deviations between the two series. However, in the short run the association between supply and wages is likely to be weak due to the time-lags involved in wage-setting and barriers to labor flow between sectors. The statistical distinction between the two explanations is therefore troublesome.[201, 202]

Model (3) allows for supply and between-sector demand shifts influence wages differently. The model exhibits an extremely high fit, which once again partly derives from the low number of degrees of freedom (10). All coefficients are statistically significant at the 1 percent level and display the expected sign. The estimated elasticity of substitution lies in between the estimate for the other models. The impact of demand on relative wage exceeds the impact of supply by a factor 6, indicating either (a) the demand indicator is grossly underestimated or/and (b) the labor markets adapts more rigidly to demand shocks than to innovations in supply. The interpretation of

201. Card and Lemieux (2000) observed an identical problem of colinearity in the case of Canada: "the relative supply essentially follows a linear trend [. . .], its effect cannot separately be identified from the effect from the linear trend. The large standard errors reflect this identification problem." Card and Lemieux (2000) p. 18, footnote 19.

202. For the period considered, the relative supply displays an evolution corresponding to an I(1) process similar to the time trend. Co-integration techniques could therefore be appropriate. However, the number of observation does not allow for application of this technique.

TABLE 11.2: Comparable Estimates of Elasticity of Substitution

Author	Elasticity	Country
Katz and Murphy (1992)	1.41	USA
Murphy, Riddle and Romer (1998)	1.37	Canada and USA
Card and Lemieux (2000)	1.1–1.6	USA
Santamaria (2000)	2.1	Colombia
This paper		
Model (1)	1.0	Brazil
Model (2)	4.7	Brazil
Model (3)	1.6	Brazil

Note: Card and Lemieux (2000) find a larger substitutability between the two labor types once they take into account a large but finite elasticity of substitution between age-cohorts.

the result from model (3) is less polarized than the two other models. It stresses that both the supply side and the demand side contributed to the rise in the wage of highly skilled labor.

The three models yields widely different estimate of the role that the asymmetric expansion in supply played for the rising skill-premium (and wage-inequality). From an econometrical point of view model (3) fares the best. It features the highest explanatory power, all variables highly significantly and no signs of misspecification as given by the RESET and Durbin-Watson test. Furthermore, the estimated elasticity of substitution resembles in magnitude that found on other labor markets (Table 11.2).

International evidence suggests that the elasticity of substitution lies in the interval 1.1–2.1. Hence model (1) and (2) are extremities. Assuming the Brazilian labor market works in a similar way to the Colombian and the North American, model (1) overestimates the influence of supply, while model (2) underestimate the effect. The extreme estimates likely arise from the high collinearity between the supply and the time trend. Omitting the time trend in model (1) causes the coefficient of supply to reflect the steady increase in relative demand and therefore overestimate. The oppositely occurs for model (2), the high and insignificant estimate of the elasticity of substitution likely reflects that the time-trend accounts for the impact of relative supply on relative wage, which then turns insignificant.

Hence, three factors—econometrical criteria, international evidence and balanced economic common sense—concurrently indicate that model (3) most appropriately estimates the elasticity of substitution. As a robustness test for the role played both other education groups weighted in the supply series, we carried out an estimation without added the supply of workers with lower secondary and primary education. As shown in Table 11A.8, the exclusion of other education groups has no influential bearing on the findings.[203] Although a precise estimate of the impact of

203. The size and significance levels remain unchanged. Only the size of the constant changes, which reflects that the supply or workers with primary or lower secondary education essentially develops similarly to that of upper secondary education. The inclusion of lower levels of education hence amounts to a multiplication of the supply of workers with upper secondary education, by a factor Z. Technically:

$$\frac{w_1}{w_2} = \alpha + \beta\left[\ln\left(\frac{NS_1}{NS_2 * Z}\right)\right] = \alpha + \beta[\ln(NS_1) - (\ln(NS_2) + \ln(Z))] = \alpha - \ln(Z) + \beta\left[\ln\left(\frac{NS_1}{NS_2}\right)\right]$$

relative supply of tertiary educated labor on relative wage in Brazil is handicapped by the time trend behavior of the supply series, we conclude from the analysis in this section that the economy wide elasticity of substitution between upper secondary graduates and tertiary graduates lies in the vicinity of 1.6.

This implies that the asymmetric expansion in the educational composition of the labor supply accounts for 54 percent of the increase in the relative wage of tertiary graduates while changes in demand answer for the remaining 46 percent. We found that the change in the sectoral composition decreased the relative demand for workers with tertiary education by 34 percent of the observed increase. However, a constant increase in skill-biased demand for highly skilled labor of 83 percent of the observed wage-change more than fully off-sat the equalizing effect from the between-sector demand shifts.[204]

What If? Alternative Paths for Supply and Wage-inequality in the Past

The estimated model of the relationship between educational composition of the labor supply and relative wage between education groups provides information on the mechanics of the labor market. In this section, we take advantage of the previous findings. By rearranging the estimated model, we illustrate how policymakers through the influence on the output of the education system can affect relative wage. Specifically, we ask the question: How much should the tertiary education system had expanded for the skill-premium to remain constant at the 1981 level?

Model for Counter factual Analysis

We apply model (2) from the last section, which includes a time trend and restricts demand and supply to impact relative wage in the same magnitude.

$$\log\left(\frac{w_{ter,t}}{w_{u\sec,t}}\right) = \alpha + \beta_1 \log\left(\frac{NS_{ter,t}}{NS_{\sec,t}}\right) + \beta_2 t_t \tag{9}$$

Our policy variable, the explained variable, is the supply of hours worked by workers with tertiary education. We turn around the model in order for the policy variable, the (net) supply of tertiary graduates to be expressed as a function of the estimated coefficients, the exogenous variables and the desired level for relative wage. Consequently, we assume explicitly that upper secondary education and lower levels of education expanded as observed.

$$NS_{ter,t} = NS_{u\sec,t} * \exp\left[\frac{1}{\beta_1}\left[\log\left(\frac{w_{ter,t}}{w_{u\sec,t}}\right) - \beta_2 t_t - \alpha\right]\right] \tag{10}$$

Turning around the model and performing counterfactual simulation requires a strong assumption of the exogenous character of the model. That is, the economic relationship estimated between

---

204. The relative supply of tertiary graduates fell by 0.21 and the relative wage increased by 0.24, figure 7. Additionally, we estimated the coefficient to 0.62. The fraction explained by supply thus equals $0.21^* 0.62/0.24 = 0.54$. For demand, the between-sector demand shifts reduced the wage gap by $3.55^* - 0.024/0.24 = -0.36$ whereas the skill-biased change in labor demand accounts for $0.011^*18/0.24 = 0.825$.

the time-series (the estimated coefficients) is assumed to remain stable even though the time series counterfactually change.[205]

Required Expansion in Tertiary Education for a Constant Skill-premium

How much should the labor supply of workers with tertiary education have expanded in order to keep the skill-premium constant at the 1981-level? In terms of the above model framework, we set the relative wage through out the period to be constant at the 1981-level. In 1981, tertiary graduates earned 14.1 *reais* per hour compared to 6.1 *reais* for graduates of upper secondary education, hence a log relative wage of 0.84. This is around the double of the U.S.-level in 1981, 0.41; Katz and Murphy (1992). We estimate (10):[206]

$$S_{ter,t} = S_{usec,t}{}^* \exp\left[\frac{1}{-0.62}[\log(RW_{1981}) - 0.005{}^*t - 0.34]\right] \qquad (11)$$

Estimating the model yields the following figure.

Figure 11.8 shows that the share of working hours supplied by tertiary graduates should have expanded from 6 percent in 1981 to 13.5 percent in 1999 in order for the relative wage to have remained at the 1981-level. As shown the share increased by a meager 2.5 percentage point to 8.5 percent. In 1999, the difference between the two series approximately corresponds to 5 percent of the labor force or a staggering shortfall of four million graduates from the tertiary education system. In 1997, only 254,000 graduated from tertiary education while an impressive 1,3 million graduated from upper secondary education. World Bank (2000b) estimates that in order to keep the current continuation rate from secondary education constant an additional 400,000 extra seats in the tertiary education is necessary. Given labor demand plausibly continues to favor highly skilled labor, as indicated by the significance of the time trend, even such a major expansion would prove insufficient to stop the relative wage and wage-inequality to widen.

Summary

This paper seeks to inform policymakers about the role of the skill-premium for wage-inequality and the available policy instruments and their impact on the skill-premium. The paper finds that:

---

205. Assessing the seriousness of the bias due this shortcoming is complex. Murphy, Riddle and Romer (1998) perform stability tests on the elasticity of substitution and the time trend of the skill-bias of labor demand. Interestingly, they found two statistically significant breaks in the time trend: A slow-down in skill-biased labor demand in 1976 and a speed-up in 1981. They interpret the breaks to be caused by variation in the introduction of general purpose technologies. If such technological breaks depend on the evolution of supply of education, such as the number of highly educated workers, then the model's parameters are path dependant. Furthermore, the output of secondary education is highly likely to influence later outputs of tertiary education. Therefore, the supply series of secondary and tertiary education might not be independent as assumed in this policy analysis. These considerations emphasize that the findings should serve as educated indications for the impact of education policy, not final exact results. In the case of Brazil, it would make less sense to test for similar breaks since (a) the limited number of observations complicates the test and (b) the very high fit of the model signals that the linear specification is a correct specification. Arbache, Green and Dickerson (2001) find no breaks in demand. Similarly, we find no sign of a trend break, see residual plots appendix figure 6 and 8.

206. Additionally, the estimated equation takes into account the change in demand and the evolution of supply of other education groups than the two reference groups; upper secondary and tertiary.

FIGURE 11.8: REQUIRED SUPPLY OF TERTIARY GRADUATES FOR A CONSTANT SKILL-PREMIUM CONSTANT

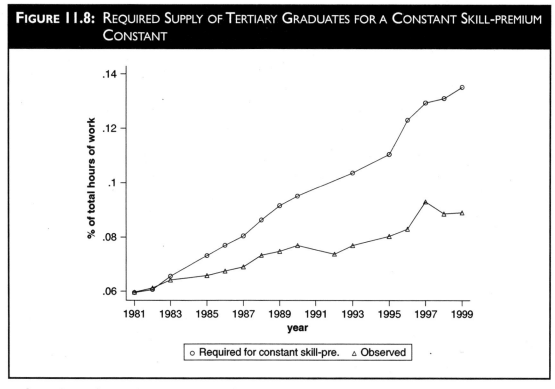

Source: Authors' own calculation based on PNAD.

■ *Graduates from Brazilian colleges are highly rewarded for their education.* The reward, the skill-premium, has risen constantly for two decades now. The returns to tertiary schooling, 23.9 percent, tops the list of returns in Latin America and is almost the double of the returns in the United States and Canada. The extremely high wage presents policymakers with an opportunity for economic growth that can be capitalized by expanding the tertiary education system and thereby satisfy the high demand for highly advanced educated workers.

■ *The rising wage of workers with tertiary education exacerbates wage-inequality.* The paper shows that if the returns to schooling in Brazil decreased to levels found in North America, the wage-inequality would decline by around 4 gini-points. Additionally, we showed that the decline in the reward of primary and secondary education accounted for half the reduction in wage-inequality that took place after 1988. This fact indicates the importance of the reward of education for wage-inequality.

■ *An asymmetric expansion in the Brazilian education system and a constant skill-biased change in labor demand fully explain the rise in the skill-premium.* The tertiary education system was unable to accommodate the surge of graduates from upper secondary education during the 1980s and 1990s. Consequently, the supply of workers with tertiary education dropped 20 percent relative to the supply of workers with upper secondary education. Our application of the Katz and Murphy model in the case of Brazil fully explain the rise in relative wage. The analysis suggests that the elasticity of substitution between the two types of labor is in the vicinity of 0.61. This implies that the asymmetric expansion in the educational composition of the labor supply accounts for 54 percent of the increase in the relative wage of tertiary graduates while labor demand answer for the remaining 46 percent.

■ *A major expansion in the tertiary education system could reverse the rising relative wage that deteriorates wage-inequality.* We find that in order for the relative wage to have remained at the 1981 level, the share of workers with tertiary education should have more that doubled from 6 percent in 1981 to 13.5 percent in 1999. However, the share only reached 8.5 percent. Currently, about 12 percent of an age-cohort enters tertiary education in Brazil. Hence, at the current speed, it would take around 40 years for the share of workers with tertiary education to reach a meager 12 percent of the workforce. Policymakers face a daunting task in order to reverse the current trend of rising relative wage. For example, a doubling of the current rate of enrollment into tertiary education, from 12 percent to 24 percent, demands the creation of 2.5 millions extra seats in the tertiary education system, Hauptman (1998). A such major expansion in the tertiary education system would not only reduce the skill-premium and lead to a more equitable income distribution, but simultaneously increase higher labor market incomes and improved living standards. Furthermore, an aggressive expansion potentially could propel Brazil into the knowledge economy by revolutionizing the technological capabilities of the labor market force benefiting domestic producers.

Appendix

TABLE 11A.1: VARIABLE CODING

Statistic	Computed from
	(Vxxxx refers to the variable coding in the 1999 PNAD-questionnaires)
Monthly wage (fixed 1997 R$) (Including wage from second job, if applicable)	Nominal monthly wage (sum of V9532 and V9982) deflated by IPCA
Hourly wage (fixed 1997 R$) (Including wage and working hours from second job, if applicable)	$\frac{\text{Monthly wage}}{\text{Working hours per week}^*4} = \frac{V9532+V9982}{(V9058+V9101)^*4}$
Gender	V0302
Age	V8005
Schooling	V4703
Labor market status	V9029 and V9042
Region of residence	V5030
Rural residence	V4728

TABLE 11A.2: Descriptive Statistics for Entire Population 1976–1989

Year	1976	1981	1982	1983	1985	1986	1987	1988	1989
Age (mean)	32.7	32.9	32.9	33.0	32.9	32.8	33.1	33.3	33.3
Female participation rate	29.5%	32.3%	33.0%	33.6%	34.2%	34.4%	35.2%	35.4%	35.8%
Years of schooling (mean)	4.75	5.24	5.25	5.35	5.57	5.63	5.72	5.80	5.92
Hourly wage (mean)	3.03	3.01	3.00	2.56	2.85	3.56	2.85	3.01	3.57
Monthly wage (mean)	550	527	526	448	500	617	489	515	603
Hours worked weekly (mean)	47.7	46.3	46.3	45.8	46.0	45.7	45.5	45.3	44.3
Rural residence	23.8%	17.6%	17.7%	18.3%	17.5%	18.1%	18.1%	18.4%	17.5%
% living in North	4.4%	6.9%	7.2%	7.2%	8.0%	8.5%	8.8%	8.5%	8.8%
% living in North East	20.3%	26.6%	25.9%	26.7%	27.4%	28.3%	28.2%	28.6%	27.9%
% living in Center-West	16.6%	12.9%	13.2%	13.3%	11.0%	11.9%	12.1%	12.5%	12.9%
% living in South	13.2%	16.9%	16.9%	16.4%	16.7%	15.8%	16.2%	16.1%	16.2%
% living in South East	45.5%	36.7%	36.8%	36.4%	37.0%	35.6%	34.8%	34.3%	34.3%
Number of observations	118,282	154,330	167,105	167,713	179,392	101,834	106,750	107,311	109,224

Year	1990	1992	1993	1995	1996	1997	1998	1999
Age (mean)	33.5	33.8	34.0	34.3	34.5	33.9	34.9	35.1
Female participation rate	36.2%	36.8%	36.6%	37.8%	38.0%	41.3%	38.2%	38.6%
Years of schooling (mean)	5.99	5.96	6.17	6.33	6.59	6.82	6.82	6.91
Hourly wage (mean)	2.65	2.10	2.79	3.16	3.26	3.17	3.18	2.96
Monthly wage (mean)	444	349	464	522	528	512	520	481
Hours worked weekly (mean)	44.1	44.5	44.1	44.1	44.4	43.7	44.2	43.9
Rural residence	18.0%	15.2%	15.0%	14.5%	14.3%	14.0%	14.7%	15.0%
% living in North	8.7%	6.6%	6.9%	6.8%	7.0%	6.9%	7.2%	7.0%
% living in North East	28.3%	27.2%	27.3%	28.0%	27.5%	27.4%	28.2%	28.7%
% living in Center-West	12.9%	11.3%	10.9%	11.0%	11.0%	11.4%	11.7%	11.6%
% living in South	16.0%	18.5%	18.0%	18.0%	18.4%	17.9%	18.2%	17.9%
% living in South East	34.1%	36.4%	36.8%	36.3%	36.2%	36.3%	34.6%	34.8%
Number of observations	111,456	111,136	114,969	123,215	119351	106504	125052	128384

Source: PNAD.

TABLE 11A.3: DESCRIPTIVE STATISTICS BY EDUCATION LEVEL 1976–1989

Year	1976	1981	1982	1983	1985	1986	1987	1988	1989
Hourly wage by education level									
No schooling	1.3	1.3	1.2	1.0	1.1	1.5	1.1	1.1	1.3
Incomplete primary	2.0	1.9	1.8	1.6	1.7	2.3	1.7	1.7	2.1
Complete primary	3.2	2.8	2.8	2.3	2.5	3.3	2.5	2.5	3.0
Complete lower secondary	5.9	4.3	4.5	3.7	4.0	4.7	3.6	3.8	4.4
Complete upper secondary	6.8	6.3	6.4	5.3	5.6	6.5	5.5	5.6	6.5
Incomplete tertiary	8.7	8.8	9.2	7.6	8.2	9.6	8.1	8.9	9.8
Complete tertiary	15.5	14.0	14.1	11.6	13.1	15.7	12.3	13.4	15.3
Share of work force in numbers of workers									
No schooling	28.6%	24.4%	25.3%	23.7%	22.4%	22.0%	21.5%	20.8%	20.3%
Incomplete primary	25.6%	23.5%	22.4%	22.4%	21.2%	21.3%	20.5%	20.6%	19.5%
Complete primary	28.9%	29.9%	29.5%	29.9%	30.4%	29.9%	30.0%	29.5%	30.1%
Complete lower secondary	6.6%	8.0%	8.2%	8.5%	9.2%	9.5%	9.8%	9.9%	10.3%
Complete upper secondary	5.1%	7.4%	7.7%	8.3%	9.3%	9.4%	10.2%	10.6%	11.2%
Incomplete tertiary	1.5%	2.3%	2.3%	2.3%	2.3%	2.4%	2.5%	2.6%	2.6%
Complete tertiary	3.8%	4.5%	4.7%	5.0%	5.3%	5.4%	5.7%	6.0%	6.0%
Sum	100.0%	100.0%	100.0%	100.0%	100.0%	100.0%	100.0%	100.0%	100.0%

(Continued)

Note: Wages are in fixed September 1997 prices.

TABLE 11A.3: DESCRIPTIVE STATISTICS BY EDUCATION LEVEL 1976–1989 (COUNTINUED)

Year	1990	1992	1993	1995	1996	1997	1998	1999
Hourly wage by education level								
No schooling	1.0	1.0	1.1	1.2	1.3	1.2	1.2	1.1
Incomplete primary	1.5	1.4	1.6	1.7	1.8	1.8	1.7	1.5
Complete primary	2.2	1.8	2.2	2.4	2.4	2.3	2.2	2.0
Complete lower secondary	3.1	2.6	3.2	3.4	3.4	3.1	3.1	2.9
Complete upper secondary	4.7	3.6	4.6	5.0	5.0	4.8	4.5	4.3
Incomplete tertiary	7.4	4.8	6.7	7.2	7.2	7.1	7.3	6.5
Complete tertiary	10.9	6.6	11.5	12.9	12.8	12.0	12.4	11.5
Share of work force in numbers of workers								
No schooling	19.5%	19.5%	18.2%	17.0%	16.8%	15.6%	15.3%	14.7%
Incomplete primary	19.3%	18.4%	18.3%	17.9%	16.4%	16.4%	16.2%	15.9%
Complete primary	30.1%	30.2%	30.6%	31.1%	30.3%	30.4%	30.5%	30.6%
Complete lower secondary	10.5%	11.0%	11.3%	11.6%	13.1%	12.6%	13.1%	13.0%
Complete upper secondary	11.7%	11.7%	12.2%	12.9%	13.6%	14.3%	14.7%	15.4%
Incomplete tertiary	2.6%	3.0%	2.9%	2.9%	2.9%	3.2%	2.9%	3.0%
Complete tertiary	6.3%	6.2%	6.4%	6.7%	6.9%	7.5%	7.4%	7.5%
Sum	100.0%	100.0%	100.0%	100.0%	100.0%	100.0%	100.0%	100.0%

Note: Wages are in fixed September 1997 prices.
Source: PNAD.

TABLE 11A.4: EDUCATION WEIGHTS USED TO COMPUTE RELATIVE SUPPLY

	Average wage Card and Lemieux (2000)	Average difference in returns (from mincer wage regression)	Average wage (fixed demographic groups)	Regression (fixed demographic groups) Katz and Murphy (1992)
To complete upper secondary				
Primary	0.47	0.44	0.42	0.26
Lower secondary	0.70	0.64	0.7	0.74
Incomplete tertiary	0.66	0.65	0.61	0.98
To complete tertiary				
Primary	0	0	0	0.07
Lower secondary	0	0	0	−0.02
Incomplete tertiary	0.34	0.35	0.39	0.22

Source: PNAD.

TABLE 11A.5: SECTOR LABOR INTENSITY, AVERAGE 1976–1999

Sector	No Schooling	Incomplete Primary	Complete Primary	Complete Lower Secondary	Complete Upper Secondary	Incomplete Tertiary	Complete Tertiary	Sum
Agriculture & mining	40.3%	29.9%	24.0%	3.1%	1.8%	0.3%	0.6%	100%
Low tech	9.9%	17.7%	44.5%	15.3%	8.9%	1.7%	2.1%	100%
Basic manufacturing	6.3%	12.7%	38.1%	19.7%	14.2%	3.7%	5.4%	100%
High tech	**5.2%**	**10.1%**	**28.9%**	**16.9%**	**20.9%**	**6.5%**	**11.5%**	**100%**
Construction	18.9%	26.6%	39.5%	8.3%	3.8%	0.8%	2.0%	100%
Utility, Transport, and Communications	7.8%	15.2%	38.3%	16.6%	14.3%	3.1%	4.7%	100%
Whole and retail sale	7.7%	13.1%	34.8%	21.1%	17.4%	2.9%	3.1%	100%
Financial services	**1.1%**	**2.6%**	**10.2%**	**18.0%**	**33.7%**	**15.2%**	**19.1%**	**100%**
Services	12.5%	19.4%	39.7%	13.8%	9.0%	2.0%	3.6%	100%
Public education, medical, and social sector	3.0%	6.2%	18.5%	14.0%	26.3%	10.2%	21.9%	100%
Public administration and law enforcement	5.1%	8.0%	20.9%	18.3%	23.6%	7.5%	16.7%	100%

Source: PNAD.

TABLE 11A.6: SECTOR EMPLOYMENT SHARE 1976 TO 1999

Sector	1976	1982	1985	1988	1990	1992	1995	1997	1999	Change 1976–1999 %-points
Agriculture & mining	21.9%	17.3%	17.7%	16.7%	14.8%	15.1%	13.6%	12.1%	12.7%	−9.2%
Low tech	8.0%	7.7%	8.1%	7.7%	7.7%	7.6%	7.2%	6.8%	6.7%	−1.4%
Basic manufacturing	7.1%	6.5%	6.1%	6.3%	6.2%	5.5%	5.3%	5.2%	4.9%	−2.3%
High tech	**0.9%**	**0.9%**	**1.0%**	**0.9%**	**0.9%**	**0.9%**	**0.8%**	**0.8%**	**0.7%**	**−0.2%**
Construction	8.9%	8.8%	7.2%	7.3%	7.2%	7.6%	7.3%	7.2%	7.8%	−1.1%
Utility, Transport, and Communications	6.0%	6.0%	5.6%	5.5%	5.5%	5.6%	5.6%	5.4%	5.7%	−0.3%
Whole and retail sale	9.3%	11.9%	12.6%	13.0%	14.1%	13.9%	14.8%	15.1%	15.0%	5.6%
Financial services	**2.8%**	**3.1%**	**3.4%**	**2.7%**	**2.7%**	**2.1%**	**1.9%**	**1.8%**	**1.6%**	**−1.1%**
Services	20.0%	22.4%	22.8%	23.2%	23.8%	25.1%	26.7%	27.9%	27.6%	7.6%
Public education, medical, and social sector	8.7%	9.1%	9.6%	10.4%	10.4%	10.5%	10.8%	12.0%	11.4%	2.8%
Public administration and law enforcement	6.4%	6.2%	6.0%	6.2%	6.5%	6.1%	6.1%	5.8%	5.9%	−0.4%
SUM	100.0%	100.0%	100.0%	100.0%	100.0%	100.0%	100.0%	100.0%	100.0%	0.0%

Source: PNAD.

Table 11A.7: Between-Sectors Labor Demand Shifts

Education Level	1976–1981	1981–1985	1985–1990	1990–1995	1995–1999	1976–1999
No schooling	−8.6%	0.6%	−4.9%	−2.4%	−2.0%	−14.0%
Incomplete Primary	−2.7%	−0.4%	−2.1%	−0.3%	−0.7%	−5.7%
Complete Primary	2.8%	−0.6%	0.7%	1.1%	0.1%	2.6%
Complete Lower secondary	6.7%	0.4%	2.9%	1.0%	0.6%	12.6%
Complete Upper secondary	7.3%	1.1%	3.2%	−0.2%	0.8%	20.8%
Incomplete Tertiary	5.3%	1.2%	2.5%	−1.8%	0.6%	10.3%
Complete Tertiary	4.2%	0.3%	4.3%	−0.6%	1.5%	13.6%

Note: Based on hours of work.
Source: PNAD.

Table 11A.8: Robustness: Estimation Disregarding Other Education Groups

Model	(1)	(2)	3
Time Sample	1981–1999	1981–1999	1981–1999
Constant	0.586 (0.038)	0.773[*] (0.083)	0.778[**] (0.068)
Net Supply $(-1/\sigma)$	−0.80[**] (0.080)	−0.039 (0.32)	−0.64[*] (0.34)
Time trend	—	0.012[*] (0.0050)	0.0016 (0.0056)
Demand	—	—	4.52[**] (1.84)
R^2	0.89	0.92	0.95
Observations	15	15	15
Tests for misspecification			
Durbin-Watson test	1.87	2.28	1.46
RESET test	0.31	0.97	0.21
Implied Elasticity (σ)	1.25	25.6	1.56

Note: The Durbin-Watson test for model (3) falls in the inconclusive range.

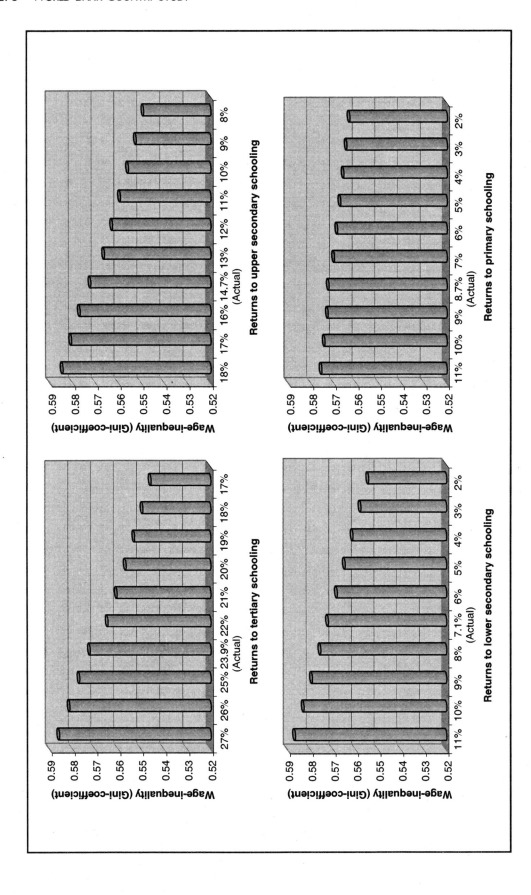

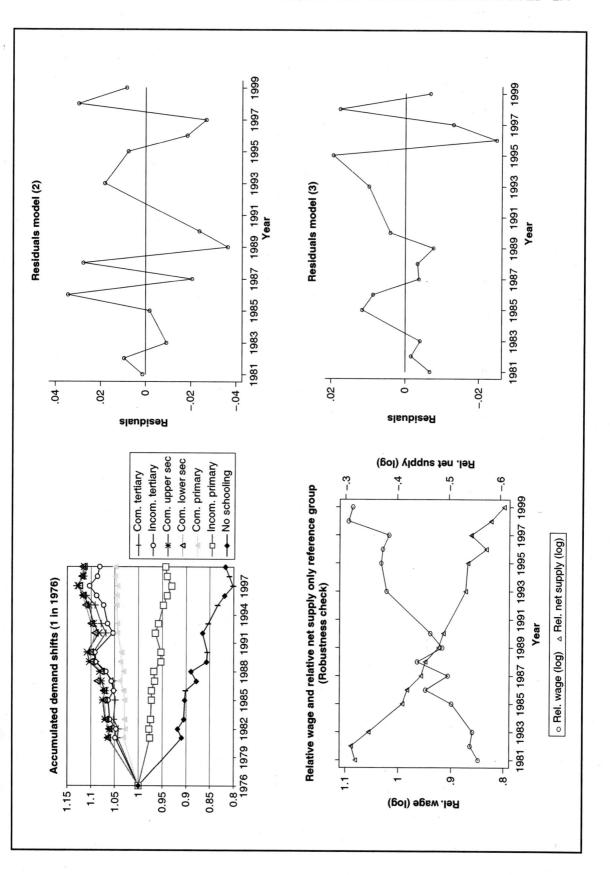

References

Arbache, J.S., F. Green, and A. Dickerson. 2000. "A Picture of Wage Inequality and the Allocation of Labor in a Period of Trade Liberalization: The Case of Brazil." Universidade de Brasilia.

Arias, O., K.F. Hollack, and W. Sosa. 1999. "Individual Heterogeneity in the Returns to Schooling: Instrumental Variables Quantile Regression Using Twins Data." University of Illinois. Processed.

Barros, R., and L. Ramos. 1996. "Temporal Evolution of the Relationship between Wages and Educational of Brazilian Men." In N. Birdsall and R.H. Sabot, ed. *Opportunity Foregone; Education in Brazil.* Washington, D.C.: Inter-American Development Bank.

Birdsall, N. and R.H. Sabot, ed. 1996. *Opportunity Foregone; Education in Brazil.* Washington, D.C.: Inter-American Development Bank.

Behrman, J.R., N. Birdsall, and R. Kaplan. 1996. "The Quality of Schooling and Labor Markets Outcomes." In N. Birdsall and R.H. Sabot, ed. *Opportunity Foregone; Education in Brazil.* Washington, D.C.: Inter-American Development Bank.

Blom, Verner, and Holm-Nielsen. Forthcoming. "Education, Earnings and Inequality in Brazil 1982–1998; Implications for Education Policy." Policy Research Working Paper, World Bank, Washington D.C.

Bound, J., and G. Johnson. 1992. "Changes in the Structure of Wages in the 1980's: An Evaluation of Alternative Explanations." *American Economic Review* 82(3):371–392.

Card, D. 1998. "The Causal Effect of Education on Earnings." In O. Ashenfelter and D. Card, eds. *Handbook of Labor Economics.* Vol. 3.

Caselli, F., and W.J. Coleman. 2001. "Cross-Country technology Diffusion: The Case of Computers." NBER working paper 8130.

Deaton, A. 1997. *The Analysis of Household Surveys—A Microeconometric Approach to Development Policy.* Baltimore: Johns Hopkins University Press.

Ferreira, F., and R. Paes de Barros. 1999. "The Slippery Slope: Explaining the Increase in Extreme Poverty in Urban Brazil, 1976-1996." Policy Research Working Paper No. 2210, World Bank, Washington, D.C.

Feenstra, R., and G. Hanson. 1997. "Productivity Measurement and the Impact of Trade and Technology on Wages." NBER Working Paper No. 6052.

Gonzaga, M. G. 1996. "The Effect of Openness on Industrial Employment in Brazil." IPEA, Serie Seminarios No 27/96.

Hauptman, A. 1998. "Accommodating the Growing Demand for Higher Education in Brazil: A role for the Federal Universities?" Discussion Paper, World Bank Latin America and the Caribbean Regional Office, World Bank, Washington D.C.

Katz, L. and K. Murphy. 1992. "The Change in Relative Wages 1963-1987; Supply and Demand Factors." *Quarterly Journal of Economics* 107 (February).

Juhn, C., K.M. Murphy, and B. Pierce. 1993. "Wage Inequality and the Rise in Returns to Skills." *Journal of Political Economy* 101(3).

Lam, D. 1999. "Generating Extreme Inequality: Schooling, Earnings, and Intergenerational Transmissions of Human Capital in South Africa and Brazil." Research Report, No. 99-439, Population Studies Center, University of Michigan.

Lam, D. and R. Schoeni. 1993. "The Effects of Family Background on Earnings and Returns to Schooling: Evidence from Brazil." *Journal of Political Economy* 101(4):710–740

Lächler, U. 1998. "Education and Earnings Inequality in Mexico." Policy Research Working Paper No. 1949, World Bank, Washington, D.C.

Lee, J. 2001. "Education and Technology Readiness: Prospects for Developing Countries." Working Paper, Korea University, 2001.

Levey, F. and R. J. Murnane. 1992. "U.S. Earnings Levels and Earnings Inequality: A Review of Recent Trends and Proposed Explanations." *Journal of Economic Literature* 30:1333-1381.

Mankiw, N.G., D. Romer, and D.N. Weil. 1992. "A Contribution to the Empirics of Economic Growth." *Quarterly Journal of Economics* 107(2).

Mincer, J. 1974. "Schooling, Experience and Earnings." NBER Working Paper, New York.

Murphy, K.M., W.C. Riddle, and P.M. Romer. 1998. "Wages, Skills, and technology in the United States and Canada." NBER working paper 6638.

Neri, M.C., and C.M. Camargo.1999. "Distributive Effects of Brazilian Structural Reforms." Texto Para Discussao, No. 406, Departamento de Economia, PUC-Rio.

Prichett, L. 2000. "An Economist's Midnight Thoughts on Education: The Puzzle of Government Production." Kennedy School of Government.

Rosembaum,D.T 2000. "Ability, Educational Ranks, and Labor Market Trends: The Effects of Shifts in the Skill Composition of the Educational Groups." Department of Economics, University of North Carolina at Greensboro.

Robbins and Gindling. 1999. "Trade Liberalization and the Relative Wages for More-Skilled Workers in Costa Rica." *Review of Development Economics* 3(2):155–169.

Sachs, J.D., and H.J. Shartz. 1996. "U.S. Trade with Developing Countries and Wage Inequality." *AEA Papers and Proceedings* 86(2).

Santamaria, M. 2000. "External Trade, Skill, Technology and the Recent Increase of Income Inequality in Colombia." Dissertation paper.

Tinbergen, Jan. 1975. *Income Differences: recent research.*

Vélez, C.E., J. Leibovich, A. Kugler, C. Bouillon, and J. Núñez . 2001. "The Reversal of Inequality Gains in Colombia, 1978-1995: A Combination of Persistent and Fluctuating Forces." World Bank and IDB. Processed.

Verner, D. 2000a. "The Dynamics of Poverty and its Determinants: The Case of Pernambuco and the Northeast Brazil."

———. 2000b. "Wage Determination in Pernambuco, Bahia, Ceará and the Northeast: An Application of Quantile Regressions." World Bank policy working paper, Washington, D.C.

Wodon, T.Q. 2000. *Poverty and Policy in the Latin America and the Caribbean.* World Bank Technical Paper No. 467. Washington, D.C.: World Bank.

Wood, A. 2000. "Globalization and Wage Inequalities: a Synthesis of Three Theories." Department for International Development, London.

World Bank. 2000a. "Brazil, Secondary Education in Brazil." World Bank, Washington, DC.

———. 2000b. "Brazil, Sector Study Higher Education in Brazil." World Bank, Washington, DC.